CONTENTS

CONTENTS 3

FOREWORD 5

THE THREAT ENVIRONMENT 7

    THE GLOBAL JIHAD AND ITS IDEOLOGICAL WELLSPRING: SHARIAH 9

    RUSSIA 39

    CHINA 75

    IRAQ 93

    IRAN 115

    NORTH KOREA 127

    LATIN AMERICA 135

    IMMIGRATION AND BORDER INSECURITY 147

    YUGOSLAVIA 153

    VIETNAM 159

    THE GRID/EMP 171

SPEAKING TRUTH TO POWER 183

    GEORGE H.W. BUSH 187

    BILL CLINTON 195

    GEORGE W. BUSH 209

    BARACK OBAMA 221

HOW TO WAGE AND WIN THE WAR FOR THE FREE WORLD 241

    PEACE THROUGH STRENGTH 243

    MILITARY READINESS 259

    NUCLEAR DETERRENCE 281

    SOVEREIGNTY 313

    WAR OF IDEAS 333

    MISSILE DEFENSE 347

    ISRAEL 377

    ENERGY SECURITY 403

    ECONOMIC SECURITY 413

    TECHNOLOGY SECURITY 431

    SPACE 445

    INTELLIGENCE 459

AFTERWORD 485

FOREWORD

Twenty-five years is, in the great scheme of things – say, the history of powerful nations, great civilizations and especially the cosmos, a mere blink of an eye. It feels like a long time, however, in the life of this mere mortal.

The chance I was afforded, starting in 1989, to write a column every week for two-and-a-half decades for an important newspaper in the capital of the most powerful of nations at a critical moment in the history of Western civilization was more than a privilege. It also amounted to a splendid platform from which to contribute materially to the debate about the national security and foreign policy issues of that era.

Seen in hindsight, the resulting columns, published by the *Washington Times* from 1989-2014, represent a kind of geological core sample on those issues. I have tried to down-select for this volume from more than 1200 of them the ones that seem to me either to retain interesting insights into important past events and/or to be of continuing relevance to those still unfolding.

This selection, taken together, amounts to a mosaic of commentary on the threats America has been facing, evaluations of the efforts – or lack of such efforts – to address them and my own prescriptions as to what should be done. They provide, moreover, a sort of prism through which to calibrate the trajectory we have been on for some time and to make informed assessments of where we are likely to find ourselves *if we don't learn from and apply the lessons to be drawn from our recent history*.

One thing is clear from these snapshots and, indeed, from the tale of humankind writ large: Deferring action in the face of aggressive evil is a formula for worse outcomes at higher costs, in terms of national treasure and, more importantly, lives.

Each of these columns bespeaks in its own way the philosophy personified and practiced by Ronald Reagan, a man I was privileged to serve for four-and-a-half years in senior ranks of the Defense Department. He called it "peace through strength." Even before Mr. Reagan assumed the presidency, I had an opportunity to be imbued with this approach by two of my other bosses and mentors: two great legislators, Senators Henry M. "Scoop" Jackson (D-Washington) and John Tower (R-Texas).

Promoting peace through strength has also been the purpose of the organization that I helped found and have run over the 26 years since I left the Pentagon: the Center for Security Policy, now doing business as Secure Freedom. Over the years, my colleagues at the Center and those with whom we have worked in coalitions on a broad array of subjects – many of which have been the focus of my columns – have enormously enriched my understanding of these topics.

I would like to express appreciation in particular to several of these longtime friends and muses. Rinelda Bliss, Roger Robinson, Mike Reilly and Christine Brim are among the many from whom I learned much and upon whom I relied at critical moments in the establishment and evolution of the organization in which we collaborated for so long and to such great effect. I am grateful as well to the present staff of Secure Freedom, and all those who preceded them, for unfailingly inspiring me with their love of our country and their commitment to its security.

Needless to say, this collection, and the larger body of work from which it is drawn, would not have been possible without the extraordinary support and editorial gifts of Mary Lou Forbes, one of America's most accomplished newspaperwomen, and two of her indefatigable lieutenants at the editorial desk of the Commentary Section of the *Washington Times*, Ben Tyree and Frank Perley. Their encouragement, appreciation of my contributions and unfailing help with favorable placement, artwork and accommodations of my requests for extra space, made the crafting of these columns infinitely easier and vastly more pleasurable.

I am also grateful to the *Washington Times'* current Managing Editor, John Solomon, for his gracious permission to publish this compilation and for initiating in 2015 the "Frank Gaffney's Threat Assessment" feature in the *Times'* online edition.

As the selection of columns in this book suggests, I was given free rein to tackle controversial subjects, offer provocative recommendations and otherwise speak truth to power. It was enormously gratifying, and frankly highly therapeutic, to be able to do so, year upon year. There was only one topic about which I was not permitted to write over roughly thirteen of those years. But that is the subject of another book, not this one.

I was greatly aided in assembling and sifting through these columns by a series of gifted assistants and interns of the Center for Security Policy: Lisa Firestone, Megan Mueller, Ada Osborn, Michael Boyden, Alex McAnenny, Sylvie Staines, Megan Schultz, Adam Savit, Jordi Chervitz and Alex VanNess. Without their patience, enthusiasm and professionalism, such an undertaking would have remained for me an unfulfilled dream. Each and every one of them has my deep appreciation.

Finally, my heartfelt thanks to all the women in my life whose love and enabling of my professional pursuits, including long hours spent writing and unavailable to them, can never fully be recompensed. Still, I pray that my wife, Marisol, and our five daughters – Camelia, Jandri, Eugenia, Sarah and Elizabeth – will find in this collection some small measure of the gratitude I feel for what would never have been possible to accomplish without them in my life.

-Frank J. Gaffney, Jr.

THE THREAT
ENVIRONMENT

In the course of two-and-a-half decades, the United States has faced myriad threats. Columns in this section chronicle how successive administrations of both parties have contended with them during that period – including President Obama's dangerously delusional or, more accurately, his deluding stewardship of the defense and foreign policy portfolio.

A particular focus of my work – both in Washington Times columns and elsewhere – has been the threat posed by totalitarian ideologies. These have included: Soviet communism; the equally repressive and kleptocratic variant nostalgically practiced in Vladimir Putin's autocracy; the modified Maoist version pursued by Deng Xiao Ping and his successors in Beijing; the cult of personality of the Kim dynasty in North Korea; and the Islamic supremacist doctrine its adherents call shariah, much in evidence in Shiite Iran, Sunni Muslim nations and increasingly in the West.

These columns illuminate various developments on each of these fronts in what I call the "War for the Free World" – a descriptor that best conveys the global character of the challenges we are facing, or shortly will, and what is at stake: nothing less than the Western civilization that has given rise to and nurtures the Free World.

Of particular and ongoing importance has been successive columns' call for increased vigilance about, understanding of and counter action against shariah's adherents. We have tried – arguably since the Iranian revolution in 1979 – a more-or-less acquiescent posture toward this ideological threat, without appreciable success and despite the heroism of countless of our men and women in uniform.

It is high time that a new approach were adopted – one rooted in the practice of peace through strength. The Center for Security Policy in mid-January 2015 unveiled a "Secure Freedom Strategy" for the purpose of providing

The Global Jihad And Its Ideological Wellspring: Shariah

Events of the past week have dramatically concentrated American minds on the problem of international terrorism. And rightly so. After all, the 30 synchronized attacks by Kurdish terrorists in Europe, the FBI's interception of an Islamic extremist cell as it prepared to blow up targets all over New York City and the belated U.S. retaliation for Saddam Hussein's attempted assassination of former President Bush have something in common: They are indicators of the ominous shape of things to come in the emerging New World Disorder.

Consider for a moment the international factors that have emboldened Marxist Kurdish militants to conduct their bloody warfare against Turkey and its assets overseas: Political weakness in Ankara in the aftermath of President Turgut Ozal's untimely demise; sympathetic treatment for their separatist cause from Germany and other European nations; and Washington's recent criticisms of the Turkish human rights record and its effective cutoff of grants for security assistance upon which the Turks heavily rely.

Islamic political extremists appear to have ambitiously set their sights on targets in the United States for similar reasons. Muslim fanatics supported by Iran, Sudan and Syria are enjoying considerable success in destabilizing the political systems of Egypt, Algeria and Tunisia. Israel, too, is under siege from these forces.

What is more, European nations - notably France, Yugoslavia and Greece – are still allowing these terrorists (and others) to operate from their territory, turning a blind eye to their presence and even to their use of foreign diplomatic posts and personnel to attack targets elsewhere. And increasingly those targets will be inside the United States as American power and the will to utilize it are perceived to decline.

Even President Clinton's weekend attack on the Iraqi intelligence center in Baghdad - welcome and overdue though it was - is symptomatic of the current problem. It comes after months of dithering, in which the Clinton administration first downplayed reports that there was a plot against former President Bush. Then it impugned the quality of the evidence of such a plot. Finally, the administration put out the word that the United States would wait to see if those charged by Kuwait with mounting the assassination attempt were convicted before contemplating any reaction

In the end, Washington acknowledged that the Iraqi attempt on Mr. Bush's life was real, that there was compelling evidence that it was ordered "at the highest levels of the Iraqi government" and that the United States needed to hit back even though the verdict is still out in Kuwait. To its credit, the Clinton administration acted as it had to - unilaterally - despite its endless invocation of the need for multilateralism in the conduct of foreign affairs.

The administration also properly attacked key strategic targets as opposed to the targets of previous retaliatory strikes - notably, irrelevant tactical sites like air defense batteries and radars far removed from Baghdad.

Furthermore, the operation demonstrated once again that investments in high-tech weaponry give the United States a formidable capacity to execute precision attacks over great distances with minimal unintended damage and loss of U.S. lives.

Still, coupled with periodic signals that Washington is anxious to establish better relations with Saddam Hussein, first the dithering and then the limited nature of the retaliation - aimed not at Saddam per se or even comprehensively at his base of power - have probably reinforced dangerous perceptions in Iraq and beyond: The United States remains unwilling to come to grips with the root cause of state-sponsored terrorism, namely ruling cliques like Saddam Hussein's that plot, support and otherwise facilitate deadly aggression.

If so, the recent spate of increased terrorist attacks on American citizens, institutions and assets - and those of the United States' key allies – may simply be the most immediate penalties paid for the nation's retreat from world leadership and the precipitous dismantling of much of its military power. If this country persists, however, in the neo-isolationist tendencies of the past few years and proceeds with the cashiering of its defense establishment, intelligence community and dominant global position, it is predictable that such present costs will pale compared with those that will have to be borne down the road.

If we are smart, Saddam Hussein will not be the only one who, in the words of Defense Secretary Les Aspin, gets a "wake-up call." Instead, every American should be reminded by the latest terrorist incidents that politics, like nature, abhors a vacuum. U.S. interests - for example, in international commerce and tourism, to say nothing of domestic security - will be increasingly in jeopardy if others, acting individually or in concert, sense opportunities to engage in acts of terrorism or larger-scale aggression with virtual impunity.

To be sure, a decision to end the slide toward national impotence by restoring the robustness of the U.S. military and reasserting America's commitment to be fully engaged in international affairs is unlikely to prevent all terrorist incidents. When combined with a vigorous counterterrorism intelligence effort, however, such steps will make the United States a much less inviting target than it is currently becoming.

One widespread and pernicious illusion died a fiery death on Sept. 11: The notion that the United States - the "world's only superpower" - was invulnerable and its people secure within their own borders against foreign attack was vaporized along with the World Trade Center towers, portions of the Pentagon and the hijacked jet aimed at the Capitol.

It appears that two other dangerous illusions linger on, however.

One involves the belief clung to by diehard opponents of President Bush's efforts to develop and deploy effective missile defenses that we can safely perpetuate our complete vulnerability to another, far more deadly attack from ballistic missiles.

The second is, if anything, even more preposterous: The belief that there are some "good" terrorists with whom we can prudently make common cause, at least temporarily, in waging war against the "bad" terrorists responsible for the events of Sept. 11.

At this writing, Democratic members of Congress led by Rep. John Spratt of South Carolina and Sen. Carl Levin of Michigan are expected to sunder the new-found bipartisan unity that has broken out in Washington since last week's attacks. They seek to make dramatic reductions in the levels of funding for the president's missile defense program and, in Mr. Levin's case, to impose – in coming months, if not immediately - new legislative restrictions that would grievously hinder the use of any funds that may ultimately be approved for anti-missile systems.

The proponents of such legislation evidently have a fairly low regard for the intelligence of their colleagues and the public. They apparently hope to sell the argument that, since ballistic missile defenses would not have stopped the passenger aircraft used by the terrorists this time, we should not be defended against what may be their weapon of choice the next time.

Of course, this illusion flies in the face of common sense, to say nothing of the constitutional duty to provide for the common defense. Those who perpetrated these heinous crimes went to great lengths and considerable expense to inflict grave, but still relatively limited, damage on the nation they hate. They succeeded because the United States was unready to use defenses it does currently have to shoot down domestic commercial planes.

Does anyone think for a moment, that if those waging holy war on this country, people fully prepared to die in the process of doing so, had access to weapons capable of inflicting infinitely greater death and destruction on us - and against which we had no defense - they would refrain from using them?

Even more of an illusion - no, a delusion - is the failure to appreciate a related point: The sponsors of terrorism, with whom Mr. Bush has properly declared a state of war to exist, are working feverishly to acquire long-range ballistic missiles precisely so they can deter the sort of attack against their countries he has promised to launch. Would the United States really contemplate retaliation against Afghanistan if it could realistically threaten within 30 minutes to lay waste to the rest of New York City via missile-delivered weapons of mass destruction - and our president could do nothing to prevent such a disaster?

No less invidious than the illusory belief that the United States should be defended against some terrifying threats but not all of them is the sentiment now in evidence in Colin Powell's State Department. Officials in Foggy Bottom seem to feel that some sponsors of international terrorism can be recruited to wage Mr. Bush's war against other terrorist organizations and their hosts. Specifically, Yasser Arafat's Palestinian Authority, Bashar Assad's Syria and President Mohammad Khatami's Iran are evidently being touted by some in the administration as candidates for the new multinational coalition.

This is one of the most impractical, not to say bizarre, ideas to come along in some time. For one thing, if Mr. Bush's oft-repeated commitment to rid the world of terrorists and those who harbor them is to have any meaning - to say nothing of any chance of producing the desired result - he cannot be put in the position of turning a blind eye to some of the world's most notorious sponsors of terrorism.

For another, U.S. officials cannot really believe that the United States would be able to mount effective strikes on Osama bin Laden's organization, Al Qaeda, and some of his friends while sharing intelligence and operational details with coalition members who are also his friends, or who have, at least, made common cause with his terrorist campaigns against the United States interests and allies.

The folly of this strategy, if it could be called such, would be greatly compounded by its corollary: In order to induce America's Arab enemies to participate in the new coalition, Israel will have to be excluded. Such a step would simultaneously deny the United States what may be its single best, and certainly most reliable, source of urgently needed intelligence and anti-terrorist skills. It would also be widely seen as implicit affirmation of the virulent attacks on Israel that the Bush administration recently and wisely declined to dignify at the U.N. conference on racism in Durban, South Africa.

After all, if Israel is deliberately excluded from the posse, there must be something to the charges that it is itself guilty of crimes against humanity.

Those murdered in cold blood on Sept. 11 will not have died in vain if we as a nation are spared the potentially far greater costs associated with these lingering illusions. It behooves Mr. Bush and Congress to work together to ensure that effective missile defenses are built and deployed at the earliest possible time and that any new alliance is made with fellow democracies who are victims of terrorism, not with terrorists who have violently assaulted them and us.

The biggest imponderable concerning the war on terror is whether the American people and their leaders are clear on a central question: Exactly who is the enemy in this war? We are, after all, not fighting some abstraction called "terror." The truth is we are engaged in a death struggle with people who use terror - usually involving the deliberate murder of innocent civilians - as an instrument to advance their agendas.

As to precisely who those people are, the past 25 months have brought to light a bewildering array of terrorist organizations pursuing a variety of stated objectives, usually with help from this or that rogue state-sponsor. But one thing should be clear after September 11, 2001: The most determined, numerous and dangerous of these enemies are radical, violent Muslims known as "Islamists."

Most experts believe the Islamists are, at present, a small percentage of the Muslim faithful worldwide. The danger is that, since there are approximately 1.6 billion Muslims, even a small percentage could mean there are millions available to serve as cannon fodder for the radicals. Worse yet, all things being equal, their numbers will continue to grow, thanks in no small measure to the assiduous efforts of Islamist regimes in Saudi Arabia and Iran [the former of the Sunni Wahhabi stripe, the latter favoring Shi'ite extremism].

All too often, such efforts are accompanied - and systematically advanced - by an insidious disinformation campaign. Its main thrust is that anyone who dares to point out the threat posed by the Islamists is a racist, bigot or ignoramus. Why? Because, we are told, such observations impugn all Muslims.

This is, of course, absurd. Law-abiding and tolerant Muslims first and foremost understand there are real differences between themselves and the Islamists - so much so the radicals view their peaceable co-religionists with at least as much hostility as they do people of other faiths.

Among those most aggressively promoting the idea that Islamists are indistinguishable from any other Muslims are a number of Arab-American and Muslim-American organizations long associated with jihadists and their causes. Since September 11, they have tried to obscure their true colors by promoting the fiction that they are defenders of all people of the Islamic faith, rather than what they actually are: apologists for the radicals among them, focused on initiatives that have the effect of excusing, protecting or otherwise benefiting the latter.

Fortunately, some of these organizations [notably several founded by or associated with Abdurahman Alamoudi - the Islamist-sympathizer indicted last month for receiving illegal funding from Libya] have recently come under increasing scrutiny from law enforcement and the Congress. The American Muslim Council, the American Muslim

Foundation, the Council on American-Islamic Relations [CAIR], the Islamic Society of North America and the Muslim Student Association have had officials arrested and/or troubling questions raised on Capitol Hill about their activities in our prisons, military chaplain corps, mosques and colleges.

In light of the arrests and worrisome revelations, it is all the more astounding that such groups enjoy any credibility at all when they denounce those who warn of Islamists hijacking and perverting the Muslim faith. The latest example of this phenomenon has been an attack mounted in the past week by the Islamists' proponents on one of the nation's most highly regarded, experienced and decorated Special Forces officers, Lt. Gen. William "Jerry" Boykin. Gen. Boykin recently assumed the post of Deputy Undersecretary of Defense for Intelligence. In that capacity, he is charged with the priority tasks of hunting down Osama bin Laden, Saddam Hussein and their ilk. This respected Pentagon official became the subject of intense and mostly hostile media attention after an inveterate leftist activist-turned columnist and TV commentator named William Arkin circulated videotaped and other materials. In them, the general professed his Christian faith and reviled Muslim extremists - yes, extremists - on both religious and strategic grounds.

Whatever one thinks of Gen. Boykin's obviously deeply held personal beliefs, he must be credited with one thing: He understands that Islamists have declared war on this country and that we have no alternative but to defeat them.

For stating this truth, the general has been roundly criticized by the Islamists' admirers and their friends. Notably, one of the most visible of the professional Muslim agitators - CAIR's executive director, Nihad Awad – has accused Gen. Boykin of "ignorance," having "extremist views" and exhibiting sufficiently defective judgment as to require his reassignment.

To their credit, President Bush, National Security Adviser Condoleezza Rice, Defense Secretary Donald Rumsfeld and Joint Chiefs Chairman General Richard Myers have thus far declined to accede to this sort of pressure. While the administration's party line remains that the United States has no interest in waging war against Islam, it would be a significant breakthrough if American officials can now frankly address the nature of our most dangerous foes: Radicals seeking to justify their terror by masquerading as bonafide adherents to the Islamic faith.

If we are to fight the Islamists effectively, we need to appreciate and highlight the threat they pose not only to non-Muslims but also to the non-jihadist Muslim world. This will, in turn, require the sharpest possible clarity about whether, to paraphrase President Bush, Muslims - at home and abroad - are with us, or with the Islamists.

The third anniversary of the U.S.-led invasion of Iraq has been marked by antiwar demonstrations, polls suggesting evaporating public support for the effort to consolidate that country's liberation and paroxysms of doubt by America's finger-in-the-wind politicians. It seems like a good time to reflect anew on the true nature of the conflict and why we have no choice but to wage it with tenacity to a successful conclusion.

Fortunately, we are greatly aided in that task by the timely arrival of an extraordinary film: "Obsession: Radical Islam's War Against the West." Viewing this documentary should hereafter be considered a prerequisite for participating in the debate about the national security challenges we face, and what must be done to address them.

"Obsession" is an unblinking, and deeply disturbing, portrait of our most immediate and dangerous enemy, in Iraq and elsewhere - the ideology best described as Islamofascism.

The film's conclusion is as inescapable as it is well documented: Adherents to this totalitarian political movement are determined to destroy the Free World, whose nations, values and institutions are seen as impediments to the global triumph of the Islamists' preferred, Taliban-style religious rule. For our enemies, Iraq represents but one front in a world war. And we, too, must recognize it as such.

The full dimensions of that War for the Free World are laid bare in "Obsession" from an extraordinary array of sources. For example, penetrating analyses are provided by internationally renowned Western experts like Sir Martin Gilbert, Alan Dershowitz, Daniel Pipes, Caroline Glick, Steven Emerson, Robert Wistrich and Itamar Marcus.

The insights of a number of courageous anti-Islamist Muslims (in some cases, former Muslims) are, if anything, even more compelling. These include observations of the daughter of a terrorist, Nonie Darwish; a former Palestinian terrorist, Walid Shoebat; an Israeli-Arab journalist, Khaled Abu-Toameth; an American imam, Khaleel Mohammed; and two prominent expatriate writers, Salim Mansur and Tashbih Sayyed. They describe with authority our common foes' determination and ruthlessness.

Lest there be any doubt, however, about the magnitude of the challenge freedom-loving peoples face, the footage in "Obsession" drawn from Islamist sources themselves (notably, their various state-owned and terrorist-sponsored television outlets) is dispositive. It features imams calling for death to America; officials of Mideast governments making plain the destruction of the United States is God's will; even tiny children regurgitating their desire for death while killing Israelis, Americans and other infidels.

The impact of the images of Muslim kids brandishing weapons, marching in goose step and giving stiff-armed salutes in mass demonstrations underscores a point made in the film by the late Alfons Heck, a former Hitler Youth Group leader in Nazi Germany: Islamofascism is really just the latest in a series of totalitarian ideologies bent on destroying the Free World.

16

"Obsession" makes clear that, like the Fuehrer, the Islamists will not be content with denying the people of Iraq accountable, representative government. Neither would their appetites be sated by destroying the State of Israel. In fact, even seemingly less momentous forms of appeasement - such as negotiating with the Islamofascist Iranian regime - will simply confirm our avowed enemies' contempt for us, and their confidence in the ultimate victory of their cause.

The connections between the Nazis and the Islamofascists are rooted in more than shared ambitions of world domination and violent methods. As Matthias Kuntzel, a professor at the University of Hamburg and noted German expert on the two ideologies has observed, "Although Islamism is an independent, anti-Semitic, anti-modern mass movement, its main early promoters - the Muslim Brotherhood in Egypt and [Haj Amin el-Husseini,] the Mufti [of Jerusalem] and the Qassamites in Palestine - were supported financially and ideologically by agencies of the German National Socialist [Nazi] government."

As it happens, Professor Kuntzel participated last week in a Paris conference co-sponsored by the Center for Security Policy to discuss "Democracies in the face of Islamist Confrontation." The conferees - involving a number of anti-Islamist Muslims as well as non-Muslims from Europe, North America and North Africa - made plain one other ominous parallel: The rising threat of Islamofascism and anti-Semitism within Western European societies today has taken on the feel of the early 1930s, replete with political instability, mounting public unease and a misplaced confidence that accommodating violent ideologues will translate into at least temporary tranquility.

Totalitarianism's return would come as no surprise to Eric Hoffer, whose extraordinary 1951 book "The True Believer: Thoughts on the Nature of Mass Movements" reads as though written yesterday. Hoffer recognized "All mass movements generate in their adherents a readiness to die and a proclivity for united action; all of them, irrespective of the doctrine they preach and the program they project, breed fanaticism, enthusiasm, fervent hope, hatred and intolerance; all of them are capable of releasing a powerful flow of activity in certain departments of life; all of them demand blind faith and singlehearted allegiance."

We are, in short, once again under assault from such a mass movement, one that appeals to large numbers of people, calls on them to die for the cause and will stop at nothing to obtain its totalitarian goals. Unfortunately, in two respects, the threat posed by Islamofascism is even greater than its totalitarian predecessors: Many of its adherents are inside Western societies and are adept at exploiting their political movement's patina of religiosity to exploit, to the Free World's detriment, our civil liberties rooted in religious tolerance.

Consequently, as a practical matter, we have no choice but to fight the Islamofascists, both abroad and at home. Surrender, whether in Iraq or elsewhere, is not an option.

The United States is in mortal peril from a false friend: the Kingdom of Saudi Arabia. The peril emanates from the totalitarian legal-religious-military-political code the Saudis call Shariah and their assiduous efforts to impose it worldwide. The danger is enormously exacerbated by the almost-complete failure of American officials at every level of government to acknowledge, let alone act to prevent, the Saudis' true agenda.

Three examples are instructive:

A recent expose by New York Times reporter Philip Shenon of congressional and independent investigations of the murderous Sept. 11, 2001, attacks describes evidence of financial, logistical and other material support by Saudi government personnel to the perpetrators of those acts of terrorism. In "The Commission: The Uncensored History of the 9/11 Investigation," Mr. Shenon suggests the Bush White House, the FBI and, not least, Saudi Ambassador Prince Bandar went to considerable lengths to suppress such evidence.

In the end, what is known is principally circumstantial - notably, a seeming Saudi covert operative in Southern California housed and facilitated the movements of two of the Sept. 11, 2001, hijackers, was in frequent communication with a Wahhabi cleric working in the United States under Saudi diplomatic cover and received before the attacks funds drawn on an account Prince Bandar's wife used to support "charities." It nonetheless seems reasonable to conclude that, had these leads been scrupulously pursued rather than covered up, we would have a far better appreciation of the enmity felt toward this country by all too many of our so-called Saudi "friends" and "allies."

What is more, in a lawsuit brought by the insurance companies who paid out more than $5 billion dollars to the victims of the Sept. 11 attacks, lawyers from the Philadelphia-based firm of Cozen O'Connor are uncovering details of Saudi government involvement in financing "foreign" jihad to keep it out of the Kingdom. Not surprisingly, they have uncovered connections missed by the Sept. 11 Commission.

That enmity can unmistakably be found in textbooks the government of Saudi Arabia supplies religious schools (known as "madrassas") around the world, including the Islamic Saudi Academy it operates in Alexandria, Va. Last week, the U.S. Commission on International Religious Freedom (USCIRF) revealed these texts encourage children to regard non-Muslims and even other Muslims with hostility and hatred and suggests it is permissible to take "their blood and treasure." Jihad is described as "the pinnacle of Islam," without clarifying the term's meaning to be just a struggle of the spirit - rather than its typical interpretation: holy war.

Importantly, the USCIRF found itself thwarted at every turn by the U.S. State Department. Foggy Bottom endlessly ran interference for the Saudis: State blithely assured the commission that Saudi Arabia had promised to rewrite its teaching materials to eliminate offensive passages. It half-heartedly pressed Riyadh for copies of the textbooks actually used at the Academy, then withheld from the USCIRF the books it did receive.

The proof now in hand, no thanks to the State Department, makes clear the virulently intolerant nature of what the Saudis insist is the authoritative form of Islamic law or Shariah. It should be sufficient grounds for acting on an earlier recommendation by the International Religious Freedom Commission: Close the Saudi Embassy-run madrassa in our midst, once and for all.

That outcome will be the demand of community activists, champions of religious freedom and national security professionals who will be demonstrating at the Islamic Saudi Academy's Alexandria campus at 8 a.m. this morning. They are protesting a decision taken a fortnight ago by the Fairfax County Board of Supervisors to renew a county-held lease on this facility - a decision that was shameful and irresponsible then, and that is, in the wake of the IRFC findings, utterly untenable now.

Even the Saudis' reported, new-found willingness to increase oil production by half-a-million barrels per day should not be confused with acts of friendship. After all, twice in recent months King Abdullah contemptuously rebuffed pleas from President Bush for just such relief from the damage caused by soaring petroleum prices. Only when that damage appeared likely to trigger a renewed U.S. determination finally to end America's "addiction to oil" have the Saudis seen any need to bring down prices at the pump.

Fortunately, the latest Saudi gambit may be too little, too late to perpetuate our present enslavement by the Organization of Petroleum Exporting Countries, the Saudi-led oil cartel that has been waging economic warfare against the United States for decades and lately with increasingly devastating effects. Thanks to the likes of Robert Zubrin, author of the highly acclaimed "Energy Victory: Winning the War on Terror by Breaking Free of Oil," Fox New's popular prime-time host Bill O'Reilly and a growing number of legislators, the American people are awakening to the fact we have an alternative: Flexible Fuel Vehicles - cars that at a nominal cost can use existing technology to run on alcohol-based fuels (such as ethanol, methanol or butanol), gasoline or some combination thereof. (More information about these "Freedom Fuels" and the Open Fuel Standard that will allow them to help end the dangerous tyranny of Saudi Arabia and OPEC is at www.SetAmericaFree.org.)

As the Saudis are not actually our friends, they will do everything possible to prevent such a development - just as they have assiduously sought to suppress information about other aspects of the seditious, totalitarian agenda they call Shariah agenda. We can no longer pretend that Saudi efforts to impose that agenda, here as well as abroad, are consistent with our national security and other interests. And we can no longer tolerate actions by those in the U.S. government aimed at obscuring such behavior, when the practical effect of doing so is to enable it to advance our destruction.

Last week, John Brennan, the assistant to the President for homeland security and counterterrorism approvingly recalled a key point in the speech Mr. Obama delivered in Cairo in June: "America is not and never will be at war with Islam." Unfortunately, that statement ignores the fact that the decision as to whether the United States is at war with anybody is not entirely up to our leadership or people. The real question is: Is 'Islam' at war with us?

It is certainly true that hundreds of millions of Muslims the world over are not seeking to wage war against the United States, or other non-Muslim states. America has, as Mr. Brennan noted in his remarks before the Center for Strategic and International Studies (CSIS) on Thursday, a powerful interest in not making all those who practice Islam into our enemies.

Yet, it would be a grave mistake to construe the problem we face as John Brennan proceeded to do in his speech at CSIS: "We are at war with al Qaeda which attacked us on 9/11 and killed 3,000 people. We are at war with its violent extremist allies who seek to carry on al-Qaida's murderous agenda." He described that agenda as seeking "to replace sovereign nations with a global caliphate."

Unfortunately, that is the stated goal of all those who adhere to what authoritative Islam calls Shariah - a number that includes many millions of people the world over. Mr. Brennan's speech made no reference to this wellspring of jihadism.

Of course, not all those who embrace Shariah are prepared to use terror against us. Shariah requires though that if its adherents do not actually engage in violent jihad, they must support it through financial or other means. After all, according to Shariah, the purpose of jihad is to bring about the triumph of Islam over the entire world. Shariah commands that the faithful must use violence where possible to advance that objective, and non-violent means where not.

By failing to recognize this justification and catalyst for the threat we face, Mr. Obama and his administration effectively foreclose the possibility of countering it effectively. Worse yet, in their understandable desire not to give gratuitous offense to Muslims, the U.S. government has repeatedly deferred to those who are most easily and most vocally offended.

Specifically, the latter - notably, the putatively non-violent, but virulently Islamist Muslim Brotherhood and its myriad front organizations - have come to dictate what our officials can and cannot say about the danger posed not just by al Qaeda and its "violent extremist allies," but by all those who embrace the teachings, traditions, institutions and dictates of what authoritative Islam defines as "mainstream": Shariah.

This practice effectively disenfranchises American Muslims who reject this Shariah program - precisely the sorts of people we should most want to empower. Last week, I discussed this problem on our talk radio program with someone who is trying to do something about it: Rep. Sue Myrick of North Carolina.

As it happens, Ms. Myrick's district is not far from where Daniel Patrick Boyd and other alleged "homegrown" jihadists were reportedly plotting attacks abroad, and possibly here. What is more, the financial sector so prominent in the Charlotte community she represents is also a prime target of one of the most insidious forms of what author Robert Spencer calls "stealth" jihad: Shariah-compliant finance.

Congresswoman Myrick, a co-founder of the House Anti-Terror Caucus, recently convened a meeting to afford "moderate" Muslims an opportunity to interact with representatives of various federal law enforcement and other agencies responsible for securing this country. According to Ms. Myrick, some of the officials seemed to be discovering for the first time that there are practitioners of Islam who do not embrace the seditious tenets of Shariah - and who were extremely concerned about the government's almost exclusive reliance on those who do.

Fortunately, decisions in federal court in recent weeks may produce some urgently needed policy course-corrections. Judge Laurence Zatkoff in the Eastern District of Michigan recently cleared the way for accelerated and wide-ranging discovery in connection with a suit brought by a Michigan Iraq war veteran, Kevin Murray, against the Treasury Department and Federal Reserve. Mr. Murray is challenging on constitutional separation of church-and-state grounds the practice of a U.S. government-owned company, the insurance conglomerate AIG, promoting Shariah-compliant products.

It seems likely that the depositions that will now be taken by Mr. Murray's legal team - securities litigator and Shariah expert David Yerushalmi and attorneys at the Thomas More Law Center, led by its director Richard Thompson - will shed important light on the federal government's understanding of authoritative Islam's seditious program. It may also reveal the extent to which U.S. officials have, with their failure to comprehend the true nature of the threat we face, acted, either wittingly or unwittingly, in ways that have enabled it to metastasize further.

Whether through the revelations of this lawsuit or through the work of influential legislators like Sue Myrick, the time has come to recognize that even if we insist we are not at war with Islam, the authorities of Islam *are* at war with us. Only by so doing can we connect with and empower our natural allies in this war - Muslims who want to enjoy liberty in a Shariah-free America. And only by so doing, do we have a chance of prevailing.

The supremacist program authoritative Islam calls Shariah is big on symbols. Arguably, none is more effective than its practice of building mosques on its conquests' most sacred sites.

In Jerusalem, triumphant Muslims built the Al-Aqsa mosque on top of the Jews' revered Temple Mount. They transformed what had been for a thousand years the largest cathedral in Christendom, Constantinople's magnificent St. Sophia basilica, into a sprawling mosque complex. And the Moorish Ummayad dynasty in Spain, made the city of Cordoba its capital, and installed an immense mosque on the site of an ancient Christian church there.

Now, an imam in New York, who has suddenly come into $100 million from undisclosed sources, wants to build a 13-story Islamic Cultural Center adjacent to the site of Shariah's greatest triumph to date in America: Ground Zero, the place where the World Trade Center's twin towers proudly stood until they were destroyed by Shariah-adherent jihadists on September 11, 2001. It is not a coincidence that the imam, Feisal Abdul Rauf, has called his project "the Cordoba House."

Such a mosque on 9/11's hallowed ground would not only constitute a durable, symbolic taunt by our enemies about their bloody victory. In accordance with Shariah, once ground has been taken for Islam, it can never revert to the non-Muslim Dar al-Harb, literally the House of War.

In other words, the Ground Zero mosque is designed to be a permanent, in-our-face beachhead for Shariah, a platform for inspiring the triumphalist ambitions of the faithful and eroding resistence to their demands for separate and (for the moment, at least) equal treatment in America.

So why, one might ask, have Mayor Michael Bloomberg, various other elected officials and clergy and community leaders expressed support for the Cordoba House?

In part, it is a function of local considerations: Who wouldn't welcome the prospect of an infusion of $100 million into the still-suffering economy of lower Manhattan? What is more, if the mosque serves as a magnet for new Muslim residents, depressed housing prices could rebound.

The larger problem is that too few of our leaders understand the nature of Shariah and its implications. Even when an imam like Rauf explicitly says he favors bringing Shariah to America, officials at every level of government seem untroubled by the fact that such an agenda necessarily is anti-constitutional and incompatible with our freedoms.

To be sure, Imam Rauf is a skilled practitioner of the Shariah tradition of taqqiya deception for the faith. It turns out, he was to the manner born: As ace researcher Alyssa Lappen has documented, Rauf has family and other longstanding ties to the Muslim

Brotherhood.

So, in a page taken straight out of the Brotherhood taqqiya playbook, the imam and his wife and collaborator on the Cordoba House project, Daisy Khan, have been much in evidence of late, professing their commitment to interfaith dialogue and the dedication of their new facility to serving the non-Muslim as well as Muslim communities.

As it happens, similar assurances about mosque complexes built elsewhere by other Shariah adherents have amounted to the old "bait-and-switch" scam. A group called Americans for Peace and Tolerance (APT) has monitored, for example, the Islamic Society of Boston's Saudi-funded, city-enabled mega-mosque in Roxbury, Massachusetts. Despite professions of tolerance, the mosque has ties to Hamas and other terrorists. According to APT, the mosque's imam, "Abdullah Faarooq, has told his followers to 'pick up the gun and the sword' and supported local terror suspects Aafia Siddiqui and Tarek Mehanna."

In the United Kingdom, the North London Central Mosque (a.k.a. the Finsbury Park Mosque) has been embraced by the British government and is considered an archetype for its effort to counter radicalization by working with the Muslim Brotherhood's "non-violent" Islamists. Yet, this mosque hosted one of America's most wanted terrorists: Anwar al-Alwaki. According to National Public Radio, among those who attended his sermons there was the Nigerian panty-bomber, Umar Farouk Abulmutallab.

We have reason to fear that the United States government is poised to follow Britain's disastrous course - further compounding the muddle-headed thinking among leaders across the country about Shariah and the threat it poses. John Brennan, President Obama's Homeland Security and Counterterrorism Advisor has repeatedly signaled that he wants to reach out to "moderate" jihadists of the Taliban and Hezbollah. President Obama has said he intends to provide more than $400 million for Hamas-run Gaza.

Then, Brennan gave an interview in the *Washington Times* last week in which he displayed anew his profound misunderstanding of the enemy and its threat doctrine. As the Times' Eli Lake reported: "Mr. Brennan said that he opposed granting any legitimacy to what he called al Qaeda's 'twisted' interpretation of Islam. 'Clearly, bin Laden and al Qaeda believe they are on this very holy agenda and this jihad. However in my view, what we cannot do is to allow them to think, and the rest of the world to think, for the future terrorists of the world to believe al Qaeda is a legitimate representation of jihad and Islam.'"

Such denials of the centrality of violent jihad to authoritative Islam - and the obligation to engage in more stealthy forms of jihad to the same end, the global triumph of Islam, where violence is not practicable - is a formula for disaster. Unchallenged, it will produce a toxic shrine at Ground Zero to the doctrine that animates al Qaeda and the Muslim Brotherhood alike, Shariah.

The liquidation of Osama bin Laden is a cause for full-throated national celebration. It must also be the occasion for a redirection of our efforts to wage and win what has been misnamed "the War on Terrorism." At last, we must recognize the struggle we are in for what it is – the War for the Free World – and begin taking all the steps necessary to win it, not just some of them.

For starters, let's consider some of the areas in which lessons can already be learned in light of what is now known about the takedown of al Qaeda's leader:

Ferreting out bin Laden's safe haven in Abbattabad, Pakistan is the latest affirmation of the importance of human intelligence. While various technical means of monitoring his couriers' communications and movements played a role, in the end it appears there really is no substitute for old-fashioned spying and tradecraft. The need to correct continuing – and in some cases acute – shortfalls in this area should feature prominently in the upcoming confirmation hearings for the outgoing and incoming CIA Directors, Secretary of Defense-designate Leon Panetta and General David Petraeus, respectively.

That imperative is especially pressing when foreign "liaison" services are as manifestly unreliable as is now indisputably true of Pakistan's double-dealing intelligence agency, the ISI. Ever since Jimmy Carter's Director of Central Intelligence, Stansfield Turner, set about dismantling U.S. "humint" capabilities – and especially since 9/11 – America has relied to a great and unwise degree on information and agents supplied by others.

The fact that the Pakistanis could not be apprised of the operation that took out bin Laden until after it was over – to say nothing of the manner in which he was "hiding" in a million-dollar compound behind 12-foot walls in close proximity to some of Pakistan's key military installations – tells us everything we need to know about the untrustworthiness of our so-called ally, and the extent to which it is working with our foes.

These insights come, moreover, on the heels of published reports last week that Pakistan's prime minister and the director of the ISI paid a visit to Afghan president Hamid Kharzi. In its course, they are said to have pressed him to cut ties with the United States and partner instead with their country and its ally, Communist China.

Such contemptuous behavior towards us reflects in part at least the calculation in Islamabad (and doubtless elsewhere) that the U.S. is a declining power, which need not be feared because it lacks the will to punish its enemies and cannot be counted upon to protect its friends. Bin Laden's liquidation is an important corrective to such portentous impressions. It must be reinforced and built upon as a matter of the utmost national importance.

The proficiency of our armed forces in executing the kill-or-capture orders for Osama bin Laden should be a source of pride for all Americans. The fact that it was done without loss of any U.S. personnel makes the performance all the more extraordinary. Press reports served up in the wake of the bin Laden mission to the effect that special forces teams and their CIA paramilitary counterparts perform such feats on a daily basis only underscores the high quality of these units, and their value to the nation.

Such proficiency comes at a price, though; "Freedom is not free." Yet, we are now increasingly trying to defend America without making the sustained investment it requires.

Barack Obama's own incumbent Secretary of Defense, Robert Gates, has warned that we risk "hollowing out" our military if the President's announced cut of a further $400 billion cut in defense spending over the next 12 years is enacted – coming as it would on top of the nearly $200 billion already excised. Even elite units are having to operate without the requisite gear, in some cases relying on family and friends to supply some of what they need to survive the dangers associated with their assignments. Time will tell whether the helicopter lost in the latest mission was a casualty of maintenance shortfalls.

One thing is certain: We will pay in treasure or in a currency we hold more dear – lives – if the success against bin Laden is taken as a further excuse to diminish our armed forces, rather than as a reminder of the need to assure their readiness for tomorrow's wars, as well as today's.

Finally, bin Laden's welcome demise must precipitate a retooling of our appreciation of the threat we face. No matter how often our leaders insist the enemy is al Qaeda and its destruction is our goal, the reality is different. We confront a larger array of adversaries who share such terrorists' goals – the imposition worldwide of a politico-military-legal program they call shariah to be administered by a Caliph – but pursue them via different, often stealthy means.

Such enemies, including the Muslim Brotherhood, operate here as well as abroad – a point that should be a focus of Senate and House hearings this week with Attorney General Eric Holder. Ending the sort of obstruction of justice his department appears to have engaged in with respect to the prosecution of Brotherhood fronts and operatives is a good place to start the next phase of the War for the Free World.

How's this for a wake-up call: America's most cherished civil liberties and the Constitution that enshrines them are actually enabling Muslim Brotherhood operatives and other Islamists who have the declared mission of destroying our freedoms and government "from within…by [our] hands." Specifically, our enemies are using our tolerance of religion to create an infrastructure of mosques here that incubate the Islamic holy war called jihad.

If this revelation is not exactly news to those who are serious students of the Brotherhood's decades-long, stealthy "civilization jihad" in this country (for more, see the best-selling "Team B II Report" published late last year by the Center for Security Policy: *Shariah: The Threat to America*), it will almost certainly come as a shock to the average American. Yet, the phenomenon of our rights being used to pursue our destruction has become undeniable – particularly now, thanks to an assiduously researched, peer-reviewed study published on June 6th by the highly respected journal, *Middle East Quarterly*.

Entitled "*Shari'a and Violence in American Mosques*," this paper describes an ominous jihadist footprint being put into place across the nation. It is made up of ostensibly religious institutions, entities that, therefore, enjoy constitutional protection. But, according to the data examined by this study, most mosques in the United States are actually engaged in – or at least supportive of – a totalitarian, seditious agenda they call shariah. Its express purpose is undermining and ultimately forcibly replacing the U.S. government and its founding documents. In their place would be a "caliph," governing in accordance with shariah's political-military-legal code.

To be sure, some American mosques are not part of the jihadist enterprise. And most Muslims in the United States, like most adherents of other faiths, are not regular attendees at their places of worship.

Still, according to this study's two formidable authors – my colleague, David Yerushalmi, one of the nation's foremost non-Muslim experts on the totalitarian Islamic doctrine known as shariah, and a highly respected Israeli academic and expert on Islam and Arabic culture, Dr. Mordechai Kedar – on-site investigations of a random but representative sample of American mosques in fourteen states and the District of Columbia produced chilling insights into the threat posed by many such institutions.

For the purpose of their analysis, the authors examined data collected by surveyors who "were asked to observe and record selected behaviors deemed to be shariah-adherent. These behaviors were selected precisely because they constitute observable and measurable practices of an orthodox form of Islam, as opposed to internalized, non-observable articles of faith." Such behaviors included, among other readily discernible indicators: "a) women wearing the hijab (head covering) or niqab (full-length shift covering the entire female form except for the eyes); b) gender segregation during mosque prayers; and c) enforcement of straight prayer lines."

For the purpose of their study, the authors evaluated support for jihad by considering the presence in mosque bookstores, libraries and among recommended materials "literature encouraging worshipers to engage in terrorist activity, to provide financial support to jihadists, and to promote the establishment of a caliphate in the United States. These materials also explicitly praised acts of terror against the West; praised symbols or role models of violent jihad; promoted the use of force, terror, war, and violence to implement the shariah; emphasized the inferiority of non-Muslim life; promoted hatred and intolerance toward non-Muslims or notional Muslims; and endorsed inflammatory materialswith anti-U.S. view."

Employing this methodology, Mr. Yerushalmi and Dr. Kedar found that:

- More than 80 percent of U.S. mosques advocate or otherwise promote violence. "Of the 100 mosques surveyed, 51% had texts on site rated as severely advocating violence; 30% had texts rated as moderately advocating violence; and 19% had no violent texts at all."

- Mosques that were identifiable using empirical measures "as shariah-adherent were more likely to feature violence-positive texts on site than were their non-shariah adherent counterparts."

- "In 84.5% of the mosques, the imam recommended studying violence-positive texts. The leadership at shariah-adherent mosques was morelikely to recommend that a worshipper study violence-positive texts than leadership at non-shariah-adherent mosques."

- "[O]f the 51 mosques that contained severe materials, 100 percent were led by imams who recommended that worshipers study texts that promote violence."

- "Fifty-eight percent (58%) of the mosques invited guest imams known to promote violent jihad. The leadership of mosques that featured violence-positive literature was more likely to invite guest imams who wereknown to promote violent jihad than was the leadership of mosques that did not feature violence-positive literature on mosque premises."

[*See the website* **MappingSharia.com** *for more information on each of the books surveyed, including a brief analysis of each book's importance, excerpts, their availability, and even downloadable PDFs.*]

In short, such findings strongly suggest that shariah-adherence is a useful predictor of sympathy for – and, in some cases at least, action on behalf of – jihad, to include both the Islamists' violent or stealthy forms of warfare aimed at supplanting the U.S. Constitution and government. Indeed, the study confirms the anecdotal reports by Muslims themselves and earlier, less rigorous empirical studies of Saudi hate-filled literature permeating mosques in the United States.

The UK government has just announced that, pursuant to a update of its counter-terrorism program known as "Prevent," it now recognizes non-violent forms of Islamist extremism can be every bit as dangerous as the violent kinds. We need to do the same – especially since the Muslim Brotherhood and its fellow shariah-adherents are successfully using not only mosques, but academia, the media, financial institutions, political groups and interfaith "dialogue" to pursue their pre-violent yet seditious, and therefore anti-constitutional and illegal, agenda.

Last week, Vice President Joe Biden offered the latest - and arguably the clearest - evidence of Team Obama's strategy for victory in what was once euphemistically known as the "War on Terror": Define down the enemy.

In an interview with former State Department official Leslie Gelb published in *Newsweek*, Biden declared: "The Taliban per se is not our enemy. That's critical. There is not a single statement that the president has ever made in any of our policy assertions that the Taliban is our enemy because it threatens U.S. interests."

In other words, the Obama administration appears to have embraced the Taliban line that it will stop killing and maiming our people as soon as there are no more of them in Afghanistan. As one of its operatives told reporters for *The Daily Beast*: "We are not a worldwide movement. Our focus is totally on Afghan territory. Ninety-nine percent of Taliban couldn't even find the U.S. on a map."

There is a question that must be answered before we go any farther in the direction Obama-Biden and Company clearly have in mind - namely, negotiating what amounts to the surrender of Afghanistan to so-called "moderate" members of the Taliban: The issue is not whether the Taliban is a worldwide movement, but is it *part of one*?

Indisputably, the Taliban considers itself to be an element of the umma, the Dar al-Islam, the Muslim world. As such, it embraces, practices and imposes the totalitarian, supremacist political-military-legal doctrine known as shariah. It has these attributes in common with al Qaeda. It also shares them with other unsavory elements around the world such as: the Muslim Brotherhood, Lashkar-e-Taiba, Hizb ut Tahrir, Hamas, Hezbollah, the governments of Iran and Saudi Arabia, and Boko Haram, the Nigerian terrorist group that massacred dozens of Christians on Christmas Day.

The Obama administration refuses to recognize this reality. It would have us believe that the only threat we face comes from al Qaeda. In fact, increasingly, it seems to suggest that we need not be unduly concerned about its franchises in the Levant, Iraq and the Arabian Peninsula, just "core" al Qaeda. For that matter, we don't really have to worry about the core group's foot soldiers, just their leadership. And, according to senior U.S. officials, we have killed all but two of those.

Thus, we are encouraged to recognize that the war - now re-euphemized as "Countering Violent Extremism" - is just about over, to the great credit of our Commander-in-Chief.

The only problem with this rosy picture is that it bears no resemblance to reality.

In fact, our shariah-adherent enemies are not in retreat, let alone defeated. Even if the top ranks of al Qaeda now doing business out of Pakistan have been substantially depleted, neither that hydra-headed organization nor its fellow jihadists with other affiliations evidence anything but a growing determination: They see the coming of a divinely mandated opportunity to prevail over the "Great Satan," a United States that has *actually* retreated from Iraq and is signaling its determination to do the same from Afghanistan.

This ominous assessment was validated just before Christmas in federal court in the Southern District of New York. Notwithstanding the contention that the deep-seated enmity between Islam's Shia and Sunni factions precludes cooperation between them, Judge George Daniels ruled that Shiite Iran is liable, along with the Sunnis of al Qaeda and the Taliban, for the attacks that killed nearly 3,000 Americans on 9/11.

More to the present point, as the Associated Press put it, the judge also found that: "Iran continues to provide material support and resources to al Qaeda by providing a safe haven for al Qaeda leadership and rank-and-file al Qaeda members."

Put simply, our enemies who share a fealty to shariah are perfectly capable - despite differences on fine points of Islamic practice - of collaborating to the common end of seeking our forcible submission to their doctrine or, failing that, to effecting our destruction.

In the interest of achieving tactical political advantage at home, President Obama and his subordinates are studiously ignoring this reality. Worse yet, they are insisting that no one else understand it either.

At this writing, an official witch-hunt is underway to find and eliminate training materials in FBI, other law enforcement, intelligence and military files that show the immediate threat we face emanates from shariah, not the leadership of core al Qaeda. And to help ensure conformity with this dictate going forward, the administration is relying on vetting of trainers by "community leaders" affiliated with organizations the federal government has established are fronts for the Muslim Brotherhood.

Five thousand years ago, the Chinese strategist Sun Tzu famously warned: "If you know yourself but not the enemy, for every victory gained you will also suffer a defeat. If you know neither the enemy nor yourself, you will succumb in every battle."

At the moment we seem a lot closer to losing every battle than we are to winning any wars. It would be a grave disservice to our splendid men and women who fight them - and perilous to the country they sacrifice so much to defend - were the Obama administration to persist in seeking the pretense of victory by defining down the enemy, and, in the process, ensuring we succumb to defeat.

Shortly before Newt Gingrich's decisive victory in South Carolina last week, he was asked a critical question by a Palmetto State voter: Would he support a Muslim candidate for president? The former Speaker of the House answered in a way that was both characteristically insightful and profoundly helpful with respect to one of the most serious challenges our country faces at the moment.

Mr. Gingrich responded by saying it depends on a critical factor: Is the candidate "a modern person who happens to worship Allah"? Or "a person who belonged to any kind of belief in shariah, any kind of effort to impose that on the rest of us"? Speaker Gingrich observed that the former would not be a problem, while the latter would be a "mortal threat." The Georgia Republican went on to assert the need for federal legislation that would prevent shariah from being applied in U.S. courts.

Muslim Brotherhood front groups like the Council on American Islamic Relations (CAIR) are squealing like, well, stuck haram (or impure) pigs. After all, they have been working overtime to try to obscure the true nature of shariah and to prevent the enactment of legislation that would interfere with the considerable progress being made below the radar in states across the country: the insinuation of shariah into the American judiciary.

Resorting to their standard technique of ad hominem attacks, CAIR and its friends have derided Mr. Gingrich's stance as "racist," "bigoted" and "Islamophobic." Such comments evidently were not persuasive to South Carolina voters - and they should be equally dismissed by everybody else.

The simple fact of the matter is that shariah defines the fault line between people who are Muslims but can love our country, respect and enjoy its freedoms and support our form of government and Constitution on the one hand, and those who are obliged by doctrine to oppose all those things. Worse, adherents to shariah must - in accordance with that doctrine - seek, as Speaker Gingrich says, "to impose it on the rest of us."

For the latter Muslims, the preferred way of achieving such submission is, as Mohammed taught, through violence. Where that would be impractical and/or counterproductive for the moment, however, their doctrine encourages the use of stealthy techniques to advance the same, supremacist goal.

The Muslim Brotherhood in America calls this "civilization jihad." It seeks through, for example, the use of shariah in U.S. courts to insinuate their program here at the expense of our constitutional rights and state public policy.

A sense of how far along we are in this process was provided by a study conducted last year by the Center for Security Policy. Entitled *Shariah Law and American State Courts:*

An Assessment of State Appellate Court Cases, the report is a microcosm of U.S. jurisprudence. Its findings were alarming: Out of a sample of 50 cases, in 27 instances in 23 states, the courts involved allowed the use of shariah to adjudicate the dispute.

In almost all of the cases, that outcome was at the expense of the constitutional rights of American women or children. Under shariah, they simply do not enjoy the same stature and are not entitled to the same freedoms as they are under U.S. law.

In November 2010, seventy percent of the voters of Oklahoma approved an amendment to the state constitution that would have barred shariah from being used in Oklahoma's courts. No sooner had the balloting ended than the local franchise of CAIR - an unindicted co-conspirator in the Holy Land Foundation terrorism financing trial - asked for an injunction on the grounds that such a prohibition would violate Muslims' constitutional rights. A federal judge agreed, and was recently upheld by an appellate court.

Fortunately, those who concur with Newt Gingrich on the nature of the threat posed by shariah and who want to prevent its further penetration into this country have another option. Three states - Tennessee, Louisiana and Arizona - have already enacted a statute known as American Laws for American Courts (ALAC). It prohibits the use of any foreign law in the state's courts that would interfere with U.S. constitutional rights or state public policy.

While shariah would certainly be covered by ALAC, it is not singled out for special treatment. No challenge has been mounted thus far in any of the states where it is the law today. And some 20 other states are actively considering ALAC's adoption in the current legislative session.

The Muslim Brotherhood and its friends desperately hope to stave off the further enactment of American Laws for American Courts. They recognize that it can effectively thwart a key part of their civilization jihad in this country. They also have seen that, wherever ALAC is considered, more and more of our countrymen are becoming aware of the problem Newt Gingrich has helped define: the threat from shariah and the need to keep its adherents from imposing that toxic, anti-constitutional doctrine on the rest of us, whether by stealth in our courts (among other places) or through terrifying violence.

For all these reasons, we should ensure that neither shariah nor any other form of foreign or transnational law is allowed to trump our constitutional rights. To the Muslim Brotherhood's fury, ALAC is a way of doing it in a constitutionally sound and highly teachable way.

For the past two weeks, the American people have been encouraged by Team Obama — official representatives of the administration, its champions in the press and other partisans — to believe a number of national security calumnies that can be described only as surrealistically epic and dangerous deceptions. Far more than the usual political sleight of hand that can be expected in the run-up to an election, the mendacity of Team Obama is truly audacious, and the consequences of the public accepting it at face value are grave.

Take, for example, President Obama's insistence that the surging violence in dozens of countries is a "natural" response by Muslims to a video produced in America that trashes Islam's Prophet Muhammad. One can scarcely find an official or press account of these events that does not start with something to the effect that the attacks were precipitated by that (almost entirely unviewed) short film.

There are several things wrong with this proposition. First, in some places — notably Libya, where an attack on the U.S. Consulate in Benghazi resulted in the brutal killing of the American ambassador and three others assigned to that mission — there is no evidence that the film was even a pretext, let alone the real reason for what was, in fact, a disciplined, coordinated and successful act of jihad. In others, it was simply the latest excuse by Islamists to incite crowds to violence, just as Danish cartoons, burned Korans, a speech by the pope and defiled Afghan corpses have been at one time or another.

What this latest campaign of deceit by Team Obama is meant to obscure is its own national security malpractice, namely a dogged refusal to face the reality that America is at war with an enemy that it has been unwilling to name, has failed to counter and is actually emboldening. Such behavior has signaled to jihadists seeking to impose on the rest of us the totalitarian ideology they call Shariah that acts of violence — or even threats of violence — against us will be met with accommodations and concessions whenever the stated justification is outrage over some perceived insult to Islam.

The Obama administration has committed to engage in, as Secretary of State Hillary Rodham Clinton put it, "old-fashioned techniques of peer pressure and shaming" to discourage such offensive behavior. This is but a milestone along the trajectory of the White House's acquiescence to the Shariah blasphemy agenda of the Muslim Brotherhood's state-level counterpart, the Organization of Islamic Cooperation.

The course of this trajectory is utterly predictable: more violence, followed by more demands for more self-imposed restrictions on free speech, which are justified as necessitated by the national security. This pattern, in turn, translates into a rising perception of our submission to the Islamists' demands, which encourages another cycle of jihadism, and on and on. What started as the U.S. government's refusal to understand or even name the enemy for fear of causing offense may soon metastasize into a cowed submission to Shariah — all in the name of "keeping the peace," of course.

We are likely to be treated to another example of Mr. Obama's staggering national security disinformation campaign in connection with the U.N. General Assembly meetings in New York this week. The Egyptian president, the Muslim Brotherhood's Mohammed Morsi, is expected to use his appearances to repeat his demand that the United States release Omar Abdul Rahman, better known as the "Blind Sheikh," who is a convicted terrorist serving a life sentence in federal prison. The Obama administration wants us to believe that such a step is not under consideration.

Yet, Mrs. Clinton's State Department gave a visa in June to one of the Blind Sheikh's fellow terrorists, Hani Nour Eldin. The reason? To facilitate discussions of Mr. Morsi's demand in meetings at the White House, at the State Department and on Capitol Hill. Andrew McCarthy, who was the federal prosecutor who secured Rahman's conviction of conspiring to destroy the World Trade Center in 1993, warns that despite the administration's serial and artfully worded denials, Mr. Obama is likely to release the sheikh after the November election.

I have experienced another Obama calumny personally, but it touches every American who speaks clearly about the threat we face. Organizations closely aligned with the White House and supportive of its pandering to Islamists — such as the radical left's Center for American Progress, the American Civil Liberties Union, the Southern Poverty Law Center, and the Muslim Brotherhood's Council on American-Islamic Relations and the Muslim Public Affairs Council — have taken to vilifying opponents of jihadism.

Without any basis in fact, we have been called everything from "racists" and "bigots" to "Islamophobes." Our expertise on national security and threats from the Shariah agenda have been denied, basically on the grounds that we have not been approved by the Muslim Brotherhood, attended a madrassa or been trained as Islamist clerics. It has been suggested lately that if anything bad happens involving Muslims and violence, it will be our fault.

This assertion presumably is designed to set the stage for prosecution of the kind we have seen in Europe and Canada on hate speech or other charges consistent with what amount to Shariah blasphemy laws — once our First Amendment rights have been further shredded by Mr. Obama and his team.

Will we really accede to this succession of big lies, with all that portends for our freedom of expression, our situational awareness of the jihadist threat and our ability to resist it? Not if we want to bequeath to our children the America we inherited.

Authorities in Massachusetts have identified suspects in the Boston Marathon bombing on Monday as Dzhokhar and (the now-deceased) Tamerlan Tsarnaev, two brothers of Chechen descent originally from Kyrgyzstan. Many Americans haven't heard of the place; most couldn't find it on a map. Nearly all would be unable to say why people from there would want to kill people from here.

Welcome to the phenomenon of global jihad. It is time to dispense with the illusion that we are safe from foreign threats because we have put, as President Obama repeatedly insisted during the last campaign, "al Qaeda on the path to defeat," thanks to the death of Osama bin Laden and the drone-delivered thinning of the ranks of his lieutenants.

The Chechen jihadists in Boston may or may not have been associated with, or even inspired by, bin Laden's terror network. But in the days and weeks to come we are likely to discover that they identify with its goals: 1) imposing the supremacist Islamic doctrine of shariah – a totalitarian, brutally repressive and anti-Constitutional ideology – on the entire world, Muslim and non-Muslim alike. And 2) recreating a caliphate (or a similar theo-political entity) to rule according to that doctrine.

The same is true of other violent jihadists of the Sunni and Shia stripes, including, respectively, the Wahhabis of Saudi Arabia and the regime in Iran. Ditto the so-called non-violent Muslim Brotherhood. In fact, that organization – which is the mother-ship for virtually all modern Sunni jihadists – favors an approach better described as pre-violent: The Brotherhood is perfectly prepared to use violence when it will be effective. Until then, they will adopt other measures (which they call "civilization jihad") to create conditions that would be conducive to the realization of the goals they share with all other Islamists.

My preliminary read on the Brothers Tsarnaev is that they, too, were committed to the triumph of shariah. And whether they were associated with one or the other of these groups, factions, or sects, or if they were self-taught and operating alone, it seems likely that they embraced that doctrine's requirement to wage jihad against infidels – something they evidently did with pressure-cooker improvised explosive devices near the Finish Line on Monday.

Literally by the minute, we are learning more about their backgrounds and behavior. With luck, we will also know shortly whether they were aided by accomplices or organizational infrastructure that may still pose a threat.

What we know already, however, is that there are perhaps hundreds of thousands, maybe millions, of others like them around the world. Folks who believe that their god commands them to engage personally in holy war against the infidels and non-shariah-adherent Muslims (whom they call apostates).

What is particularly worrying is that this is not a new revelation. We have been on notice of this fact since well before 9/11. And yet we have at times ignored it – or, in some cases, denied it assiduously. And that is not simply true of average Americans. It has been the widespread practice within administrations of both parties, beginning in earnest under George W. Bush and metastasizing greatly in the Obama presidency. (For a detailed treatment of how this has happened and why, see www.MuslimBrotherhoodinAmerica.com and *The Muslim Brother in the Obama Administration* www.horowitzfreedomcenter.org.)

We have thus systematically violated one of the cardinal principles of warfare dating back at least to the ancient Chinese strategist Sun Tsu, who warned that you cannot defeat an enemy you do not know. Worse, we have allowed an enemy we could and should have known long ago to dictate to us what we are allowed to understand, think, and do about them.

For example, the Obama administration has purged the files and training materials of federal law enforcement, intelligence, homeland security, and defense agencies of information that might "offend" Islamists. That would include knowing such truths as that it is the orthodoxy of Islam (although a practice not embraced by all Muslims) to engage in jihad to advance the supremacy of shariah.

Even more alarming, the U.S. government now operates under guidelines for training in "countering violent extremism" (the euphemism it adopted in lieu of the Bush administration's preferred euphemism for jihad, "terrorism") that make matters infinitely more dangerous: those using federal funds for such training must now first consult with "community partners" about the trainers and their materials. Those partners appear to be Muslim Brotherhood operatives and front groups.

Whether we choose to acknowledge it or not, we are a nation at war. And not simply in Afghanistan, but worldwide. Not with every Muslim, but with every Muslim that believes shariah must reign supreme and will do whatever is necessary to bring that about.

Those enemies fully understand and embrace this war. They regard our efforts to pretend otherwise or to accommodate, placate, or appease them as submission. According to their doctrine of shariah, the appropriate response to the infidel submitting is, in the words of the Koran, to make them "feel subdued." And that is a formula for more violent jihadism, not less.

At a moment when our elected representatives are contemplating immigration "reform" that would likely have the result of enabling, among others, still more global jihadists into our country, we need to grasp the lessons of the latest Boston massacre. We must be clear about the enemy, vigilant against his jihadist techniques – both the violent and pre-violent ones – and adopt the war footing required to prevail over this threat here at home and elsewhere, before more of us suffer the perils of global holy war.

As al Qaeda raises its black flag of jihad over parts of Iraq liberated from its clutches at the cost of enormous American blood and treasure, we are getting a taste of what President Obama's serial national security fraud is wreaking around the world.

Remember back in the 2012 campaign when he told us, repeatedly, that al Qaeda was "on the path to defeat"? That was a deliberate fraud, meant to shore up his commander-in-chief credentials at a time when he (wrongly) thought they might properly be seriously challenged by Republican Mitt Romney.

Remember when the jihadists' flag was flown over the U.S. Embassy in Cairo and accompanied the murderous sacking of two American facilities in Benghazi on Sept. 11, 2012? These events were symptomatic of our nation's perceived weakness — a perception that is, as former Defense Secretary Donald H. Rumsfeld says, "provocative." (The failure of the Republican leadership in the House to hold the Obama administration accountable for such outrages — or even to establish the truth about these debacles — is the subject of a scorching letter from conservative leaders, families of the fallen and others delivered on Monday.)

Remember when Mr. Obama assured us that there were "moderates" among the Syrian opposition and that we should bomb their enemy, Bashar Assad, to punish him and, presumably, with a view to bringing them to power. As a practical matter, the only people who count among the "rebels" are Islamists, whose supremacist Shariah doctrine requires them inevitably to seek our destruction.

The same goes for Mr. Assad's Shiite backers in Iran and Hezbollah. They hate the Sunnis of the Muslim Brotherhood and its offshoots, such as al Qaeda. They are perfectly willing, though, to make common cause against us whenever the opportunity presents itself. Think Sept. 11.

I could go on and on, but you get the idea. We have been repeatedly deceived by Team Obama about the nature of the enemy we face. Our Islamist enemies have only grown more formidable and more numerous, are on the march in more places and are more emboldened by what they rightly see as our submission.

What is especially worrisome is that the wages of the ineptitude — or worse — of American leaders in the face of such threats are immensely increased by the fact that scarcely any among them are even aware that we face yet another kind of jihad: the stealthy type the Muslim Brotherhood calls "civilization jihad."

We know from a secret plan providentially discovered in Annandale, Va., in 2004 that the Muslim Brotherhood is using subversion and sedition to destroy Western civilization "from within." A new paper published by the Gatestone Institute's Soeren Kern entitled the "Islamization of Britain in 2013" documents how far advanced this destruction is in the land of our closest European ally — and what is in store for the rest of the West if we remain oblivious to this threat.

The following are among the most appalling leading indicators of the United Kingdom's inexorable submission to Shariah:

"In January, Muslim gangs were filmed loitering on streets in London and demanding that passers-by conform to Islamic Shariah law. In a series of videos, the self-proclaimed vigilantes — who call themselves Muslim London Patrol — are seen abusing non-Muslim pedestrians and repeatedly shouting, 'This is a Muslim area.' One video records the men shouting: 'Allah is the greatest! Islam is here, whether you like it or not. We are here. We are here. What we need is Islam. What we need is Shariah.'

"In April, a documentary secretly filmed inside several of the 85 Islamic Shariah Law courts operating in Britain exposed the systematic discrimination that many women are suffering at the hands of Muslim jurists. The undercover investigation proves what has long been suspected: namely, that Shariah courts, which operate in mosques and houses across Britain, routinely issue rulings on domestic and marital issues according to Islamic Shariah law that are at odds with British law. Although Shariah rulings are not legally binding, those subject to the rulings often feel obliged to obey them as a matter of religious belief, or because of pressure from family and community members to do so.

"[There has been] a wave of sex crimes involving predatory Muslim taxi drivers who are raping female passengers. The number of so-called taxi rapes is snowballing to such an extent that a British judge has issued a warning that no woman can expect to be safe while traveling in a cab.

"In June, the Central Criminal Court of England and Wales (aka the Old Bailey) sentenced seven members of a Muslim 'child-grooming' gang based in Oxford to at least 95 years in prison for raping, torturing and trafficking British girls as young as 11. According to government estimates that are believed to be 'just the tip of the iceberg,' at least 2,500 British children have so far been confirmed to be victims of grooming gangs, and another 20,000 children are at risk of sexual exploitation. At least 27 police forces are currently investigating 54 alleged child-grooming gangs across England and Wales."

Do you think these sorts of things can't happen in America? A decade ago, most British couldn't have imagined them happening there, either. Don't worry, though, the Obama administration says you have nothing to fear — except from those of us who are raising the alarm about its submissive policies and serial national security fraud.

Russia

In recent months, President Bush has sent a clear, if bizarre, message to the international community: Foreign governments can expect better treatment from the United States if they are adversaries than if they are friends. For example, contrast the President's felicitous attitude toward the Soviet Union with his increasingly strident position on Israel.

Mr. Bush has repeatedly expressed concern about the dangers inherent in "instability" in the Soviet Union and Eastern Europe. He has even gone so far as to suggest that this prospect - not our longtime adversary, the Soviet Union - is "the enemy." In fact, the Bush administration has become so preoccupied with the risks to American security interests should such instability produce a regional crisis in Europe that it is leaving no stone unturned in its effort to help prop up Soviet President Mikhail Gorbachev's increasingly tenuous regime.

In practical terms, this policy approach has taken several forms. Mr. Bush has been at pains to distance the United States from those democratic forces - from the Lithuanian nationalists to Boris Yeltsin - who are challenging Mr. Gorbachev's slow pace of reform. Instead, he is using U.S. diplomatic influence to encourage others, notably West Germany (which hardly needs much encouragement), to accommodate Soviet security, technology and economic needs. What is more, the Bush administration is positioning itself to support a significant Western financial bailout package for the Soviet Union.

At the same time, the president seems to feel that, with respect to Israel, instability - far from being the enemy - is to be encouraged. After all, the administration apparently believes, only by forcing a change in the status quo can peace in the region be secured. This reasoning holds that the sole route to lasting stability and peace in the Middle East requires: (1.) compelling Israel to make concessions in advance in order to obtain negotiations with the Palestinians (read, the Palestine Liberation Organization) and (2.) using that process to extort the Israelis to make the ultimate leap of faith - trading land for "peace."

Accordingly, where Mr. Bush has sought to weaken rivals to Mr. Gorbachev, he actually intervened personally and calculatedly to bring down the government of Israel when he equated Jewish residences in East Jerusalem with those the United States opposes in the territories of the West Bank and Gaza. Where his administration has worked exhaustively with the United States' regional partners in Europe to fashion security arrangements acceptable to Mr. Gorbachev, it has made no secret of its view that Israel must adjust its position to accommodate that of the PLO and its allies in the Middle East from Iraq to Libya. This reality has not been appreciably altered by the administration's tardy and reluctant suspension (not to be confused with cessation) of the U.S.-Palestinian "dialogue" in the aftermath of the PLO's abortive raid last month on Tel Aviv's beaches.

Perhaps most striking of all, as American policymakers have signaled a growing willingness to provide Moscow with effectively untied, direct financial assistance - in addition to the various trade concessions and flows of high technology, know-how and other forms of economic support for Moscow already underway - the U.S. government is threatening to reduce or stringently condition its assistance to Israel. Robert Dole, the Senate Republican leader, clearly was serving as a stalking horse for the Bush administration when he proposed earlier this year a 5 percent cut in Israel's foreign-aid allotment in fiscal 1991.

More recently, the administration has threatened to withhold $400 million in housing guarantees unless the Israelis cease all settlements activities. This demand was subsequently broadened by Rep. David Obey, Wisconsin Democrat and chairman of the House Foreign Operations Subcommittee, when during recent floor action on the annual foreign assistance bill he announced that he was prepared to make all U.S. aid contingent on such an Israeli step if the administration wished.

The risks of this backward policy toward the Soviet Union and Israel should be obvious to a man like George Bush who prides himself on his savoir faire in the field of foreign relations. Unfortunately, he seems unaware that propping up Mr. Gorbachev and the present Soviet system - rather than supporting those demanding radical democratic change - simply increases the prospect that the formidable military threat that system has produced to date will persist and reduces the likelihood of genuine, structural reform in the Soviet Union.

The president seems equally oblivious to the reality that undermining Israel's security (the inevitable result of negotiations on a Palestinian homeland) and weakening the U.S.-Israeli strategic relationship (the inevitable result of the current American diplomatic gambit) is a formula for regional instability of the worst kind - war. It is not a catalyst for a lasting resolution of the persistent conflict between Israel and her Arab neighbors.

It is past time for the Bush administration to treat the government of one of the United States' most important friends and strategic allies with at least the respect and solicitude currently being granted our principal adversary. Acceding to Soviet blackmail and engaging in coercion of Israel will not produce stability in either Europe or the Middle East. More likely, it will endanger U.S. interests in both areas. Such a reckless policy should be abandoned at once.

41

"ON THE ROAD TO MINSK: YELTSIN'S ATTAINMENT" | DECEMBER 11, 1991

To the urgent wake up call received Sunday from the leaders of Russia, Ukraine and Byelorussia, the Bush administration has said, "Please hold." Unfortunately, the call - in the form of an announcement that the two largest and wealthiest former Soviet republics and Byelorussia had formed a new "Commonwealth of Independent States" headquartered in Minsk, not Moscow, and had terminated the old Soviet Union - was one that cannot, and must not, wait.

After all, this extraordinary development comes against the backdrop of increasingly sinister and insistent indications of a hard-line reaction to democratic change in the former Soviet Union. Its timing appears calculated to pre-empt an impending military backed coup; its successful consolidation may be the last best hope to prevent widespread bloodshed and chaos in the old Soviet empire.

If that were not compelling reason enough to recognize the new Commonwealth and shift the focus of U.S. relations - at least symbolically - from Moscow to Minsk, there is another: As White House press spokesman Marlin Fitzwater noted Monday, "The Commonwealth communiqué that was issued yesterday reflected the five principles that we set forth on Sept. 4."

In other words, Russia's Boris Yeltsin, Ukraine's Leonid Kravchuk and Byelorussia's Stanislau Shushkevich evidently undertook explicitly to meet the tests recently enunciated by the United States for extending recognition to newly independent republics of the former Soviet Union. It offers: explicit protections to ethnic minorities; respect for each other's territory and the inviolability of borders; and acceptance of international treaty and debt obligations.

Of course, it is one thing to make commitments to such laudable goals and another to realize them. Under normal circumstances, the United States and other Western nations could be forgiven for hesitating to embrace the new Commonwealth. There are obvious uncertainties about how it will work, how many former republics will participate, etc.

It is, however, an absurd understatement to note that these are anything but normal times. Withholding recognition of the Commonwealth of Independent States and other ties with its member states pending clarification of these issues would be worse than a "bait and switch" - a reneging on our implicit, if not explicit, promise of diplomatic relations if only certain conditions were satisfied. Under present circumstances, it would represent a vote of "no confidence" in the best hopes for democratic and free market transformation of the Soviet empire.

Put simply, a wait-and-see strategy is a luxury neither we nor the democratic forces seeking to dismantle the old Soviet order can afford. The destiny of the former Soviet Union may turn on developments in the next hours and days - not weeks and months.

There was, therefore, no little irony in Secretary of State James Baker's statement on Sunday to the effect that there are dangerous parallels between the former Soviet Union and the crisis in Yugoslavia. After all, Mr. Baker is the same man whose visit to Belgrade earlier this year helped set the stage for Serbian aggression against Croatia - and the West's hapless response. What is more, the Bush administration seems prepared to take essentially the same stance toward the dissolution of the Soviet empire that as it has taken - with such disastrous results - concerning the collapsed Yugoslav empire. That is, to require those with the most to lose (the communist-rooted central authorities, be they in Moscow or Belgrade) to assent expressly to the dismantling of their power.

By conveying the United States' determination not to "reward" independence-minded republics bent on altering the "territorial integrity" of the empire in which they involuntarily were incorporated, the Bush administration previously sent a powerful, if subliminal, signal to Belgrade: The central, Serbian-dominated authorities there were encouraged to maintain control throughout the country, no matter what the cost.

Mr. Baker is right to point to the carnage that ensued in Croatia. But he is as wrong in the lessons he draws from it for the Soviet situation as he is in eschewing responsibility for the consequences of U.S. and Western policy in Yugoslavia.

If America now makes the same mistake it made in Yugoslavia, regarding the choice of former Soviet republics seeking their independence and forming new voluntary alliances with others, it is absolutely predictable that the consequences will be similar - if not far worse. This is, of course, an argument for adopting a different and far more proactive strategy, not for standing pat.

Such a strategy should start with a long overdue decision to "cut and cut clean" (as Paul Laxalt once advised with regard to Ferdinand Marcos), breaking once and for all with Mikhail Gorbachev and his discredited, abandoned central authorities by: recognizing the Commonwealth of Independent States; posting a competent ambassador to its new headquarters in Minsk; and making the breakaway states that comprise it the beneficiaries of U.S. assistance and the focus of Western policies to the extent that they embrace sweeping democratic and free market structural reforms.

This is not to say that such actions alone will prevent a renewed effort by Moscow center and/or the military to try to retain power through violence. To the contrary, the indicators continue to mount that a Coup II is in the works, and this time around there will probably be no question about Mr. Gorbachev's full complicity with the perpetrators.

Such a prospect should not be an argument for inaction, however. Rather, it should be a catalyst for a new U.S. strategy clearly aligned with the alternatives to Moscow center, not with those determined to prop it up.

Neither does the fact of nuclear weapons in the Soviet equation – something blessedly absent from the Yugoslav one - justify the administration's present course. It goes without saying that these weapons must be carefully controlled; every effort should be made to assist in their early, wholesale destruction.

That said, the immediate object of U.S. policy ought to be to maximize the number of entities in the former Soviet Union whose permission is required to release or physically relocate nuclear arms - not to reconsolidate that power with Mr. Gorbachev and company. After all, such an arrangement minimizes the chances that authority to employ "nukes" will ever be granted. Importantly, this sort of "triple-key" veto mechanism has reportedly been made a part of the new Commonwealth accord.

For all these reasons, the time has come for Washington to answer the call from the new Commonwealth of Independent States with the welcoming response: "On to Minsk!"

President Bush has taken great pride in his personal involvement in U.S. diplomacy. Inevitably, it will be cited as the single quality that most distinguishes him from his rivals in the 1992 election. Ironically, the consequences of his penchant for "personal diplomacy" may prove to be among his greatest political liabilities.

To a greater degree than at any time since his mentor, Richard Nixon, occupied the Oval Office, this president has been directly engaged in the conduct of American foreign policy. The phone calls between heads of state - with all their potential for spontaneous commitments, unscripted concessions, miscommunications and misunderstandings - have, under the Bush administration, ceased to be an extraordinary tool of last resort. Today, scarcely a day goes by without Mr. Bush personally ringing up foreign leaders, great and small.

This "hands-on" approach has been credited with enabling Mr. Bush, for example, to fashion and maintain the odd assortment of countries that formed the grand anti-Saddam coalition. It appears he expected that "personal diplomacy" would similarly serve as his ace in the hole during the recent high-profile trip to Japan. No one seems more surprised than the president that Prime Minister Kiichi Miyazawa balked at granting meaningful trade concessions framed as necessary favors to his old friend, George Bush.

Arguably, personal diplomacy served Mr. Bush - and the nation - even more poorly to the extent it contributed to his disastrous policy toward the late Soviet Union. Long after it was apparent that Mikhail Gorbachev was part of the problem and not the solution to the Soviet people's aspirations for an end to communist misrule, the president insisted on propping up his counterpart in Moscow. For instance, considerations of friendship, rather than objective assessments of creditworthiness (as required by law) or American strategic interests (as dictated by common sense), prompted the Bush administration to grant $3.75 billion in agricultural credit guarantees over the last year of Mr. Gorbachev's rule in a blatant effort to preserve his regime.

Predictably, these taxpayer-underwritten loans had the effect of simply postponing the inevitable: Moscow center persisted for a few months more to despoil the Soviet Union and to squander its resources and those provided by the West. In the end, however, Mr. Bush's great friend was pushed over the side by Boris Yeltsin and others determined to implement radical political and economic reforms to which Mr. Gorbachev had merely paid lip service.

With the fall of Mikhail Gorbachev, however, the dark side of Mr. Bush's personal diplomacy became more evident. Administration officials made no secret of their displeasure at Mr. Gorbachev's removal from power and expressed considerable pique at the demeaning way in which it was effected. Perhaps this was just an understandable - if short-sighted - manifestation of the president's disappointment that the horse he had backed for so long lost the race while the horses he had assiduously resisted being associated with had triumphed.

The Bush administration's continuing antipathy to Mr. Yeltsin, on the other hand, is less easily explained. After all, the Russian president has actually begun to implement structural reforms that will transform his nation - reforms long sought by the United States. In the process, his popularly elected government has risked everything - challenging politically powerful constituencies with liberalized prices, sharply reduced defense spending, withdrawal of forces from the Baltics, proposals for deep cuts in nuclear arms and the dismantlement of apparatuses and policies it inherited from the ancien regime.

As this inevitably turbulent transformation has gotten under way, Mr. Bush has remained strikingly aloof and unforthcoming. Apart from his brief and reportedly amicable meeting with Mr. Yeltsin at Camp David 10 days ago, the administration's attitude toward aiding the efforts of democratic reformers in the former Soviet Union has been unremittingly cool. Consider the following recent indicators:

- During a Feb. 1 meeting in Washington with Yegor Gaidar, Mr. Yeltsin's key deputy and economic guru, Treasury Secretary Nicholas Brady offered plenty of skeptical questions - but no new U.S. commitments to help the reformers succeed in Moscow.

- The Bush administration appears to be siding with our European allies in opposing extending further export credit guarantees for manufactures to Russia in the absence of a new central bank. This has not only dried up desperately needed imports of consumer goods; it has also undercut the Japanese government that has been willing to extend such guarantees in cooperation with Russia's foreign trade bank.

- The administration has also resisted providing meaningful debt relief, let alone conditioned forgiveness of debts incurred under the Gorbachev regime. While the Group of Seven major industrial countries has agreed to a modest – and short-term - rescheduling of part of the Soviet-bequeathed debt, the sort of generous and long-term relief that is required is nowhere in sight. The president's men regard any discussion of this idea - one whose time has clearly come - as "counterproductive."

These developments beg the following questions: Does the personal antipathy Mr. Bush long felt toward Mr. Yeltsin and his democratic colleagues persist? Could it be that, notwithstanding the display of hospitality at Camp David, Mr. Bush remains unreconciled to the idea of the reformers' success? Could this downside quality of "personal diplomacy" be such that the president would actually be willing to deny the Yeltsins of the former Soviet Union the tools they so desperately need to consolidate an as yet unrealized victory for democracy and free-market economic opportunity?

Needless to say, were the answers to these questions to be in the affirmative, the United States would be making an historic strategic blunder. The alternatives to Mr. Yeltsin and his colleagues are likely to be what Vladimir Bukovsky calls "communist mutants" (e.g., Eduard Shevardnadze and Anatoly Sobchak) or still less appetizing autocrats (e.g., Alexander Rutskoi, Boris Gromov and Yevgeni Primakov).

If Mr. Bush wishes to demonstrate his commitment to democracy in Russia and other former Soviet republics engaged in genuine structural reform, he should immediately call for generous, long-term debt relief (and even selective forgiveness). This will do much to alleviate the critical hard-currency cash-flow crisis gripping the Commonwealth states without requiring massive new sums from Western taxpayers. Combined with genuinely humanitarian aid, such a restructuring could also go a long way toward aligning his administration, at last, with the right side in the former Soviet empire.

Last week, President Bush pleaded poverty when criticized by former President Richard Nixon for his "pathetically inadequate" assistance to democratic forces in the former Soviet Union. Contending that "we're living in a time of constrained resources," Mr. Bush averred that "there isn't a lot of money around" with which to help Boris Yeltsin and others struggling to consolidate the political and economic transformation of the old Soviet Union.

There is, however, one initiative that is readily available, that would have an immediate and powerful effect in Russia and other qualifying former republics, and that would not cost the American taxpayer another dime in new outlays: substantial long-term debt rescheduling and selected forgiveness. Not surprisingly, such debt relief featured prominently on the list of actions recommended by Mr. Nixon in a memorandum he recently circulated on the eve of an extraordinary conference sponsored by his presidential library on March 11-12.

Once the Soviet regime that incurred the bulk of this debt - some $50 billion under the stewardship of Mikhail Gorbachev alone - was formally supplanted by a democratically elected government in Russia and a commonwealth of sovereign states, it became appropriate to consider immediate action on debt relief. Indeed, generous, multiyear rescheduling of the inherited debt would be the single most important, near-term and affordable step the West could take to give tangible expression to its solidarity with the struggling democratic and free-market reformers in the former Soviet Union.

Unfortunately, to this point the Bush administration has evinced little willingness to lead a coordinated Western effort on Soviet debt relief. Instead, it appears to be toadying to the German bankers and foreign governments who foolishly and irresponsibly lent Moscow center the bulk of its foreign debt. For example, Ed Hewett - the senior director for Russian and Eurasian Affairs at the National Security Council and a longtime enthusiast for Western lending to the Gorbachev regime - intimated at the Nixon Library Conference last Wednesday that the administration was reluctant to push for debt relief lest it jeopardize the opportunity for new borrowing by Russia and other reforming successor states in the future.

That pretext for denying Mr. Yeltsin and like-minded reformers relief from the crushing costs of even the $44 billion provided just in 1990-91 - Mr. Hewett noted ruefully "no one is quite sure where it went" - is, at best, disingenuous and, at worst, self-fulfilling. With their vast natural resources and economic potential, Russia and Ukraine at the very least are unlikely to be denied Western future loans, particularly if they are project-specific or collateralized.

Were the United States and other Western governments now to exercise leadership with respect to long-term debt rescheduling and selected forgiveness, other lenders (virtually all of whom are believed, sensibly, to have begun discounting or writing off these devalued assets) will follow suit without prejudice to new money flows. On the other hand, if sovereign lenders fail to exercise such leadership, the banks and inordinately exposed governments naturally will press their claims.

The inevitable result: Billions of dollars in precious hard currency - money that could otherwise go toward importing needed consumer goods or critical investment - will be sluiced from the former Soviet republics to Western creditors. It may even be, ironically, that some of whatever new money flows the West does provide now will wind up going to pay German bankers and taxpayers instead of appreciably helping the Russian people!

While the party line on debt relief for qualifying Soviet successor states is concern about their future borrowing potential, another consideration is probably determinative for the Bush administration. The president's men may fear that any action that focuses attention on the $3.75 billion in U.S. taxpayer resources loaned to Mr. Gorbachev during his last year in office would vindicate Mr. Bush's critics - who said at the time the money would be misspent, constitute life-support for a communist regime and never be repaid.

Under present circumstances, however, Mr. Bush cannot afford to let such considerations preclude action on debt relief. As Mr. Nixon and some on Capitol Hill have properly observed, the costs of failing to act decisively on behalf of those engaged in wholesale structural reform in the former Soviet Union may prove unacceptably high.

An initiative on debt relief, moreover, should enjoy a higher priority for the United States and other governments than some of the steps being considered, notably a $4 billion to $6 billion ruble convertibility fund. After all, such a fund (assuming it works as it is supposed to) will not be expended. By contrast, were $40 billion to $60 billion worth of cumulative principal and interest payments to be generously rescheduled or partially forgiven, it would mean that that money would be physically in the hands of the reformers – and available, therefore, to be spent in a disciplined way to meet other pressing needs.

Two other considerations argue for a prompt adjustment in the relative priority being accorded by the Bush administration to debt relief on the one hand and a new fund to prop up the old Soviet ruble on the other. First, the former would cost the West no new money, whereas the latter will require substantial new contributions from the already beleaguered American taxpayer. And second, generous, multiyear rescheduling or debt forgiveness can alleviate otherwise intense pressure to generate hard currency revenues through the export of advanced Soviet-designed weaponry, something a partially convertible ruble is unlikely to accomplish.

Western creditors who knowingly bet their taxpayers', shareholders' and depositors' money on an unworkable, centrally controlled economic system for political or commercial reasons - should be accorded little sympathy in weighing appropriate rescheduling or forgiveness. Such creditors entered into these transactions with their eyes wide open concerning the dubious prospects for full repayment. It is only sensible and fair - and in the West's long-term interests - that the true democratic forces in the former Soviet Union not now be penalized by the very creditors who did so much in the past to perpetuate the detested communist ancien regime.

Arguably, among the most important of the many bits of unfinished foreign policy business Bill Clinton will inherit from George Bush is the question of relations with Ukraine. If the incoming administration follows the lead of the outgoing one in this area, however, chances are bilateral ties will become dangerously strained. If so, the principal beneficiary will the ascendant hard-liners in Moscow.

The Bush administration is currently using intense diplomatic, financial and political pressure to try to coerce Ukraine to turn over to Russia strategic nuclear weapons Kiev inherited with the breakup of the old Soviet empire. The reasons for such heavy-handedness are said to include concerns that:

- A failure by Ukraine to do so might create grave instabilities insofar as it will destroy the foundation upon which the START I Treaty was predicated (namely that only Russia would retain the former Soviet strategic arsenal) and, in the process, tube the recently signed follow-on agreement, START II.

- Ukrainian insistence on retaining such weapons would undercut its stated commitment to subscribe to the Nuclear Non-Proliferation Treaty and, it is argued, create a new impetus for other nations to acquire atomic and/or thermonuclear arms.

- Ukraine's nuclear chauvinism may provide pretexts for hard line elements in Russia to steer Kremlin policy in more militaristic and hegemonistic directions.

Are these concerns well-grounded? Do they justify the kind of knee-breaking the Bush team is engaged in? And, more to the point, if the present U.S. approach ultimately succeeds, will this country's long-term strategic interests be advanced - or will they actually be disserved?

My own heretical view is that the answer to each of these questions may be "No." At the very least, the assumptions that have prompted the Bush administration to answer them in the affirmative should be analyzed and debated more carefully than they have been to date - certainly before the Clinton administration starts shaping policies predicated upon them, too.

For starters, Ukraine is one of the most important countries of the "post-Cold War" Europe. Its geographic size (equivalent to France), its rich agricultural potential, large (if, as with all of Soviet industry) overly militarized industrial base and its well-educated and reasonably productive population would make Ukraine a significant player - even without nuclear weapons. What is more, Ukraine also has, at present, physical control over the world's third largest inventory of strategic arms.

Incredibly, despite these factors, U.S. policy toward Ukraine has not changed appreciably from the days when it was a vassal state of the Soviet empire. This policy was best characterized - even caricatured - by President Bush's notorious "Chicken Kiev" speech in July 1991, a month before the coup in Moscow.

On that occasion, he questioned the sanity of Ukrainians who yearned for independence from Moscow and strenuously urged that Ukraine give up its nationalist aspirations and remain part of the Soviet Union. Seemingly spiteful at having been proven wrong, the Bush administration has scarcely deviated in the post-Gorbachev period from its Moscow-centric approach. When Ukraine is considered at all, it appears to be as an afterthought - or, worse, as a nasty impediment to smooth relations with the Kremlin.

This attitude has not been improved by Kiev's mounting unease over political developments in Russia. Washington has been infuriated that its own dubious arms control agenda might be jeopardized by Ukrainians challenging the wisdom of surrendering their stockpile of powerful nuclear arms to a historical enemy - particularly one increasingly dominated by the sorts of people who have previously used military power to enslave Ukraine.

Whether the United States likes it or not, Ukraine has serious and, to a considerable extent, legitimate concerns about Russia's future course. Particularly with the ascendancy of enemies of structural reform in Moscow, Ukrainians have ample grounds for adopting a cautious attitude toward Western-promoted policies that may, at best, reduce Kiev's negotiating leverage and, at worst, put its sovereignty at risk.

The time has come to challenge the assumption that U.S. and Western interests will necessarily be best served by insisting that Ukraine turn over all remaining, longer-range nuclear weapons to Russia. An independent, strong Ukraine may in fact prove to be the best bulwark against revanchism from Moscow - something we have as much to fear, as do the Ukrainians. Kiev's continued physical control of nuclear arms may prove a deterrent to renascent aggressiveness in Russian foreign policy.

At the very least, before a new U.S. administration takes up the Bush team's cudgel against Kiev, it must demonstrate that the strategic implications of disarming Ukraine have been thought through. If it does so, the conclusions just may be that renewed militarism is on the rise in Russia - whether Ukraine retains its nuclear weapons or not, that the reductions called for in START I and II are not likely to assure the desired stability or U.S. deterrent capability in the face of those developments in Moscow, and that the proliferation of nuclear weapons is a function of the appetites and resourcefulness of people like Saddam Hussein or Kim Il-sung - forces not appreciably influenced by ineffectual, unverifiable treaties or well-intentioned breast-beating from Washington.

The most portentous item to come out of last week's G-7 effort to help Boris Yeltsin was not the much ballyhooed $3 billion aid package. Pledged to assist Russian privatization efforts. Rather, it was the decision taken at Mr. Yeltsin's request virtually to eliminate multilateral export controls on the transfer of militarily relevant technologies to Russia.

The truth of the matter is that there are not many such restrictions left after four or five years of "liberalization" (read dismantling) of the export control regime known as CO-COM - an acronym derived from the name of the organization established during the Cold War to monitor and promote that regime, the Coordinating Committee for Multilateral Export Controls. Indeed, those multilateral export controls still in place govern the most sensitive technologies, equipment and know-how that are particularly susceptible to abuse by those inclined to apply them to strategic purposes.

Still, Mr. Yeltsin made the final evisceration of COCOM one of the priority agenda items for his visit to the Tokyo economic summit. His G-7 hosts, faced with severe political and economic constraints that inhibited their ability to respond to Russian demands for vast new financial assistance, were accommodating. After all, doing so helps them appease domestic business interests who have also long campaigned for an end to these impediments to the sale of lucrative, if potentially dangerous, technologies to Russian buyers.

Unfortunately, in so doing, the United States and its allies have agreed to stop controlling the flow of dangerous dual-use equipment and know-how to Russia before Moscow has demonstrated either a willingness to safeguard technologies of mass destruction or the capacity to do so. Interestingly, such preconditions were expressly stated in the Charter for American-Russian Partnership and Friendship signed on June 17, 1992, by then-President George Bush and Mr. Yeltsin. It stipulates that:

"The United States and Russia agree that the process of normalization of technology trade is based on Russia's determination to adhere strictly to world standards of export controls in the area of nonproliferation of weapons of mass destruction and related technologies, missiles and missile technology, destabilizing conventional armaments and dual-use goods and technologies."

On Dec. 15, 1992, however, Director of the Central Intelligence Agency Robert Gates described Russia's failure to implement this commitment starkly:

"Moscow publicly opposes the illegal transfer of technology that would lead to the proliferation of weapons of mass destruction. But the economic incentives are great - especially if the equipment for sale is dual-use with civilian applications."

There are three systemic problems that prevent Russia from exercising reliable control over technology exports:

- The lack of an effective customs system: While the Soviet Union once had a strict system of border controls, the breakup of the U.S.S.R. created 15 new independent states and 5,400 miles of new frontiers. In addition to Russia's proximity to such proliferation-threat nations as North Korea and China, corridors to former Soviet client states and other nations aspiring to nuclear weapons capabilities such as Iran, Iraq and Pakistan are now more easily traversed by smugglers.

- Wholly inadequate export control system: While the United States employs approximately 600 export licensing officials, Russia's export licensing staff numbers a paltry 15 persons - none of whom are trained in accordance with international standards. In the words of a recent U.S. National Academy of Sciences report, "[There is no] competent civil authority with the will and capabilities to enforce the laws, decrees, operating regulations, licensing procedures and enforcement practices recently adopted by the government of the Russian Federation."

- Rampant corruption: Soviet-era apparatchiks and former Communist Party bosses still control the vast majority of state mechanisms, resources and assets. Of these, one of the most lucrative is the ability to issue export licenses. Russian smugglers have been notoriously successful in crossing borders with the help of both forged export licenses and authentic ones obtained with the help of bribes.

No less worrisome than the possibility that Russia might recklessly transfer sensitive Western technology is the significant risk that such equipment and know-how might wind up enhancing the offensive power of the Russian military. The former Soviet Union well understood the immense savings that could be realized in this way, and there is no reason to believe that the leaders of Russia's armed forces - many of whom previously led the Soviet military-industrial complex - will miss such opportunities as they confront severe budgetary pressures.

Remarks by Yeltsin adviser Mikhail Malei that appeared in the Feb. 24 edition of the Current Digest of the Soviet Press were instructive on this point:

"Conversion does not mean the destruction of high-level technologies for the sake of producing primitive articles. Conversion means the transformation of the military-industrial complex through the sale of its products that are bought on the world market. Conversion means freeing the meager Russian budget from the need to make outlays on the military-industrial complex and supplementing the budget with hard cash."

While it is seductive to believe that removing COCOM restrictions would serve to draw Russia more closely into the family of democratic nations, the practical effect of such a move under present circumstances would be only to exacerbate the transfer of militarily critical technologies to undesirable parties. Without a rigorous Russian export control system in place and a high degree of confidence that Russia has successfully weathered the challenges to its present democratic path, there is a strong probability that the end of COCOM will simply mean that heretofore protected dual-use technologies will end up in the wrong hands and put to the wrong uses.

Of the many international traditions for marking the Christmas season, none is more inconsistent with the spirit of the holiday than that periodically observed by Russian leaders: For years, the Kremlin's autocrats have exploited the West's Yuletide distractions to take reprehensible actions against their own or other's citizens.

For example, Andrei Sakharov's banishment to a living hell in Gorky occurred at this time of year, as did the Soviet-directed crackdown on Poland's Solidarity movement and the invasion of Afghanistan. And in 1990, a man widely believed in the West to be an engine of democratic reform in Moscow, Mikhail Gorbachev, found the year-end period an opportune one to turn the screws on the restive Baltic States.

So it is not particularly surprising that late December was the moment chosen by the erstwhile democrat, Boris Yeltsin, to crush a secessionist effort by Chechnya, one of the Russian Federation's many "autonomous republics." What is puzzling, however, is why Mr. Yeltsin chose this Christmas brutally to bring Chechnya's Muslim population to heel. After all, the Chechens declared their independence three years ago - a stance Mr. Yeltsin treated, until recently, largely with benign neglect.

[On Tuesday, Mr. Yeltsin offered to pull back Russian troops from the outskirts of the Chechen capital and said it was time to end Moscow's military campaign in the breakaway Russian republic, according to the Associated Press. The move appeared to be an invitation for Chechen leaders to resume peace talks.]

The factors giving rise to this decision say much about the man Boris Yeltsin has become - and about the direction he is intent on taking Russia. One such factor appears to be domestic politics. Mr. Yeltsin may have calculated -wrongly, as it turns out - that a swift, crushing action against the Muslim people of Chechnya would be highly popular with the Russian people. After all, within days of his storming of the Russian White House in October 1993, Mr. Yeltsin issued a decree ordering the roundup and expulsion from Moscow of persons of Caucasian nationality - a diktat ominously reminiscent of Josef Stalin's anti-Semitic actions at the time of the "Doctors' Plot" in 1952-53, when persons of Jewish background were incarcerated and, in many cases, eliminated.

Mr. Yeltsin probably reckoned that, while members of parliament would howl at his unilateral decision to strike in Chechnya, the public would support him. The Duma would, as a result, lose power to the executive, facilitating at a minimum further movement toward a Gaullist-style presidency - if not, effectively, a dictatorship. In the event, the Russian public has largely responded in much the same way as its elected representatives: with horror at the prospect of a long and bloody Afghanistan-style conflict, perhaps compounded by a campaign of terror that might be unleashed throughout Russia by the tens of thousands of Chechens estimated to live outside of Chechnya.

Another factor may have been economic and strategic in nature: Moscow is angling to participate in and dominate the potentially enormously lucrative oil exploitation deal Western companies have recently struck with neighboring Azerbaijan. A major pipeline from the Caucasus through Russia transits Chechnya. If Mr. Yeltsin were motivated by such considerations, however, the violence he has unleashed in Chechnya will almost certainly backfire. It has had the effect of uniting Chechen opposition to Moscow and will likely result in vicious guerrilla war against Russia. Such developments are sure to send a chilling message to any investors considering relying on that pipeline project or planning to build another one in the region.

Another, perhaps decisive factor may have been the perception in Moscow that what was already a weak American administration was now essentially a lame-duck one, following the midterm elections last month. It would be understandable if Mr. Yeltsin reckoned that he had nothing to lose by moving against Chechnya. On the one hand, the Clinton-Talbott team is apparently constitutionally incapable of criticizing Russian misbehavior. On the other, the new Congress was likely to be more insistent on making U.S. assistance conditional on real Russian progress toward political and economic reform at home and good conduct internationally - tests the Yeltsin regime is ever less likely to satisfy.

The U.S. response to date to provocative Russian actions - including, in addition to its violence in Chechnya, its threats and obstructionism at two recent meetings in Europe and its subversion of efforts to punish Serbia and keep the pressure on Saddam Hussein - has largely been characterized by a determined effort to accentuate the positive and minimize the growing signs that U.S. policy is out of synch with the emerging Russian reality. This stance can only serve to encourage the Kremlin's worst instincts.

In fact, the Chechnya campaign is just the latest indication that the prospects are declining for democratic reform in Russia. To the contrary, a growing effort to respond to chaos in the North Caucasus and elsewhere is likely to give rise to a greater degree of authoritarianism - with grave implications for Russia's approach to individual liberties, economic liberalization, remilitarization and foreign policies contrary to Western interests.

The United States must demonstrate convincingly its opposition to such trends in Russia. The place to start is with Chechnya. Washington must stop dismissing this odious military crackdown there as a legitimate, if regrettable, response to an internal problem.

The United States should, instead, be making it clear that Russia's failure to act in a manner consistent with democratic practices and Western norms in dealing with the Chechen independence movement will inevitably have adverse consequences for U.S. and allied assistance to Moscow and for efforts to integrate Russia into the West. If President Clinton cannot bring himself to make such a principled statement, the Congress must do so at the first possible opportunity.

Of all the mistakes President Clinton appears poised to make in his summit with Russian President Boris Yeltsin - including legitimating Mr. Yeltsin's Stalinesque genocide in Chechnya, his nuclear proliferation to Iran and his NATO-wrecking operation - one is in a class by itself: Mr. Clinton's efforts to impede, if not preclude, effective anti-missile defenses threatens not only to jeopardize U.S. national security interests; it could also produce a constitutional crisis.

This singularly portentous problem arises from communiqué language the Clinton administration has developed with the Russians. The plan is for the two presidents to pronounce the 1972 Anti-Ballistic Missile (ABM) Treaty the "cornerstone" of U.S.-Russian relations and strategic stability.

The administration hopes with this statement to lock in the U.S. commitment to an agreement that effectively bans missile defenses for the American people, notwithstanding that it was forged with a country (the Soviet Union) that no longer exists and was drafted in a strategic environment that no longer pertains (namely, one in which essentially only the Soviets' nuclear weapons and ballistic missiles posed a threat to the United States and its troops and allies overseas). Despite these dramatic changes, the United States remains without deployed, effective anti-missile defenses. And, if the Clinton team has its way, this will remain the case indefinitely.

Worse yet, the summiteers are expected to embrace written commitments that would have the effect of dramatically expanding the ABM Treaty's scope. By agreeing not to deploy "regional defenses" against each other's ballistic missiles and to assure "non-circumvention" of the treaty, Mr. Clinton would give the Kremlin important rights. Three key leaders of the House of Representatives -Appropriations Committee Chairman Robert Livingston, National Security Committee Chairman Floyd Spence, and Appropriations Defense Subcommittee Chairman Bill Young - wrote the president last Thursday, warning that:

"[These limitations] suggest unacceptable geographical limitations on U.S. theater missile defenses [TMD] and could open the door for Russia to oppose any U.S. TMD deployments. In addition, the reported 'non-circumvention' language could cause Russia to challenge our international cooperative theater defense programs."

The legislators went on to note their continuing opposition to the Clinton administration's efforts to negotiate the "multilateralization" of the ABM Treaty. That initiative would open the treaty to additional signatories, a step calculated to make it more difficult to change its terms in the future. They also reiterated their opposition to the current U.S. negotiating position which would "place velocity limits on TMD interceptors ... [and]

hamstring our ability to provide the most capable missile defenses to our forward-deployed forces." Messrs. Livingston, Spence and Young concluded by observing:

"President Yeltsin must be made to realize that we are ready to act cooperatively [with Russia] if we can, but unilaterally if we must when it comes to missile defenses. The importance of this issue to U.S. security is simply too great to extend Russia or any other nation a veto."

Such a warning to the president of the United States from senior members of the House of Representatives who control the government's purse strings cannot prudently be ignored. It would be more than foolish, however, for the administration to ignore a letter sent on May 2 by 50 members of the U.S. Senate - including Majority Leader Robert Dole and virtually every other member of the Republican leadership. This letter served formal notice on Mr. Clinton:

> "We are deeply troubled by indications that you intend to proceed, in the face of clearly stated congressional opposition, to make commitments in Moscow that would impede U.S. efforts to provide American troops with effective protection against missile attack. We find particularly troubling press reports describing the draft communiqué language being developed for that meeting... We want you and the Russians to be fully aware of our determination to prevent the creation of new impediments to missile defenses."

The 50 signatories to this letter represent more than enough to defeat any new missile defense treaty or ABM amendment that President Clinton might submit for Senate advice and consent, as required by the U.S. Constitution. Therefore, the administration seems to believe it can do as it did with the notorious North Korean "agreed framework" - namely, ignore altogether the Senate's role in treaty making. Mr. Dole and his colleagues must not allow an administration bent on "dumbing-down," if not altogether precluding, U.S. missile defense capabilities to dumb-down the Constitution in the process.

It is noteworthy that in addition to Mr. Dole, three other Senate Republicans - Phil Gramm, Dick Lugar and Arlen Specter - who share Mr. Dole's desire to bring an early end to the Clinton presidency, are among those who signed the May 2 letter. If Mr. Clinton will not be deterred from making a serious mistake on missile defenses at the summit by virtue of either the strategic dangers or the potential constitutional crisis it may precipitate, perhaps the political risks associated with leaving the United States exposed to missile attack will do the trick.

After all, the president has been at pains in the wake of the Oklahoma City bombing to promise the populace that he would take every step to protect it. Does he really mean he will do so unless the attacker uses a ballistic missile, in which case the public is on its own? If so, Mr. Clinton will be roughly as vulnerable politically as he would leave the American people.

Roughly 50 years ago, two Soviet spies, Julius and Ethel Rosenberg, participated in one of the most portentous espionage operations of all time: They gleaned for Moscow critical information about the techniques and technology that underpinned the then-fledgling U.S. atomic weapons program. Thanks to the Rosenbergs and their partners in treason, Josef Stalin was able to cut years off the time it would otherwise have taken the U.S.S.R. to obtain "the Bomb." The rest, as they say, is history. The Rosenbergs were caught, tried and executed for their crimes as the Kremlin exploited first its atomic, then its thermonuclear capabilities to discourage American resistance, to the consolidation of Uncle Joe's evil empire.

Incredibly, President Clinton's trip to Moscow this week may produce the greatest transfer of U.S. nuclear secrets to the Kremlin since the Rosenbergs. A decision document prepared for the president's consideration offers, among other ill-advised concessions, what might be called the "Rosenberg Option" – a proposal for the United States to provide Boris Yeltsin's government with the crown jewels of the American nuclear weapons program.

These include computer programs that enable sophisticated modeling of radiation transport phenomena and implosion physics, exotic phenomena that must be well under-stood to validate existing weapon designs and to create new ones. Also proposed for release to the Russians would be test cases that would enable the Kremlin to confirm performance of the models. Unfortunately, the advanced supercomputers needed to run such demanding software are also now available to Russia, thanks to earlier, reckless Clinton decisions relaxing export restrictions on such dual-use technology.

The computer programs in question are at the core of what the Clinton administration calls its "Science-based Stockpile Stewardship" program. Administration officials like Energy Secretary Hazel O'Leary have made much of this program as a hedge intended to protect the U.S. nuclear deterrent against the cumulative, ravaging effects of other priority "denuclearization" initiatives such as: foregoing nuclear testing, halting the production of nuclear weapons and dismantling the Energy Department's nuclear weapons complex.

While the options paper suggests that only "unclassified" information will be conveyed to the Russians, those with expertise in this area appreciate that, even if one could somehow isolate such information from its extremely sensitive context, the insights gleaned from the "unclassified" data would be of enormous value to potential adversaries. For example, once these powerful tools are in others' hands, all that will be required to have very precise knowledge about the performance - and vulnerabilities - of U.S. nuclear weapons will be the inputting of certain data concerning their characteristics. If such data are not already in the KGB's files, they will certainly be given high priority in future tasking. Russia also will be able to use such tools greatly to improve their own weapon systems.

Of course, the Clintonites cannot bring themselves to consider Russia as a potential adversary. Too much political capital - not to mention U.S. taxpayer funding -has been invested in Boris Yeltsin and the shibboleth that he remains an engine for the assured democratic, free market transformation of the former Soviet Union in the face of growing authoritarianism and resurgent state-domination of a shaky Russian economy. Too many American defense budget cuts have been premised on the irreversibility of the dissipation of the old Soviet threat, especially its nuclear manifestation. And too much of President Clinton's architecture (such as it is) for the post-Cold War world, from Bosnia to joint space exploration, assumes that Russia will prove to be a reliable "partner for peace." Needless to say, even if such a see-no-evil policy could be justified while Mr. Yeltsin remains in power, it is utterly untenable since he may not be just a few months from now.

The fact remains that the Clinton team feels unencumbered by security concerns as it pursues the president's top arms control objective – the negotiation of a Comprehensive Test Ban (CTB) Treaty by September 1996. It wrongly construes such a treaty as a critical component of the effort to curb nuclear proliferation. Nuclear testing is demonstrably not a prerequisite to the acquisition and deployment of nuclear weapons, however, as the Pakistani and Israeli nuclear programs have shown.

What is more, the administration is undeterred in its pursuit of a CTB by evidence that the Russians recently conducted a secret underground nuclear test. This event foreshadows how problematic it will be detect, let alone to prove, that covert testing is occurring in a CTB environment.

It is this reality that makes the Rosenberg Option especially perverse. Its proponents in the Clinton administration want to give the Kremlin sensitive U.S. nuclear weapons-related software and hardware as an inducement to Moscow to forswear even testing that cannot be detected by American intelligence. After all, the Russians already profess a commitment to the CTB. To date, they have similarly balked at proscribing their right to conduct the sorts of very low-yield tests that we will not, in any event, be able to tell whether they have performed.

In short, the United States is poised to offer Russia nuclear capabilities that it could otherwise have only dreamed of stealing so that Moscow will promise to agree to arms control terms that we will be unable to determine they are observing. Haven't we learned enough from Moscow's systematic non-compliance with the Biological Weapons Convention, the Conventional Forces in Europe Treaty, the Anti-Ballistic Missile Treaty and too many other accords to name to recognize that the Russians are unlikely to honor even provisions we can monitor, let alone those we cannot? For more such commitments we are prepared to give up our nuclear seed corn?

The Rosenberg Option - and indeed the larger Clinton administration denuclearization agenda of which it is a part - could only be in play because of the general inattention of the Republican Congress to these matters. With the notable exception of a few key legislators like Sens. Jon Kyl and Dirk Kempthorne, Republicans of Arizona and Idaho, respectively, there has been altogether too little concern expressed about Clinton policies that are degrading the future safety, reliability and credibility of the U.S. nuclear deterrent and that may be contributing to the nuclear threat posed to us by others. Sen. Robert Dole's willingness to take Mr. Clinton to task over these policies will be an important test, not only of his sensitivity to their dire national security ramifications, but also of his readiness to take corrective action if elected president next November.

Vladimir Putin's opening foreign policy gambit, after his victory at the polls last month, says a lot about what sort of leader of Russia he will be. President Clinton, British Prime Minister Tony Blair and others have been quick to portray the newly elected president's success in securing ratification of the START II Treaty - after seven years of studied inaction by the Duma – as evidence that Mr. Putin is a man with whom we can safely do business.

On closer inspection, however, this action is evidence less of a heartening sea change in Russia than the sort of maneuver - jujitsu - that one would expect from a man who prides himself not only on his black belt in martial arts, but on his career in the front lines of Soviet intelligence in Cold War operations against the West. We should take little comfort from signs that the most dangerous master of the Kremlin since the last KGB man to rule there, Yuri Andropov, is now able to bend the Duma to his will as he shrewdly works to undermine our advantages and turn Russia's liabilities into strengths.

Take, for example, Mr. Putin's machinations on the START II Treaty. In its original form, this accord - while defective in important respects - could be said to have had some redeeming features from the U.S. point of view. In particular, it was supposed to result in the early elimination of all of the former Soviet Union's vast arsenal of SS-18s, heavy ballistic missiles capable of preemptively attacking the United States with large numbers of independently targetable warheads. This was the treaty ratified by the U.S. Senate in January 1996.

Unfortunately, the Clinton-Gore administration agreed in September 1997 to defer the dismantling of these and other threatening Russian missiles until as late as 2007. And that was the arrangement the Duma approved last Friday. Lest the impact of this change be lost on anyone, Mr. Putin subsequently indicated that none of Russia s long-range missiles will be retired until they reach the end of their useful service life. Some deal.

What is more, Mr. Putin has asserted that Russia will not implement the START II Treaty at all, unless and until the United States ratifies what the Duma has just done. That would mean accepting several other troubling provisions, notably steps aimed at breathing new life into the strategically obsolete, legally defunct 1972 Anti-Ballistic Missile Treaty.

For example, the Russians have attached to their resolution of ratification two other ill-advised agreements also signed by the Clinton-Gore administration in September 1997. One would effect an extraordinary makeover of the ABM Treaty, from the bilateral accord signed with the Soviet Union - a country that ceased to exist nine years ago - into a multilateral accord between Russia, Ukraine and Belarus on the one hand and the United States on the other. An insight into the Clinton-Gore administration's actual attitude toward defending the United States against missile attack may be found in its motivation for seeking this change: Creating multiple foreign vetoes would make it even more difficult for the ABM Treaty to be modified so as to permit U.S. missile defenses to be deployed.

The second agreement addresses the question of demarcation: Where is the technological line to be drawn between so-called theater missile defenses that were not supposed to be covered by the ABM Treaty and strategic defenses that were? In practice, this accord would have the effect of imposing new limitations on a whole class of promising anti-missile systems. It has already contributed to actions that have dumbed down the Navy's sea-based theater wide missile defense program, rendering it less capable of providing near-term protection for U.S. forces and allies overseas than it could – and than it needs to do.

In addition, at Mr. Putin's direction, the Duma has served notice that if the United States withdraws from the ABM treaty, Russia will abrogate not only the START I and II treaties but from other arms-control accords as well. This audacious move takes advantage of the Clinton-Gore administration's refusal to acknowledge the fact that the ABM treaty is no longer in effect as a matter of international law. It also would, as a practical matter, eliminate a right the United States was explicitly afforded by the ABM Treaty, namely that of withdrawing from the accord on six-month notice if U.S. supreme interests are jeopardized.

As the New York Times reported on Saturday: "Washington has a choice, Mr. Putin said. The United States will have to renounce its plans to develop a national ABM system in order to preserve START II and the agreement limiting conventional forces in Europe. If it does not and discards the ABM treaty, Mr. Putin said, the United States will become in the eyes of the world the party that is guilty for destroying the foundations of strategic stability.

It remains to be seen what Mr. Putin's jujitsu will mean for the Clinton-Gore administration's highest foreign policy priority: negotiation of a grand compromise on strategic arms. This would package a follow-on START III agreement (involving far more radical, unverifiable and ill-advised reductions in U.S. offensive nuclear arms) together with Russian permission for an exceedingly limited American anti-missile deployment in Alaska, provided Washington foreswears any interest in more comprehensive layered defenses.

Before President Clinton makes matters worse - either in negotiations leading up to or during the summit he plans to hold with Mr. Putin sometime next month - he should heed a lesson offered by the bruising fight that led to rejection of his 1996 Comprehensive Test Ban Treaty: Under the Constitution, the Senate is a coequal partner with the executive branch in the making of international treaties. It would be a serious mistake to enroll, without serious debate let alone prior agreement from the Senate, in a new agreement effecting dubious reductions in U.S. nuclear forces and precluding the sort of layered missile defenses that even the director of the Clinton Pentagon's Ballistic Missile Defense Organization, Lt. Gen. Ronald Kadish, says are likely to be necessary.

Alas, a president more interested in securing an arms-control legacy irrespective of the cost is likely to prove an easy mark for a cunning, ruthless operative like Vladimir Putin. The Senate must therefore promptly step into the breach, performing the vital check-and-balance role envisioned for it by the Founding Fathers. It should insist upon Mr. Clinton finally submitting for the Senate's advice and consent the September 1997 agreements the Duma has now approved. By rejecting these accords on the grounds that they will make it harder for the United States to achieve the missile defense required by it and its forces and allies overseas, the Senate can make clear the unacceptability of the grand compromise that Mr. Clinton now seeks - a deal that might just be sufficiently inimical to U.S. national security interests to be acceptable to Mr. Putin.

As president-elect, George W. Bush is going to have to swiftly address a number of vital foreign policy questions.

A number of these are obvious, such as the escalating war in the Middle East, the emerging threat from China and the urgent need to defend the American people against ballistic missile attack.

Other decisions are perhaps less evident, but arguably no less momentous for long-term U.S. interests. Among these is the question of U.S. ties with one of the most important nations in Eurasia: Ukraine.

Since the end of the Cold War, Washington has mostly gotten it wrong on Ukraine, a freedom-loving nation of 55 million on the border of Russia.

Successive administrations have seen Ukrainian independence and sovereignty as an unwanted irritant to good relations with the Kremlin.

President George H.W. Bush voiced this infamous view in what came to be known as his "Chicken Kiev" speech of Aug. 1, 1991 - an appeal to Ukraine to remain part of the Soviet Union.

Unfortunately, after the Soviet Union's demise, the Clinton-Gore team has persisted in the pursuit of a Moscow-centric approach to the former Soviet Union.

The only time during the past eight years that the United States has seriously engaged Ukraine was for the dubious purpose of securing its denuclearization. Otherwise, the United States has exhibited what can charitably be called "benign neglect" toward Ukraine and her people.

The effect has been to exacerbate problems for the Ukrainians at home and to make Kiev more susceptible to the combination of seductive overtures and threatening pressures emanating from Moscow.

The time has clearly come for a different approach. The Russia of Vladimir Putin is exhibiting behavior that is ever more problematic.

Among the most worrisome are Russia's transfer to China of untold billions of dollars worth of advanced weapons, the Kremlin's increasingly domineering behavior toward its neighbors, an unbridled hostility toward a free press and the persecution on trumped-up espionage charges of an innocent U.S. citizen, Edmond Pope.

Against the dark backdrop, the necessity of strengthening Ukraine as a counterweight to Russia is increasingly apparent.

Specifically, the next U.S. president should immediately set about forging a strategic partnership with Ukraine aimed at establishing a strong U.S. commitment to the latter's independence, sovereignty and economic growth.

If the United States' words are backed by deeds - notably, political support, military cooperation, broadened trade opportunities and encouragement for U.S. investment in Ukraine and Ukraine's integration into Europe - the signal would be unmistakable: Russia can no longer feel free to engage in intimidation, coercion and other predations against its erstwhile colony.

For a new U.S.-Ukrainian strategic partnership to work, however, Kiev must be willing to undertake at long last genuine democratic political and free market reforms.

The rule of law - an indispensable ingredient not only to individual freedoms but to real economic growth - must be established and faithfully honored.

Among other things, the United States should make clear that the Ukrainian government must enact the sort of genuine privatization, property rights and other economic reforms needed to curb rampant corruption, facilitate and reward entrepreneurship and secure popular support for change.

If the next president makes a priority of pursuing such a strategic partnership with Ukraine, he can secure a bulwark against Russia's emerging revanchism - attempts to regain former territories by Mr. Putin or his successor. He may also be able to help effect a transformation in Ukraine that will enable her to become a force for the further flowering of individual rights and economic opportunity in Eastern Europe and Central Asia.

On the other hand, in the event the next president fails to provide such visionary leadership, when the question is inevitably asked "Who lost Ukraine?" he may have to answer, "I did." Given the current opportunity, that would be a shameful mea culpa for either Mr. Bush.

At the end of 1940, President Franklin D. Roosevelt delivered a powerful "fireside chat," a fitting backdrop to the visit to Europe this week by his successor, George W. Bush.

In his radio address, Roosevelt summoned a reluctant America to sacrifice to produce the arms urgently needed by freedom-loving people in Britain and elsewhere at risk of being overrun by Nazism and other forms of tyranny. He called the United States "the great arsenal of democracy."

In his travels, Mr. Bush will meet with leaders of a number of countries whose national survival in World War II depended critically upon the industrial output of democracy's indispensable arsenal. He will try to restore with these allies relations strained in recent years by disagreements over liberation of Iraq and other matters.

Unfortunately, the president's "fence-mending" efforts with Russian President Vladimir Putin and his French, German and British counterparts seem likely to founder over these states increasingly becoming arsenals for tyranny.

Take Russia. Since the end of the Cold War, the old Soviet military-industrial complex has been kept a going concern largely by selling its products to Communist China and other regimes unfriendly to freedom.

Mr. Putin's Russia has approved sale of a vast array of advanced aircraft, missile systems, submarines, other seagoing vessels and armored equipment. Worse yet, the Russians have in many cases transferred not only end-items but manufacturing know-how, enabling the Chinese to produce even more such sophisticated equipment in the future - for its own use and for sale, in turn, to other despotic regimes.

Mr. Putin's list of client tyrannies does not end with China. Just last week, he reaffirmed his decision to allow the Iranian mullahocracy to complete construction of a Russian-designed and -supplied nuclear power plant at Bushehr. In this, he blithely dismissed U.S. and other concerns the Iranian regime will use this facility to amass fuel for nuclear weapons.

Mr. Putin has been no more responsive to appeals to forgo sale of advanced surface-to-air missiles to the Syrian despot, Bashar Assad. Such weapons may well end up in the hands of the terrorist Hezbollah organization that enjoys safe haven and sponsorship from Syria and its patron, Iran. This would greatly escalate the risk of conflict between Israel and Syria and the possibility Russian-made weapons will be used in efforts to shoot down American pilots operating in and from Iraq.

In addition, the Kremlin has recently agreed to sell as many as 100,000 AK-47 assault rifles to one of this hemisphere's most worrisome, and ambitious, despots: Venezuela's Hugo Chavez. Mr. Chavez will use these arms to equip his allies in fomenting anti-

American revolutions throughout Latin America - including, notably, in Nicaragua, where the Sandinistas seem poised to retake power.

If Mr. Bush's Russian interlocutor is indifferent to appeals for greater restraint in such sales to freedom's enemies, so it appears are France's Jacques Chirac, Germany's Gerhard Schroeder and Britain's Tony Blair.

The Three EU Musketeers seem determined to end the arms embargo the European Union imposed on China after the Tiananmen Square massacre, thereby allowing Europe's military-industrial capacity also to be put in the service of China's evermore offensively oriented armed forces.

The sorts of technology transfers that could flow from the EU's arsenal to the Chinese are particularly troubling, insofar as they would complement nicely the formidable weapon systems already provided by Russia. As the American Enterprise Institute's Daniel Blumenthal and Thomas Donnelly pointed out Sunday in an Outlook article in The Washington Post: "The missing pieces of the People's Liberation Army puzzle are exactly the sorts of command and control, communications, intelligence, surveillance and reconnaissance systems that the Europeans are getting ready to sell."

The negative consequences of such sales for U.S.-European relations are hard to exaggerate. Chinese military doctrine posits the inevitability of conflict with the United States. Preparations by Beijing are not compatible with mere self-defense or even threats to Taiwan. China's blue-water navy capabilities, long-range ballistic and cruise missiles and space-control technologies would, if combined with command and control and other equipment designed to NATO standards, be much more threatening and greatly increase the odds such gear will be used in the future to kill Americans.

In his "Arsenal of Democracy" address 65 years ago, Roosevelt warned his countrymen: "Frankly and definitely there is danger ahead - danger against which we must prepare. But we well know that we cannot escape danger, or the fear of danger, by crawling into bed and pulling the covers over our heads." He argued America could prevent "the danger" from afflicting us directly only by arming the British and others already fighting the fascists.

Today, it is no less important we confront the danger to us from actual or prospective enemies, armed this time by those we previously helped secure their freedom.

President Bush may be reluctant to remind his hosts in Europe this week that they are "either with us or against us." But if they serve as arsenals for tyranny, the Europeans and Russians should understand Americans will clearly see them for what they are: "Against us."

Chess is the national sport of Russia. It is, therefore, as Soviet Communists like Vladimir Putin used to say, "no coincidence, comrade" that the proposal on missile defense he rolled out at last week's G-8 meeting was a sophisticated gambit, a crafty effort not to advance the protection of Europe and the United States from future Iranian missiles, but to block such anti-missile defenses. Call it Putin's ploy.

In fact, in the manner of an accomplished master of the game - for example, his democracy-advocating nemesis, Garry Kasparov - Mr. Putin is playing on several different chessboards simultaneously.

First, there is the U.S.-Russian relationship. An enemy is required by every would-be totalitarian - and it is increasingly clear that, despite his laughable claim to being "the last democrat," Mr. Putin's behavior has the hallmarks of a new czar. For Vladimir Putin, it is us. By building up the notion we are a threat, he is able to garner popular support for his growing consolidation of power and even repression at home. He is also able to justify a new military build-up and adventurism abroad in league with the likes of world class anti-Americans like Iran's mullahs, China's communist leadership, Venezuela's Hugo Chavez and Kim Jong-il of North Korea.

Then, there is the Russian-European "board." Mr. Putin has reverted to traditional Kremlin behavior toward Europe: bullying, coercing and blackmailing, using threats of nuclear attacks and energy cut-offs and other forms of economic pressure. Taking a move out of Josef Stalin's playbook, the man-who-would-be-czar has even attacked one of the Baltic States, Estonia, albeit with cyber-warfare, not the old fashioned kind.

Finally, Vladimir Putin is trying to affect U.S.-European relations. His service in the KGB during the American-led effort to place intermediate-range nuclear missiles in Europe nearly a quarter-century ago clearly left its mark on him. He is not only nostalgic for the Soviets' superpower status that began to unravel when that deployment went forward. He is also well versed in the type of divide-and-conquer strategy that narrowly failed to topple key NATO governments and prevent the INF missiles from being fielded.

Today, the Kremlin hopes to capitalize on U.S.-European strains over Iraq and to use the wedge of opposition to Bush administration plans to deploy a very modest anti-missile capability in Poland and the Czech Republic to create, and fill, a vacuum of power on the Continent.

The Putin ploy seeks to advance these purposes in several ways:

The Russian president has offered a Russian radar in Azerbaijan as an alternative to the detection and tracking radar slated under the Bush plan for the Czech Republic. Never mind that the Kremlin's obsolescent radar is not designed for the sophisticated discrimination of warheads from decoys inherent in the proposed, modern American system. The idea is not to do the job, rather to confuse the issue, give Czech opponents an apparent alternative to having the new radar based in their country and make the U.S. appear unreasonable.

Similarly, Mr. Putin has proposed that instead of 10 anti-missile interceptors slated for deployment in Poland, the United States put interceptors in Turkey, Iraq and at sea on warships equipped with the Aegis defensive system. This gambit gives Polish critics an out, while affording a chance further to roil the United States' relations with Turkey and Iraq.

The Kremlin has long sought to undermine the incalculably important strategic alliance between America and Turkey - already frayed by the anti-U.S. agenda of the Islamist government in Ankara and the growing tensions between the two countries over Iraq's Kurdistan. And at a moment when the idea of "getting out of Iraq" is all the rage in American elite circles, committing to the long-term basing there of anti-missile systems is clearly not on.

The idea of making Aegis warships all they can be when it comes to anti-missile defenses is, of course, a great idea. That is not what Mr. Putin has in mind, however. And, unless a man who does - the new chairman of the Joint Chiefs of Staff-designate, Adm. Mike Mullins - has his way, these missile defense ships will remain incapable of providing the sort of robust protection to Europe and the United States that they could, and that we need.

For good measure, Mr. Putin has thrown in two other problematic ideas:

(1)   There is no need to rush on European missile defenses, since he claims the Iranians have no missiles that can reach Europe, nor any plans to build them.

(2)   And Russia must be involved in the decision making about any anti-missile deployments.

The first is patently untrue. Iran's current Shahab-3 missile could reach parts of NATO territory. And there are unmistakable signs the mullahs in Tehran intend to develop a Shahab-4 that will be able to attack much, if not all, of the European Continent.

The most insidious aspect of Mr. Putin's ploy is his insistence, through seduction or intimidation, that Russia be a party to any decisions about the deployment - and perhaps the employment - of missile defenses for Europe. This would be tantamount to allowing one of the Tehran regime's most important allies and one of its nuclear enablers to determine whether and how our European partners and interests will be protected against the threat posed by Mr. Putin's friends in Iran.

All this is expected to be discussed further in July when Vladimir Putin is honored with a trip to the Bush family compound in Maine. President Bush will be under greater pressure to surrender American freedom of action on missile defense there than any U.S. leader since Ronald Reagan, who was tempted to do so by Mikhail Gorbachev at Reykjavik two decades ago. Now, as then, the response to the Kremlin's gambit must be "Thanks, but not thanks."

Sixty years ago, President Franklin Delano Roosevelt announced to the nation in one of his famous "fireside chats" that America must be "the great arsenal of democracy." It was a visionary and, at the time, controversial declaration that a nation dead-set against becoming entangled in the war then consuming Europe must nonetheless help arm democratic nations fighting for their survival. This initiative proved critical to Britain's defense in the run-up to Pearl Harbor, at which point the United States became decisively not just the Free World's armory, but its savior.

Today, we find another country putting its formidable military-industrial complex in the service of others around the globe. The arsenal is Russia's; the recipients are virtually without exception the world's most dangerous enemies of freedom. This practice is making a mockery of President Obama's much touted "reset" of relations with the Kremlin - including, notably, the new, bilateral START Treaty. It also increases exponentially the dangers associated with his policy of "engaging" rogue states, a practice that is simply affording them time to buy ever more advanced and deadly weapons from Moscow.

Consider just a few examples of the Arsenal for Roguery at work, and its implications for our security, and that of what's left of the Free World:

- Even as the President continues to claim that the Russians are willing to be more helpful in getting tougher UN sanctions on Iran, the Kremlin is allowing the nuclear reactor it previously sold Tehran to be brought on line. It is pledging to complete the transfer of advanced S-300 air defense systems, which will greatly complicate - if not effectively preclude - aerial attacks by the Israelis or U.S. forces aimed at destroying that facility and others associated with the Iranian nuclear weapons program.

- Russia is also selling the S-300 to Syria. This is important because the Syrians have justly been put on notice by Israel that they would be subjected to retaliatory strikes in the event Russian-designed (and perhaps supplied?) Scud missiles transferred recently by Damascus to Hezbollah in Lebanon are used against the Jewish state. Such Russian protection may embolden Syria to believe that it can unleash with impunity death and destruction on Israel (perhaps by using Scud delivered biological or chemical weapons) via its terrorist proxies - and Iran's.

- The Russians have also been marketing to international customers a family of deadly sea-skimming anti-ship cruise missiles with air-, surface- and submarine-launched variants. These Brahmos rocket/ramjet missiles were jointly developed with the Indians and can fly at up to 2.5 times the speed of sound. The proliferation of such missiles constitutes a serious threat to American naval and other vessels given the difficulties of defending against a weapon with these flight characteristics.

- Then, there is the up-to-$5 billion in arms sales that Russian Prime Minister Vladimir Putin claims to have concluded with our hemisphere's most dangerous dictator, Hugo Chavez of Venezuela. What exactly is on offer is unclear. But the purchase reportedly includes T-72 tanks and S-300 missiles. This comes on top of Chavez's earlier acquisitions of 100,000 Kalashnikov automatic rifles, helicopters, fighter jets and submarines. Evidently, a Russian nuclear reactor is also being promised.

But, not to worry. According to the Associated Press, Putin declared during his most recent sales visit to Caracas earlier this month: "Our objective is to make the world more democratic, make it balanced and multi-polar. The cooperation between Russia and Venezuela in this context has special importance." Feel better?

If any further evidence were needed that the Russians are enabling through their arms sales a grave new threat to American interests and those of other freedom-loving peoples, there's this: The London Sunday Telegraph reported on the April 25th that Moscow was marketing a new "Club-K container missile system." For just $10 million, one can acquire a launcher and four sea- or land-attack cruise missiles concealed in what otherwise appears to be a standard shipping container.

The newspaper reports that "Iran and Venezuela have already shown an interest in the Club-K...which could allow them to carry out pre-emptive strikes from behind an enemy's missile defenses."

As President Obama is fond of saying, let me be clear: Vladimir Putin's Russia - yes, he still runs the place - is cynically exploiting the U.S. administration's fecklessness in blindly pursuing improved relations. So far, this has gotten Moscow, among other things: the cancelation of a near-term deployment of U.S. missile defenses in Europe; American acquiescence to increasing Russian aggressiveness in reestablishing a sphere of influence in the "near-abroad"; and no objection to the Kremlin's acquisition of a French amphibious assault ship well-suited for that purpose.

Worse yet, Russia has pledged it will abrogate the START accord should the United States improve "qualitatively or quantitatively" the sorts of missile defenses Moscow's arms sales to rogue states (and perhaps others) are making ever more necessary.

History will show that the metastasizing danger of the Russian arsenal for roguery's world-wide operations has been greatly compounded - if not fundamentally enabled - by the assiduous application of the Obama Doctrine: "Embolden our enemies. Undermine our allies. Diminish our country." If the latter doctrine is not swiftly corrected, and the former not effectively thwarted, America and the rest of the Free World may soon find themselves confronting threats even greater than those at large when first we rose to the challenge of being the indispensable arsenal for democracy.

To the uninitiated, Vladimir Putin has seemingly just undertaken what President Obama might call a "reset" of the Russian political landscape. In fact, the prime minister's announcement Saturday that he would swap offices with the current president, Dmitry Medvedev, just clarifies an abiding reality: There is not, and since at least 2000 never has been, any power center in Moscow other than Putin, the former KGB operative-turned-authoritarian kleptocrat.

The real question is whether that revelation will make it impossible for the Obama administration to persist in its delusion that a conciliatory U.S. policy towards Russia will encourage the Kremlin to moderate its repression at home and its aggressiveness abroad?

To date, this American reset with Russia has certainly done nothing to ameliorate the plight of journalists, human rights attorneys and activists, independent businessmen and other opposition figures who have become, under the de facto Putin regime, literally endangered species. Neither has it dissuaded the Kremlin from: using energy weapons to force what Putin calls "the near abroad" and even Europe to submit to his demands; selling vast quantities of advanced arms to the world's most dangerous regimes; meddling in the Middle East, Central Asia, Latin America, Europe and anywhere else that the Kremlin's influence can be expanded at the United States' expense; and exploiting U.S. dependence on Russia for everything from access to Afghanistan to access for our astronauts to the space station.

In particular, Obama's reset with Putin's Russia has failed to diminish the Kremlin's continuing commitment to the modernization of its arsenal of strategic and tactical nuclear weapons. While the former has shrunk with the retirement of Soviet-era long-range missiles and submarines, what remains is being systematically upgraded with modern warheads and platforms. As my Center for Security Policy colleague, Ben Lerner, observes in a forthcoming white paper on the misbegotten New START Treaty, U.S. negotiators ignored this reality and gave away the store in the hope of persuading Moscow to join in the President's fantasy of "ridding the world of nuclear weapons."

Notably, Team Obama gave up on long-range missile defenses of Europe and the United States based in Poland and the Czech Republic to appease Moscow. His representatives reportedly approved language the Russians drafted giving them what amounts to a veto over future "quantitative or qualitative improvements" to U.S. anti-missile systems.

Obama and Company also agreed to terms in New START that forced us to dismantle strategic weapons, but not the Russians. Worse yet, the Kremlin got to keep its entire, vast arsenal of shorter-range, relatively low-yield "tactical" arms. By some estimates, they enjoy a 10-to-1 advantage in such weapons.

Even more ominous is the fact that some of those weapons are believed to be aboard cruise missile-armed submarines known to operate within striking distance of our coasts. And like Russia's strategic forces, these tactical weapons are being upgraded - in some cases with advanced technologies whose military effects, and therefore lethality, are not fully understood by our weapons designers.

In the course of what passed for the Senate ratification debate on New START during the lame duck session late last year, administration spokesmen blithely assured skeptics that the next treaty with Moscow would capture tactical weapons and otherwise correct the myriad deficiencies of the 2010 accord.

On the basis of such dubious promises, Senator Lamar Alexander and a handful of other Republicans joined all Senate Democrats to provide the necessary two-thirds majority. Sen. Alexander evidently enjoyed so much the favorable press and other accolades he achieved for breaking ranks with the rest of the GOP leadership that he has just announced that he will give up his post as chairman of the Senate Republican Policy Committee - presumably in the interest of having more latitude to engage in such defections in the future.

As with other Obama delusions, there has never been any basis for believing the Russians would give up weapons that they assert could be used to shape and prevail in tomorrow's battles. Even if, against all odds, the Kremlin were to agree to curbs on tactical nuclear weapons, their relatively small size and ease of portability means that any such limitations would be inherently unverifiable.

No worries. According to the Washington Times' invaluable "Inside the Ring" column, the administration will not be dissuaded from its goal of ridding at least America of its nuclear arms by Vladimir Putin's continuing recalcitrance or other obstacles. Columnist Bill Gertz reports that Gary Samore, the top arms control guru on President Obama's National Security Council, "noted that if there is no agreement or treaty, 'even unilateral' cuts are being considered."

In other words, despite the fact that Russia's once-and-future president is not going along - and, for that matter, neither is any other nuclear weapon state, the Obama administration blithely plans to reset America's deterrent. Gone will be the time-tested strategic Triad of intercontinental-range bombers and land- and sea-based missiles. If we are lucky, we will be left with a far-less-resilient "Dyad" equipped with obsolescing, untested weapons. Never mind that the world is becoming more dangerous by the day; a new study dubbed a mini-Nuclear Posture Review has been ordered up to justify such unilateral disarmament.

With the successive budget cuts eviscerating our conventional forces, it is not clear how much of a fight the military leadership will put up to preserve weapons that may be the ultimate guarantor of our security but that some deem unusable. Expect no complaints from Vladimir Putin and his friends. This is just the sort of reset - read, self-inflicted American wound - that he relishes most.

China

There are many compelling reasons for opposing renewal of Most Favored Nation (MFN) status for communist China. But there is one overarching factor that demands such a step: China is utilizing much of the huge trade surplus that it enjoys thanks to this privileged trading status to mount a strategic threat to the United States and its vital interests in Asia, the Middle East and beyond.

To be sure, MFN is a blunt instrument - affecting, if it is denied, millions of innocent Chinese workers, the economy of Hong Kong, U.S. jobs associated with exports to and imports from China, etc. Yet, it is the only measure currently on the table remotely proportionate to the magnitude of the danger Beijing is creating, to a considerable degree with resources it is garnering from trade with the United States.

As Ross Munro and Richard Bernstein put it in their critically acclaimed book published earlier this year, "The Coming Conflict with China": "Before, Beijing saw American power as a strategic advantage for the PRC; now, it has decided that American power represents a threat, not just to China's security but to China's plans to grow stronger and to play a paramount role in the affairs of Asia."

The enormous impetus behind China's determined effort to acquire a modern military capable of decisively projecting power derives from this zero-sum view of the U.S.-P.R.C. relationship. The Chinese leadership believes, after all, that it must be able not only to dominate the nations of East Asia and the South China Sea. It sees China as having to exercise control over the Pacific out to what the Chinese call "the second island chain" (i.e., the Philippines, Japan and even the U.S. territory of Guam). The larger purpose appears to be even more ambitious: to render the United States incapable of exercising influence in Asia that would compete with, let alone counter, Chinese hegemony in the region.

The Chinese are pursuing a multifaceted campaign to accomplish these strategic objectives. The following are among the means the P.R.C. is pursuing toward such ominous ends:

- Strategic force modernization: The Washington Times recently reported that China is expected to begin deploying by the year 2000 an advanced intercontinental-range ballistic missile, designated the Dong Feng-31 (DF-31). This missile will give Beijing the ability to deliver nuclear warheads with great accuracy throughout the Pacific and parts of the Western United States.

  A foretaste of the use to which China may be willing to put such a capability can be seen in a report published on Page One of the New York Times on Jan. 24, 1996. It described how a senior Chinese official had signaled Beijing's willingness to engage in "nuclear blackmail" against the United States by suggesting that American interference in China's coercion of Taiwan could result in an attack on

Los Angeles. In the absence of any deployed U.S. ability to intercept a Chinese ballistic missile launched at Los Angeles – or any other target in the United States - such threats may well have the desired effect.

- Buildup of other aspects of China's military: Beijing is also pouring billions of dollars into what might be called a "Great Leap Forward" for other elements of the People's Liberation Army, notably its power-projection capabilities (long-range aircraft, blue-water naval units, precision-guided munitions and unconventional weapons). Such capabilities pose, most immediately, a danger that China will be able to control transit of the South China Sea and access to its energy and other strategic resources.

- Espionage: The illegal acquisition of U.S. technology - especially that of the dual-use variety - is a priority assignment for the hundreds of People's Liberation Army-owned or - affiliated front companies operating in the United States. Together with large numbers of intelligence operatives, 40,000 graduate and undergraduate students and Overseas Chinese entrepreneurs doing business in this country or with its companies, America faces a literally unprecedented risk of penetration and espionage and, consequently, an immense counterintelligence challenge.

- Arming U.S. gangs and drug lords: China has been caught shipping AK-47s and other lethal firepower to criminal elements in this country with the potential to sow mayhem in American society. PLA-affiliated companies have offered to sell undercover U.S. law enforcement officers posing as drug lords not only automatic weapons - whose lethal effects were evident when the streets of Los Angeles were recently turned into a war zone by bank robbers wielding AK-47s manufactured by the Chinese firm Norinco - but rocket-propelled grenade launchers, light armored vehicles and shoulder-fired surface-to-air missiles.

- Financial Penetration: Since 1988, China has issued some 80 bonds on the U.S. and Western securities markets. While the bulk of these have been yen-denominated bonds, the total amount of dollar-denominated Chinese bonds (primarily issued in the U.S. market) has now reached at least $6.7 billion.

This preferred borrowing venue provides major Chinese state-owned enterprises and banks intimately connected with the PLA and Beijing's security services with access to large sums of undisciplined, unconditioned and inexpensive cash. This money can be easily diverted to finance activities inimical to U.S. security interests - not to mention American principles and values. Worse yet, in the process, Beijing is successfully recruiting numerous politically influential constituencies in this country that will have a financial vested interest in ensuring China is not subject to future U.S. economic sanctions, containment strategies or other forms of isolation and/or penalties. It adds insult to injury that Chinese efforts to suborn or otherwise influence this country's elected leaders might have been underwritten, at least in part, by the proceeds of undisciplined bond sales to American companies and citizens.

- Proliferation: Beijing has, for years, been aggressively and irresponsibly facilitating the spread of weapons of mass destruction (WMD) and other deadly ordinance to rogue states capable of using them against U.S. personnel, interests and/or allies. The picture that emerges is one of a nation systematically seeding the Middle East, Persian Gulf and South Asia with chemical, biological and nuclear weapons technology - together with ballistic and cruise missiles with which such arms can be delivered over increasingly long ranges.

  If Beijing is using proliferation as an integral part of a campaign to diminish U.S. presence and influence in the Western Pacific, the possibility that its clients might use Chinese-supplied arms to precipitate conflict in regions far removed from Asia could seen as desirable by the Chinese leadership. After all, it would almost certainly preoccupy the United States – substantially tying down and drawing down its military, political and strategic resources.

While the United States would prefer to avoid confronting China, it has no responsible choice under present and foreseeable circumstances but to stop engaging in activities that will have the effect of making it ever more difficult - and far more costly - to challenge the P.R.C. The place to start is by non-renewal of MFN for China.

By the time this column appears, there will be no such address. Thousands of Chinese troops will have arrived via armored vehicles, helicopters and warships to secure for communism its first territorial acquisition since the fall of the Berlin Wall - and arguably its most precious one ever: the pearl of the Orient, Hong Kong.

The strategic import of this moment is being deliberately overshadowed by the forced gaiety of round-the-clock "celebrations." One cannot, however, help but feel - surrounded by the red-and-yellow banners, dragons, lamps, flags and other regalia of the new masters of Hong Kong - the alarm experienced by those who saw Adolf Hitler's troops welcomed into Austria and the Sudetenland with swastikas and brown shirts.

The innumerable television cameras in town to record the surrender of Hong Kong seem largely distracted by the pomp of various ceremonies attended by high-ranking U.S. officials and their counterparts from other free nations. These foreign representatives are content to mouth platitudes about "orderly transitions" and their intentions to "hold the People's Republic of China accountable" for preserving Hong Kong's freedoms.

For their part, the leaders of the PRC and the quislings they have anointed to govern Hong Kong are only too willing to play back what the West would like to hear. "One country, two systems" is the mantra of the day. This evidently is meant to convey the idea that Hong Kong will be "free" - free to be a capitalist police state along the lines of Singapore. China will pursue its own brand of "state capitalism" with a less-than-human face.

It is already clear, however, that Hong Kong will not be "free" in any other sense of the word. Everyone agrees that Asia's most vigorously independent press has already begun to exhibit self-censorship, even before China's jackboots are present to enforce the party line.

So too will economic freedom prove elusive in the absence of the other liberties Hong Kongers have come to know. Already, businessmen here who lack guanxi ("connections") to Beijing's corrupt power structure are finding themselves seriously disadvantaged in business. What is more, those who do have connections are increasingly discovering that one day's guanxi can disappear the next. In the absence of the rule of law, businessmen are finding themselves at the losing end of China's wired system of "justice" and - in some cases at least - in jail.

Against this gloomy backdrop, the words and courage of a leader of democratic Hong Kong, Martin Lee, stand out brilliantly. As he put it in an op-ed article published in the South China Morning Post on Monday, the last day of his service as a popularly elected member of the Legislative Council:

"Imagine yourself in a large well-lit room. Suddenly all the lights go out. But if you have a candle and a box of matches, light can be brought about by a single flame. And if other people follow your example and also light their candles, then the light will return. In short, the degree of autonomy we will enjoy is only as high as our level of determination to defend it.

"But imagine yourself in a room with many lit candles. If you extinguish your candle, others may do so as well and darkness will come. So we must all remember, that if we exercise our freedom today, others are watching and will follow. But equally, if we practice self-censorship, the chances are that others will restrain themselves, too... "

"It is often said that a society gets the government it deserves. If we fail to stand together, if we fail to continue exercising the freedoms we enjoy today - then we will have no one to blame but ourselves for we will have voluntarily tied our hands.

"But if we resolve as a community to continue living freely and we remain determined to fight for the freedoms we are promised, it will be all the more difficult for them to be taken away. Are we up to the challenge?"

The question might well be asked of the American people, as well. Those like President Clinton who insist that the PRC is no longer communist or like Madeleine Albright who advocate "engagement" with Beijing seemingly at any cost may be unable to appreciate how much is riding on the continued personal safety and visible public presence of Martin Lee and his fellow democrats in Hong Kong. There will, however, be no clearer indication of the real future of Hong Kong or of the quality of the U.S. commitment to liberty than whether Martin Lee and his colleagues are allowed to keep their candles burning brightly, no matter how damning the reality they illuminate.

Make no mistake; this is a defining moment for America. The Chinese communists are transparently banking on the Clinton administration and the majority of the "business first" U.S. Congress to fail to rise to this challenge. They are discounting Washington's stated commitment to Hong Kong's freedom as more empty rhetoric, America's threats of dire repercussions if that freedom is jeopardized as meant for domestic consumption only. If they are right, then more than Hong Kong will surely be embarking upon what Winston Churchill once termed "a new dark age." It behooves us, no less than Martin Lee's people, to prove them wrong.

As Chinese President Jiang Zemin's makes his victory lap around the United States this week, I keep wondering: What if the real motivation for the 21-gun salutes and lavish feting of the Butcher of Beijing is not really the Clinton administration's enthusiasm for an appeasement policy dubbed "engagement," or even its slavish pursuit of foreign sales on any terms? What if it amounts to the ultimate quid pro quo for China's help to the 1996 Clinton-Gore campaign, or perhaps in its aftermath, a form of hush money for keeping Charlie Trie and his damning secrets away from U.S. investigators? Could President Clinton be that cynical, that self-absorbed, that indifferent to long-term national interests that China seems determined to threaten?

Unfortunately, everything about the Sino-U.S. relationship at the moment reeks of cynicism. Take Mr. Clinton's speech Friday at the Voice of America, a speech designed to justify his policy toward the People's Republic. Throughout his remarks, the president described the "common interests" the United States has with China in a manner seemingly designed to mislead the American people about the extent to which Beijing has been assiduously jeopardizing those interests.

For example, Mr. Clinton spoke of a shared stake in "stability" in the Persian Gulf, as though China has not been selling Iran advanced anti-ship cruise missiles and weapons of mass destruction - military capabilities sought by Tehran precisely for the purpose of exercising a destabilizing control over Western oil supplies. He applauded China's participation in a series of arms control agreements governing nuclear, chemical and biological weapons and ballistic missile technology without mentioning that the Chinese have been violating every one of those accords.

And Mr. Clinton pledged "intensified" law enforcement cooperation with China to fight "drug-trafficking and international organized crime." Since this administration never misses an opportunity to exploit children, he used the fact that "too many of our children are still killed with guns, too many of our streets are still riddled with drugs" to establish a certain moral equivalency with China and rationalize a redoubled, joint, effort to fight these plagues.

Curiously, he failed to mention that Wang Jun - the well-connected Chinese tycoon brought by Mr. Trie to one of the president's White House fund-raising coffees - has been associated with gun-running (remember the AK-47s used to shoot up the LAPD a few months back?) and drug-smuggling in this country. We have already seen one federal "sting" that might have demonstrated Beijing's complicity in such operations compromised by a leak, apparently from a State Department source. It is hard to fathom how more "cooperation" with Chinese authorities will result in anything other than an improved ability on the part of the PRC's suppliers of guns and drugs to avoid interception by American authorities.

Similar cynicism is at work in Mr. Clinton's expected certification that Beijing is no longer contributing to the proliferation of weapons of mass destruction, a precondition to sales by the U.S. nuclear power industry of its wares to China. This certification is predicated on a new round of "assurances" that it will stop proliferating, assurances that are worth no more than the ones previously offered and repeatedly violated. The simple fact is that the PRC is - and will remain - up to its eyeballs in trade in dangerous technologies in order to: earn hard currency and/or access to oil; increase its influence in strategic locales; and create conditions, for example in the Persian Gulf, that will divert American forces and attention from the sphere of influence China seeks to carve out in Asia.

The corrupting effect of such cynicism is also evident in the other side of this transaction. One offer from American industry will be the fruits of roughly $1.1 billion worth of U.S. investments in a new generation of inherently safe nuclear power technologies - some $350 million of which have come from the taxpayer, the rest from the private sector. A chilling article last Saturday in The Washington Post titled "China Plays Rough: 'Invest and Transfer Technology, or No Market Access,'" describes how American companies are being forced to transfer state-of-the-art manufacturing know-how and hardware to the PRC if they want to do business there.

In case after case, Chinese companies have promptly ripped off the U.S.-supplied technology and engaged in cutthroat competition with the American concern. It is predictable that this will happen with any new reactor technology, as well; the $60 billion market said to exist in China for U.S. products will be filled with this country's technology, all right, but supplied by indigenous Chinese copycats.

One of the shrewdest and most critical observers of the Clinton policy toward the PRC - the New York Times' former editor and nationally syndicated columnist, A.M. Rosenthal - noted last July the cumulative effect of such cynicism and the corruption it breeds in high places:

"The men of the [Chinese] Politburo know [the United States'] heavy-duty thinkers still have not grasped the new historic reality that Beijing has brought about: China is remodeling America. Beijing has changed the thinking and behavior of America's president, political parties, top business executives, journalistic and academic seers, even of the guardians of its security. Most delicious to the communists, China has reshaped and diminished the value America places on itself - its democratic and religious values, even its military security values."

Fortunately, some American leaders are still resisting China's cynical corruption. One of them, Rep. Christopher Cox, California Republican – whose courageous, principled leadership in the Congress will be recognized tonight when he receives the Center for Security Policy's prestigious "Keeper of the Flame" award - is spearheading legislation aimed at thwarting some of the Chinese most abusive practices.

Senate Intelligence Committee Chairman Richard Shelby has expressed entirely appropriate concern, given Beijing's past track record, about accepting at face value Chinese assurances their future non-proliferation policies. Sen. Thad Cochran, Mississippi Republican, is trying to stop the sales of powerful U.S. supercomputers to China's nuclear weapons and other military facilities. Sen. Lauch Faircloth, North Carolina Republican, has just introduced important legislation to ensure closer monitoring of Chinese (and other foreign entities') efforts to penetrate the U.S. bond and equities markets. And Sen. Arlen Specter, Pennsylvania Republican, and Rep. Frank Wolf, Virginia Republican, are leading an initiative that would penalize China for its systematic persecution of religious minorities.

We can only hope such voices will be heard above the din of cynical appeasers and corrupt sycophants likely to be much in evidence during President Jiang's official meetings and his public appearances this week.

Hong Kong's still-independent press is having a field day with an unusual PDA (public display of aggressiveness) by the new master of the former British colony: China's President Jiang Zemin.

Evidently, Mr. Jiang was upset at the impertinence of a journalist who asked whether Beijing's endorsement of a second term for the highly unpopular shipping magnate it had installed to run Hong Kong amounted to "an imperial order."

According to yesterday's edition of The Washington Post, the communist emperor - furious that someone had accurately described the nature of his clothes - "flew into a rage. 'You media need to raise your general knowledge level, got it? You should not say we have an imperial order and then criticize me. Got it? Naive. I am so angry.' "

Tung Chee-wha, the chief executive of Hong Kong in question, subsequently demonstrated his subordination to China by telling the press: "President Jiang actually loves you all very much. He merely gave you a kind of encouragement." Like their journalists, the people of Hong Kong are under no illusion: The kind of "encouragement" Beijing's emperor has in mind would give "tough love" a whole new meaning.

Americans - journalists, politicians and the public alike - should take to heart Mr. Jiang's call for "raising the general knowledge level" about his government and what it is doing. Yet there is strong resistance to any such educational effort, as was evidenced by the reaction from both the two presidential campaigns and the Fourth Estate to the one, fleeting focus on China in the entire 2000 campaign.

Last week, a mysterious group had the temerity to run a television ad suggesting viewers vote Republican because Al Gore had received illegal campaign contributions from Communist China and the PRC had, under the Clinton-Gore administration, secured access to sensitive military secrets that have greatly increased the Chinese threat to the United States. It concluded by reprising one of the most effective political spots in the history of television advertising - the "Daisy" ad employed against Barry Goldwater's 1964 presidential bid that showed a little girl whose enumeration of flower petals morphs into a countdown to a nuclear detonation.

The Gore campaign denounced it; the Bush campaign asked that it be pulled; and the press gave it huge quantities of free air time in the course of expressing its shock, shock that someone would run such a spot – often sneeringly declaring that the ad's allegations had never been proven.

This episode is a terrible indictment of the "general level of knowledge" about China. The American people are entitled to be reminded that Al Gore did indeed raise money from illegal Chinese sources, as did his mentor, Bill

Clinton. To be sure, he maintains he did not know he was doing so. Yet, e-mails from his office, conveniently unavailable until very lately, suggest he did.

Neither is there any doubt that Communist China secured highly secret information about U.S. weapon systems and militarily relevant technology during the Clinton-Gore years. An indication of just how much has become evident now that the U.S. intelligence community has finally gotten through the laborious process of translating 13,000 pages of information about Chinese nuclear and missile programs provided unsolicited in 1995 by a so-called "walk-in" – an individual whom it had dismissed, until very recently, as a Chinese double-agent.

Information in the public domain makes clear some of what China received was transferred with the explicit permission of President Clinton (for example, supercomputers that wound up in the PRC's nuclear and military-industrial complex). Other equipment and know-how either were stolen or diverted. How much the administration knew about the latter may never be fully known. There can be no doubt, however, that the cumulative effect of this hemorrhage of high technology was very detrimental to American security interests.

After the revelation of the secret agreement Vice President Gore signed in 1995 with then-Russian Prime Minister Viktor Chernomyrdin to conceal from Congress information about Kremlin weapons deals with Iran that, under U.S. law, would otherwise have triggered sanctions, the question must be asked: Was there a similar agreement between the Clinton White House and Beijing to withhold from the legislative branch documentation about technology transfers to China that would have adversely affected bilateral relations?

The "general knowledge level" about China could also be usefully raised with respect to two other items:

(1) On Oct. 10, one of the most influential members of the U.S. Senate on national security matters, Sen. Jon Kyl, Arizona Republican, placed in the record 14 pages of quotes - which he described as "but a small sample of the bellicose statements that China's government has made recently." On that occasion, he remarked:

"Time and time again, Chinese officials and state-sponsored media have made bellicose and threatening statements aimed at the United States and our longstanding, democratic ally, Taiwan. They have even gone so far as to issue-implied threats to use nuclear weapons against the United States. The question is, will we take them at their word on these defense matters as we did when they made trade commitments?"

(2) Even as China is making such threats, it is displaying the vulnerability of its economy by mounting a renewed effort to secure billions of dollars in largely un-

disciplined, non-transparent stock and sovereign bond offerings on the U.S. capital markets. As has been observed by former National Security Council official Roger Robinson, who now chairs the Center for Security Policy's William J. Casey Institute, there is reason to believe Beijing is coming to Wall Street to fund technology theft, espionage, proliferation and repression of human rights and religious freedom at home and in places like Sudan and Tibet. Since the Securities and Exchange Commission has declined to date to insist on full disclosure of the uses to which such proceeds are being put, American institutional and other investors may actually unwittingly wind up subsidizing these activities.

It has been reported that Communist China prefers that Al Gore rather than George W. Bush be the next American president. It would help raise the standards of the American people's understanding of what China is about if, in the final week of the campaign, the Texas governor would help explain why.

If Pakistan and India go to nuclear war in coming days, each country will be blamed for precipitating that calamity. The real responsibility, however, will lie elsewhere - with Communist China.

After all, it was the People's Republic that put Pakistan in the atomic weapons business. Had it not been for Chinese know-how, personnel and technology, Islamabad would almost certainly not have "the Bomb" today.

Beijing and its North Korean proxy have also been instrumental in Pakistan's ballistic missile delivery systems for such weapons. According to The Washington Times' Bill Gertz, Chinese-supplied M-11 missiles - which the Pakistanis have renamed the Shaheen and armed with atomic if not crude thermonuclear weapons - have been readied for use against India.

To be sure, even if China not decided years ago to play the Pakistani "card" against the PRC's democratic enemy, India, by arming the Pakistanis to the teeth, the present circumstances in Kashmir may still have produced yet another war between the two countries. But it would almost certainly have remained conventional in character, and the casualties on both sides relatively small.

Unfortunately, China's rampant proliferation of weapons of mass destruction has not only brought democratic India to the brink of nuclear war with her neighbor. According to the Associated Press, the Pakistani government recently detained two individuals, Sultan Bashir-ud-Din Mahmood and Abdul Majid, "on suspicion of sharing technical information with Osama bin Laden. They worked for Pakistan's Atomic Energy Commission until retiring in 1999."

Evidence accumulating from liberated enemy compounds, bunkers and hard drives attests to the keen interest bin Laden and Company have had in acquiring weapons of mass destruction WMD. It is hard to believe that Chinese-trained and-empowered Pakistanis, who were clearly sympathetic to his cause, were not forthcoming. If so, Americans may have even more direct reason to fear the effects of the PRC's nuclear trade than deadly Indo-Pakistani missile duels.

Matters are made even worse by the prospect that Pakistan has acted upon its longstanding desire to be the source of the "the Islamic Bomb." Iran, Iraq, Libya, Syria, Algeria, Egypt and Saudi Arabia are among the countries of the Muslim world who would love to get their hands on the technology and materials needed to put themselves into the atomic or nuclear weapons business. Islamabad may well have served as a willing cutout for Chinese help to some or all of these nations, and perhaps others as well.

Of these, Iraq is probably the most dangerous in the near-term. Baghdad's ever-increasing WMD inventory - and Saddam Hussein's willingness to use them - is the subject of a compelling new study by Dr. Kathleen Bailey entitled "Iraq's Asymmetric Threat to the United States and U.S. Allies," (published by the National Institute for Public Policy.)

The threat posed by Iraq is compelling the Bush administration, finally, to bring about the end to Saddam's reign of terror against his own people and others around the world. The increasingly compelling, if circumstantial, evidence of Iraqi involvement in recent terrorist acts against the United States - the subject of a newly released book, "The War Against America: Saddam Hussein and the World Trade Center Attacks," by Laurie Mylroie - makes clear that we defer such action any longer at our extreme peril.

When the administration does move against Iraq, it - and the American people - will be confronted once again with an unhappy reality temporarily obscured by the war on terrorism and the strange (and often unsavory) bedfellows coalition cobbled together by Secretary of State Colin Powell to prosecute it: Communist China is no friend of the United States.

To the contrary, the PRC is a growing problem. Its burgeoning demand for energy has translated into troubling partnerships with unsavory regimes not only in Iraq but in Iran, Sudan and even Venezuela in our own hemisphere and into imperialistic aggression in the Spratly Islands. Beijing is buying an array of advanced weapons designed by the Soviets/Russians to destroy American military hardware and personnel. And, to add insult to injury, it is seeking to underwrite such activities either directly or (given the fungibility of money) indirectly on our own capital markets, unbeknownst to most American investors.

Add into the mix China's systematic dissemination of WMD technologies and delivery systems to countries we call "rogue states" and they call "clients" and you have a disaster waiting to happen. It would be reckless for America to ignore these developments - or their longer-term implications.

Still worse would be for our leaders to succumb to the siren's song emanating from "Friends of China" like former U.N. Ambassador Richard Holbrooke who recently urged President Bush (a man whose leadership Mr. Holbrooke has assiduously worked to undermine around the world) to negotiate a fourth "communiqué" with Beijing, based on a putative "common strategic concern with terrorism."

Unfortunately, our strategic concern should be with a China that has been abetting terrorism in Pakistan, North Korea, Iran, Iraq, Libya and elsewhere for years. Beijing may want us, in the name of the war on terror, to legitimate its repression of long-suffering minorities like Muslim Uighurs, Tibetans, Falun Gong or Christians. But we must not ignore the not-so-hidden dragon role China is playing in greatly exacerbating the costs and dangers associated with that war.

Almost exactly six years ago, Hong Kong was surrendered by Great Britain to Communist China. There to bear witness the turnover of the Crown Colony to the PRC, I wrote:

"The strategic import of this moment is being deliberately overshadowed by the forced gaiety of round-the-clock 'celebrations.' One cannot, however, help but feel surrounded by the red-and-yellow banners, dragons, lamps, flags and other regalia of the new masters of Hong Kong the alarm experienced by those who saw Hitler's troops welcomed into Austria and the Sudetenland with swastikas and brown shirts.

"The innumerable television cameras in town to record the surrender seem largely distracted by the pomp of various ceremonies attended by high-ranking U.S. officials and their counterparts from other free nations. These foreign representatives are content to mouth platitudes about 'orderly transitions' and their intentions to 'hold the People's Republic of China accountable' for preserving Hong Kong's freedoms.

"For their part, the leaders of the PRC and the quislings they have anointed to govern Hong Kong are only too willing to play back what the West would like to hear. 'Two systems, one country' is the mantra of the day. This evidently is meant to convey the idea that Hong Kong will be 'free' free to be a capitalist police state along the lines of Singapore. China will pursue its own brand of 'state capitalism' with a less-than-human face...

"The Chinese communists are counting on the Clinton administration and the majority of the 'business first' U.S. Congress to follow past practice. If so, it would seem a safe bet that the United States empty rhetorical warnings aside will look the other way as Beijing crushes Hong Kong's freedoms, so long as the PRC does so in a stealthful, incremental fashion. Will they be proven right? Is this what we have become as a people? If so, then more than Hong Kong will enter what Winston Churchill once termed 'a new dark age.' "

This pregnant question is now confronting not the Clinton administration, but its successor and the Republican-controlled 108th Congress. For the PRC is poised to effect its latest and perhaps terminal effort to strip the people of Hong Kong of their freedoms: a legislative initiative expected, all other things being equal, to be adopted on July 9 by the Beijing-controlled Hong Kong Legislative Council under Article 23 of the so-called "Basic Law." It could be used to deny freedom of religion, press and expression guaranteed by the Chinese when Britain agreed to turn over its colony in 1984.

One of the most courageous of Hong Kong's minority of democratically elected legislators, Martin Lee, has warned that "It is no overstatement to say that this is truly a last opportunity to preserve the freedoms of the people of Hong Kong."

After a meeting with Mr. Lee last week, the chairman and vice chairman of the bipartisan U.S.-China Economic and Security Review Commission, Roger Robinson and Richard D'Amato, respectively, warned in a letter sent Friday to the Senate and House leadership that the "legislation ... would give the Beijing-sponsored Hong Kong government the ability to criminalize a wide range of religious, political and journalistic activities without due process or basic legal standards." The congressionally mandated commission urged that "Congress take strong action as soon as possible opposing the proposed legislation and requesting that the Hong Kong government withdraw the bill from consideration" and that "the president and secretary of state should argue forcefully against the bill with their Chinese counterparts."

As during the Clinton years, of course, there are countervailing pressures. The trade lobby will resist anything that might upset Beijing. President Bush is, moreover, being told that China can be helpful with its ever-more belligerent client, North Korea [although the PRC appears to enjoy the leverage that flows from the bad behavior of a proxy it equipped with nuclear and missile technology].

Mr. Bush also wants Beijing's help on the war on terror [even though China, like Russia, has long had ties with all the state-sponsors of terror and some of the organizations they harbor and abet]. And the administration wants the Chinese government to stop its companies, like Norinco, from proliferating ballistic missile and other dangerous technology to the likes of Iran [as if this could have happened in China's police state without government knowledge and clandestine approval].

Unfortunately, were Mr. Bush now to turn a blind eye to the crushing of what remains of Hong Kong's freedoms, it is predictable that the Chinese communists' ominous aspirations to extend their sway still further will be greatly encouraged. Coercive pressure will be applied against democratic Taiwan; it is even possible that an avoidable cross-strait war might be inspired by the West's failure to stand up for Hong Kong. Inevitably, Beijing will be reinforced in its belief that, in due course, it will be able displace the United States as the preeminent Asian power and once again dominate that landmass and the Western Pacific.

China's new power on Hong Kong's Article 23 play thus poses a momentous challenge for President Bush: As he commendably seeks to bring freedom to those around the world who have never known it, will he sit idly by as freedom is taken away from those in Hong Kong who yearn to continue to enjoy it?

At this point in our history, do we really need a Treasury secretary who is a pedigreed "Friend of China"? That is a term the Communist Chinese apply to individuals who have proven their affinity for the People's Republic by service of one kind or another. Communist China arguably has no better or more powerful "friend" in the whole of the Western world than the man President Bush has just appointed to be this nation's chief financial officer: Henry Paulson.

Mr. Paulson has made a very successful career, an immense personal fortune and an astounding financial empire at the New York-based investment house, Goldman Sachs. In no small measure, those accomplishments are a product of his extensive personal and professional dealings with the People's Republic of China.

In fact, in his role as chairman of that enormously successful firm, Mr. Paulson proudly notes he has made about "70 trips to China since late 1990." No one logs that kind of time or enjoys the kind of entree to the communist power structure it suggests unless he is considered a true "friend of China."

Why should we be concerned that an individual who has played, according to Goldman Vice Chairman Robert Hormats, a "very crucial" role in the company's many China-related financial transactions including "really immers[ing] himself in a lot of activities in China" would become Treasury secretary?

The U.S.-China relationship is complicated and is likely to become considerably more so in the years ahead. On the one hand, China is a very important trading partner, albeit one that engages systematically in unfair practices, often in violation of obligations it assumed upon entry to the World Trade Organization, at enormous cost to this country's balance of payments. The PRC is also the largest holder of U.S. debt; its unwillingness to buy more Treasury notes, let alone to unload even a portion of the hundreds of billions worth it now holds could have profound, adverse repercussions on our economy.

On the other hand, as a Pentagon report issued shortly before the Paulson nomination was announced makes clear, Communist China is translating some of its vast new wealth into activities and capabilities clearly antithetical to U.S. interests and security. These include: rapid modernization of the People's Liberation Army and its air, naval and space warfare elements, to give the PRC vastly increased offensive capacity against even modern militaries like ours; the acquisition of forward-operating facilities in key strategic choke-points and regions around the world, including the Caribbean and Latin America; close ties with every despotic regime on the planet; and direct control of, or at least assured access to, an ever-larger percentage of the world's energy resources.

Against this backdrop, what sort of role will a "friend of China" like Henry Paulson play in a Bush Cabinet where he has been assured he will shape policy, not simply flack for it?

Let us stipulate that, as his spokesman at Goldman Sachs put it recently, "When Mr. Paulson becomes secretary of the Treasury, he will have totally divorced his interests from those of Goldman Sachs." Even were he to liquidate his huge holdings of Goldman stock (as opposed to merely placing them in a "blind trust"), he will have a difficult time avoiding a conflict of interest in addressing issues that will have huge implications for his friends and former colleagues at the firm and for the United States.

Consider the following items that clearly fall within his prospective portfolio, to say nothing of his possible input on matters directly related to national security policy and China:

- Revaluation of the Chinese currency to reflect more accurately its true value and reduce its contribution to the PRC's competitive trade advantage. Friends of China have long made excuses for Beijing and resisted efforts to pressure it to float its currency.

- The offerings of PRC state-owned enterprises on the U.S. capital markets many of which are economic dinosaurs that use the proceeds of such often-Goldman-managed and -wildly oversubscribed stock sales to prop up their operations and free up Chinese government funding for other, nefarious purposes.

- This is especially true of Chinese "banks" which the blue-ribbon U.S.-China Economic and Security Review Commission last year established amounted to "slush funds" available for Beijing to use to finance not only the business ventures of well-connected "princelings," but all manner of other nefarious activities in which the PRC engages overseas. These include: technology theft, espionage, intelligence operations, arms sales, alien smuggling and drug running. Goldman is the lead investment bank for the IPO of one of the most egregious of such state-owned enterprises, the Bank of China.

- Chinese acquisitions of U.S. assets will fall under the ambit of the secretary of Treasury in his department's capacity as chairman of the dysfunctional Committee on Foreign Investment in the United States (CFIUS). CFIUS has been reluctant if not utterly unable to see threats to U.S. interests and security posed by acquisitions, some of which have been managed or endorsed by Goldman Sachs. It seems unimaginable it will do better under the direction of one of China's best friends.

Henry Paulson is clearly a capable man and, but for his ties to China, would bring to Treasury stature and skills that are much needed. Those ties have earned him the right to be a Friend of China. They should disqualify him from being Treasury secretary.

Iraq

"'PAUSE FOR PEACE' OR CAT'S-PAWS?; CEASE-FIRE PRESSURES" | FEBRUARY 14, 1991

The nation is understandably preoccupied at the moment with the prospect of eventual ground action in the war with Iraq - and the American casualties it will entail. A far greater danger to U.S. long-term interests, however, is that the war will be stopped before the necessary objectives have been realized.

These objectives are, simply put, the toppling of Saddam Hussein's regime and the complete neutralization of its offensive power-projection capabilities. The good news is that the Bush administration appears to have embraced these as its de facto - if not formally stated - war aims.

The bad news is that the administration is dangerously exposed to the mounting pressure for an immediate cease-fire that would prevent the accomplishing of these war aims.

This pressure has been manifested within the past week in appeals by King Hussein of Jordan, Iranian President Ali Akbar Hashemi Rafsanjani and the Soviet President Mikhail Gorbachev, appeals demanding a "pause for peace." A more appropriate characterization of the machinations of these self-appointed intermediaries might be "cats-paws for peace." For even the Iranians, whose cease-fire proposal has for the moment been rebuffed by Saddam, are serving the Iraqi tyrant's cause. After all, they - like Saddam - are determined to deny the United States a decisive political, as well as military, victory. To accomplish this, they understand that it is necessary to preserve Saddam's hold on power. A cease-fire under present circumstances - with or without the liberation of Kuwait - would almost certainly realize both of these goals.

It is against this backdrop that the ever more assertive peace initiatives from Moscow, Tehran and Amman must be considered, particularly the associated contention that the allies are exceeding the U.N. mandate in their attacks against Iraq. By so doing, Iraq's proxies hope to deny President Bush what he believes to be his trump card: the international community's seal of approval for the campaign against Saddam.

Incredibly, new Soviet Foreign Minister Alexander Bessmertnykh recently snookered Secretary of State James Baker into making a joint statement that plays directly into the hands of those hoping for a stalemate in the Gulf. It expressly committed the U.S. government to accept such a cease-fire with Iraq.

This communiqué was an unmitigated disaster on both substantive and procedural grounds. Substantively, it directly undercut Mr. Bush's sensible post-Jan. 16 policy of "no negotiations." Under the terms of this joint statement, all Saddam needs to do to qualify for a cease-fire is to make an "unequivocal commitment to withdraw from Kuwait" and take unspecified "immediate, concrete steps leading to full compliance" with U.N. Security

Council resolutions. In other words, the United States would be obliged to suspend hostilities even before Kuwait is completely liberated.

In terms of process, the joint statement was equally deplorable. No one at the White House or any other agency was given advance warning of the contents of Mr. Baker's deal with his Soviet counterpart. As a result, there was no opportunity for sanity-checks or course-corrections. The president only learned of the joint statement after it had been quietly posted on a State Department pressroom bulletin board, crowed over publicly by Mr. Bessmertnykh and handed as a fait accomplis to him in his limousine on the way to the State of the Union address. It is a vivid example of Mr. Baker's high-handed and over-reaching approach to foreign policy.

In the aftermath of the Baker-Bessmertnykh communiqué, two key points should be kept in mind: First, the deal now being offered to Saddam is a trap – the same one from which we were only delivered prior to Jan. 16 by the Iraqi dictator's sheer recalcitrance. Had he simply relented on Kuwait, he could have written his own ticket: no war crimes trials, no reparations, the effective end of the embargo against his country, negotiations with Kuwait sure to produce territorial and oil concessions and an international peace conference designed to coerce Israel into making risky territorial concessions of its own.

Such generous terms are not the stuff of idle speculation; they are what Saddam was offered by Mr. Baker and other interlocutors before the U.N.-imposed deadline expired on Jan. 15. Fortunately for all of us - whether out of arrogance, miscalculation or sheer contempt for the West only history will explain - Saddam refused to accept the opportunity these terms afforded to enhance his stature, redouble his military capabilities and expand his hegemony far beyond Kuwait.

It would be a tragedy of epic proportions if, in deference to Soviet – or others' - demands, the United States were now to re-extend to Saddam essentially the same opportunity. Presumably, the punishment inflicted by tens of thousands of allied bombing missions has markedly reduced Iraq's arsenal of weapons of mass destruction (chemical, biological and nuclear arms) and the threat posed by its other offensive forces. Still, if Saddam can survive this conflict and reasonably claim to have dictated satisfactory conditions for its termination, there is little doubt that his larger-than-life position in the Arab world, the enormous oil resources of his country and the residual capabilities of the Iraqi military will make him a formidable threat down the road.

The second worrisome upshot of the joint communiqué is the further evidence it offers that Moscow is actively promoting such an undesirable outcome. Evidently, the Bush administration has invested so much in Mr. Gorbachev – and so trumpeted the Soviet role in this crisis as a prototype for the much ballyhooed "New World Order" - that it cannot bring itself to come to grips with the true, and rather sinister, thrust of Soviet policy.

To make matters worse, Moscow has successfully parlayed its double-dealing policy on the Gulf into Western acquiescence to the Soviet central authorities' repression at home. The fact that we are being had by the Soviet Union on Iraq makes all the more reprehensible the U.S. willingness to look the other way on the crackdown in the Baltics.

The bottom line is this: The Bush administration, having staked as much as it has on multilateralism and Soviet cooperativeness in dealing with the Iraqi crisis, is dangerously vulnerable to having the rug pulled out from under it. Before the trap of a "pause for peace" springs closed, the United States had best make it clear that it will not be a party to any cease-fire so long as Saddam remains in power and capable of shattering the peace at will in the future.

The announcement by President Bush on Wednesday of a "no-fly" zone over Iraqi territory south of the 32nd parallel represents a welcome departure from his administration's past indifference to the brutal repression by Saddam Hussein of his population - including its Shi'ite majority. This action is, however, tragically too late and far too little.

Too late: Think what might have happened had the Bush administration's stated concern for the victims of Saddam's predations - and its ire over his contemptuous disregard for related U.N. Security Council resolutions - translated into U.S. military activity before now. Millions of Iraqi citizens might have been spared great hardship, if not death.

Even the least risky of armed interventions, such as an air cap (or no-fly zone) over southern Iraq, would have had a profound effect. It would have prevented armed helicopters from being used decisively and in violation of the cease-fire agreement to destroy those who rose up against the ruling clique at the end of the Persian Gulf war - and at Mr. Bush's urging. It may even have enabled that uprising to succeed.

Too little: Unfortunately, the decision to establish such a no-fly zone at this late date seems a product of the same incoherence that has afflicted U.S. policy toward Iraq since the war was halted precipitously and prematurely. Now, as then, the Bush administration is preoccupied with the symptoms of the problem rather than its root cause: Saddam, his megalomania and the absolute, despotic control exercised by him and his ruling clique through an as-yet intact police state apparatus.

This incoherence was much in evidence in the White House and Pentagon briefings at which the no-fly initiative was announced. First, the "senior administration official" who back grounded the press corps explained that the action was being taken now in light of: (1) a disturbing report from the U.N. Human Rights Commission's rapporteur, Max Van der Stoel; (2) a "qualitative difference in the level and the form of repression" on the part of Iraqi forces against the Shi'ites; and (3) assurances from the Iraqi opposition about their commitment to democracy and the territorial integrity of Iraq.

In fact, none of these points stands up to scrutiny:

- Mr. Van der Stoel first reported his findings in February, not on Aug. 11; he observed then that there have been few parallels since World War II to the level of state-inflicted inhumanity and brutal repression in evidence in southern Iraq.
- The victims of that repression probably have not noticed the "qualitative" difference in the violence; helicopters, artillery and ground forces have been used with devastating effect from the outset of Saddam's post-war campaign against those seeking refuge in the southern marshlands.
- The Iraqi opposition was making the same commitments to anyone who would

listen prior to, during and after the Gulf war; unhappily, the U.S. administration was not among those listening.

By its own logic, the administration should be establishing a no-fly zone throughout Iraq. For example, the unnamed senior administration briefer cited Mr. Van der Stoel as saying that: "There exists no reason to believe that the human rights situation has improved anywhere else in Iraq."

Worse yet, the administration's spokesmen have repeatedly acknowledged that Saddam was systematically violating the U.N. resolutions on a countrywide basis. Scud missiles are being illegally retained; the Kurds in the north are being subjected to an economic embargo; U.N. monitors and associated security personnel are being forced out of the country; food and medical supplies are not being distributed to the population at large; imports are continuing to find their way into Iraq despite U.N. sanctions; etc.

The new no-fly zone has many of the risks and few of the potential benefits of the approach the United States ought to be pursuing: a clear and explicit policy aimed at removing Saddam Hussein and his despotic regime from power. Either one may lead to disaffection of allies and international criticism; either one might result in the de facto (if not de jure) partitioning of Iraq; either one might expose U.S. military personnel to capture or death in combat.

Still, a policy that has as its purpose correcting the systemic problem instead of its symptoms is far more likely to enjoy the support of the American people - just as it is far more certain to produce long-term Iraqi compliance with the U.N. requirements and a lasting improvement in the condition of the people of Iraq.

Adoption of such a coherent policy should be moved to the top of the Bush administration's agenda. If it is not, the failure to do so should be made a matter of rigorous debate in the presidential election.

Among the many distressing aspects of what passes for President Clinton's foreign policy - from the abdication of leadership concerning Bosnia to the imminent normalization of relations with the unreconstructed and unapologetic communist rulers of Vietnam, to the accommodationist approach apparently at work with respect to North Korea's nuclear weapons program - one initiative has been particularly troubling: Mr. Clinton's stated determination to "depersonalize" the conflict with Saddam Hussein.

From its unveiling shortly before the Clinton Inauguration, this policy has been seen as an attempt to differentiate the new team's approach from what it saw as the Bush administration's preoccupation with Saddam. As Mr. Clinton put it in an exclusive interview with Tom Friedman of the New York Times on Jan. 13, 1993 - an interview the then-president-elect told Mr. Friedman he wanted to use to send a signal to Saddam Hussein:

"Certainly based on the evidence we have, the people of Iraq would be better off if they had a different ruler. But my job is not to pick their rulers for them. I always tell everybody I am a Baptist. I believe in deathbed conversions. If [Saddam] wants a different relationship with the United States and the United Nations, all he has to do is change his behavior."

In the wake of the firestorm of criticism precipitated by this conciliatory pronouncement, both Mr. Clinton and his Secretary of State-designate, Warren Christopher, disassociated themselves with any notion of taking a softer line toward Saddam than the Bush administration had done. The president-elect said on Jan. 14 that "I have no intention of normalizing relations with [Saddam]"; for his part, Mr. Christopher pronounced himself "no Baptist" and deeply skeptical of "death-bed conversions."

Still, in its first five months in office, the Clinton policy toward Iraq seems, at best, to have been one of benign neglect. With the exception of allowing a few utterly ineffectual air strikes on missile batteries and the like in response to Iraqi provocations, the administration has generally appeared determined to ignore the abiding malevolence emanating from Saddam Hussein's Iraq - and the need to complete unfinished business with respect to his continued hold on power.

The most ominous manifestation of this phenomenon has been the Clinton administration's response to date to the Iraqi despot's effort to blow up former President Bush and most of the other key U.S. Gulf war policy-makers who were traveling with him in Kuwait about a month ago. While the official line is that this matter is still under investigation, the unmistakable signal being sent is that the Clinton team is so determined to avoid becoming bogged down in its own crisis with Iraq that it is inclined to overlook the failed assassination attempt.

Toward this end, administration sources have put out the word that the case against Iraq's assassins now in Kuwaiti custody is less than airtight; that their interrogation at the hands of the authorities in Kuwait had been botched and direct evidence of Saddam's complicity not established. Such leaks are exceedingly pernicious.

The truth of the matter is that U.S. investigators are, I am told, satisfied that the evidence is compelling of official Iraqi involvement in the attempt to kill Mr. Bush. As this fact becomes public knowledge, the leakers are not going to have thwarted demands for appropriate retaliation – demands already being volubly expressed on Capitol Hill. They will simply have given aid and comfort to those disposed to challenge the legitimacy of any such U.S. retribution when it comes.

The really scary part about this inept U.S. response to the Iraqi assassination attempt is that it is doubtless emboldening Saddam to contemplate further outrages even as it is terrifying America's allies in the Persian Gulf who have no interest in opposing the Butcher of Baghdad by themselves. Absent a new policy direction from Washington - including strong and effective action aimed at punishing Saddam and his clique for this latest act of aggression – the United States will find itself facing a far more dangerous situation in this strategic region even than that which prevailed prior to Desert Storm.

The one ray of hope on this front is that Martin Indyck, the top Middle East policymaker at the Clinton National Security Council, unveiled last week a major new initiative that he dubbed "dual containment." In an address to the influential Washington Institute for the Near East, Mr. Indyck put a very different spin on the idea behind "depersonalizing" the conflict with Iraq:

"We seek full compliance for all Iraqi regimes. We will not be satisfied with Saddam's overthrow before we agree to lift sanctions. Rather we will want to be satisfied that any successor government complies fully with all U.N. resolutions. Nor do we seek or expect a reconciliation with Saddam Hussein's regime... Our purpose is deliberate: It is to establish clearly and unequivocally that the current regime in Iraq is a criminal regime, beyond the pale of international society and, in our judgment, irredeemable."

Strong words. And welcome ones - particularly since they are accompanied by equally strong comments about the need to contain Iran and the administration's determination to do so without falling prey to the oft-repeated mistake of building up Iraq as a counterweight. Indeed, the Indyck speech is one of the most important and impressive foreign policy addresses in recent memory; it should be required reading for anyone with an interest not only in the region most immediately involved, but with U.S. security policy more generally.

The question is: Will the administration actually implement the policy so well enunciated by Martin Indyck? The place to start is with a powerful blow in retaliation for the attempted murder of a former American head of state. Ideally, this would involve an air strike aimed at destroying some of the as-yet largely unscathed bases of Saddam's power - his security apparatus, the Republican Guards, the Air Force and other military headquarters.

Question: Which of the following is the most dangerously absurd?

(1) The United States allowed Saddam Hussein and his Russian friend, KGB thug and Foreign Minister Yevgeny Primakov, to get away with murder in conjuring up, and then formulating a "solution" to, the latest crisis with Iraq.

(2) The Clinton administration is trying to claim that its management of the affair was a complete success, thanks to the president's effective dual track strategy of diplomacy backed by a military buildup in the Persian Gulf.

(3) Or the administration evidently has so little regard for the intelligence of the American people as to try to deny the first and sustain the second.

The choice is complicated by the fact that all three of these developments are very dangerous and thoroughly absurd. Consider the following particulars:

First, the Clinton administration allowed itself to be completely outmaneuvered by Saddam and Mr. Primakov, demonstrating in the process an inability to marshal and use military force effectively in a circumstance that clearly demands it. It has been compelled publicly and repeatedly to declare that the Iraqi regime is not the problem. It says the issue was simply the unacceptable expulsion of U.S. inspectors. By definition then, the now-accomplished return of these courageous individuals (or at least four out of the six that left) allows Washington to declare victory.

Now, this is rather like saying that, having left somebody holding your ice-cream cone three weeks ago, you will be satisfied with coming back and picking it up. You can come back, but the situation will have permanently changed: Either he will have eaten the ice cream or it will have long since melted away.

So, too, with Saddam Hussein's covert weapons program. During the 21 days in which there were no U.N. inspectors in Iraq, previously identified assets relevant to ongoing Iraqi chemical and biological weapons and ballistic missile programs have almost certainly been moved and returned to service. The Iraqis have also taken advantage of the situation to relocate and redouble concealment of the as-yet-undiscovered parts of these and its nuclear weapons programs.

It should be noted that, even if the status quo ante could be fully restored, it was not all that satisfactory. The formal review of the inspection program conducted by a U.N. advisory committee last week confirmed that Iraq has systematically interfered with, sabotaged and otherwise tried to defeat the UNSCOM effort. Currently, Baghdad claims the United Nations acceded last June to its demand that so-called "presidential sites" - one of which is reported to be the size of Washington, D.C. - are off-limit. While the Clinton administration now claims that it will settle for nothing less than the right to visit all sites, as long as Saddam is in power, such visits will always be a losing game.

This is particularly true if, as William Safire and others have reported, the increased representation on UNSCOM teams of Russian, Chinese and other foreign nationals friendly to Iraq - one of the indisputable achievements of Mr. Primakov's hat trick - means the Iraqis will get more early warning with which to defeat the inspectors.

Second, the Clinton administration was reduced to contracting out its foreign policy to someone who is, arguably, the least reliable man on the planet when it comes to showing (in the laughable expression of State Department press spokesman James Rubin) "the steeliness of the will of the international community" to resist Saddam. Mrs. Albright has been reduced to declaring, as she did last Sunday, that the United States remains the "dominant power" in the region. Such a statement calls to mind the president's peevish utterance "I am still relevant" in the wake of an earlier defeat - the Republican conquest of Capitol Hill in 1994.

Matters are being made worse -potentially much worse - by the administration's panicky response to Arab excuse mongering. Our erstwhile regional partners in the grand coalition against Saddam Hussein claimed they were going to sit out any military confrontation with him over unhappiness about the collapse of the Israeli-Palestinian "peace process."

Euchring Benjamin Netanyahu into surrendering more territory to Yasser Arafat, when the latter already has 98 percent of the Palestinian Arab population under his despotic control and persists in allowing his areas to be used to conduct terrorist operations against Israel, will make peace less likely in the Levant, while doing nothing to promote it in the Persian Gulf. In fact, such thinking is completely backward: Few things could do more to advance a real peace between Israel and the Palestinians than toppling Saddam's regime and converting Iraq from an agent of regional instability into a force for stability.

Third, most Americans intuitively recognize that it was a mistake to have left the Butcher of Baghdad in power at the end of Operation Desert Storm. They also understand that the latest round of "Iraqi Roulette" was no "victory" for the United States. Just because our brains were not splattered this time by the revolver Saddam has pointed at our head, common sense tells us that a chemical, biological or possibly nuclear "bullet" remains in the cylinder.

Politicians who seek to cover their failures by transparently phony declarations that they have "kept Saddam in his box" and implausible assurances that they will be able to do so indefinitely, invite public cynicism and alienation. By so doing, they not only insult the intelligence of our countrymen. Worse, they jeopardize the popular support needed to accomplish the hard work of toppling Saddam Hussein that remains to be done.

Whether you chose dangerous absurdity 1, 2 or 3, the bottom line is the same: Saddam's regime must be removed from power. Anything less is sure to be absurdly ineffective in dealing with the increasingly dangerous threat posed by that regime.

On the eve of what is being billed as a major address to the United Nations, President Bush is being advised to emulate his father's approach on Iraq 12 years ago by making the cobbling together of a broadly based international coalition a precondition to taking on Saddam Hussein.

It can only be hoped that - under today's, very different circumstances - Mr. Bush will base his diplomacy and actions on a very different model: his recent, hugely successful disentangling of the United States from the 1972 Anti-Ballistic Missile [ABM] Treaty.

Interestingly, there are several noteworthy similarities between the two initiatives. In both cases, George W. Bush's guidance comes from the law of the land. When Mr. Bush became president, he inherited statutory direction adopted by overwhelming bipartisan majorities and signed by Bill Clinton in 1999 that made it the policy of the United States government to deploy effective missile defenses "as soon as is technologically possible."

Another policy was also on the books, having been approved by Congress the year before and signed into law as well by President Clinton. It called for toppling Saddam and provided $97 million to equip the Iraqi opposition to help us accomplish that goal.

As was his wont, Mr. Clinton paid lip service to these initiatives and took credit for enacting them, yet refused to take the steps necessary for the implementation of either one. Fortunately, Mr. Bush not only took an oath faithfully to uphold the law of the land; he is actually determined to do so.

A second parallel involves the courage required to realize these policies. It is useful to recall that in the run-up to his decision to exercise America's right to withdraw from the Anti-Ballistic Missile Treaty - a right conferred by the Treaty itself - President Bush faced heated domestic and international criticism. Then, as now, he was warned of the dangers of acting "unilaterally," over the adamant objections of the international community and especially the United States' closest allies.

The prospects that he would unleash grievous instability and perhaps even Armageddon by proceeding with missile defenses prohibited by the ABM Treaty are not too different from the threats Mr. Bush is told will emerge in the Arab world, and beyond, if he proceeds without a U.N. mandate for removing Saddam Hussein from power.

In a characteristically lucid and bracing address to the Center for Security Policy last week, syndicated columnist Charles Krauthammer noted that this nation's Founding document, the Declaration of Independence, calls for "due regard for the opinion of mankind." As with the intense consultations that preceded the Bush announcement last December that the United States would cease to adhere to the ABM Treaty, there is much to be said for thoroughly explaining our policy of regime change in Iraq and the factors that impel it to the leaders of other countries. That is not the same thing, however, as subordinating vital national interests to their "opinion."

Our experience in the months since the ABM Treaty expired last June is surely relevant to the president's Iraq initiative, as well. Once it is clear that the United States is going to act pursuant to its perceived national requirements, and that it has both the capability and the leadership to see the policy through, most of the world gets with the program. Today, one scarcely hears about the ABM Treaty and the notion that Mr. Bush's action was actually going to propel the world into cataclysmic arms races, or worse, is seen by those candid enough to admit it for what it always was: Utter nonsense.

To be sure, had the Russians behaved worse, they might have increased the political costs to Mr. Bush of U.S. withdrawal from the ABM Treaty. Some will argue that the lesson for "W." is that the Kremlin must be bought off if he wants to bring down the former Soviet Union's client in Baghdad without grave difficulty from Moscow. This would, however, be a misreading of recent history.

While President Bush gave his Russian counterpart Vladimir Putin political cover by agreeing to a new treaty formalizing mutual, unilateral commitments to cut strategic forces, as bribes go, it did not amount to much. [Of course, if the President so much as hints at a willingness to pay this time for Russia's acquiescence, Mr. Putin will try to charge him dearly.] What actually brought the Russians along on the ABM issue - and what will prompt them to go along on Iraq - is the appreciation of American resolve, and a recognition that there is no up-side to opposing us.

Now some will argue there is a crucial difference between these two politico-military-diplomatic initiatives. One involved rejection of a clearly outdated, albeit talismanic treaty, the other will involve a potentially highly destructive war. This conveniently ignores the assertions from some of the ABM Treaty's particularly hysterical supporters that destroying that "cornerstone of strategic stability" could lead not only to spiraling arms races but actual conflict.

More importantly, the reality is that both Mr. Bush's decision to adhere to the law of the land by withdrawing from the Anti-Ballistic Missile Treaty and his commitment to liberate the Iraqi people and end Saddam's weapons of mass destruction program by achieving regime change in Iraq spring from a single source: His determination to defend the American people.

That happens as well to be his constitutional responsibility, and he will fulfill that duty once again on Iraq if his due regard for the "opinion of mankind" on the ABM issue - consultations, but no veto - serves as the model for dealing with the U.N. about changing Saddam's regime.

The current buzz is that the Saudis, Egyptians, Turks and others are plotting to have Saddam Hussein removed from power - either voluntarily with a "golden parachute" exile package for him and his family, or involuntarily via possibly violent action. Either way, the promoters of this initiative reportedly contemplate offering amnesty for Iraqi generals who help effect "regime change" in Baghdad so as to preclude having the U.S. military accomplish it.

Over the weekend, top Bush administration officials expressed enthusiasm for this idea. As Secretary of State Colin Powell put it on CBS News' Sunday morning program "Face the Nation": "[If it worked,] we would have an entirely new situation presented to the international community and we might be able to avoid war."

Presumably, the Bush team is encouraging what might be called a coup in Baghdad in keeping with the president's oft-stated position that war is the last option. A coup also happens to be the outcome that the CIA and State Department have been haplessly trying to engineer in Iraq for more than a decade.

Before addressing the demerits of this proposal, the cynicism of several of the foreign governments now said to be working to topple Saddam cannot go unremarked. In particular, Saudi Arabia and Egypt have been among the most adamant members of the United Nations in declaring their respect for the sovereignty of Iraq and their conviction that interference in its internal affairs by any outside power is impermissible. At least the Bush administration has made no bones about its belief that regime change is required.

Still, the question occurs: Will a coup do? Would either Saddam Hussein's voluntary or unwilling displacement from the seat of power in Baghdad accomplish the needed regime change and its necessary consequences - namely, the liberation of the Iraqi people and an end to Saddam's weapons of mass destruction programs?

Unfortunately, the answer is almost certainly no. For starters, there is a grave danger that the only change that will occur would be to replace Saddam Hussein with some other ruthless thug. Even if the latter did not come from the Butcher of Baghdad's immediate family [given what is known about Saddam's sons, this is a singularly horrifying prospect], an amnesty for his subordinates would probably ensure that the next Iraqi leader is one of his henchmen, Takriti clansmen or senior officers. Such an outcome is particularly likely in view of the Saudi and Egyptian governments' ill-concealed preference for despots.

An amnesty would also amount to a free pass for people who must, like Saddam Hussein, be held accountable for war crimes and unimaginable human-rights abuses. Without such accountability and a more general program of "lustration" aimed at purging the political system of the ancien regime's adherents, a post-Saddam Iraq will be denied the chance for real freedom.

This chance was fully realized by Germany and Japan, at U.S. insistence, where lustration occurred. It remains, at best, a fragile opportunity for countries of the former Soviet empire where lustration has largely not transpired.

If anything, a "regime change" that amounts to a change of face, but not of character, may give rise to an even greater danger down the road.

Those who were willing to do business with Saddam will surely demand that U.N.-imposed sanctions on his successor's regime be removed at once. With unchecked use of Iraq's immense petro wealth, the next Saddam could rapidly finish whatever build-up of weapons of mass destruction his predecessor failed to complete. And it strains credulity that such a regime will afford international inspectors, let alone U.S. military personnel, with the sort of unencumbered access to Iraq's secret files needed if we are to learn, at last, the true status of these activities.

Worst of all, if the United States is seen by the people of Iraq as once again favoring their continued enslavement, albeit by someone whose record of brutality may be less well-known than Saddam's, we risk their permanent alienation. In the process, we would lose not only the opportunity to free one of the most industrious and capable populations in the Middle East, perhaps transforming Iraq into a prosperous and peace-loving nation. We would also squander the chance to create a model for bringing real democracy and economic opportunity to a region desperately in need of both.

While such an arrangement may suit the Saudi royal family, the dictators of Syria and Egypt, the murderous mullahs in Iran, etc., it should not be seen by Americans as an acceptable substitute for the true liberation of Iraq - the only hope for genuinely disarming that country.

There are worse things than an American-led war against Saddam Hussein's regime in the next few weeks. Chief among them would be a war that will have to be waged later, against either Saddam or a no-less-dangerous successor whom the world has foolishly allowed to pursue his tyrannical domestic policies, weapons programs and ambitions for regional domination.

It has been clear for many months that the wild card in any campaign to liberate Iraq would be not the quality of American military might or the malevolence of Saddam Hussein's resistance. Rather, it would be the role played by the Iraqi people in helping to free themselves from one of the world's most despotic tyrants.

In the course of the past fortnight, the awesome application of the power of U.S. armed forces has been on display minute-by-minute, thanks in no small measure to the basically real-time reporting of correspondents "embedded" with various combat units. These reporters have also served greatly to amplify the ruthlessness and brutality with which the Iraqi regime is clinging to power notably, by forcing civilians at gunpoint to attack coalition troops, executing its own personnel for wanting not to fight and inviting "collateral damage" on non-military populations by collocating weapons with hospitals, mosques, schools, etc.

What has been inexplicable thus far, however, is why a vastly more robust effort has not been made to date to secure the active support of the Iraqi people? As things stand now, they appear, by most accounts, to be uncertain of the true purpose of American and allied troops in their country. Iraqi propaganda and other Arab media warn of Western imperialism and "Crusader" threats to the Muslim faith. The amazingly few instances in which civilians have been harmed under circumstances attributed by the regime to coalition forces [whether rightly, due to an accident, or deceitfully] has unhelpfully given resonance to nationalist appeals to support Saddam.

The people of Iraq are also terrified by the continuing predations of Saddam's Fedayeen and other enforcers, which Secretary of Defense Donald Rumsfeld has properly called "death squads." They remember only too well the harsh reprisals against those who dared to respond to President George H.W. Bush's 1991 call to rise up against the regime. The various videotaped images of Saddam and his cohort broadcast from time to time may seem stilted and inauthentic to our eyes but they are seen by conditioned Iraqis as paralyzing evidence that he remains in control and a threat.

As a result of these factors, the Iraqi people have yet to play any significant role in their liberation. Should they continue to do so, estimates of a protracted and bloody fight are much more likely to prove correct. At worst, the United States and its allies could find themselves fighting a regime that manages to secure a measure of popular support to which it is certainly not entitled and that would be exceedingly detrimental to the goal of regime change.

What is to be done to correct this unsatisfactory, and potentially disastrous, state of affairs? The answer: "Embed" Free Iraqis.

This would, of course, mean more than simply having Iraqis who support Operation Iraqi Freedom along for the ride, like the journalists.

While that would be desirable in and of itself [for example, tangibly demonstrating Iraqi support for our troops' efforts and facilitating translations in the latters' interactions with local populations], there are myriad other ways in which Free Iraqis' help could be instrumental to the "hearts and minds" dimension of this conflict.

Opportunities should be afforded to U.S.-trained Iraqi freedom fighters to participate in operations in the southern and central parts of the country, just as the Kurds are now being given roles to play in liberating the North. Having Free Iraqis at checkpoints could help with the challenging task of defending against Saddam-loyalists masquerading as civilians, without harming bonafide non-combatants. Using such allies to penetrate enemy-held cities and positions could greatly facilitate their seizure with minimum loss of life and destruction on both sides.

Particularly needed are the voices and faces of Free Iraq on the media most Iraqis can receive. As a prominent Iraqi exile, Professor Kanan Makiya, observed in The Washington Post on Sunday: "Eliminating [Saddam's] image is not enough. An alternative image must be projected and by Iraqis, not Americans." Broadcasting the message of hope and liberation from within Iraq is essential to winning not only the confidence and active assistance of the Iraqi people. It could be of incalculable importance in dissipating sympathy for Saddam elsewhere in the Arab and Muslim worlds.

Needless to say, Free Iraqis need to be fully "embedded," as well, in the development and constituting of a transitional authority capable of governing Iraq once its liberation is secured. While some work toward this end has been undertaken, largely at the initiative of the Iraqi National Congress and opposition groups working with it, more much more needs to be done to establish an effective interim Iraqi alternative to the present, odious regime.

Unfortunately, these ideas, so central to empowering anti-Saddam Iraqis and securing the assistance of millions of their like-minded countrymen, remain anathema to the U.S. State Department and CIA. As a result, far less has been done to prepare to meet today's urgent need for an organized, disciplined and reliable Free Iraqi component to serve as an integral part of Operation Iraqi Freedom. There is no more time to waste.

Many lives, Iraqi and American, are at stake, as may even be the ultimate success of the mission. "Embed" Free Iraqis now.

Suddenly, the heretofore unthinkable seems not so impossible. Domestic political considerations driven by declining polls and negative reporting have prompted the Bush administration to take a series of dubious tactical decisions in Iraq. These have, in turn, contributed to a worsening situation on the ground there, featuring continuing physical insecurity, political turmoil and demoralization of U.S. forces. Amplified by relentlessly unfavorable press accounts and increasingly shrill Democratic criticism, these developments have given rise to still more dubious tactical decisions, an emboldened opposition on the ground and more bad news to report.

This dynamic has produced in the midst of this election year a sense in some quarters that an early U.S. exit may not only be inevitable but desirable. After all, a growing number of Americans seem to be under the illusion that, as with Vietnam, we can end the war simply by bailing out of Iraq.

If only fences are mended with the United Nations, they have been encouraged to believe, the world will once again leave us alone. At the very least, we could then go back to fighting international terror as more or less a police action.

Three developments of the past few days, however, make clear that we live in a very different sort of world - one that will become infinitely more dangerous for the United States if it is perceived to have "lost" Iraq:

- Last week's murder and hostage-taking of indigenous and foreign workers in Saudi Arabia's oil sector was a strategic attack not only on the kingdom but on the world economy. It underscores the fragility of what is currently the only rapidly expandable source of the crude, which if taken off-line would precipitate an immediate end to any recovery, and probably serious and lasting economic dislocation.

  Even before this attack, perceptions that disruptions may be in the offing at the hands of al Qaeda or other terrorists - possibly involving the destruction of key parts of the Saudi fields' infrastructure - had contributed to soaring prices on the spot market and at gas pumps.

- The other main driver in petroleum-related price rises of late is the emergence on world oil markets of growing demand from China. Most analysts believe the only way Beijing can maintain the sorts of economic growth and rising living standards essential to the Communist Party's continued hold on power is for vastly greater imports of energy from the international oil patch. In the absence of massive new finds of oil, technological or other impetuses for reduced U.S. and Western demand, the Chinese competition will not only further increase the cost of a barrel of oil. It may also contribute to the sort of mentality that political scientists call a "zero-sum" game - where one side can only benefit at the other's expense, a mindset that, when it comes to vital and scarce natural resources, frequently leads to conflict and war.

Unfortunately, the Associated Press reported on May 30 that a new Defense Department report perceives an ominous Chinese interest in waging war swiftly and decisively against the United States. For some years, party and military leaders have used a term that translates into English roughly as "Assassin's Mace." The wire service quotes the Pentagon analysis as saying this "concept appears to include a range of weapon systems and technologies related to information warfare, ballistic and antiship cruise missiles, advanced fighters and submarines, counterspace system and air defense."

There is reason to fear that the Chinese believe some such capabilities could be successfully employed, possibly in the relatively near term, to attack Taiwan and assert Chinese hegemony in East Asia, with little warning while the U.S. is tied down elsewhere.

- One of the things that could tie the United States down considerably would be the emergence of a terrorist Fifth Column here at home. As columnist Michelle Malkin has noted, a new study done at the request of Sens. Jon Kyl, Arizona Republican, and Chuck Schumer, New York Democrat, by the Justice Department's inspector general has confirmed earlier, frightening press reports: U.S. and state prison systems have been penetrated for years by proselytizers for the radical subset of the Muslim faith known as Islamism - notably, the virulently intolerant, jihadist strain associated with Saudi Arabia's state-sanctioned Wahhabi cult.

Incredibly, neither their interactions with prisoners nor even those of incarcerated Islamist terrorists have been adequately supervised out of what the I.G. deemed to be misplaced concern about "privacy rights" and "religious freedom." Worse still, released felons are but one source, if a particularly dangerous one, for attacks in this country by al Qaeda sympathizers that have been cultivated over the past three decades by institutions tied to Saudi Arabia.

Taken together, these developments confirm that a withdrawal from and loss of Iraq will hardly be the end of our travails. If anything, the attendant perception of diminished U.S. power and loss of will would exacerbate the threats we face in the years ahead from terrorists, their state sponsors and others who would exploit the damage that might be inflicted by America's enemies on the West's oil supply, in East Asia and here at home.

These dangers will not be eliminated by success in Iraq, but they will be made more manageable as Iraqi oil comes on line, U.S. forces are freed up for duty elsewhere and Islamism is dealt a strategic defeat. This is, as Margaret Thatcher famously put it, "no time to go wobbly."

Suddenly, the Democrats have found their voice on Iraq. It is the sound of defeatism.

Would-be Speaker Nancy Pelosi, Senate Minority Leader Harry Reid and 10 of their colleagues in leadership positions have proclaimed that it is time to begin withdrawing U.S. forces from Iraq. They want to start by the end of the year, without regard for the conditions on the ground. And they want all American troops out by some unspecified time, without regard for the consequences that would follow such a retreat.

Among those who have endorsed what might be called "the Contract for Defeat" is the putative front-runner for the 2008 Democratic presidential nomination, Sen. Hillary Rodham Clinton of New York. Mindful of the ascendant power within her party of anti-war activists evident in their vicious campaign to unseat former vice presidential contender and three-term Sen. Joe Lieberman of Connecticut, this one-time supporter of the liberation of Iraq is becoming increasingly strident in her criticism of the war and those responsible for it. Last week, she triangulated her way to the head of the parade of those hoping to make Secretary of Defense Donald Rumsfeld a scapegoat for the Iraqis' difficulties and demanding his resignation.

There is a certain irony here. Arguably, whatever mistakes Don Rumsfeld might have made or were made by others on his watch that are contributing to the present violence in Iraq pale by comparison with the effect Democratic defeatism is having on the so-called "insurgents."

Think about it: Our Islamofascist enemies and their allies are convinced that they can defeat us politically. The means by which they seek to do that is by producing a steady stream of bloodletting and mayhem. The results are then incessantly beamed into American living rooms by mainstream media transparently hostile to President Bush and his Iraq campaign.

Then, Democratic critics (and, in fairness, a few Republican politicians like Sen. Chuck Hagel of Nebraska who have figured out that it is more fun, or at least more conducive to favorable press reviews, to talk and occasionally vote like an anti-Bush Democrat) seize upon the suicide bombings in Iraq as proof that success there is impossible. Therefore, they solemnly intone, we should stop wasting lives and treasure trying to achieve it.

It is hard to imagine a greater incentive to more attacks against Iraqi civilians, security personnel, government officials and their families and, yes, against our own and other Coalition forces. Call it the "cycle of violence."

To be sure, the fact that the opportunities continue to exist for such attacks is not necessarily the fault of the critics. They and, for that matter, supporters of the war effort can legitimately feel frustration that the "security situation in Iraq" (as it is euphemistically known) has not been stabilized before now in Baghdad and other persistent areas of insurgent activity.

That said, it is virtually impossible in any but the most totalitarian of societies to prevent determined people from inflicting casualties on targets of opportunity, particularly when such people are willing to kill themselves in the process. But we must also hold accountable those who are, in effect, rewarding our enemies for engaging in such behavior by translating the latters' murderous actions into the realization of political objectives.

Unfortunately, Democratic defeatism is not only encouraging our enemies in Iraq. Since that conflict is but one front in a far larger, indeed global war (one best described as the War for the Free World), those insisting that we cut our losses with respect to Iraq are also fueling dynamics elsewhere that are likely to give rise to a number of other, deeply problematic strategic outcomes.

One need look no farther than the Mideast's other flash point du jour: the conflict in Lebanon between the Free World's outpost in the region, Israel, and Hezbollah. Even though nearly all Democrats have expressed support for Israel's efforts to neutralize this virulent terrorist organization, they cannot escape a grim reality: The Democrats' incessant, partisan efforts to undermine President Bush's authority that are diminishing the prospects for victory in Iraq are also weakening his administration's ability to resist mostly foreign pressure to adopt a more neutral stance vis-a-vis the Jewish State in the midst of its death-struggle with our common, Islamofascist enemies.

Terrorists in the Fertile Crescent are not the only ones attuned to the perceived dissipation of domestic support for the fight for the future of Iraq. The Iranian and Syrian regimes, which take pride in having destabilized the nascent Iraqi democracy, have clearly been emboldened to precipitate and fuel a second front in Lebanon.

American defeatism will breed still more setbacks if, as seems the case at the moment, freedom's enemies get their way by inducing the Bush team to: impose a premature cease-fire on Israel; insert an international peacekeeping force that will surely prove to be hostile to the Jewish State and protective of her foes; and reward Hezbollah for its outrages by compelling the Israelis to cede to Lebanon strategic territory (dubbed "Shabaa Farms") taken from Syria in the 1967.

Hard experience tells us that defeatism is an indulgence great nations cannot afford in time of war. Its full costs may not become apparent immediately. But the Free World, including the United States itself, will suffer grievously for encouraging our enemies' conviction that we lack the will and resolve to stand with our friends when the going get gets tough.

This is a tale of three men, all prominent figures on the world stage. Two of them Saddam Hussein and former President Gerald Ford have died in recent days; the third, President George W. Bush, is struggling for his political life. How successful Mr. Bush is in recasting and reinvigorating his wartime presidency will depend, in part, on the lessons he draws publicly from the two lately departed.

Of course, the former Iraqi despot and the one-time American president lived very different lives and, appropriately, came to very different ends. Saddam's was dancing from a gallows, in the company of hangmen and witnesses who expressed the sentiment of millions of Iraqis and other freedom-loving peoples in damning him to hellfire. Mr. Ford's demise came quietly in his sleep; surrounded by his loved ones and remembered fondly by the nation he served for decades in war and peace.

Still, the two men constitute bookends of a sort for a Mr. Bush finalizing the strategy he will shortly present for winning the War for the Free World a war that did not begin and will not end in Iraq, especially if the United States were to be seen as losing there.

There is but one reason that the late "Butcher of Baghdad" and his tyrannical regime are no more, and with them the threat they once posed to Saddam's people, their neighbors and, yes to us: Civilized nations, led forcefully by President Bush, acted to remove him from power and thereby enabled free Iraqis to bring him to justice.

By contrast, a year after the liberation of Iraq, Mr. Ford told The Washington Post's Bob Woodward (in an interview embargoed until after the former president's death), "I don't think I would have gone to war [with Iraq]." According to Mr. Woodward, his 92-year-old subject declared: "Well, I can understand the theory of wanting to free people... I just don't think we should go hellfire damnation around the globe freeing people, unless it is directly related to our own national security."

Of course, Mr. Bush and those of us who supported his efforts to free the Iraqi people would argue that doing so was indeed "directly related to our national security." The fact-finding Iraq Survey Group determined Saddam was continuing to produce small quantities of chemical and biological agent right up to the end and intended to ship them "in aerosol cans and perfume sprayers" to the U.S. and Europe. The death toll created by such a state-sponsored acts of terror could have been horrific.

A no less compelling case can be made that our national security would be well-served if dangerous despots like Mahmoud Ahmadinejad and Ayatollah Ali Khameni of Iran and North Korea's Kim Jong-Il were also hung by the neck until dead. It should be the object of American policy to help the long-suffering people of those two countries bring about regime changes that would lead to justice being served on such individuals.

We should do so not out of some fuzzy moral sentiment of the kind often sneeringly dismissed by so-called "foreign policy realists" like the Ford administration's Brent Scowcroft and James Baker. Rather, we should be working to bring about regime change in Iran and North Korea because it is vital to American security that tyrants who have made no secret of their wish to hurt this country as Mr. Ahmadinejad likes to put it, "a world without America is not only desirable, but achievable" are as unable to act on their ambitions as Saddam Hussein.

The alternative of allowing these threats further to metastasize is to ensure not only that the tyrannies in Tehran and Pyongyang be more dangerous in the future. They will help still other threats to become more formidable, as well.

Accordingly, when President Bush addresses the nation in the days ahead, laying out his vision for "the way forward," he must explicitly remind all of us that we are in a war that is not confined to Iraq. If he chooses to "surge" into Iraq more troops, their mission must be part of a larger plan for defeating Iranian activities and proxies in that country, and working to rebuild what Tehran has helped destroy there.

At the same time, Mr. Bush must firmly reject the views of "stability" and accommodation with despotic regimes that we associate with President Ford's time in office. Assisting the peoples of Iran and North Korea to end (with apologies to Mr. Ford) their "long national nightmares" inflicted by the Islamofascist mullahs and the Stalinist Kim dynasty, respectively, is essential to the survival of the Free World's.

President Bush should provide such assistance in the comprehensive way his predecessor pursued the downfall of Soviet Communism in sharp contrast to the Ford administration which effectively sought to perpetuate it via "detente." In fact, Reaganesque economic and financial measures led by the Treasury Department's Under Secretary Stuart Levey are already having a salutary effect by constricting the cash flow of both Tehran and Pyongyang. These steps need to be complemented by political warfare initiatives, information operations, expanded intelligence activity and, as appropriate, covert action.

In the spirit of "not a Ford but" the Gipper, and with a view to ensuring that more tyrants meet Saddam's fate, George Bush should ask the nation: "If not we, who? If not now, when?"

Iran

In recent days, senior U.S. military figures have expressed a concern voiced in this space a few weeks back: The international environment bears an increasingly worrisome resemblance to the period between World Wars I and II. As Gen. Binford Peay put it on the occasion of his retirement Sept. 26 as commander in chief of the U.S. Central Command:

"I am convinced that we are living in the 'interwar years' - a period akin in so many ways to that of the 1920s and '30s, when Americans failed to recognize the war clouds gathering in Europe and Asia, embraced isolationism and refused to maintain a properly equipped, trained and ready military."

Interestingly, the term "interwar" was also used to describe the present era by several top generals and admirals still on active duty in the course of their remarks before a symposium on military planning held in Washington last week under the sponsorship of, among others, the Institute for Foreign Policy Analysis (IFPA) and the U.S. Army.

The "gathering war clouds" seem particularly ominous at the moment in one of the regions for which Gen. Peay was, until recently, responsible: the Persian Gulf. Air attacks by Iran against opposition bases in Southern Iraq, in violation of the U.S.-enforced "no-fly" zone there, have prompted the United States to divert the U.S.S. Nimitz and her battle group from the Western Pacific to the Gulf. This action will significantly increase the American assets available to make good the Clinton administration's threats to shoot down Iranian jets if such attacks continue.

It also highlights two other facts: First, thanks to the cumulative effects of 12 years of defense budget cuts, the U.S. Navy no longer has sufficient force structure to keep at least one aircraft carrier permanently on station in the Indian Ocean/Persian Gulf region. There are simply too few carriers, too many other requirements for the unique U.S. presence and commitment that they communicate on the world's oceans and too real concerns about adverse impact on morale and retention occasioned by long deployments.

As a result, the Navy is reduced to hoping that, should push come to shove in the vital waterways of the Persian Gulf, it won't happen at an inopportune time. Unfortunately, that is generally the moment that adversaries prefer to strike.

Second, when the Nimitz finally arrives on station, she will be but the latest vessel to run the gauntlet arising from Iran's burgeoning land-, sea- and airborne anti-ship missile capabilities. As it happens, some of the most intense alarms about these Iranian threats to international shipping – including vessels carrying a large percentage of the world's oil supplies as well as American and allied warships - were sounded a few years ago by one of the influential military figures who participated in the IFPA symposium last week: Vice Adm. "Scott" Redd. In his previous incarnation as the commander of the U.S. 5th Fleet, with responsibility for ensuring safe passage through the Gulf for such shipping, Adm. Redd minced no words about the danger arising from Iran.

As recent revelations by this newspaper's intrepid national security reporter, Bill Gertz, have made clear, that danger will shortly extend well beyond the Persian Gulf. Thanks to ongoing technology transfers from Russia and China, the radical Islamic theocrats that continue to run Iran – notwithstanding the election of a so-called "moderate" as the Iranian president - will within a few years have ballistic missiles capable of delivering nuclear, chemical, biological or radiological weapons against targets throughout the Middle East and in Europe. It is absolutely predictable that, in due course, Tehran will obtain missiles of sufficient range to threaten not only American forces and allies in these regions but the United States, itself.

Last month, Russian Prime Minister Victor Chernomyrdin contemptuously dismissed Vice President Al Gore's halfhearted protests of such assistance to Iran, knowing full well that his rebuff would entail no costs in Moscow's favorable treatment by the United States. This month, Chinese President Jiang Zemin is expected to do the same. In fact, Jiang will actually be rewarded by the Clinton administration with a presidential certification that China's behavior with respect to proliferation is satisfactory.

If collusion between potential adversaries in intensifying the threat to U.S. and Western interests is an eerie reminder of the last interwar period, so too is the spectacle of an allied nation appeasing a likely aggressor - and, in the process, helping to underwrite the latter's ability to engage in such aggression. The French oil company Total, with the outspoken backing of its government and the European Union, has decided to invest $2 billion in Iran. This represents the largest foreign investment there since the U.S. Embassy was sacked in 1979 that is sure to whet the appetite of others for similar ventures. In partnership with the Russian government-owned monopoly Gazprom and the Malaysian company Petronas, Total hopes to profit handsomely from developing vast new Iranian offshore natural gas deposits. In so doing, though, it will be creating an important new hard currency revenue stream for Iran.

Just as the United States has been inclined to look the other way on malevolent Russian and Chinese behavior in Iran, the Clinton administration is signaling a deplorable willingness to waive legislation adopted last year at the instigation of Sen. Alfonse D'Amato, a statute that would otherwise require the imposition of sanctions against Total. While Secretary of State Madeleine Albright blusters that America's "friends and allies don't get it" concerning the folly of strengthening Iran, she and the rest of the Clinton team are giving them no reason to do so.

Among those who clearly do get it are key legislators like Al D'Amato, Jon Kyl and Sam Brownback in the Senate and Ben Gilman in the House. With their leadership, we may just see the sort of firm action needed to respond to those who would arm a country as likely as any to bring this interwar period to a costly close.

One could be forgiven, in light of recent headlines and press accounts, for wondering precisely who the enemy is in this war on terror. For some people, it clearly seems the list should include - if not be headed by - a democratic ally that has been subjected, per capita, to considerably more sustained and deadly terrorist attacks than the United States: Israel.

This argument requires Israel to be seen not for what it is - namely, a longstanding U.S. partner in a strategically vital region of the world where few exist, one that shares America's values and is a bulwark against the rising tide of anti-Western Islamist extremism. Israel must, instead, be portrayed as perfidious, pursuing an international agenda divergent from (if not actually at odds with) that of the United States and a liability, rather than an asset.

Those who would portray Israel in such an unflattering light doubtless are gleeful over leaks claiming the Jewish State surreptitiously obtained state secrets from a U.S. government employee working for the Pentagon. At this writing, no evidence has been provided to support such charges. Nor has anyone been apprehended - although, for several days, the FBI has been described as poised to arrest someone employed by the Defense Department's policy organization. Only time will tell whether anyone actually is taken into custody, the type of charges and whether he is actually found guilty.

In the meantime, these leaks have already diverted attention from a nation that genuinely should head the list of America's foes: the terrorist sponsoring, nuclear arming and ballistic missile wielding Islamist government of Iran. This effect has been all the more ironic insofar as, according to press accounts, the classified information the FBI thinks was improperly purveyed to Israel involved documents shedding light on America's evolving policy toward the Iranian mullahocracy.

Strategic analyst Steven Daskal recently offered a reminder of the peril posed by Iran: "While the Islamic Republic of Iran as a state is technically not at war with the U.S., Ayatollah Khomeini's fatwa calling for total war by all Shi'ites, regardless of citizenship, against the 'Great Satan America' remains in effect - it has never been rescinded, and in fact was expanded to include killing Americans as being a necessary part of a defensive jihad to make the world safe for Islam. Khomeini's pioneering pseudo-theology was later picked up by Sunni extremists, including Osama bin Laden."

In a thoughtful article in the Aug. 23 New York Post, Amir Taheri recounted how Khomeini and his successors have translated that fatwa into a 25-year-long war against the United States - waged asymmetrically, both directly (for example, in attacks against U.S. embassies and personnel) and indirectly (through terrorist proxies like Hezbollah in Lebanon, Sheik Muqtada al-Sadr in Iraq and Shi'ite warlords in Afghanistan). Mr. Taheri correctly observes "the Khomeinist revolution defines itself in opposition to a vision of the world that it regards as an American imposition. With or without nuclear weapons, the Islamic Republic, in its present shape, represents a clear and present threat to the kind of Middle East that President Bush says he wants to shape."

Therefore, for the U.S., stopping Tehran's Islamist government before it obtains the means to carry out threats to attack Americans forces in Iraq and elsewhere should be an urgent priority. For Israel, however, denying the ruling Iranian mullahs nuclear arms is literally a matter of national life and death.

Israel's concern about the growing existential threat from Iran can only be heightened by overtures Sen. John Kerry and his running mate have been making lately to Tehran. In remarks Monday, vice presidential candidate John Edwards said a Kerry administration would offer the Iranians a "great bargain": They could keep their nuclear energy program and obtain for it Western supplies of enriched uranium fuel, provided the regime in Tehran promised to forswear nuclear weapons. According to Mr. Edwards, if Iran did not accept this "bargain," everyone - including our European allies - would recognize the true, military purpose of this program and would "stand with us" in levying on Iran "very heavy sanctions."

There is just one problem: Based on what is known about Iran's program and intentions - let alone its history of animus toward us - only the recklessly naive could still believe such a deal is necessary to divine the mullahs' true purposes.

While it may be inconvenient to say so, Iran is clearly putting into place a complete nuclear fuel cycle so as to obtain both weapons and power from its reactor and enrichment facilities. And a deal like that on offer from Messrs. Kerry and Edwards failed abysmally in North Korea.

If the United States is unwilling to take concrete steps to prevent the Iranian Bomb from coming to fruition, its Israeli ally will likely feel compelled to act unilaterally - just as it did with the 1981 raid that neutralized Saddam Hussein's nuclear infrastructure. At the time, the Reagan administration joined the world in sharply protesting Israel's attack.

A decade later, however, the value of the contribution thus made to American security was noted by then-Defense Secretary Dick Cheney, who said he thanked God every day during Operation Desert Storm that Israel had kept Iraq a nuclear-free zone. If such a counter proliferation strategy becomes necessary once again, it will be in all of our interests to have Israel succeed.

"The advance of hope in the Middle East ... requires new thinking in the capitals of great democracies - including Washington, D.C. By now it should be clear that decades of excusing and accommodating tyranny, in pursuit of stability, have only led to injustice and instability and tragedy.

"It should be clear the advance of democracy leads to peace, because governments that respect the rights of their people also respect the rights of their neighbors. It should be clear the best antidote to radicalism and terror is the tolerance and hope kindled in free societies. And our duty is now clear: For the sake of our long-term security, all free nations must stand with the forces of democracy and justice that have begun to transform the Middle East." So said President George W. Bush at the National Defense University a week ago.

Even as President Bush drew this lesson from the past, Europe's leading nations - Britain, France and Germany - were inveigling his administration to join them in the latest example of great democracies "excusing and accommodating tyranny" in the pursuit of what passes for "stability."

Within days of the president's powerful address at NDU, the Eurofaustians had induced him to join their effort to do a deal that would, as a practical matter, legitimate, perpetuate and enrich the despotic mullahocracy of Iran.

To hear Secretary of State Condoleezza Rice and National Security Adviser Stephen Hadley tell it, U.S. policy toward Iran has not changed. Rather, the U.S. has - in the interest of getting the Iranian regime to abandon its nuclear ambitions - simply "withdrawn its objections" to Europe's paying Tehran with currency we control (Iran's entry into the World Trade Organization, and spare parts for aging 737 airliners).

In exchange for these seemingly modest concessions, we are assured new, common "red-lines" have been drawn with the Europeans. If the Iranians don't agree to give up nuclear weapons ambitions, we can count on the so-called EU-3 to join us in taking the matter to the U.N. Security Council for action.

We should be clear, however. We have entered the bazaar and the offer on the table should be understood by everyone to be but the opening bid. The mullahs have already responded by saying they will not abandon their uranium-enrichment program, seed corn for nuclear weaponry. Clearly, they expect more Western offers to induce them to be more tractable.

Unfortunately, it is predictable the Europeans will be all too willing to make such further offers, in the interest of "keeping the dialogue going" and avoiding a rupture with Tehran that would be seen as clearing the way for the Iranian bomb. (A similar logic impels the Eurofaustians to resume arms sales to Communist China, even as China inexorably moves forward with its plans to re-annex Taiwan, by force if necessary.)

The futility of the Eurofaustians' deal-making is assured, however, since there is no way to make sure Tehran complies any more fully with future promises to freeze its nuclear weapons program than it has with previous ones.

For example, we recently learned part of the vast Iranian covert nuclear weapons complex involves facilities in hardened tunnels half-a-mile underground. It is roughly as difficult to know what is going on inside such sites, as it is to destroy them.

Deal-making with a repressive, dishonest and aggressive Iranian regime buys the mullahs the one thing they need most: Time. That is, time to complete their covert nuclear program. Time to mate nuclear warheads with Iran's growing arsenal of longer- and longer-range ballistic and cruise missiles. Time to ensure Iran's Chinese and Russian friends will thwart any Security Council resolution the United States might actually be able to persuade the EU-3 to support.

Arguably even more insidious is the prospect the Bush administration will be seen by the Iranian people as having decided, at least implicitly, that a deal with the Iranian regime is more important than "standing with the people" of Iran, who yearn for freedom from the mullahs. This is all the more regrettable since it not only calls into question the president's central organizing principle for the war on terror; it would also seem to preclude, or at least greatly to impede, the only tool that might actually prevent Iranian nuclear armament: regime change in favor of freedom.

In a meeting with The Washington Times editorial board last Friday, Miss Rice confirmed this dilemma: "Our challenge is to continue to speak to the aspirations of the Iranian people even as we deal with near-term issues like the Iranian nuclear program. And the president is determined to do that, determined not to lose the emphasis on the rights and the aspirations of all people, including the Iranian people, to live in freedom. We don't want to do anything that legitimizes this government - the mullahs - in a direct way. And so there isn't any indication here of 'warming of relations.' "

The problem is that, even if Miss Rice is correct and - despite all appearances and, frankly, expectations - these European-led negotiations do not wind up euchring the United States into legitimating the regime and abandoning the aspirations of the Iranian people, they will make it more difficult to do something about those aspirations. We need to wage political warfare against the mullahocracy if there is to be any chance of freeing its people and denying terror's friends the Bomb. And neither time nor the Eurofaustians will be on our side in such warfare.

The Iranian mullahocracy has been at war with this country since it came to power in 1979. The problem is that the weapons available to Tehran for prosecuting its jihad against "the Great Satan" are no longer simply truck bombs and suicide vests. Its proxy army, Hezbollah, has taken over Lebanon and operates terror cells from Iraq to Latin America and even inside the United States. With help from Communist China and Russia, its Iranian Revolutionary Guard Corps wields an array of anti-ship missiles, mines and go-fast boats capable of discouraging oil traffic from transiting the Straits of Hormuz - if not actually sealing that vital waterway for protracted periods.

Not least, Iran is now armed with ballistic missiles of ever-longer range. Those missiles have been developed with help from North Korea for delivering the nuclear weapons the mullahs have been developing covertly for more than 20 years. Once such weapons are in hand - perhaps in just a matter of months now - Tehran will be in a position to execute its threat to wipe Israel (a k a "the Little Satan") off the map.

As a blue-ribbon commission told the House Armed Services Committee last Thursday, moreover, by launching its nuclear-armed ballistic missiles off a ship, the Iranian regime could soon be able to make good on another of its oft-stated pledges: To bring about "a world without America."

The commissioners warned that, by detonating a sea-launched nuclear weapon in space over the United States, Iran could unleash an intense electromagnetic pulse (EMP) that would have a "catastrophic" effect on much of the nation's energy infrastructure. In short order, the ensuing lack of electricity would cause a devastating ripple effect on our telecommunications, sanitation and water, transportation, food and health-care sectors, and the Internet. Iranian missile tests suggest an emergent capability to execute such an attack.

If we are already at war with the Iranian regime and our enemy's destructive power is about to increase exponentially, what can we do to about it? For various reasons, it remains undesirable to use our own military force against the mullahs if it can possibly be avoided. If that alternative is to be made unnecessary, five things must be done as a matter of the utmost urgency. Three have to do with greatly intensifying the financial pressure on Tehran:

(1) We need to discourage investments in companies that provide the advanced technology and capital essential to the oil exports that underpin the Iranian economy. The campaign aimed at divesting such stocks from private and public pension fund portfolios and, instead, investing "terror-free" had a signal victory last week when the head of the French oil conglomerate Total said, "Today, we would be taking too much political risk to invest in Iran."

By moving billions of dollars into certified terror-free funds like those offered by the United Missouri Bank, U.S. investors can effect more of this sort of corporate behavior-modification. Sen. Joseph Lieberman is expected shortly to introduce legislation that will offer federal employees a terror-free option in their Thrift Savings Plan. Every American should have such a ready choice - and be encouraged to exercise it.

(2) We need to deflate the price of oil that sustains the Iranian regime. We can do so by ending the monopoly oil-derived gasoline enjoys in the global transportation sector. (This imperative is the subject of a hilarious video by David and Jerry Zucker at www.NozzleRage.com). By adopting an Open Fuel Standard, Congress can set a standard assuring new cars sold both in America and the rest of the world will be capable of using alcohols that can be made practically anywhere (for example, ethanol, methanol or butanol), as well as gasoline. Long before vast numbers of such Flexible Fuel Vehicles are on the roads, the Organization of Petroleum Exporting Countries-induced speculative bubble that has contributed to the recent run-up in the price per barrel of oil will be lanced.

(3) We must counter the effort being made by the Iranians and other Islamists to use so-called Shariah-Compliant Finance (SCF) as a means to wage "financial jihad" against us. Before SCF instruments proliferate further in our capital markets, in the process legitimating and helping to underwrite the repressive, anti-constitutional and subversive program the Iranian mullahs (among others) call Shariah, that program must be recognized for what it is - sedition - and prosecuted as such. The effect would be chilling for Iranian and other SCF transactions in Western markets worldwide.

(4) We need to deploy as quickly as possible effective anti-missile defenses - both in Europe and at sea. Russian objections notwithstanding, we cannot afford to delay any further in protecting ourselves and our allies against EMP and other missile-delivered threats.

(5) Finally, we must mount an intensive, comprehensive and urgent effort to aid the Iranian people in liberating themselves from the theocrats that have afflicted their nation for nearly 30 years and made it a pariah internationally. Supplying information technologies, assistance to students, teachers, unionists and others willing to stand up to the regime, aid to restive minorities and covert operations should all be in play.

By adopting these measures, we may yet be able to bring about regime change in Iran - the only hope for avoiding full-fledged combat against the Islamic Republic there. But we should be under no illusion: We will not avoid war; it has been thrust upon us by the mullahs for many years now. We may, however, be able to avoid the far worse condition they wish to inflict by unleashing the weapons now coming into their arsenal.

A troubling pattern of putting U.S. and allied security interests second to the Obama administration's political priorities is now well established. If allowed to continue, it not only will make the world more dangerous, it is going to get people killed - probably in large numbers and some of them may be Americans.

A prime example of the phenomenon was the disclosure of minute details of the 2011 raid by SEAL Team 6 within hours of its successful liquidation of al Qaeda leader Osama bin Laden in Pakistan. The revelation of special operations tradecraft horrified those in and out of the U.S. military who appreciate that safeguarding the secrecy of such techniques is essential to ensuring their future utility and the safety of those who employ them.

The really galling thing, though, was that such secrets were compromised for the transparent purpose of touting Mr. Obama's decisiveness and competency as commander in chief. Regrettably, such qualities have not been much in evidence, either before or after that raid. For that matter, notwithstanding Vice President Joseph R. Biden's characteristically preposterous description of the operation as "the most audacious plan in 500 years," it is not entirely clear what his boss' role was in the execution, let alone the conception.

Still, given the importance now being attached to this narrative of vision and courage in the Obama re-election campaign, it is clear that the serial disclosure of state secrets by, most notably, the president's counterterrorism guru, Deputy National Security Adviser John Brennan, was in the service of a political cause. Call it the ends justifying the means.

More recently, "four senior diplomats and military intelligence officers" reportedly fed Foreign Policy magazine contributor Mark Perry a salacious story about Israel enlisting Azerbaijan in its plans for staging aircraft in an attack on Iran. Mr. Perry claims that "a senior administration official told [him] in early February, 'The Israelis have bought an airfield, and the airfield is called Azerbaijan.' "

If true, such a disclosure would fit the pattern of deliberate, concerted and damaging leaks of exceedingly sensitive information in order to advance Team Obama's political agenda. In this instance, that agenda would be to prevent any strike on Iranian nuclear and perhaps other targets by the Jewish state before the November elections.

True or not, the revelation has had the desired effect: It put the Azeri government of President Ilham Aliyev on the spot and forced it to disavow any such collaboration with Israel. While some have questioned the integrity of the author and the logic of his thesis, the trouble is, it certainly sounds like the Obama administration to see such a stunt as a highly desirable twofer: an opportunity to undermine Israel's security while effectively protecting Iran.

It seems that a similar calculation moved the Obama administration to divulge what appeared on the front page of The Washington Post's Sunday edition: An article citing unnamed White House and intelligence sources, including "a senior U.S. official involved in high-level discussions about Iran policy," that revealed details about the intelligence operations and capabilities the United States is said to have brought to bear lately against Iran.

The ostensible purpose of these initiatives has been the monitoring and disabling of the Iranian nuclear weapons program. Among the insights: the CIA has stood up and greatly expanded a unit dubbed "Persia House" for the purpose of monitoring and running covert actions against Iran.

In the article, much was made of the growth of this organization, its use of stealthy unmanned drones to collect signals and other intelligence deep in Iran and U.S. involvement in computer worms, assassinations of Iranian nuclear scientists and explosions in certain sensitive facilities involved in Iran's weapons program.

The point of these leaks of exceedingly sensitive activities - at least some of which could constitute acts of war, however, seemed once again to be cynically manipulative: It appears designed to show the American people that everything is under control. Team Obama is working the problem, skillfully employing intelligence assets to prevent Iran's nuclear ambitions from being realized without using military force.

The Post story also served as a vehicle for reiterating the administration's party line: The mullahs have not decided to acquire an actual weapon and are at least a year away from getting one. What's more, we will know should that decision be taken in plenty of time to do something about it.

We would all wish these assurances to be accurate. Unfortunately, the problem with the Obama administration's practice of playing fast and loose with information that is secret for a reason - it might be called "political compromise," but that would be the only sense of the term this president seems to favor - is that it almost certainly will jeopardize our security and the security of other freedom-loving people.

North Korea

There ought to be a "Famous Last Words" Hall of Fame. If there were, Jimmy Carter's pronouncement following his mission to Pyongyang last week - "The crisis [on the Korean Peninsula] is over" - would clearly qualify.

If such an institution properly organized, moreover, it would situate this statement next to a similarly fatuous and misleading September 1938 utterance by Neville Chamberlain. Upon his arrival back in London from a summit meeting in Munich where he tried to appease Adolf Hitler by legitimating Nazi territorial designs on Czechoslovakia, the British prime minister declared: "[I have] returned from Germany bringing peace with honor. I believe it is peace for our time... Go home and get a nice quiet sleep."

What gives special distinction to the Carter and Chamberlain statements is not just that they are absurdly naive and wrongheaded. These pronouncements are also noteworthy because of the soporific effect they tend to have on the national security decisions of democracies whose publics and press are all-too-willing to embrace an illusion, rather than confront a frightening reality.

Even though the Clinton administration is now trying to put some daylight between itself and the former president, Mr. Carter is nonetheless being widely credited with having achieved a "breakthrough" in the increasingly dangerous crisis over North Korea's acquisition of nuclear weapons. Mr. Carter assures us that Pyongyang has agreed to "freeze" its nuclear program and that it is committed to improving relations with the United States and South Korea. And President Clinton suggests he is cautiously optimistic on both scores.

In fact, far from accomplishing a genuine breakthrough, by precipitating the unwarranted resumption of direct negotiations between the United States and

North Korea and by undermining Washington's already flaccid campaign for economic sanctions against Pyongyang, the former president's meddling in the crisis will soon be seen for what it really is: yet another breakdown of American policy, yet another demonstration of American impotence and unreliability.

Such results have, of course, been predictable ever since Mr. Carter – an icon of American weakness and indecision - announced his mission to North Korea. After all, during his failed presidency, Jimmy Carter so misunderstood the abiding danger posed by the North Korean regime that he sought to pull U.S. forces out of South Korea. Had he been allowed to implement this appeasement policy, freedom might already have been extinguished throughout the Korean Peninsula and endangered elsewhere in Asia.

Now, Mr. Carter is once again communicating to the thugs who run the nation-sized concentration camp known as North Korea that the United States has neither the will, the leadership ability nor the resources to confront them. Like Chamberlain at Munich, he has achieved not "peace for our time" but more time for a dangerous totalitarian state to prepare to threaten the peace.

To be sure, there are no easy or risk-free solutions to the North Korean nuclear crisis. But the course of action urged by Mr. Carter and evidently being embraced by Mr. Clinton - a course of more pandering to Pyongyang, more wishful thinking about the North's trustworthiness, more postponement of military preparations and diplomatic coercion - will only serve to embolden Kim Il-sung. It will certainly not persuade him to abandon his menacing nuclear weapons program.

Worse yet, there are many others around the globe carefully monitoring the Carter-Clinton performance vis-a-vis North Korea. Those who regard the United States as an impediment (whether actual or potential) to their ambitions to acquire territory, to secure weaponry of mass destruction or otherwise to destabilize their regions or the globe, can only be encouraged by the latest developments.

From Belgrade to Beijing to Baghdad and Tehran, dangerous conclusions are being confirmed: As was the case a generation ago, negotiations can be used to sap the will of Western democracies, buying time and latitude to achieve sinister purposes. Talk - or the prospect of it - can often induce freedom-loving people to pursue a "nice quiet sleep" rather than the painful steps actually required.

The bankruptcy of Jimmy Carter's bid for "peace for our time" may not become evident as quickly as did that of Neville Chamberlain, whose accord was demonstrably undone when Hitler expropriated not just the ethnic German-populated Sudetenland but all of Czechoslovakia. It may be difficult, for example, to prove that North Korea's nuclear program has not, in fact, been "frozen"; international inspectors may be allowed to stay in the North but remain unable to verify the scope of Pyongyang's bomb-building activities; and high-level bilateral talks will likely continue to be frustrating but inconclusive.

Accordingly, unless President Clinton uses the period ahead to put into place the means by which South Korea can be defended and the North's nuclear program disrupted - if not destroyed, the United States may be even less prepared for the consequences of a false peace than was Great Britain as it treated with an unappeasable Adolf Hitler. It is not enough to appear somewhat skeptical about the Carter mission; effective hedges to its inevitable failure must be established at once.

A perfect example of the New World Disorder Bill Clinton and Al Gore are bequeathing to their successors can be found north of the 38th Parallel on the Korean Peninsula.

On the one hand, impoverished, Communist North Korea is leading its rich, democratic neighbor to the south in a diplomatic dance that is mesmerizing Western policymakers with visions of sugar-plum treaties, economic engagement and "peace in our time."

On the other hand, North Korea continues to prepare for war. Worse yet, with its burgeoning proliferation of ballistic missile and weapons of mass destruction technology, Pyongyang is sowing the seeds for mayhem elsewhere around the world. Nowhere does this appear to be more menacingly true than in that most explosive of tinderboxes: the Middle East.

The latest round of bilateral diplomacy will occur this week as defense ministers Cho Song-Tae of South Korea and Kim Il-chol of North Korea meet on the South Korean island of Cheju. This meeting is expected to address issues such as trans-border railroad construction, a security hotline between the two countries and "confidence-building measures."

Unfortunately, there appears to be precious little basis for "confidence" that North Korea has actually changed course; if not, the upshot of this latest bilateral fandango may be to exacerbate the likelihood of conflict on the Korean Peninsula.

Indeed, last Friday's New York Times reported that a new, leaked Pentagon study concludes that: "While the historic summit between the North and the South holds the promise of reconciliation and change, no evidence exists of the fundamental precursors for change. There is little or no evidence of economic reform or reform-minded leaders, reduction in military or a lessening of anti-U.S. rhetoric."

Worse yet, each passing day seems to bring fresh evidence of North Korea's determined contribution to a more disorderly - if not a vastly more dangerous - planet. Its dictator, Kim Jong-il, regards ballistic missiles as an export commodity, one of the few things his country produces that can provide its bankrupt regime with infusions of hard currency. He recently acknowledged that his country is selling missile technology to its fellow rogue states. These include:

- Iran. Tehran has just conducted its latest flight test of the so-called Shahab-3 ballistic missile, believed to have been derived from North Korea's No Dong missile. When deployed, it will be capable of delivering chemical, biological or even small nuclear weapons against Israel.

  In the past, the Iranian government paraded a Shahab-3 through the streets of Tehran, accompanied by posters that said, "Israel should be wiped from the map" and "The U.S.A. can do nothing." While the most recent test apparently failed shortly after liftoff, it is unlikely the Islamists in Tehran will be dissuaded from pursuing the means by which they can threaten immense harm to the "Great Satan," its friends and interests.

- Libya. On Sept. 24, the London Sunday Telegraph revealed that Libya has completed its own, ominous missile deal with North Korea. According to the Telegraph, Moammar Gadhafi's unreconstructed, terrorist-sponsoring regime has secretly taken delivery of the first of 50 No Dong missiles and seven mobile launchers from Pyongyang:

"Despite co-operating closely with Iran and Yugoslavia on developing missile technology, both the Libyan missile projects have encountered severe development problems. The deal with Pyongyang will enable Col. Gadhafi to bypass his own development programs as the North Koreans will provide him with ready-made ballistic missiles which will soon be able to pose a significant threat to the security of Israel and Southern Europe."

North Korea is said to have supplied, in addition to the missiles themselves, nine engineers who will presumably not only abet Libya in wielding the threat its No Dongs represent but will assist Col. Gadhafi in acquiring still longer-range delivery capabilities for his weapons of mass destruction.

- Syria. On Sept. 25, the Israeli daily Ha'aretz reported that "Syria successfully tested its first North Korean ground-to-ground Scud-D missile early Saturday morning" and that Israel's "military establishment was somewhat surprised by the model of missile fired." The longer range and mobility of the Scud Ds mean that Syrian forces will be able to hold Israel at risk from a much larger area, considerably decreasing the likelihood that the vaunted Israeli air force will be able to locate and disable these weapons before they are used to rain weapons of mass destruction down on the Jewish State.

- Iraq/Sudan. North Korea also is reportedly helping Iraq to build a Scud missile manufacturing plant near Khartoum in the Sudan. Such a facility will presumably greatly facilitate the proliferation of ballistic missiles in Africa, the Middle East and beyond.

In light of these developments, it is mind-boggling that the Clinton-Gore administration persists in seeking normalized ties with North Korea and downplaying - the newly leaked Pentagon report to the contrary notwithstanding - the real risks associated with its continued appeasement of Pyongyang.

No less disturbing are two other, related Clinton-Gore policy mistakes: First, the administration is trying to nail down a multilateral agreement creating a so-called "Global Action Plan Against Missile Proliferation (GAP)." This initiative was spawned by Russian President Vladimir Putin who, during a visit to Pyongyang, cooked up the idea of paying the North Koreans to give up their ballistic missiles and space launch vehicles (rockets inherently capable of being used to deliver not only payloads into space but weapons to Earth-bound targets thousands of miles away) as a means of derailing U.S. missile defenses. Even though Kim Jong-il subsequently dismissed the idea, the U.S. and others are actively proposing to launch satellites for the North (and other ballistic missile wannabe states), perhaps even paying for the privilege of doing so.

Second, President Clinton has deferred to his successor any action on deploying competent American missile defenses. By so doing, he has compounded the danger already made too real by his earlier, adamant opposition to fielding effective anti-missile systems: The likelihood that the United States will be obliged to deploy such defenses after they are needed, rather than before.

Of course, if Israel or someplace else we care about - to say nothing of the United States, itself - is struck by a ballistic missile-delivered weapon of mass destruction, the debate about deploying missile defenses will be over. In its place will be a national commitment to a Manhattan Project-style crash program imbued with the utmost national priority and a charter to put an array of protective layers in place at the earliest possible moment.

But by then, the true, menacing nature of the New World Disorder that is going to be Bill Clinton's most dangerous legacy will have become evident to all Americans.

For several years, North Korea has said it had nuclear weapons and the world has generally assumed it did. With Pyongyang's apparent underground detonation of such a device on Monday, whatever lingering uncertainty there may have been has dissipated. Call it Kim Jong-il's coming-out party. Now the question of what to do about one of the most dangerous regimes on the planet a state-sponsor of terror who has expressed a willingness to sell its nuclear technology to those with the cash to buy it recurs with fresh urgency.

Let's get one thing straight at the outset: The threat North Korea poses today is actually not appreciably different from that which the Stalinist regime constituted last week. The difference is we no longer have the luxury of ignoring it, or dealing with it through feckless "six-party talks" amounting to the same thing.

Instead, we need to approach the danger posed by a nuclear-armed North Korea as though it presents a mortal peril to American strategic interests in Asia and, perhaps, to this country directly. For, indeed, it does. The idea that a regime that has permitted some 2 million of its own people to starve to death will better treat others including ours is untenable and risky in the extreme.

Consequently, we need now to hold accountable those responsible for the North Korean nuclear program. Communist China has played a double game for years. Without Beijing's military technology, to say nothing of its financial support, strategic protection and food and energy lifelines, Kim Jong-il's regime would have been toast long ago and its people likely reunited with prosperous South Korea. To a lesser degree, the same can be said of the role of Vladimir Putin's Russia.

Pakistan was the cutout for much of the nuclear weapons know-how and equipment that flowed from China to Pyongyang. Nukes-R-Us impresario A.Q. Khan appears to have been used in transfers for which the Pakistani regime sought plausible deniability.

More recently, Iran has been an enabler of North Korea's nuclear and missile programs. Call it the oil-for-weapons program. Pyongyang has been trading mass destruction wherewithal and delivery systems to Tehran in exchange for energy supplies and, presumably, cash. The deal has helped lubricate Mr. Kim's steady progress toward ever-longer-range missiles and acquisition of weapons to go on them. It has also greatly shortened the time it is taking Iran, the other charter member of the "Axis of Evil," to get up the learning curve in both areas.

Unfortunately, even our nominal ally South Korea has become increasingly vital to propping up Mr. Kim's regime. It has been investing substantially in the North, creating industrial zones for which it has sought special treatment in trade arrangements with the U.S. and otherwise demanding that the West appease Pyongyang.

133

These sorts of activities can no longer be ignored or tolerated. While the United States has to pick its shots, it must now adopt the sort of strategy Ronald Reagan employed to destroy the Soviet Union: a concerted campaign aimed at cutting off the funding to, neutralizing the threat from and delegitimating a hostile regime. Elements of such a campaign would include:

- Joining with Japan, Australia and others who share our view of the danger posed by North Korea to deny Pyongyang the financial life-support it must have to survive. International corporations operating in the North should be given a choice: Do business with Mr. Kim or with the Free World. Those who opt for the former should be denied government contracts, subjected to financial sanctions and import controls and made the focus of divestment initiatives like that which ultimately brought down the South African Apartheid regime 20 years ago.

- Greatly ramping up the U.S. effort to deploy the sort of effective antimissile defenses first sought by Reagan in 1983. Thanks to President Bush's leadership, the United States now has the latitude to protect its people against ballistic missile attack. To date, unfortunately, the effort to do so has mostly been confined to a limited, land-based missile defense system. In light especially of the North Korean threat, we need to augment that deployment immediately by modifying the Navy's Aegis fleet air-defense ships with the capability to shoot down ballistic missiles of various ranges — whether launched from places like North Korea or from tramp steamers off our coasts.

- In addition, now that the North Koreans have joined the Indians and Pakistanis in demonstrating that our restraint in nuclear testing does not prevent such experiments by others, we need to resume the sort of periodic underground tests essential to ensuring that our deterrent remains as safe, reliable and credible as we can make it. President Reagan strenuously argued such testing is a nonnegotiable requirement. We can no longer responsibly persist in the moratorium on nuclear testing we have observed since 1992.

- Finally, the United States must stop pretending we can live with Kim Jong-il's regime. Rather than legitimating the regime by negotiating with it — even in multilateral (to say nothing of bilateral) settings, every effort should now be bent toward discrediting this odious dictatorship, making pariahs of those who perpetuate it and encouraging freedom throughout the Korean Peninsula.

President Reagan demonstrated the peoples enslaved by the Soviet superpower need not be consigned to such a state in perpetuity. So in our time we must bend every effort to ending the tyrannical misrule of the nuclear club's newest, and arguably most dangerous, member: Kim Jong-il.

Latin America

What would appear on the surface to be a welcome announcement by Fidel Castro - to the effect that the dangerous, Soviet-designed VVER-440 nuclear power project at Cienfuegos has been canceled - is probably just another in a long list of ruses perpetrated by the Cuban despot. In fact, there is important evidence that suggests Mr. Castro is merely postponing the completion of work on this ticking nuclear time-bomb - not scrapping it.

It has long been obvious that, were the two Cienfuegos reactors to come on line, they would create just 90 miles off the American coast a threat akin to, if not greater than, that posed by the Chernobyl disaster to those downwind. In the view of leading experts, a nuclear accident would be inevitable given the serious problems with the design and construction of the Cuban reactors.

These include: faulty seals and defective welds; long exposure of sensitive equipment to corrosive salt water-saturated tropical air; substandard materials; incompetently designed safety features; and insufficiently trained operators and technicians. The consequences of such a disaster for the United States would make those of Hurricane Andrew pale by comparison.

In his annual Sept. 5 speech commemorating Cuba's communist revolution, Mr. Castro lambasted Russia for altering its payment terms connected with the project that has already cost a reported $2 billion. Since April, Russia has insisted that payment for nuclear equipment and technicians associated with the project be made in hard currency, rather than as a part of the subsidized barter arrangement in effect during Mikhail Gorbachev's tenure.

Mr. Castro lamented that "We don't have any other alternative than to halt the construction of this project ... The Russian authorities ... have proposed continuing the electronuclear plant under terms and conditions which make this totally impossible."

It would be wholly out of character, however, for Fidel Castro to use the occasion of the anniversary of Cuba's "glorious" revolution to publicize one of his regime's most monumental failures. Far more in keeping with his modus operandi would be the utilization of such a forum and such a dramatic denunciation of his partners in the Cienfuegos project as a device to euchre them into granting more favorable terms.

Mr. Castro may also be serving notice on Moscow that his government will consider arrangements with other potential collaborators - such bad actors as Iran, China or North Korea - in the absence of a more forthcoming Russian stance. In this connection, it is worth noting that delegations from all three of these countries have paid visits recently to Cuba's nuclear facilities.

Mr. Castro's pronouncement may also have another intended audience: the U.S. Congress. His highly visible statement that the Cienfuegos project was being dropped could have been timed to encourage conferees on HR 4547, the so-called "Freedom Support Act," to drop a provision included in the Senate version at the initiative of Sen. Connie Mack, Florida Republican. The Mack amendment would condition future U.S. economic assistance to the former Soviet Union on the willingness of Soviet successor states to halt the sale of key components to the Cienfuegos project.

It must be noted, however, that within the last four months, a Ukrainian team of technicians has moved to the inside of the plant all of the nuclear system components from locations exposed to the elements. Such a step is consistent with an effort to mothball the structure - not to shut it down. What is more, according to a report in The Washington Post, a Russian delegation left Moscow last week for Havana to discuss the resumption of work on the Cienfuegos project.

At this juncture, 90 percent of the reactors' structures have been completed - not 70 percent, as Mr. Castro claimed last weekend - and approximately 60 percent of the associated electrical work has been done. According to Dr. Nils Diaz, professor of engineering at the University of Florida, the plant could be completed within two years with sufficient assistance and technical support from Russia or Ukraine.

In addition, some $2 billion - not the $1 billion acknowledged by Mr. Castro - has been invested in the project. As a practical matter, the Cuban regime cannot afford to write off the Cienfuegos nuclear program. Given the radical reduction in energy supplies Havana receives from the former Soviet Union, Mr. Castro has no alternative but to find some way to bring on line these two nuclear reactors, each of which is expected to save 600,000 tons of fuel annually.

In short, there is ample reason to expect that Fidel Castro will try to keep his ambitious - and highly dangerous - nuclear power program on life-support as long as he remains in office. Were he to succeed, his regime will present a greater danger to the security of the American people than at any time since the Cuban missile crisis.

The prompt termination of Mr. Castro's despotic hold on power is, therefore, a more urgent priority than ever. Toward this end, steps aimed at undermining his despotic regime - like those called for by the Cuban Democracy Act sponsored by Rep. Robert Torricelli, New Jersey Democrat - should be implemented at once.

By the same token, the Mack amendment must be made part of any final congressional action on the Freedom Support Act. It is absolutely essential that U.S. tax dollars not be spent to support governments in the former Soviet Union who may yet prove indifferent to the vital U.S. national interest in terminating the Cienfuegos project once and for all.

Cuban dictator Fidel Castro is at it again: With at least $800 million in help from his friends in Moscow and Europe, he hopes at last to bring on line a troubled nuclear reactor 180 miles off the U.S. coast. It has been clear for years that, should he succeed in doing so, it is just a matter of time before this reactor melts down with catastrophic Chernobyl-style consequences for much of the United States. Today, concerned Members of Congress led by Reps. Robert Menendez, New Jersey Democrat, and Ileana Ros-Lehtinen, Florida Republican, will offer the first of possibly numerous legislative initiatives aimed at blocking efforts to complete the Juragua reactor complex - and at penalizing those who propose to assist Havana in doing so.

Among the most lethal detritus left behind by the collapsed Soviet empire are a string of poorly designed, ill-constructed and/or incompetently operated nuclear reactors that pose a risk of human and environmental calamity. Most of these are within the former Soviet Union itself and Eastern Europe and have been subject to chronic, unscheduled shutdowns for safety reasons. Many are regarded as nothing less than ticking time bombs. Indeed, the German government was so concerned about the four VVER 440 reactors it inherited from East Germany that it shut them down within days of reunification.

The two partially completed VVER 440 reactors near Cienfuegos, Cuba, are in a class by themselves, however. Experts, including defectors previously involved in what passed for a "quality control" program at the construction site, have identified the following, fatal defects:

- Sixty percent of the Soviet-supplied materials used in these reactors are defective. Soviet advisers reportedly told Cuban officials they could not guarantee that valves installed in the first reactor's emergency cooling system would function under certain conditions. Worse yet, much of the reactor's equipment was left exposed to the elements and sea air for as long as 18 months. In tropical areas, such machinery must be stored in climate-controlled facilities to avoid serious corrosion and other damage.

- The first reactor's dome would not be able to contain overpressures associated with meltdown conditions. The upper portion of the containment dome has been designed to withstand pressures of seven pounds per square inch -vs. some 50 pounds per square inch required of U.S. reactors.

- As many as 15 percent of the 5,000 welds joining pipes used in the reactors' auxiliary plumbing system, containment dome and spent fuel cooling system are known to be flawed. According to Vladimir Cervera, the senior engineer responsible for overseeing quality control at the Juragua reactor, X-rays showed welded pipe joints weakened by air pockets, bad soldering and heat damage.

Bear in mind that, if a single weld in a U.S. reactor were suspected of being defective, the Nuclear Regulatory Commission would suspend its operations. What is more, Cuban intelligence services are reported to have destroyed x-ray imagery and other documentation concerning safety violations, making corrective action problematic.

Taken together, these and other defects make it impossible to create safe nuclear power plants out of the partially constructed Juragua facilities. No amount of sophisticated Western instrumentation, know-how or training will rectify fatal physical deficiencies that can, as a practical matter, only be corrected by razing the site and starting afresh.

Should one or more of these defects cause a failure of the cooling system in a Juragua reactor, there would likely be a nuclear meltdown and release of substantial quantities of radioactivity. Such fallout would not be confined to Cuba, though. Indeed, according to a National Oceanographic and Atmospheric Agency analysis:

"Based on climatological data for summer 1991 and winter '91-'92, the summer east-to-west trade winds would carry radioactive pollutants over all Florida and portions of Gulf states as far west as Texas in about four days. In winter when trade winds are weaker and less persistent, pollutants would encounter strong westerly winds that could move the pollutants toward the east, possibly as far north as Virginia and Washington, D.C., in about four days."

If ever there were a vital U.S. interest, preventing Fidel Castro from turning his rusting reactor sites at Juragua into Chernobyl qualifies. Under no circumstances should the United States be euchered into paying for this outcome - either directly or indirectly. Reps. Menendez and Ros-Lehtinen are right to seek to dock Moscow's foreign aid account by one dollar for every dollar it sends to Mr. Castro's nuclear program. They are also right to pursue every other avenue - from blocking launches of U.S. satellites on Russian rockets to deferring rescheduling Moscow's international debt to suspending American taxpayer-guarantees for energy exploitation in Russia - to bring pressure to bear on the Kremlin to stop this transaction at once.

Congress should also squarely address the malevolent behavior of companies based in allied nations. Much as Sen. Alfonse D'Amato and Rep. Peter King propose to do in legislation aimed at stopping dangerous trade with Iran, such companies should be offered a choice: You can do business with Fidel or do business in the U.S. market, but not both. The threat of import controls on European companies involved in bringing the Juragua reactors on line would almost certainly dry up capital and technology from Europe, without which it seems unlikely the Russians could go forward.

Finally, Members of Congress need to make it unmistakably clear to the Clinton administration that its sub rosa bid to improve relations with Fidel Castro's Cuba is at an end. A despotic government that is determinedly trying to create a nuclear time bomb - in utter disregard of the safety of its own citizens, to say nothing of the detested Americanos 180 miles to the north – is not one with whom the United States can or should do business.

An unlikely gaggle of businessmen, retired military officers, leftist activists and a few prominent conservatives have formed a truly unholy alliance. Their purpose: to relax, and ultimately to abandon altogether, economic sanctions the United States has long maintained against Fidel Castro's Cuba.

The unholiness is due only in part to the strangeness of the bedfellows who have taken up this cause. To be sure, they seek cover for their campaign in Pope John Paul II's recent visit to the island. And yet, they are making common cause with Mr. Castro in focusing on the pontiff's relatively perfunctory critiques of the U.S. sanctions, while effectively ignoring the pope's calls for "Each person [in Cuba], enjoying freedom of expression, being free to undertake initiatives and make proposals within civil society, and enjoying appropriate freedom of association, [to] be able to cooperate effectively in the pursuit of the common good."

What is more, as demonstrated by two symposiums held last week in South Florida by the Center for Security Policy's William J. Casey Institute, were the sanctions regime to be eased under present circumstances, it would not only make respect for these fundamental human freedoms in Cuba less likely. It would also give Mr. Castro's regime a new lease on life in political, economic and moral terms and, in the process, endanger vital U.S. strategic interests.

The campaign to do business with Cuba - despite the sorry record of such practices under the rubric of "detente" with the former Soviet Union and "engagement" with communist China and Vietnam - has seized upon evidence that Cuban women, children and the elderly are unable to obtain needed medical drugs and treatment. The "engagers" accept Mr. Castro's disinformation that this humanitarian crisis is the fault of the U.S. "embargo" on Cuba to justify their demand that it be ended or eased.

In fact, as Frank Calzon, director of the Washington-based Center for a Free Cuba, reminded the Casey Institute audience last Thursday, there is no shortage of medical care on the island for rich foreigners. In fact, "medical tourism" has become one of the few growth industries in Cuba; well-appointed hospitals with ample supplies of medications are readily available to non-Cubans. It's just that, in the words of Ambassador Josi Sorzano, former Special Assistant to President Reagan for National Security Affairs and U.S. representative to the United Nations, Mr. Castro practices a form of "Cuban apartheid": Foreigners and members of the Communist elite can obtain goods and services, even necessities, routinely denied the average citizen of Cuba. This is a function of Mr. Castro's policies, however, not American economic sanctions.

It bears special emphasis that, under Mr. Castro, the Cuban people are not the beneficiaries of foreign investment. Canadian and European companies doing business in Cuba are obliged to contract with the state for workers. The companies have to pay the regime annual wages on the order of $9,500 per worker. Typically, the workers see only a small portion of that, though - in many cases as little as $10 per month. The rest is skimmed off to sustain Mr. Castro's regime.

Moreover, if the opportunity to exploit Cuban workers were not inducement enough, Mr. Castro makes doing business in Cuba attractive to unscrupulous mining and other businesses by allowing toxic waste dumping and environmental degradation that is prohibited in places like Canada. It is hard to square such practices with the high-minded altruism the "engagers" profess.

Relaxing the U.S. sanctions on Cuba as long as Mr. Castro remains in power would be inimical in a number of other ways, as well, to the interests of both the Cuban and American peoples. For example, Mr. Castro's pride-and-joy is the nuclear power complex in which he has invested some $1.2 billion to date to build near Juragua, Cuba. If allowed to come on-line, though, this complex will almost certainly experience a catastrophic failure due to fatal, and irremediable, flaws in the design and construction of these Soviet-era VVER- 440 reactors.

Should a Chernobyl-like disaster occur, millions of Cubans and - according to the U.S. National Oceanographic and Atmospheric Administration - a sizable portion of the American mainland (inhabited by as 50 million to 80 million Americans) downwind could be exposed to a dangerous radioactive plume. (Incredibly, the same Russians who plead poverty to secure U.S. taxpayer largesse have just extended a $350 million line of credit to the Cubans for "priority installations" on the island, including presumably Juragua's.) Mr. Castro would surely use the relaxation of sanctions to seek additional outside financing and technology to complete construction of these nuclear time bombs, something that must not be allowed to happen.

If the United States were to stop impeding economic life-support for Cuban totalitarianism, moreover, Castro and Co. would surely find new opportunities to underwrite and otherwise expand his involvement in drug-trafficking, electronic eavesdropping, terrorism and anti-democratic movements throughout Latin America and biological weapons. According to Rep. Lincoln Diaz-Balart, Florida Republican, the Clinton administration is, to varying degrees, aware of Fidel's continuing sponsorship of these malevolent activities. Knowing that the truth would be counterproductive to its preferred policy of normalizing relations with Cuba, however, the president has chosen (once again) not to level with the American people.

Mr. Diaz-Balart told the Casey Institute meeting that he believed Cuba would probably enjoy, in due course, a transition to democracy and free enterprise. He warned, however, that the effect of weakening the U.S. sanctions policy now would be, first, to help Fidel stave off that day and, second, to increase the chances that a like minded successor will be able to impose a "Little China" model on the Cuban people in the post-Castro era. Under the latter scenario, Havana, like Beijing before it, would insist upon fascist-style capitalism - requiring the state's approval of and involvement in foreign investments - while using repressive techniques to retain absolute political control.

The United States must not yield to the seductive appeal of those who urge "engagement" with Mr. Castro's Cuba. There will be plenty of time and occasion for engagement when the island gains its freedom. Engagement now will only help those who oppose such freedom to deny the Cuban people the chance to secure it.

Millions of illegal immigrants are marching in America's streets and boycotting jobs, schools and merchants. Their explicit purpose is to blackmail our government into granting rights to which they are not entitled.

These activities demonstrate two realities: First, life is good in this country and the opportunities for economic advancement are extraordinary for those willing to work hard.

Second, life is typically not so good in Mexico and the other Latin American nations from which these illegal aliens principally come. Unfortunately, if present political, economic and social trends continue south of our border, there will likely be many more immigrants coming here unlawfully in search of better lives, and to flee increasingly hard ones in their own countries.

In fact, a prospective surge in illegal immigration - perhaps coupled with a further radicalization of those already in this country - are just some of the reasons why these worrisome trends should command far greater attention from American policymakers and citizens alike. Despite the serious and almost-without-exception adverse implications of events throughout Central and South America for our strategic, trade and security interests, however, neither the Bush administration nor either party in Congress is doing much to address them.

Among the indicators of trouble ahead are the following ominous developments:

- Fidel Castro has been rescued from oblivion by the oil wealth and vaulting strategic ambitions of his most promising protégé, Venezuela's Hugo Chavez. The two authoritarians have adopted a new strategy, born of the realization that radical anti-American leftists can be brought to power throughout the hemisphere the same way Mr. Chavez was - by ballots, rather than bullets.

  Funding and organizational support from Venezuela is making the electoral playing field uneven across the region, giving a formidable advantage to populist revolutionaries over their democratic opponents. Once in office, the latter can rely not only on money from Mr. Chavez and his Islamofascist (for example, Iranian) and Chinese friends. They can also elicit muscle from Mr. Castro's foreign legion (communist Cuban special forces, police, praetorian guards, doctors and teachers) to help consolidate control and eliminate their opponents.

- This phenomenon is already well advanced in Bolivia, where Evo Morales was elected president in December, after fomenting populist upheavals to topple not one but two elected governments. He has moved rapidly in ensuing months to neutralize the parliament, constitution and judiciary that might check his steady accretion and exercise of power.

- In Peru, another would-be dictator, Ollanta Humala, has won the first round of balloting to replace outgoing President Alejandro Toledo. While it is not clear at this writing whether he will prevail in the upcoming runoff, Mr. Humala's inflammatory rhetoric (threatening the country's political elite and its constitutional democracy, admiring the violent terrorist group known as the Shining Path and signaling a willingness to go to war with neighboring Chile) represents a frightening prospect for Peru, the region and U.S. interests. Even if Mr. Humala loses, it is not clear he will refrain from fomenting trouble for the new government - and the rest of us.

- Bolivia and Peru are relatively distant and it is seductive to discount them as security problems for the United States. The same cannot be said of Mexico, which will hold a presidential election in July. Polls have long suggested the likely winner will be Andres Manuel Lopez Obrador, the rabidly anti-American former mayor of Mexico City.

Like others of his persuasion, Lopez Obrador's bid appears to have benefited from financial and help on the ground from his soul mates in Caracas and Havana, who clearly relish the prospect of extending their axis to the border of the United States. While the race has of late become increasingly competitive, as the conservative PAN Party's candidate Felipe Calderon has gained ground, Washington confronts the distinct possibility of an explicitly hostile government in Mexico.

The implications of such an outcome could be far-reaching for the integrity of our southern frontier, illegal immigration, drug trafficking, terrorism, trade and the radical "reconquista" movement (which is intent on "taking back" at least parts of the United States for Mexico).

- Then, there is Nicaragua. All other things being equal, the Marxist Sandinista party still led by Comandante Daniel Ortega is poised - with help, ironically, from both the Venezuelan and American governments - to win national elections in November. For his part, Mr. Chavez is pumping money and possibly agents into his allies' campaign.

The Bush administration is unabashedly and ham-handedly backing Eduardo Montealegre, a foreign minister under discredited former President Arnoldo Aleman. Mr. Montealegre has fractured the anti-Sandinista democrats and his candidacy seems likely to precipitate their defeat. Yet, Washington refuses to reconsider and either support the candidate of the largest and best organized pro-democracy party, the Constitutionalist Liberals, because of its association with Mr. Aleman - or at least to remain neutral.

The consequence of all these elections may well be the complete undoing of Ronald Reagan's legacy of successfully countering and, with the notable exception of Mr. Castro's Cuba, defeating totalitarianism in our hemisphere. At some point in the not-too-distant future, the question will be asked, probably with political repercussions: "Who lost Latin America?"

There is still time for the Bush administration and Congress to avoid this stigma by countering these trends and their strategic implications. But to do so, they will have to engage far more vigorously against Latin America's enemies of freedom, investing considerably greater human and financial resources, high-level attention and political capital in once again securing our hemisphere.

Immigration and Border Insecurity

Hundreds of "Minuteman" volunteers are fanning out this week across the Arizona-Mexico border. They hope, by so doing, to help the authorities reduce somewhat the human tsunami of illegal aliens crossing into America.

More important, perhaps, they seek to focus the our leaders' attention on the public's rising anger about this invasion of our territory - and its huge national security, social, economic and other costs.

The full extent of those costs may yet to be tallied. By some estimates, there were 75,000 "other-than-Mexican" illegals among those who sneaked into the United States last year. A growing number are from the Middle East and may well be Islamists using well-established alien-smuggling routes as the first step to perpetrating new acts of terror in this country.

Lest there be any lingering doubt, however, that politicians need the sort of pointed reminder the Minutemen are offering that, as they say in the movies, the American people are "mad as hell and not going to take it any more," consider the likely scenario on the floor of the U.S. Senate this week.

The scheduled business is urgent action on an emergency supplemental appropriations measure to provide funding needed now by our troops in harm's way in Iraq and Afghanistan. Without such funding, critical war materiel will begin running short - jeopardizing the mission, and possibly the lives, of our servicemen and women on the front lines.

This priority legislation became the vehicle the House of Representatives used last month to fulfill a promise made in December by its leadership and by President Bush: In exchange for passing last year a bill intended to carry out the recommendations of the September 11 Commission, but that failed to address several of the most important ones - in particular, those dealing with the need to enhance the authenticity and security of drivers' licenses, the "REAL ID" bill fixing the latter would be given expedited consideration.

The REAL ID legislation is aimed at denying future terrorists the ability exploited by the September 11, 2001, hijackers (even those in this country illegally) - namely, to hold numerous valid drivers' licenses, which they used to gain murderous access to airports and their targeted aircraft. It is no small irony, therefore, that the presence of the REAL ID provisions on the military's supplemental funding bill is being cited by the Senate parliamentarian as grounds for Sen. Larry Craig, Idaho Republican, to try to attach to it legislation that would help eviscerate what passes for restrictions on illegal immigration.

Mr. Craig, an otherwise very sensible and responsible Republican legislator from Idaho, has an idee fixe he shares with, his co-sponsor, Sen. Teddy Kennedy: The agricultural sector of the U.S. economy needs cheap labor. So, let's legalize the presence in this country of anyone who can claim to have once worked for a little more than three months in that sector.

If that were not bad enough, their families would be allowed to become legal residents, too, even if they are not now in the United States. The same would apply for illegals who had ostensibly been agricultural workers here in the past, but who have gone home. They can all become "temporarily" legit, a status the notoriously left wing, yet federally funded, Legal Services Corp. will be happy to help them subsequently adjust to permanent resident status.

In short, S.359, the Craig-Kennedy Agricultural Job Opportunity, Benefits, and Security Act of 2005 (better known as the AgJobs bill), amounts to an amnesty for a class of illegal aliens. While the proponents insist it is something else - for example, "hard-earned legalization" - there is no getting around the fact it hugely rewards people for coming to this country illegally. And, as we have seen with previous, misbegotten immigration amnesties, the effect is to encourage more people to do so.

That will surely be the case with the Craig-Kennedy AgJobs bill, too. Though it requires the illegal alien's 100 days of agricultural work in the U.S. to have occurred during any 12-month period between February 2002 and August 2003 - and, therefore, is not something new "invaders" could cash in on – this legislation further reinforces the expectation that, if you can get into this country by whatever means, you will at some point likely be allowed to stay legally.

Interestingly, Messrs. Craig and Kennedy have significantly fewer co-sponsors (43) on their legislation this year than in the last session of Congress (62). At this writing, it is unclear if many of those senators who no longer want to be publicly associated with this amnesty bill will nonetheless vote for it.

We can only hope they have heard the Minutemen's message on behalf of the vast majority of Americans of just about every walk of life and political persuasion:

The time has come to take effective action to secure our borders against the swelling tide of people trying to get into this country illegally; to find ways to decrease, not increase, those already here unlawfully; and to ensure that documents needed to access airports, government buildings, bank accounts, etc. are valid and held only by those entitled to carry them. And get all this done now, without hurting our troops.

The Congress has received lots of free advice lately from Mexican government officials and illegal aliens waving Mexico's flag in mass demonstrations coast-to-coast. Most of it takes the form of bitter complaints about our actual or prospective treatment of immigrants from that country who have gotten into this one illegally - or who aspire to do so.

If you think these critics are mad about U.S. immigration policy now, imagine how upset they would be if we adopted an approach far more radical than the bill they rail against that was adopted last year by the House of Representatives - namely, the way Mexico treats illegal aliens.

In fact, as a just-published paper by the Center for Security Policy's J. Michael Waller (www.centerforsecuritypolicy.org/Mexicos_Glass_House.pdf) points out, under a constitution first adopted in 1917 and subsequently amended, Mexico deals harshly not only with illegal immigrants. It treats even legal immigrants, naturalized citizens and foreign investors in ways that would, by the standards of those who carp about U.S. immigration policy, have to be called "racist" and "xenophobic."

For example, according to an official translation published by the Organization of American States, the Mexican constitution includes the following restrictions:

- Pursuant to Article 33, "Foreigners may not in any way participate in the political affairs of the country." This ban applies, among other things, to participation in demonstrations and the expression of opinions in public about domestic politics like those much in evidence in Los Angeles, New York and elsewhere in recent days.

- Equal employment rights are denied to immigrants, even legal ones. Article 32: "Mexicans shall have priority over foreigners under equality of circumstances for all classes of concessions and for all employment, positions or commissions of the Government in which the status of citizenship is not indispensable."

- Jobs for which Mexican citizenship is considered "indispensable" include, pursuant to Article 32, bans on foreigners, immigrants and even naturalized citizens of Mexico serving as military officers, Mexican-flagged ship and airline crew, and chiefs of seaports and airports.

  Article 55 denies immigrants the right to become federal lawmakers. A Mexican congressman or senator must be "a Mexican citizen by birth." Article 91 further stipulates that immigrants may never aspire to become cabinet officers, as they are required to be Mexican by birth. Article 95 says the same about Supreme Court justices.

  In accordance with Article 130, immigrants - even legal ones - may not become members of the clergy, either.

- Foreigners, to say nothing of illegal immigrants, are denied fundamental property rights. For example, Article 27 states, "Only Mexicans by birth or naturalization and Mexican companies have the right to acquire ownership of lands, waters and their appurtenances, or to obtain concessions for the exploitation of mines or of waters."

- Article 11 guarantees federal protection against "undesirable aliens resident in the country." What is more, private individuals are authorized to make citizen's arrests. Article 16 states, "In cases of flagrante delicto, any person may arrest the offender and his accomplices, turning them over without delay to the nearest authorities." In other words, Mexico grants its citizens the right to arrest illegal aliens and hand them over to police for prosecution. Imagine the Minutemen exercising such a right.

- The Mexican constitution states that foreigners - not just illegal immigrants - may be expelled for any reason and without due process. According to Article 33, "the Federal Executive shall have the exclusive power to compel any foreigner whose remaining he may deem inexpedient to abandon the national territory immediately and without the necessity of previous legal action."

As the immigration debate in the Senate moves into a decisive phase this week, legislators who believe America's southern border must be secured, the nation's existing immigration laws enforced and illegal aliens not rewarded with permanent residency and a direct path to citizenship are being sharply criticized and, in some cases, defamed as bigots and xenophobes. Yet, even their maximalist positions generally pale in comparison with the treatment authorized by the Mexican constitution.

So the next time such legislators - and the majority of Americans for whom they speak - are assaulted by Mexican officials, undocumented aliens waving Mexican flags in mass demonstrations here in the United States, clergy and self-described humanitarians, businessmen and other advocates of illegal immigration, ask them this: Would they favor having the U.S. impose the same restrictions on immigrants - legal and illegal - that Mexico imposes on their counterparts there?

Nothing of the kind is in the cards, of course. Nor should it be. Legal immigration and the opportunity for foreign investors and other nationals to contribute to this country are not only one of its hallmarks - they are among the reasons for its greatness.

Still, we should not allow the hypocrisy of others' treatment of undocumented aliens in their countries to induce us to refrain from taking effective steps to prevent further illegal immigration: by building a fence along our southern border; by enforcing immigration laws in the workplace and elsewhere; and by discouraging more such violations - with potentially grave national security implications - by dealing effectively with those who have already broken those laws by coming here without permission.

Yugoslavia

As the international community at last starts to move toward long-overdue military intervention in Bosnia-Herzegovina, one conclusion is becoming inescapable: It had better do so quickly.

Otherwise, the United Nations will face more than just a rapidly deteriorating situation on the ground, with countless thousands of innocent civilians added to the 128,000 Bosnians estimated to have died to date - and the likelihood that the horror will spread to still other flash points like Kosovo, Macedonia and Vojvodina. It may also find itself once again prevented from acting due to a veto from Moscow.

In recent days, as hard-line elements of the former Soviet Union have begun to reassert themselves in Russia, representatives of the Yeltsin government have launched what appears to be a coordinated effort to signal solidarity with the totalitarian Serbian government of Slobodan Milosevic. The timing, as well as the content, of such interventions is ominous.

The most dramatic of these statements was made by Russian Foreign Minister Andrei Kozyrev at the Conference on Security and Cooperation in Europe (CSCE) on Dec. 14:

"We see ... essentially unchanged goals of NATO and the Western European Union, which are working out plans to strengthen their military presence in the Baltic States and other regions on the territory of the former Soviet Union, and to interfere in Bosnia and in the internal affairs of Yugoslavia.

"This course, evidently dictated the sanctions against [Yugoslavia]. We demand their removal and, if this does not happen, we assume the right to undertake necessary unilateral measures to defend our interests, all the more since they are causing us economic harm. In its struggle the present government of Serbia can count on the support of Great Russia."

To the enormous relief of the civilized world, Mr. Kozyrev subsequently disavowed this statement, suggesting that it was merely a "rhetorical device" designed to alert the international community to "the real threats on our road to a post communist Europe." Unfortunately, no such disclaimers have followed similar presentations by other Russian officials:

- According to The Washington Post, a few days prior the Kozyrev remarks in Stockholm, a Russian representative to the International Monetary Fund threw one of the organization's executive committee meetings into turmoil when he launched into a diatribe against the West's sanctions on Serbia.

- On December 16, Vitali Churkin - a veteran and thoroughly cynical public relations flack for Soviet communists - used an international conference in Geneva to denounce the international pressure being brought to bear on Serbia and expressed Moscow's solidarity with Belgrade.

- A Russian diplomat recently tried to intimidate the Japanese government into backing off the Western consensus against Serbia, making clear that this was a matter of considerable importance to Moscow and threatening unspecified retaliation if Tokyo was not cooperative. To its credit, the government of Japan sent the Russian packing. It must be assumed that similar bilateral approaches have been made in other allied capitals, with unknown results.

In short, whatever the explanation for Foreign Minister Kozyrev's bizarre performance at the CSCE conference last week, it seems clear that he spoke the truth at least when - as part of his retraction statement - he told his stunned audience: "The text I read out earlier is a fairly accurate compilation of the demands of what is, by no means, the most extreme opposition in Russia."

Indeed, far from being the policy of the "most extreme opposition," the pro-Serbian line appears to be increasingly that of the nominally reformist government headed by Boris Yeltsin. If the events of the past fortnight are any guide, as the hard-line communist-nationalist-fascist factions ascendant in Moscow consolidate their "creeping coup," the Russian government will become ever more strident in its opposition to the current sanctions on Belgrade – to say nothing of ideas of intensifying those sanctions or complementing them with long-overdue military actions.

Consequently, if the West is serious - at long last - about persuading Serbia to halt its aggression in Bosnia and Croatia, ending the attendant atrocities and "ethnic cleansing" there and preventing a reprise elsewhere in the former Yugoslavia, it had best get on with enforcing a no-fly zone and lifting the arms embargo that keeps the victims from defending themselves. A 15-day waiting period on the former and further deferral of the latter may mean that neither materialize in the face of a Russian veto - the first expression of the all-too-familiar "new" look of Moscow's post-reform foreign policy.

Of course, moving swiftly now to the deal with Bosnia's trauma will not necessarily prevent a confrontation with Russia. Had the West acted a year ago, as it should have, a crisis with the former Soviet Union could almost certainly have been prevented. At the very least, the devastation of much of the Balkans and the present prospect for a wider regional war might have been avoided. What is more, the tangible evidence of Western solidarity with freedom-loving people and willingness to resist oppression inherent in such an action might have helped to undermine the appeal of authoritarian elements in Moscow.

Failing that, it is probably better to determine where those forces plan to take Russia sooner rather than later. In particular, we would do well to know it before the Bush administration extends $2 billion in taxpayer-guaranteed loans for the Russian oil and gas industry, before it issues hundreds of millions of dollars worth of credit guarantees for grain purchases, and before it signs onto further, possibly unverifiable arms reduction agreements.

The torrent of international criticism that followed last week's decision by the so-called Bosnian Serb assembly to seek a popular referendum on the Vance-Owen peace plan has begun to approximate the Muslim blood flowing in the streets of Zeppa, Gorazde, Sarajevo and other communities still holding out against the Serbian onslaught. No one should be surprised, however, either at the "parliament's" decision or at the continuing genocide and territorial consolidation that are going to continue over the next 10 days prior to the referendum.

After all, such outcomes were made virtually inevitable by the Europeans' unwillingness to implement or enforce what the United States hoped would be the three basic pillars of allied action - the lifting of the arms embargo against Bosnian Muslims, airstrikes and a total shutdown of the Danube and other essential supply lines for the Serbian war machine and economy.

What is surprising, however, is the international community's sudden readiness to portray Belgrade's ruthless dictator, Slobodan Milosevic, as a man of peace. After all, it has been Mr. Milosevic who has assiduously promoted the concept of a "Greater Serbia" - a concept that has animated and made possible the Bosnian Serbs' aggression. It is Mr. Milosevic who has been properly charged by the U.S. government with being a war criminal who should be brought to justice. It is Mr. Milosevic who has repeatedly lied to the very negotiators and allied leaders who now seem ready to take him at his word.

Mr. Milosevic's efforts to differentiate his position from that of his proxies in Bosnia should be treated with no less contempt than is being accorded the "parliament's" referendum scam. Even his latest promise to cut off material aid to the Bosnian Serbs - a commitment he should have made two years ago and that is likely to be honored in the breach - does not alter the historical record: Mr. Milosevic has been up to his flat-top hairdo in genocide in Bosnia-Herzegovina and Croatia. It demeans the international community and makes a mockery of the "peace process" to accord him a pivotal role in it.

As things stand now, however, Mr. Milosevic has reason to believe that – by obscuring the continuing, direct relationship between Serb policy and the Bosnian Serbs' malevolent activities - further progress can be made toward his goal of establishing a "greater Serbia" even as he seeks relief from international sanctions against Belgrade and protection of Serbia proper from Western military strikes, should they occur.

The pressure on President Clinton to acquiesce to the Milosevic-Bosnian Serb good cop-bad cop routine will, of course, be intense. Still, Mr. Clinton must understand that his options will only be made worse by further postponing military measures aimed at punishing the Serbian aggressors, protecting their victims, creating conditions on the ground that are conducive to genuine, constructive peace negotiations - as opposed to the charade presided over by Cyrus Vance and David Owen; and, in their absence, establishing territorial arrangements in Bosnia-Herzegovina that are defensible and sustainable (something that cannot be said for the Vance-Owen gerrymandered arrangements).

The president's continued insistence upon coordinated multilateral action and allied consensus as the sine qua non for U.S. intervention against Serbian aggression will inevitably translate into a consolidated and irreversible Serb victory, with ominous implications for the region and beyond.

The United States must act now - if necessary unilaterally - to achieve the aforementioned objectives. Ironically, if the United States does so under present circumstances and outside of an effort to "enforce" the hapless Vance-Owen plan, such objectives actually stand a much better chance of being achieved and with less loss of American lives.

Toward these ends, the following, specific military and other steps should be taken: silencing the powerful artillery pieces that have been the principal instrument for the devastation of Sarajevo and other Bosnian enclaves and refugee centers; denying use of the airspace of the entirety of the former Yugoslavia to Serbian warplanes and helicopters; disrupting the Serbian communications, command and control infrastructure supporting combat operations in Bosnia and Croatia; destroying loading ramps, oil reserves, arms depots and other logistic nodes employed by Serbian and/or former federal forces in support of their combat operations and those of their proxies in Bosnia and Croatia; and using Radio Free Europe's assets to inform the Serb people that the conflict is not with them but with their totalitarian ruler.

None of these actions would require the United States to deploy large numbers of ground forces in the former Yugoslavia. They could be accomplished with reasonable confidence of success by employing aircraft, naval and missile assets. Ground combat can, and should be, left to the Bosnian and Croat forces who are more than ready to defend their homelands - and to secure the liberation of those areas currently under brutal Serbian occupation - once the current disparity between the firepower available to the aggressors and to their victims is corrected. Toward this end, Bosnia and Croatia should be given access to military equipment currently being denied them and necessary for their defense and the liberation of Serb-occupied territories.

Most importantly, the foregoing steps must be accompanied by an ultimatum warning Serbia and its surrogates that a failure promptly to cease hostilities and begin immediate disengagement from Bosnia and Croatia will result in strikes against military and economic targets in Belgrade and other rear areas in Serbia. Carrying - for the first time - the costs of brutal aggression to Slobodan Milosevic's power base may help produce the end of his tyrannical regime.

The costs of such actions are not inconsequential. Unfortunately, the dangers involved are almost surely smaller than allowing the present flash fire in the Balkans once again to set alight a larger, and far more costly conflict in the region - and perhaps beyond.

Vietnam

In the next few weeks, the International Monetary Fund will vote on roughly $140 million in bridge loans that will allow communist Vietnam to clean up its arrearages to the Fund. Should these loans go through, the practical effect would be to re-establish Vietnam as a member of the world community in good standing.

Such an action would, after all, clear the way ultimately for billions of dollars in assistance from both the IMF and the World Bank for infrastructure development in Vietnam and other purposes. It also would encourage massive new infusions of aid from Western government and private sector sources.

The IMF loans can only be approved with the Clinton administration's acquiescence - if not its active, open or covert, support. The question is: Can President Clinton actually go along with the political and economic rehabilitation of Vietnam - in effect, normalizing relations with Hanoi – under present circumstances? News reports indicate that his National Security Council staff has recommended that he do so. Still, developments on two fronts argue powerfully against it:

Vietnam's continuing lies about U.S. Prisoners of War/Missing in Action: Yet another congressional mission to Hanoi has recently been conducted, aimed at stifling once and for all concerns about Vietnam's truthfulness on the POW-MIA issue. Still, new information keeps coming to light that raises additional questions about the Americans left behind in Southeast Asia at war's end.

For example, last February Harvard researcher Steven Morris discovered a possible "smoking gun" in the Soviet Communist Party's files in Moscow. This document revealed that Hanoi held 700 more U.S. prisoners than it had heretofore acknowledged. Now, despite feverish efforts by both U.S. and Vietnamese officials to discount the Morris memo comes a further revelation: In 1979, a key North Vietnamese defector named Le Dinh gave highly credible testimony to the Defense Intelligence Agency - testimony that appears to have validated the Soviet memo's central contention. According to Le Dinh, after all POWs were supposed to have been returned in 1973, Hanoi held back as many as 700 U.S. prisoners as " 'strategic assets' to be used to force the U.S. to pay reparations."

What is more, Soviet files have also yielded up a top secret cable dated March 14, 1967, from the Soviet Embassy in Hanoi, reporting on difficulties that Moscow's technical assessment teams in Vietnam were having gaining access to and exploiting a downed U.S. aircraft. It confirms that there was an active competition in this area between the Soviet Union and China and that the latter's personnel would actually blow up planes to which they had first shot so as to deny the Russians an opportunity to benefit from them.

Despite a systematic and violent effort to influence the outcome of the U.N. monitored elections held last month in Cambodia, Vietnam's puppet government in Phnom

Penh was denied a popular mandate to govern. In response, the senior leadership of the communist Cambodian People's Party (CPP) - a rogues' gallery of former Khmer Rouge military commanders and commissars with longstanding ties to Vietnam - has done everything imaginable to ensure its continued hold on power.

Hun Sen, the Vietnamese-installed communist premier, has announced his government would defy the electorate and "remain in place." Many members of the CPP's Politburo were involved in a thus-far abortive effort to destroy Cambodia by declaring the secession of the country's seven eastern provinces. Were it to succeed, such a move would likely lead to the annexation of this valuable real estate by Vietnam, one of Hanoi's longstanding objectives. The communists are now angling to retain control of key security portfolios in a new coalition government; the sort of arrangement the Sandinistas have shown in Nicaragua can permit them to "rule from below."

Against this backdrop, one thing should be clear: This is no time to be normalizing relations with Vietnam. Re-establishing diplomatic and economic ties and otherwise extending life-support to this unrepentant, brutal and aggressive regime would be morally repugnant and strategically inane.

This is all the more true insofar as pressure is inexorably building inside Vietnam proper for systemic reform. For example, on May 24 - as reports of a massive voter turnout in Cambodia suggested that the communists there were going to be defeated - a huge demonstration occurred in front of the Hue police station in Central Vietnam. In the course of this event, a Buddhist monk self-immolated in the presence of some 10,000 pro-democracy Vietnamese, sending shock waves through a regime that remembers vividly that such events presaged the demise of South Vietnam's corrupt Diem government in 1963.

In short, Vietnam is now following the well-worn path trod by other despotic regimes - from Mikhail Gorbachev's Soviet Union to Fidel Castro's Cuba to Kim Il-sung's North Korea to Jose Eduardo dos Santos' Angola. In each case, international intervention in the form of economic assistance, financial aid or political support is desperately sought even as domestic repression intensifies.

Unfortunately, such Western intervention simply serves to perpetuate these odious regimes and postpone the day when genuine freedom and respect for human rights take root in their nations. Hanoi must not be allowed a new lease on life - and the upcoming IMF vote offers an early opportunity to demonstrate that the U.S. government will not give it one.

At this writing, the heavy betting is that today will be "D-Day" for President Clinton's decision to lift the trade embargo on Vietnam. Should he take this step under present circumstances, however, the president will probably see his already serious Vietnam problem turned into an even greater personal political quagmire.

To draw on the World War II parallel, Sept. 14, 1993, is more likely to prove a "day of infamy" than the heroic turning point that sealed the fate of America's mortal enemies. Consider the following bill of particulars:

Item: There is new evidence that Vietnam has lied about the fate of U.S. servicemen unaccounted for at war's end. Last Tuesday, another politically portentous document emerged from the archives of Soviet military intelligence. It appears to offer further confirmation that Hanoi deliberately misled the United States about the number of prisoners it held.

The document, which is said to be the translation of a December 1970 report to the North Vietnamese Communist Party Central Committee by one of its officials states:

"Now, I want to stop on one more issue - about the captured American fliers. The total number of captured American fliers in the Democratic Republic of Vietnam consists of 735 people. As I have already stated, we published the names of 368 fliers. That's our diplomatic step.

"If the Americans will agree to withdraw their forces from South Vietnam, we will, for a beginning, return these 368 people to them; and when the Americans finish withdrawing their forces, we will give the rest back to them. The issue of the captured American fliers, by virtue of what has been said above, is of great importance to us."

Item: Charges that the U.S. government has long known that American prisoners were left behind in Vietnam when the war ended and has systematically dissembled about the truth have recently been raised to a new level by Sen. Robert Smith, New Hampshire Republican.

According to the New York Times, Mr. Smith in a June 29 letter to Attorney General Janet Reno has formally accused 10 government employees of "crimes aimed at covering up what he considers the government's botched efforts to find the truth." Those alleged to have engaged in such activities include a senior Bush administration political appointee as well as civilian officials of the State and Defense Department and several military officers.

Item: Ross Perot has served notice that lifting the embargo at this point will squander America's leverage over Hanoi for a full accounting of the true fate of Vietnam-era POWs and MIAs.

On the "Larry King Live" program Sept. 7, Mr. Perot said:

"We left men behind. There are still men alive. There is overwhelming evidence. Now, if you ever lift that embargo and you don't account for our men - the reason we never got them is we never paid the reparations money. They gave us part of our men, they kept the rest until they got the reparations money. That's not being too dumb, right? Then we never paid the reparations money. Watergate hit, we dropped it. They kept our men all these years - people just like you...

"It's our hope that the president will not lift the embargo. If he does, they'll kill whoever's left. Dead men tell no tales... We don't know how many [are still alive], but let's assume there's one. The principle is the same."

Item: The Clinton administration now seems to be implicated in the POW-MIA cover-up. Despite President Clinton's repeated promises to the families of those unaccounted for - most notably his commitment made on Memorial Day 1993 to "provide not just the prayers and memorials, but also to the extent humanly possible, to provide the answers you deserve" - his administration has been taking steps that actually help to reduce any chance that ongoing field investigations in Southeast Asia might ascertain the truth.

Specifically, personnel are being assigned to lead and conduct the field investigation effort who have no background in intelligence or in the region. At the same time, the most competent and experienced investigators are being ordered to relocate to the Joint Task Force headquarters in Hawaii. From there, they are unlikely to be able to make any discoveries about Vietnamese dishonesty or the ultimate disposition of U.S. POW-MIAs that could complicate the administration's objective of achieving early normalization of U.S.-Vietnamese relations.

Item: A federal grand jury has reportedly begun to investigate allegations that Commerce Secretary Ron Brown was paid $700,000 by the Vietnamese government to lift the trade embargo. According to U.S. News & World Report, Mr. Brown - who dismisses the allegations as "ridiculous" - has nonetheless retained a former federal prosecutor who served in the Justice Department's Public Integrity section to represent him. At the very least, until this matter is resolved, any decision by Mr. Clinton to lift the embargo would be unseemly, not to say suspicious.

Mr. Clinton would be well advised, in light of the foregoing, to put the idea of improving relations with Vietnam on hold for at least another year. Should he do otherwise, he will almost certainly have cause to regret adding to the baggage he already carries regarding this painful chapter in American history - if not the damage he will do in the process to the search for American POW-MIAs and to U.S. long-term interests in democracy and stability in Southeast Asia.

The Clinton administration recently announced its response to the massive cheating scandal that has rocked the U.S. Naval Academy: Heads will roll.

In addition to more than 20 midshipmen who are being expelled for breaking Annapolis' honor code on an engineering exam, one of the Navy's most senior admirals - the four-star Commander-in-Chief Pacific, Charles Larson –will replace the present superintendent, (two-star) Rear Adm. Thomas Lynch, with a mandate to instill a new sense of honor, integrity and discipline at the Academy.

Even for a president who has raised the practice of lying for political advantage to an art form, the choice of Adm. Larson for such a role is an improbable one. After all, during his tenure as CINCPAC, the admiral has played a direct and pivotal role in one of the most pernicious lies of our time – the cover-up of information about U.S. prisoners of war and missing in action (POW/MIAs) left behind in Indochina after the Vietnam War.

Adm. Larson's most public contribution to this cover-up has been his repeated assertion that Hanoi has been cooperating fully in U.S. efforts to achieve the fullest possible accounting for its personnel.

Since his command included the organization charged with establishing the truth about hundreds of so-called "discrepancy cases" -Joint Task Force-Full Accounting (JTF-FA) - statements from Adm. Larson to the effect that communist Vietnam's cooperation in ferreting out human remains and other information was "superb" have carried particular weight. Indeed, his claims in this regard gave crucial political cover to the Clinton administration and its congressional supporters in the process of deep-sixing the trade embargo against Vietnam.

The truth is that Vietnamese cooperation has been, at best, quite circumscribed. Hanoi has shown an increasing willingness, for example, to assist U.S. teams - for a hefty price - in scouring hellish jungle crash sites for dog tags, teeth and other fragmentary evidence about American servicemen who apparently died before being captured.

Vietnam has been almost completely unforthcoming, however, concerning the fate or disposition of Americans who did fall into Hanoi's hands or those of its proxies in Laos and Cambodia. Evidently, this does not constitute a lack of cooperativeness, however. Perhaps this is so because Adm. Larson and other arbiters of Vietnam's helpfulness have regarded continuing questions about the status of such individuals - some of whom went to Annapolis with the admiral - as an embarrassment to the U.S. government and an impediment to the Clinton administration's priority business of normalizing relations with Vietnam.

Adm. Larson has apparently not contented himself with mere distortion of Hanoi's record concerning the most sensitive POW-MIA cases. Under his command, information has actually been destroyed that might have helped establish the extent to which Vietnam was not cooperating.

On March 24-29, 1993, then-Brigadier Gen. Thomas Needham (the commander of Joint Task Force-Full Accounting), Adm. Larson's intelligence officer and a CIA official descended upon the U.S. Embassy in Bangkok for the purpose of personally shredding tens of thousands of primary documents concerning U.S. POW-MIAs in Indochina. The exalted rank of the shredders is noteworthy; even the Rose Law Firm presumably would acknowledge that such individuals must have been assigned the task of destroying very sensitive papers.

Indeed, these documents dated back to before Operation Homecoming in 1973 and took up some 30 linear feet of wall space in the embassy. They included detailed POW-MIA case histories, live-sighting reports and vast information obtained from refugees.

Most importantly, they contained some 20 years of handwritten notes by U.S. field investigators with comprehensive cross-references to other documents. Those who compiled this archive considered it to contain "the most important historical files in existence on the POW-MIA of Vietnam, Laos and Cambodia."

The Bangkok records were destroyed even though they were "one of a kind" and indispensable to present day investigations on discrepancy. They were destroyed even though the U.S. ambassador to Thailand at the time, David Lambertson, formally objected to the use of his mission and its shredder for this purpose. They were destroyed even though an executive order had been issued declassifying these and other documents and despite the fact that they had been subpoenaed by the Senate Select Committee on POW-MIA Affairs.

When the chairman of the Joint Chiefs of Staff, Gen. Colin Powell, ordered an investigation of this action, Adm. Larson's inspector general whitewashed the affair, claiming it involved nothing more than the "routine shredding of duplicate documents." In fact, an internal review subsequently determined that at least 119 reports were now missing after CINCPAC dispatched personnel to Washington and Bangkok to try to locate their so-called "duplicates."

The Senate Armed Services Committee will shortly have an opportunity to review the Clinton selection of Adm. Larson to serve as a role model for young military leaders and to guide the Naval Academy out of the morass of dishonor into which it has recently stumbled. The present cheating debacle at the Naval Academy is likely to prove but a foretaste of worse crises in the U.S. armed forces if a man like Adm. Larson is not held accountable for his own record of duplicity.

One would think that, if a picture is worth a thousand words, 2,000 photos recently displayed at a national convention in Crystal City should be worth 2 million words. In fact, these pictures should translate into much more than a voluminous book's worth of wordage. They should clear the way for a final, honest accounting of what happened to the hundreds of men left behind at the end of the Vietnam War.

The photographs, which were presented publicly for the first time at the annual Washington meeting of the National Alliance of POW-MIA Families, were taken more than 20 years ago by the North Vietnamese army and news agency. They show American prisoners of war, aircraft crash sites and pilot identification cards.

Some of the subjects are among those prisoners who returned at the end of the war. But many others are servicemen - photographed alive or dead - who are still officially considered "unaccounted for."

Incredibly, these materials were secretly withheld from the public - including family members of some of those servicemen appearing in these photographs who claim the U.S. government had not previously informed them about the existence of these photos, even though the Defense Department now acknowledges having them for more than two years. The National Alliance obtained these formerly "TOP SECRET" photos from a former agent of the Defense Intelligence Agency.

The explanation for this stunning withholding of information relevant to the POW-MIA issue may lie in the fact that these photos represent damning new evidence of the extent to which the American and Vietnamese governments have covered up critical information on missing U.S. servicemen. Among other things, they document the great lengths to which North Vietnam went to document its inventory of captured or dead American prisoners and their equipment – to the point of labeling and warehousing prisoners' uniforms, flight helmets and aircraft identification numbers.

In addition, hundreds of pilot identification cards - including those of men still listed as missing - are shown in pristine condition. There are also photos depicting Vietnamese searching through crash sites together with Soviet bloc advisers, indicating there is much more information in Hanoi and Moscow that can and must be made public.

Importantly, these photos also appear to put to rest several, long-disputed issues:

- Some American servicemen officially listed as missing in the Vietnam conflict were captured alive. Consequently, it is no longer possible to accept Hanoi's excuses - or those of its apologists - to the effect that it has no knowledge of the fate of these individuals.

- American servicemen listed as missing or deceased "with body unrecoverable, " were at one point in the hands of Vietnamese and Soviet bloc officials. The remains of such servicemen can no longer be considered irretrievably lost.

- The Vietnamese government was meticulous in its record-keeping about captured or deceased American pilots. Claims that Hanoi has been fully forthcoming with what little documentation it had concerning U.S. POW-MIAs - or, alternatively, that worm- or water-damage or carelessness resulted in everything else being lost - should be seen for what they are: part of a long-running, cynical manipulation of such information by Vietnam.

- Vietnamese excavation teams examined downed aircraft even in extremely remote areas. This proves that most crash sites - now being excavated by joint American and Vietnamese military teams at great cost to U.S. taxpayers – were scoured during the war and any prisoners, or their bodies, were removed long ago. Consequently, the illusion of great cooperation from Hanoi in investigating these sites should cease to be a justification for further steps toward normalizing bilateral relations.

- The U.S. government has still not come clean about all that it knows concerning our unaccounted for servicemen. Notwithstanding its professed commitment to declassify all relevant information, the Clinton team appears to be continuing the practice of past U.S. administrations in resisting full disclosure, for example, of electronic intercepts that support the National Alliance's photo collection on two points: (1) American servicemen were abandoned in Vietnam at the war's end and (2) that fact was assiduously covered up in the years since. And Clinton personnel choices make an early end to the cover-up unlikely: a virulent anti-war activist, Charles Searcy, was the president's choice to run POW-MIA affairs at the Pentagon, and the most respected field investigator, Garnett Bell, was replaced by young officers who have no background in the issue or in Southeast Asia.

Addressing the questions raised by Hanoi's photographs should be the sole focus of meetings like that between Secretary of State Warren Christopher and his Vietnamese counterpart in Bangkok this month. This effort should be accompanied by a new and independent evaluation of all available information related to the missing Americans. Clearly, unless and until Hanoi and Washington are fully forthcoming, there must be no further progress toward establishing full diplomatic and economic relations with communist Vietnam.

At a minimum, the National Alliance's photo exhibit ought to be displayed in the House and Senate office buildings, where it would be readily accessible to members of Congress, journalists and the public at large. It is especially important that this reminder of unfinished business be kept squarely in mind as President Clinton puts a new generation of Americans in uniform at risk of a similar fate in places like Bosnia, Haiti and the Golan Heights.

Last Sunday marked more than just the 20th anniversary of the United States' humiliating abandonment of an ally to hard-line Vietnamese communists that America had tired of fighting. It also served as the focus of a concerted effort to complete our capitulation by normalizing relations with the victors on their terms. Should we do so, we risk losing the Vietnam War twice.

That conclusion, of course, runs counter to the arguments - some overt, some implied - being advanced by those urging the formal re-establishment of diplomatic ties with Vietnam so as to permit the use of U.S. taxpayers in underwriting investments there. Such steps would, we are told, heal the wounds on the home front. (The depths of those wounds have been much in evidence as former Defense Secretary Robert McNamara has relentlessly hawked his memoirs via every imaginable media outlet.)

For some who opposed U.S. involvement in the Vietnam War at the time, this step is the ultimate acknowledgment of America's wrongdoing, a long overdue reparation. For others, it is portrayed as a move that will actually enable the capitalist United States to triumph over the communist Vietnamese by consolidating their society's conversion to entrepreneurism and consumerism.

Shouldn't we just declare the war "over" - as Sen. John McCain and others have repeatedly urged in recent days -and allow American businesses to cash in? For several reasons, the answer is "No":

- Why we were in Vietnam: The most painful aspect of the McNamara book is the extent to which it demeans the sacrifice of those who fought and were killed or wounded in Vietnam. In claiming he knew at the time the war was unwinnable and should not have been waged, the former defense secretary makes patsies of those who answered the call when told their country needed them to protect freedom and democracy against communist aggression in Indochina. While in April 1975, we elected as a nation to stop resisting that aggression physically on the ground, we chose to keep faith with those who had made the ultimate sacrifice for these objectives by continuing to resist its perpetrators through an economic embargo and non-recognition.

President Clinton earlier ended the embargo without insisting that Hanoi allow its people free and fair elections, a free press, freedom of religion or any other basic liberties. Were he now to move toward the unconditional normalization of relations, he would not be aiding the "healing" process. Instead, he will be pouring salt in the wounds reopened by Robert McNamara and demeaning afresh those tens of thousands of Americans who suffered and died for the Vietnamese people.

- We must not legitimate a brutal communist regime: Try as some might to romanticize Hanoi's conduct in the Vietnam War as a campaign of national liberation, it is hard with 20 years of hindsight to ignore reality: The communists brutally subjugated the people of South Vietnam by force, violating international agreements in the process. They have made systematic use of barbaric "re-education camps" to incarcerate and, in many cases, dispose of South Vietnamese who erred in being friends of the United States. Their reign of terror has sent tens of thousands into exile or to their deaths on the high seas and continues to suppress dissent. It is morally repugnant to contemplate the U.S. Treasury rewarding the perpetrators for these crimes with economic assistance and investment.

- Exploitation is neither in the United States' interest nor the Vietnamese people's: It is true that, like China before it, Vietnam is today experimenting with economic liberalization. In so doing, Hanoi is making the same gamble as Beijing: Despite long-cherished Marxian beliefs about "economic determinism," the communist power structure is betting that it can open up the economy to capitalism without jeopardizing its authoritarian hold on the society. The jury is still out in both countries as to whether Western economic engagement will, over time, make such an arrangement unsustainable or whether it will simply serve to perpetuate odious regimes.

  In the short term, however, American companies doing business in Vietnam are more likely to help prop up the repressive old order than to assure its downfall. Worse yet, by joining in the exploitation of cheap Vietnamese labor for manufacturing and assembling jobs, they will be contributing to the further hemorrhage of such employment opportunities from the United States. Is that really what American tax dollars should be used to encourage?

- There has been no full accounting - and won't be under communist Vietnam: There is ample evidence that both the Vietnamese and U.S. governments have more information about U.S. POW/ MIAs than has been made public to date. A few days in Hanoi's archives would almost certainly provide more information about the fate of missing Americans than have all the field searches and parlays that have taken place over the past decade, at a cost of many millions of dollars. The missing servicemen and their loved ones are entitled to a full accounting and better treatment from those who view their suffering as but an intolerable impediment to normalization.

Mr. McCain has argued that President Clinton should take this step now, before the issue becomes ensnarled in election-year politics. Mr. McCain is one of Sen. Phil Gramm's closest friends and advisers; he certainly knows the political season is already well under way. The question really is: Will Mr. Gramm - and his rivals for the Republican nomination - endorse Mr. McCain's stance? Or will they try to ensure that the United States does not lose the Vietnam War twice by insisting on real political reform as well as economic liberalization as the price for normalized relations with Hanoi?

The Grid/EMP

Despite its inherent illogic, the notion that last week's massive, cascading electrical blackout was a "wake-up" call seems now to have become as much a part of the political landscape as has the effort to assign blame for this costly man-made disaster. The question occurs, however: To what exactly is it that we have awakened?

The obvious answer is that there is an acute and long-neglected need to upgrade the nation's power grid. Since Thursday's crisis, much of the finger-pointing has been about who saw this need most clearly and how many years ago and who was most responsible for so little being done about it. Let us stipulate that there is enough blame to go around and that a concerted, multi-year [if not multi-decade] and bipartisan effort is going to be required to modernize the Niagara Falls grid and the rest of the U.S. electrical infrastructure.

This is, of course, much easier said than done. The costs associated with such an initiative have been estimated to start at nearly $60 billion. A federal government in deficit is reluctant to strap on such an expenditure; energy companies will surely pass their share on to consumers. Critics of the U.S. liberation of Iraq have, predictably, seized already on the irony that U.S. tax-dollars are restoring and upgrading the Iraqi electrical system when they could, and it is argued should, be spent on doing the same for ours.

In the final analysis, we will pay as a nation - one way or the other – what has to be paid in order to try to prevent a repetition of the calamitous blackout of 2003. This will become ever more self-evident as the American and Canadian costs associated with that power disruption are tallied and the need to avoid its recurrence is seen to be an absolute economic, as well as political, necessity.

The second thing to which we better have awakened is the possibility that was on everyone's mind as the lights went out across much of the northern tier of the United States and Canada's most populous cities: Could terrorists have perpetrated this disaster? And, if so, was the blackout but the first blow in a lethal one-two punch?

The good news is that this episode apparently was not the work of Osama bin Laden or his ilk. The bad news is that, given the extensive vulnerabilities of the U.S. power grid - for example, the vast numbers of unguarded power-line towers that snake across the landscape - it has only been a matter of time before someone decided to exploit them. And, having witnessed over the past few days what the immensely destructive effect of even minor disruptions of that system could be, is there any doubt that from now on the terrorists' target lists will surely include attacks on our critical infrastructure?

To make matters worse, those attacks need not be in a physical form.

Computers whose second-by-second control of the distribution flow of electricity has been shown to be indispensable to the grid's functioning can also be subjected to "cyber warfare." Unfortunately, the same is true of other parts of our critical infrastructure. Even if the power didn't go off, water and sewage systems, gas pipelines, transportation, telecommunications and so on could also be targeted and seriously disrupted.

We had better be awakened, though, to one other, particularly ominous prospect: Determined terrorists could inflict lasting, if not actually permanent, damage on the United States' electrical and other computer-based systems by employing small nuclear or non-nuclear devices that generate what is known as electro-magnetic pulse [EMP]. The short, intense spike of energy that these EMP weapons create can do irreparable harm to electronic devices [even those not in use, such as replacement microcircuits, chips and memory boards in warehouses] unless expensive measures have been taken to shield them. It is believed that human beings and other forms of life would not be directly harmed by such a burst of EMP.

No one can say with certainty at the moment how devastating or widespread the effects of an EMP strike might be. The U.S. military, which used to pay serious attention to the question, largely stopped doing so after a moratorium was imposed in 1992 on all nuclear testing [including that done for EMP effects]. Since then, the vulnerability of the armed forces' satellites, communications gear and other hardware has become largely a matter of conjecture, if it is addressed at all.

Matters are infinitely worse with respect to civilian electronic equipment, essentially none of which was designed with the costly features that would protect against EMP. Today, the best that can be said is that the extent and duration of future EMP-induced blackouts would depend on whether the emitter generates a small or large pulse, and whether it is detonated at ground level or from high altitudes. Under a worst-case - but not implausible - scenario, a large, ballistic missile-delivered EMP weapon could within seconds reduce half the country to pre-industrial age conditions for many months, if not years.

Thanks to the tenacity of one of Capitol Hill's few bona fide scientists, Rep. Roscoe Bartlett, Maryland Republican, who has long warned of the EMP threat, a blue-ribbon commission led by President Reagan's science adviser, William Graham, is now conducting a congressionally mandated study to assess this danger. If anything, the recent grid failure adds urgency to the completion of the Graham Commission's work.

As the nation rouses itself to address the lessons learned from last week's blackout, it better focus not only on how to avoid a repetition but also on a possibly vastly more serious blackout next time.

Statements out of North Korea and Iran last week confront the United States and other freedom-loving nations with a frightening prospect: Two of the world's most dangerous regimes are determined to wield nuclear weapons.

North Korea's claim to have "nukes" followed an Iranian mullahocracy announcement nothing will prevent its achieving nuclear goals. Should we worry? The short answer: Absolutely.

After all, the state policy of these two governments is hatred of America. Nuclear weapons in the hands of megalomaniacal tyrannies animated by this hatred and armed with ballistic missiles poses a unique - and intolerable - threat.

The danger is not simply the prospect one or more rogue states' nuclear weapons could be used to destroy an American city - or perhaps an allied capital in the Middle East or Europe. Such an attack could be conducted by other means, with more prosaic means of delivery such as trucks, ships or aircraft.

A blue ribbon, congressionally mandated commission recently described an altogether different sort of nuclear attack, one made possible by the detonation high above the United States of a ballistic missile-delivered weapon. The panel was charged with "assessing the threat to the United States from an electromagnetic pulse (EMP) attack."

It concluded the EMP effects of such an attack at 40 to 400 miles above this country could so severely disrupt, both directly and indirectly, electronics and electrical systems as to create a "damage level ... sufficient to be catastrophic to the nation." Worse, the commission concluded "our current vulnerability invites attack."

The EMP Threat Commission recommends urgent steps taken to reduce that vulnerability by protecting electrical, water, telecommunications and other infrastructures against crippling by electromagnetic pulse. The same needs to be done with our military, also woefully unprepared for EMP attack.

Failure to take such steps could mean a single North Korean or Iranian missile, possibly launched from a ship off the U.S. coast, could instantly transform this country from an advanced 21st century to an 18th-century society. It is hard to imagine a more devastating form of terror than that entailed in the dislocation, hardship and destruction that would accompany an America returned to a pre-industrial state - but with its population crowded into cities that could not function and with a military unable to protect us or to maintain order.

We are very acutely vulnerable to EMP attack because we largely stopped worrying about it 13 years ago. In 1992, the United States adopted a moratorium on nuclear testing, thus precluding the most rigorous and reliable way to determine electronic systems' susceptibility to electromagnetic effects.

Forgoing such has also been very deleterious to our nuclear deterrent. For example, we no longer can be certain the weapons in our arsenal will work as they should. We are reduced to relying on what amounts to informed scientific guesswork based on computer simulations. Guesses are no substitute for certainty in such life-and-death matters.

One thing is certain: Our stockpile is not as safe and reliable as we could make it. Without realistic testing, we can only make changes in the components or designs of existing weapons at the risk of degrading our confidence they will work.

Moreover, we are unable to introduce new designs better suited to countering threats posed by the likes of Iran and North Korea than are the hugely destructive weapons developed more than 20 years ago to counter targets in the Soviet Union.

Worst of all, these costs have been incurred for no good reason. Neither North Korea nor Iran have, as far as we know, conducted nuclear tests on their way to joining the "nuclear club." Consequently, it is now indisputable that the United States' forswearing underground testing has not had the promised effect - impeding proliferation.

In an important analysis published recently by the Center for Security Policy, retired Navy Vice Adm. Robert Monroe, a former director of the Defense Nuclear Agency, argues persuasively that to have any hope of preventing proliferation in the future, the United States must maintain a credible nuclear deterrent - and undertake the associated testing, developmental and industrial actions.

Finally, notwithstanding the latest setback in testing the nation's preliminary anti-missile defense system, the perfecting and fielding of such capabilities must continue - and be expanded to include sea-, air- and space-based assets.

An EMP threat is hardly the only reason to ensure ballistic missiles cannot be used to harm this country, but it is particularly compelling.

In the end, only regime change in Iran and North Korea is likely to diminish the threat from these nations. We had better do everything possible to encourage such an outcome.

Meanwhile, it would be irresponsible to invite EMP-induced disaster by remaining unable either to defend against or deter such an attack and its effects.

Amidst all the congressional to-ing and fro-ing associated with the President's controversial health care, cap-and-trade and "hate crimes" initiatives, it would be easy for most legislators to overlook a hearing the House Homeland Security Committee has scheduled for Tuesday afternoon. If Congress fails to address the subject of that hearing, however, it literally will not matter whether the government addresses any of those other, disproportionately prominent agenda items.

The title of the hearing - "Securing the Modern Electric Grid from Physical and Cyber Attacks" - fails to communicate the magnitude of the danger, and the imperative for urgent corrective action. One thing is sure, though: By the time the lead-off witness, Dr. William Graham, is finished testifying, no one present will be under any illusion on either score.

Dr. Graham formerly served as President Reagan's Science Advisor and has in recent years chaired the congressionally mandated Commission to Assess the Threat to the United States from Electromagnetic Pulse (better known as the EMP Commission). This panel, made up of many of the nation's most experienced and eminent scientists, has produced several reports that should have jarred our leaders into action on the EMP threat long before now.

After all, the Commission has concluded that the present electric grid is profoundly vulnerable to massive surges of electromagnetic energy. It has summed up the magnitude of the problem such surges could cause to the United States with a single, shocking word: "Catastrophic."

This prospect arises from the fact that today's electrical infrastructure has not been "hardened" to make it more resilient against EMP effects. Thus, if key components of the grid were to be subjected to one or more pulses of electromagnetic energy, the EMP Commission concluded that at least some of them would be susceptible to extensive damage or destruction.

Catastrophe would ensue as a result of the ripple effect that would occur as widespread disruptions occur in the supply of electrical power to other infrastructures that depend on it to operate. For example, food distribution, transportation, telecommunications, medical services and access to clean water and management of sewage would be among those affected almost immediately and for long periods of time.

Matters would be made worse by the likelihood that electronic devices so integral to modern life would also be damaged or destroyed, making reconstitution of the status quo ante profoundly problematic even if, somehow, power could be rapidly restored. And, under present circumstances at least, that won't happen.

The EMP Commission has warned that the cumulative effect of such disruptions would be to transform almost immediately our 21st Century superpower into a preindustrial nation, unable to provide for its own people let alone afford security to others. Dr. Graham estimates that within a year, nine out of ten Americans would be dead, as the population returns to what can be sustained by a subsistence society.

The Homeland Security Committee will hear tomorrow that this unimaginable horror can be triggered by a scenario examined at length by the Commission on the EMP Threat - namely, a ship-launched, ballistic missile-delivered nuclear weapon detonated outside the atmosphere high above the United States. Russia and China already have the capability to engage in such attacks. The North Koreans and Iranians are busily trying to acquire it. Despite this reality, opponents of missile defenses that could prevent such an attack have downplayed the associated risk, and thereby contributed to the perpetuation of our present vulnerability.

It turns out that EMP can also be inflicted by the sun. The last time a "great geomagnetic storm" unleashed such energy on the earth (thereafter known as a Carrington Event for the British scientist who first detected it) was September 1, 1859. A NASA release issued in May, described how the solar flare "electrified transmission cables, set fires in telegraph offices, and produced Northern Lights so bright that people could read newspapers by their red and green glow."

At the time, of course, America was not today's massively wired and electricity-dependent nation. The NASA paper went on to note that, "A recent report by the National Academy of Sciences found that if a similar storm occurred today, it could cause $1 to 2 trillion in damages to society's high-tech infrastructure and require four to ten years for complete recovery." According to NASA, such a storm will happen - possibly as soon as May 2013.

The Homeland Security Committee hearing will take testimony that makes plain one other frightening reality: Unfortunately, our unrobust electrical infrastructure is also vulnerable to non-EMP disruptions. Cyber warfare has already been unleashed on the computers that form the central nervous system of today's grid. To date, the effect has been a nuisance. If we don't take corrective action, cyber attacks in the future could be as devastating as the "man-caused disaster" of an EMP attack or the naturally occurring variant.

The good news, as the Committee will also establish, is that billions of dollars have been allocated in the economic stimulus bill for upgrading the grid. Doing so in a way that builds in the sort of resiliency to EMP and cyber warfare that we so clearly need is a no-brainer and should be eminently doable, provided appropriate priority is assigned to that use of the already appropriated funds. The alternative is an absolutely predictable - and avoidable - catastrophe

With hurricane season upon us once again, the recent anniversary of one of the most deadly and destructive in our nation's history - the mega-storm called Katrina - was an occasion for remembering what can happen if we are unprepared. Unfortunately, what was arguably the most important lesson of that hurricane has still not been addressed: the truly catastrophic vulnerability of all of the infrastructures upon which our society critically depends to interruptions of the electrical grid.

Worse yet, there are both looming man-induced *and* far more devastating natural means of precipitating such interruptions that we have not begun to address. Should these eventuate, the aftermath of Hurricane Katrina will look like, well, a day at the beach. It is no exaggeration to say that the effect of one or the other of these assaults on our electrical grid could be to engender what Iran's President Mahmoud Ahmadinejad has called "a world without America."

As Katrina demonstrated, if the electricity goes off for any protracted period of time, there is a cascading ripple-effect which takes down the means by which we communicate, get food and water, access financial resources, receive medical services, dispose of sewage and move from one location to another. The longer the time without electricity, the more difficult it is to bring such other infrastructures back on line. As the news reports marking the occasion of Katrina's landfall have made clear, some of the areas that received the brunt of that storm are still not fully back to their pre-hurricane condition.

Should some of the roughly 300 transformers that are the backbone of our electrical grid be damaged or destroyed, the interruption to the electrical grid will not be brief. Today, we have few back-ups in place. These large and complex pieces of equipment are all produced overseas and it takes at least a year to take delivery of even one, let alone many.

Dr. William Graham, President Reagan's Science Advisor, estimates that, if the electricity is off in large sections of America (far more than the relatively small part of the country afflicted by Katrina) for as long as a year, the effect will not simply be on the quality of life here. He says as many as nine out of ten of our men, women and children will die from starvation, disease and/or exposure.

Dr. Graham knows whereof he speaks. He has served for years as the chairman of a congressionally empanelled commission made up of many of the most knowledgeable scientists in the United States. Their job has been to examine in detail a phenomenon known as electro-magnetic pulse (EMP) that could be used by our enemies like Iran to effect such devastation.

The Graham panel has come to be known as the EMP Threat Commission and it has developed a particularly worrisome scenario. A non-descript freighter off one of our coasts could launch with no warning a relatively short-range ballistic missile. If that missile were armed with even a relatively small and crude nuclear weapon and that warhead were detonated in space high over the United States, it would unleash large quantities of gamma rays.

As those rays interact with the upper atmosphere, the effect would be to create an immense burst of electromagnetic energy. Any electrical or electronic device - including the grid's transformers - not shielded against this pulse would be, at best, taken temporarily off-line. More likely, they will be made permanently unusable.

It turns out, however, that other assaults on our grid might have a similar effect:

- Radio-frequency weapons could be used to go after critical nodes of the electrical infrastructure in a more tactical way.

- Cyber-warfare has increasingly been waged against the computers that control the grid and other vital parts of our economy's electronic underbelly. The perpetrators have not been positively identified, but those responsible for protecting against such cyber attacks suspect Chinese and Russian sources.

- Then there is the mother of all threats to the electrical grid: a naturally occurring phenomenon known as geomagnetic solar events. These intense solar flares were observed by a British scientist named Richard Carrington back in 1859 who correlated them as the cause of spontaneous combustion of telegraph wires and offices - the relatively tiny telecommunications infrastructure then-available to be disrupted. Scientists say we are overdue for another of these sorts of super solar storms. The destruction they could cause to the world's unprotected grids could run to the trillions of dollars to repair and the loss of countless lives.

The good news is that there are things that can be done to make our electrical infrastructure less vulnerable to these sorts of Katrina-on-steroids assaults. That is especially true now, as the stimulus package enacted earlier this year this year makes billions of dollars available to effect long-overdue and much-needed upgrades in the U.S. grid. The question is: Will we take those steps in time, *before* hostile forces or further natural phenomena devastate this country?

This week a large number of Americans determined to take such preventive action now are convening in Niagara Falls, New York - a community that knows something about hydro-electric power and its importance for the country. This meeting will be the first-of-its-kind on this subject, a large conference open to the public and aimed at educating the rest of us about these threats, and *impelling* the adoption of prophylactic measures.

Presentations will be made by Newt Gingrich and several key serving legislators, as well as many of the country's most knowledgeable scientists, security policy experts and industry leaders. Organized by a new group, EMPAct America (www.empactamerica.net), this meeting represents the best opportunity to date to translate the warnings of the EMP Threat Commission into action.

The time has come to do just that.

In 1987, Ronald Reagan mused that, if the world were about to be devastated by an alien force – perhaps a collision with a large asteroid, peoples of all nations, ideological persuasions and political parties would come together to save the planet and our civilization. We may be about to test that proposition.

At the moment, no asteroid is known to be hurtling our way. But a naturally occurring phenomenon is, one that may be as fatal for modern industrial societies and for the quality of life they have made possible – thanks principally to electrification. The technical term for this threat is geomagnetically induced currents (GMIC) generated by the coronal mass ejections (CMEs) that laymen call solar eruptions or flaring.

Think of it as "space weather." And there is a strong possibility that some of the heaviest such weather in hundreds of years is headed our way.

GMIC engenders intense bursts of electromagnetic energy. No fewer than five studies mandated by the executive or legislative branches have confirmed that such electromagnetic pulse (EMP) is lethal for the electronic devices, computers and transformers that power everything in our 21st Century society. Since these things are generally unprotected against EMP – whether naturally occurring or man-induced, they would almost certainly be damaged or destroyed. The U.S. electrical grid could, as a result, be down for many months, and probably years.

We know that this EMP-precipitated effect could also be achieved by the detonation of a nuclear weapon high over the United States. And actual or potential enemies of this country – notably Russia, China, North Korea and Iran – understand our acute vulnerability in this area, and have taken steps to exploit it.

"Catastrophic" is a term often used to describe the repercussions for our country of the cascading shut-down, first of the key elements of the grid, then inexorably, all of the electricity-dependent infrastructures that make possible life as we know it in this country. That would include those that enable: access to and distribution of food, water, fuel and heat; telecommunications; finance; transportation; sewage treatment and cooling of nuclear power plants.

President Reagan's Science Advisor, Dr. William Graham, who chaired a blue-ribbon congressional commission on the EMP threat, has calculated that within a year of the U.S. electrical grid being devastated by such a phenomenon, nine out of ten Americans would be dead.

Did that get your attention? Or, as Dirty Harry would say, do you feel lucky?

Unfortunately, – any more than we could if we knew an asteroid were headed our way. Persisting in our present state of vulnerability is an invitation to disaster, if not at the hands of some foe, then as a result of the cycle of intense solar storms in which we now find ourselves.

The good news is that there are practical and affordable steps we can take to mitigate these threats, if only we have the will and the wit to adopt them *before* we are hit by heavy space weather or its man-caused counterpart.

The present danger and our options for defending against it will be the subject of an extraordinary conference in Washington this week: the Electric Infrastructure Security Summit. Many of the nation's foremost authorities on EMP will participate, including: bipartisan champions of this issue in Congress; nuclear physicists and other experts; executive branch officials from the Federal Electric Regulatory Commission (FERC) and Department of Homeland Security; and representatives from the quasi-governmental North American Electric Reliability Corporation (NERC) and from the utilities industry.

The single biggest challenge to date has been the lack of public awareness of the EMP peril. This is particularly ironic since a television program envisioning life in America after the lights go out, NBC's "Revolution," has been quite popular. But most viewers seem to think the precipitating event is the stuff of science fiction. An intensive effort is needed now to disabuse them of this comforting, but unfounded notion, and to enlist them in the corrective actions that are necessary on an urgent, bipartisan and nation-wide basis.

To that end, some discernible progress is being made. For example, on May 16th, at the instigation of Federal Energy Regulatory Commissioner Cheryl LaFleur, the FERC issued a final rule that, in the words of the trade publication *Power Magazine*, "orders the North American Electric Reliability Corporation to develop, by the end of the year, reliability standards that address the impact of geomagnetic disturbances (GMD) on the nation's bulk power system."

The Maine state legislature is poised to adopt legislation that would require the FERC to submit a plan by the end of June to insulate Maine's grid from that of the rest of the Northeastern states and harden it against EMP. This measure could serve as model for similar state-level initiatives elsewhere and help catalyze counterpart legislation at the federal level along the lines of that introduced in the last session of Congress by Representatives Trent Franks (R-AZ) and Yvette Clarke (D-NY), dubbed the Secure High-voltage Infrastructure for Electricity from Lethal Damage (SHIELD) Act.

Important and necessary as these measures are, they are not sufficient to contend fully with the urgent threat our country is now facing. We are on a collision course for catastrophe of a magnitude, if not exactly of a kind, with that that could be inflicted by the kind of dangerous asteroid President Reagan envisioned decades ago. There is simply no time to waste in joining forces and implementing the steps needed to ensure we are not counting on luck to keep America's lights on.

SPEAKING TRUTH TO POWER

Over the years of these columns, I had the opportunity to observe, analyze and critique the national security policies of presidencies and Congresses of differing political stripes. I brought to the task a conservative perspective, but one born of my experience working for both Democratic and Republican bosses.

That service in the Reagan administration under Secretary of Defense Caspar Weinberger and previously on Capitol Hill with Scoop Jackson and John Tower on Capitol Hill was extraordinarily valuable. It gave me both substantive knowledge and experience, as well as sources of information and insights into the bureaucratic politics and decision-making processes at work in the executive and legislation branches. And, not least, generally strong opinions about their results. It was a joy, and highly therapeutic, to be able to give expression each week to my frustrations and recommended alternatives.

Some columns had the desired effect of getting inside the official decision-loop by exposing mischief afoot and, thereby, helping those inside the government or outside who were trying to prevent it from occurring. In other cases, I was able to support initiatives that either had not yet come to light or which were just being unveiled, and successfully encouraged their adoption.

Of course, there was more of the former and less of the latter in some administrations than others.

George H. W. Bush's presidency, while nominally the successor to President Reagan's, was populated and guided by those who considered "stability" and "world order" to be their principal priorities. As a general rule, they wanted no part of the sort of foreign policy activism that their predecessors engaged in pursuant to, for example, National Security Decision Directive 75 – the Reagan strategy for defeating Soviet communism and destroying the "Evil Empire" rooted in that ideology.

Even when Bush '41 did act robustly to address international challenges, it was often couched in hoary notions of "legitimacy" that had to be conferred by the United Nations, cautiousness and, to the point of parody, "prudence" that squandered opportunities for historic change – with consequences still playing out today.

A case in point, in my view, was Bush '41's failure to liberate Saddam Hussein's Iraq when he had 500,000 well-armed and well-led troops in theater. Such a force could have decisively effected the sort of regime change that would have spared the Iraqi people and the world the thirteen-year binge of domestic repression, corruption and support for terrorism that were the hallmarks of Saddam's tenure and that proved so corrosive internationally.

Bill Clinton's administration drew on individuals and policy philosophies that were considerably more problematic. His personnel choices, arms control initiatives, wholesale dismantling of our technology control arrangements, diversion of resources needed to maintain and improve the military to pay for social spending and balance the federal budget and his failure to address emerging threats in a timely and appropriate way provided much grist for my mill.

I am gratified to say that my columns helped prevent several of President Clinton's more disastrous appointments, exposed and thereby contributed to the defeat of some of his more ill-advised initiatives (notably, the Comprehensive Test Ban Treaty) and were unmistakably a thorn in the Clinton team's side.

To my pleasant surprise, President George W. Bush enlisted for senior positions on his national security team a number of my friends and colleagues – an early indication that he would not be following in his father's "establishment" policy approach. To his great credit, Bush '43 took a number of controversial steps that I considered absolutely essential to America's long-term security. For example, he withdrew from the 1972 Anti-Ballistic Missile Treaty, endorsed a plan for preserving and enhancing our nuclear deterrent and forcibly removed Saddam from power.

Unfortunately, in each of these initiatives, the follow-up left much to be desired. The United States still lacks a robust national missile defense system. Despite a good plan for preserving our deterrent, America's nuclear weapons were neither tested nor appreciably improved during the George W. Bush years. And the decision to occupy and nation-build in Iraq rather than swiftly turn it over to friendly forces and use our victory there to bring about regime change in neighboring Iran were, in my estimation, strategic mistakes of the first order.

The presidency of Barack Obama has been an unmitigated disaster. To a degree that far surpasses the ideologically driven agenda of the Clinton administration and any missteps made during either of the Bush presidents' years in the White House, we are witnessing an assault on the Constitution, an erosion of American power and prestige and escalating threats that, taken together, are fulfilling the President's pre-election promise to "fundamentally transform the United States of America."

For a national security-minded columnist, the incumbent administration has been the gift that keeps on giving. I came up with a nine-word description of the Obama Doctrine: "Embolden our enemies. Undermine our friends. Diminish our country." President Obama's relentless pursuit – whether deliberately and consciously (as I believe) or *inadvertently (as some insist who think incompetence is a more accurate explanation than deliberate malfeasance) – of these priorities has ensured that there is no lack of subject matter for my weekly output. To the contrary, most weeks it was a question of which travesty was most in need of a scathing commentary.*

The selection of columns for this section of Securing Freedom is, frankly, somewhat arbitrary. I made a point of speaking truth to power in virtually every one of those that appear elsewhere in this volume under specific topic headings. For that matter, it was the case in the thousand or so other columns that didn't make the cut.

The following columns, however, strike me as worthy of note as they address – usually critically – the broader character and direction of the four presidencies that were so often my inspiration over these twenty-five years. They also offer, at least implicitly, a set of do's and don't's that we must pray our next president follows to restore America to the posture of strength, leadership and international respect (or fear) required for our security in these perilous times.

George H.W. Bush

For many, the defining moment - and nadir - of the Bush presidency was the point last summer when George Bush abandoned his pledge against raising taxes.

The public, which had given him unprecedented popularity ratings up to that point, has indicated a marked loss of confidence in the president ever since. As a consequence, the Republican Party suffered at the polls in November, not the least in terms of missed shots at weak Democratic candidates suddenly insulated from their challengers' anti-tax assaults by none other than the president himself.

In the wake of this incident, and the fiasco over the federal budget deficit of which it was a part, the president let it be known that he distinctly preferred foreign affairs over the bump-and-grind of domestic policy. As much as he likes Dan Rostenkowski personally, he revealed dealing with the Democratic chairman of the House Ways and Means Committee and other congressional figures was less fun than conducting international relations.

The implication of this statement was that the president can be his own man in foreign policy matters to an extent not possible in the domestic arena. He can set a principled course and stick to it. Put more colloquially, Mr. Bush seemed to be saying that his lips could be read with confidence in foreign policy matters - even if that was not the case with domestic politics.

Unfortunately, the record of the Bush administration - particularly in recent months - suggests that the same cynical, opportunistic approach that is now widely perceived to be the hallmark of its approach to the political agenda at home also is at work in U.S. foreign relations. Consider but a few recent examples:

* After firmly denying that he would contemplate a direct dialogue with Saddam Hussein - perpetrator of brutal aggression and holder of hostages - Mr. Bush decided last week to exchange high-level emissaries with the Iraqi despot.

Some administration officials downplay the significance of this departure from the president's previous stance, saying that it amounts to nothing more than a formality. They attempt to put the best face on it by suggesting that these meetings in Washington and Baghdad are simply designed to clear the way for the military option, aimed at denying critics of that option grounds for claiming that avenues for a peaceful solution to the crisis remain to be explored.

Unfortunately, like most such shenanigans, this one is probably too clever by half. The practical effect of this presidential initiative will likely be to embolden Mr. Hussein and encumber the use of force sufficiently to preclude such a course of action.

At the very least, it will inflame growing congressional and public opposition to the military option and encourage already skittish allies in the anti-Iraq coalition to regard Mr. Hussein as a probable survivor of - if not the victor in - this crisis, a man with whom they would be well advised to come to terms as quickly as possible. Matters will become infinitely worse if, as seems predictable, current administration disavowals of any intention to bring the Palestinian question into the dialogue also prove insincere.

- In connection with his summit meeting with Mikhail Gorbachev last May, Mr. Bush made it clear that he viewed the Soviet parliament's enactment of legislation guaranteeing free emigration and an end to Moscow's oppression of Lithuania as necessary preconditions for a waiver of the Jackson-Vanik amendment.

- At his press conference on Nov. 30, however, Mr. Bush signaled that he was considering granting the Soviets a waiver - even though such conditions have yet to be satisfied. In fact, the promised emigration legislation is going nowhere in the Soviet parliament and a crackdown looms in the Baltic states and elsewhere in the Soviet Union, conditions that are, in all likelihood, made more certain by the president's new-found willingness to look the other way.

- In so doing, Mr. Bush also suggests a desire to clear the way for implementation of the new U.S.-Soviet trade agreement and granting to Moscow of U.S. government credits and guarantees - despite his statements of last July that such U.S. taxpayer liabilities were ill advised in the absence of genuine, structural reforms in the Soviet Union. Even as the wisdom of not exposing the federal deficit to still more losses associated with lending to an unreformed Soviet Union are becoming ever more obvious, Mr. Bush appears once again blithely to have abandoned his earlier, responsible stance.

- The president had the audacity to contend as he met with the Chinese foreign minister in the White House last week that such a session did not breach his directive against senior-level contacts with the regime responsible for the Tiananmen Square massacre. Such a preposterous statement could only lead the butchers of Beijing to assume that Mr. Bush is no more serious when he warns that stepped-up repression now occurring in China might harm U.S.-Chinese ties.

These steps, and others like them, fundamentally debase the value of the president's word in international affairs. By calling into question the dependability of the United States in this way, however, Mr. Bush does far more than simply lower his popularity rating and impair his prospects for re-election, as he does in his flip-flops on domestic policy.

By such self-initiated reversals of his stated positions, Mr. Bush seriously undercuts the nation's ability to play the role it must in global matters - the reliable friend of those seeking freedom, economic opportunity and safety from aggression.

Unfortunately, the resulting damage to U.S. interests will likely far outlast his tenure in the White House.

As the baseball season hurtles toward its exciting climax, millions of Americans wait breathlessly for those last three outs that will determine if their teams win pennants and shots at the World Series, or fade into autumn's oblivion like the also-rans from Mudville.

Such a backdrop may be a fitting one for the Bush administration, now reeling from two foreign policy fiascoes that, in hindsight, are nearly universally viewed as serious and avoidable strikes against its record. The first involved the miscalculation that Iraqi President Saddam Hussein was a man with whom the United States should do business. In due course, a policy initiated to prevent the perceived greater of two evils - Iran - from prevailing in its eight-year war with Iraq, became a formula for the present disaster in the Persian Gulf.

U.S. diplomats repeatedly kowtowed to the Iraqi despot, inevitably encouraging his expectation of American acquiescence to his regional aggression. Meanwhile, their counterparts at the Commerce Department actively pursued technology transfers that may have resulted in Mr. Hussein obtaining, according to one congressional subcommittee, "unrestricted access to nuclear, biological and missile technologies." At the same, the Agriculture Department was looking the other way on a scam that has resulted in hundreds of millions in American commodity credits being diverted by Baghdad to pay for arms.

The second strike against the Bush foreign policy team came with the decision not to act immediately and in concert with U.S. allies to deflate skyrocketing speculation on oil prices. Instead of announcing at the outset of the Persian Gulf crisis - as was done with decisive effect by the Reagan administration in the 1983-84 tanker war in the Gulf - that the United States, together with other Western nations, would tap oil stocks in the event of any disruption of oil supplies or price increases caused by speculators, the Texas oil men in the White House and the Departments of Energy and Commerce did nothing.

The damage of this grievous error - except to the Texan economy - has been compounded by the Bush administration's belated and unilateral decision last week to release unilaterally a trivial amount from the U.S. Strategic Petroleum Reserve. The United States now finds itself: confronted by a speculatively driven doubling of the price of oil; a market insensitive to its minor-league attempts to affect that price; and allies understandably reluctant to join in a broader effort to deflate the oil shock, given recent American arguments against doing just that!

My guess is that Mr. Bush's third foreign policy strike will come when the bankruptcy of his approach toward the Soviet Union becomes as apparent as is now the case with his administration's mismanagement of Mr. Hussein prior to the invasion of Kuwait and of oil prices in its aftermath.

With each passing day, the overinvestment of the president's political capital in Soviet President Mikhail Gorbachev - at the expense of developing strong ties with his democratic opposition - is a more transparent mistake. Likewise, the decisions to provide unprecedented levels of militarily relevant technology to Moscow, especially for its decrepit but strategic energy sector, are sure shortly to be seen as serious errors.

The same will certainly be true of flawed arms control agreements the administration is feverishly preparing with the Soviet Union. Haste in completing enormously complex accords affecting strategic and conventional arms is being justified by a bizarre logic: Because Mr. Gorbachev may not survive a military putsch, it is necessary while he remains in power to "nail down" treaties opposed by the Soviet armed forces. This is an exceedingly unsound basis for taking risks with American security. At the very least, it invites future Soviet non-compliance; at worst, it may result in effective U.S. unilateral disarmament.

The Bush administration's readiness to take the Soviet pitch "high and inside" will probably be on graphic display in the course of this week's visit to the United States by Gen. Mikhail Moiseyev, chief of the Soviet general staff. In what is becoming a hardy perennial of contemporary U.S.-Soviet detente, Gen. Moiseyev will tour the country with his American counterpart, Gen. Colin Powell, visiting military installations, inspecting sensitive weapon systems like the B-2 and a nuclear attack submarine and sharing the stage at public events.

Such a red carpet tour is all the more remarkable given that it provides an unprecedented platform to an individual who, on Sept. 28, just before leaving Moscow for the United States, bluntly threatened that "world war" would result if the United States used military force against the Soviet Union's client, Iraq. In stark contrast to Soviet Foreign Minister Eduard Shevardnadze's dulcet paean to U.S.-Soviet cooperation at the United Nations last week, Gen. Moiseyev conjured up images of World War I to imply that a regional conflict in the Middle East would soon engulf the great powers, presumably on opposite sides. U.S. Air Force Chief of Staff Gen. Michael J. Dugan was relieved of his command for uttering far less inflammatory statements.

Mr. Bush had best rethink his game plan vis-a-vis the Soviet Union; too much is at stake to let his presidency strike out over so clearly defective a Soviet policy. A good place to start would be by lowering the public profile of Gen. Moiseyev's visit, or better yet, sending him to the showers.

"'DEMON' LURKING IN THE DETAILS | DECEMBER 17, 1991"

I am running out of demons ... The only demons I have left are Castro and Kim Il-sung.

-Chairman of the Joint Chiefs of Staff Colin Powell

This cocky statement spoke volumes about the Bush administration's assessment of the state of world in the aftermath of the war with Iraq. For one thing, it reflected the notion that the Gulf campaign had effectively eliminated the potential of one erstwhile "demon" - Saddam Hussein - to jeopardize U.S. interests in the future. At the time he said it, Gen. Powell was still under the mistaken impression that the Iraqi weapons of mass destruction programs had been neutralized.

Subsequent visits by numerous teams of U.N. inspectors have established, however, that there was a great deal more to Saddam's nuclear, chemical and biological weapons programs than we had thought - and certainly a great deal more to it than we had destroyed in the course of the war. In fact, it is now apparent that, in the absence of further military action to root him out of power, this old "demon" is likely to be around and a substantial menace to American allies and interests for some time to come.

For another, Gen. Powell's assessment suggested that the United States no longer had any grounds for concerns about the residual military potential of the Soviet Union's armed forces. Unfortunately, while the character of that threat is in the process of changing dramatically with the breakup of the former Soviet Union, the status of tens of thousands of Soviet nuclear weapons is among the most devilish national security problems the United States faces today.

Gen. Powell's statement also had an insidious, if entirely predictable, effect on the domestic debate over defense spending. Few on Capitol Hill were inclined to carry the political baggage of being "holier than the pope" – seeing more potential threats to the United States than did the chairman of the Joint Chiefs of Staff. As a result, a powerful push was imparted to the U.S. defense budget's downward momentum (read, free fall).

It may be the dismissive character of Gen. Powell's remarks toward one of the remaining "demons," however, that will prove to have had the most insidious impact - at least over the near term. His comment was of a piece with the Bush administration's view at the time that Kim Il-sung, the ancient despot of North Korea, no longer posed sufficient threat to South Korea to justify the continued deployment of fully 40,000 U.S. servicemen on the peninsula.

The decision taken earlier this year to reduce the American presence in Korea was initially resisted by Seoul on the grounds that - despite increasing diplomatic and sports contacts with Pyongyang over the past year or so – Kim Il-sung's regime remained a serious threat to South Korea's security. So too was the President Bush's declaration on Sept. 27

that all ground-based tactical weapons would be withdrawn from overseas sites, including Korea.

As a practical matter, however, Seoul could do little but express its strong reservations about these steps in private while acceding to them publicly. Until evidence began to accumulate in the public domain that Kim's regime was swiftly acquiring the capability to manufacture nuclear weapons - evidence that last month prompted Washington to suspend temporarily its drawdown of U.S. forces from Korea (but not the withdrawal of nuclear weapons) - South Korea faced the prospect of having to deal with Pyongyang's power more or less on its own.

This portentous strategic situation contributed powerfully to the South Korean decision to negotiate the "Agreement on Reconciliation, Non-aggression, Exchange and Cooperation" signed Dec. 13. To be sure, other considerations were at work as well including: President Roh Tae-woo's desire to demonstrate his leadership by holding a summit meeting with Kim Il-sung; humanitarian interest in reunifying families divided by war and the Demilitarized Zone; and commercial interest in opening up trade and development opportunities with the North.

Still, there appears to be only one explanation for South Korea's decision to assume the considerable risks associated with this particular agreement: South Korea feared it had no choice but to accept whatever terms the North was prepared to offer. For example: The "non-aggression" pact does not end the state of war that has persisted since the armistice of 1953. Neither does it stipulate reductions in the standing forces poised north of the DMZ that are capable of swiftly moving once again against Seoul. Most striking of all, it does nothing to predicate improvements in relations on a complete, verifiable cessation of North Korea's nuclear weapons program.

Unfortunately, the net effect of this agreement may well be to increase, rather than reduce, the actual threat posed by the North to South Korean security. By setting the stage for infusions of South Korean capital into the North Korean economy, Kim Il-sung's bankrupt and tottering communist dynasty may be given a new lease on life. By opening the door to economic and other ties in the absence of transparency on the North's nuclear program, U.S., Japanese and others' efforts to bring Pyongyang to account will be seriously undercut. And by suggesting that hostilities between the two nations have effectively been brought to an end - even though North Korea's military might is unchecked and remains offensively deployed - invites a further diminution of the American commitment to Seoul's security.

The United States has paid dearly in the past for unduly discounting the importance to our interests of a stable and secure South Korea. Before we give any further encouragement to a certified "demon" in Pyongyang - or to efforts to appease him on the part of the

Seoul government - we would be well advised to take tangible steps to underscore our unflagging opposition to the former and our unwavering commitment to a free and democratic South Korea. Suspension of troop withdrawals was a good first step; a no-holds-barred approach to terminating Kim's nuclear program would be a proper second one.

Bill Clinton

.

One of the most important news stories in the past week - properly given front-page, "above-the-fold" treatment by The Washington Times - was that the Clinton administration was beginning to have second thoughts about gutting the defense budget. After meeting with President Clinton on March 16, House Minority Whip Newt Gingrich said:

"[The President] reflected maybe a sobering realization that both in human intelligence requirements and reassessing our defense requirements that the requirements of American safety might well mean a bigger budget than he had expected a few weeks ago."

Put less diplomatically, it would appear that reality is sinking in with at least some in the administration: The planned $126 billion cuts over the next five years in force structure, procurement and research and development funding, military bases and the attendant, severe contraction of the defense industry are reckless and irresponsible in light of present - and prospective - world conditions.

The truth of the matter is, those world conditions are likely to get a lot worse for American interests before they get better. This is so because the hopeful interlude begun in 1989 when pro-Western democratic forces seemed ascendant around the globe has given way to a period when those forces are under assault from radical, violent factions. These groups subscribe to many different political philosophies, agendas and creeds. They have one thing in common, however: a virulent hatred of the United States and the institutions and values it epitomizes.

What has yet to be widely recognized by the Clinton administration is the extent to which these radical, anti-Western elements are now actively collaborating with one another. In 1985, The Washington Times' columnist Arnold Beichman presciently warned of such a phenomenon, giving it the name "the radical entente." Today, such an entente is a reality with the active, reasonably systematic cooperation between the governments of pariah states, the terrorist organizations they support and various political parties or movements around the world. Consider just a few of the manifestations of this syndrome:

- Item: Even as the evidence mounts that North Korea has obtained the materials and capability to manufacture nuclear weapons - and may already have produced one or more - its willingness to sell advanced weaponry to others is becoming more obvious with each passing day. For example, North Korea is believed to have a deal with Iran whereby Pyongyang's strategic technologies (for example, ballistic missiles, fighter aircraft, tanks and perhaps nuclear know-how) are traded for Tehran's oil. As James Woolsey, the Director of the Central Intelligence Agency, noted last month: "[North Korea] is willing to sell to any country with the cash to pay."

- Item: Iran is also the beneficiary of a similar attitude among Russian hardliners who increasingly determine Kremlin policy. Submarines, Backfire bombers and turnkey facilities for manufacturing state of the art tanks and other equipment are among the assets thus flowing to Tehran.

- Item: Iran, in turn, has become a major supplier of arms, training, intelligence, logistical support, diplomatic cover and strategic direction for others in the "radical entente." Working with the Islamic extremist-dominated government of Sudan, the Iranians have set about trying to destabilize pro-Western governments in Egypt, Tunisia, Saudi Arabia and Turkey. There is also reason to suspect that Tehran, which had a hand in the destruction of the Marine barracks in Lebanon, Pan Am Flight 103 and the Israeli embassy in Buenos Aires, was also involved in the World Trade Center blast.

- Item: Despite Hafez Assad's current peace offensive aimed at recovering the Golan Heights, Syria continues to be both a major recipient of North Korean and Iranian assistance in modernizing its formidable arsenal and in aiding and abetting Islamic and other terrorist groups in their campaign against the West. For example, Damascus recently took possession - despite much huffing and puffing by the Bush administration - of extended-range Scud missiles supplied by Pyongyang, missiles capable of delivering nuclear and other weapons of mass destruction anywhere in Israel and to much of the rest of the Middle East.

- Item: Serbia's historic close ties to Iraq seem to be flourishing despite arms embargoes on both countries. The Serbian Chief of Staff, General Zivota Panic, reportedly was in Baghdad recently meeting with the Iraqi defense minister. This is but one indication that Slobodan Milosevic and Saddam Hussein are coordinating their malevolent activities.

- Item: Serbia has also shipped arms to warlords in Somalia, a distinctly unfriendly step calculated to exacerbate U.S. and U.N. difficulties in bringing peace and stability to the latter.

This list is only the beginning. Others, notably Russian nationalists, the Chinese, the Cubans, the Pakistanis and Afghan militants are also playing dangerous roles in this "radical entente." Still, it suggests the magnitude and the complexity of the problem currently facing American security policy-makers - and that likely to emerge in the years ahead.

Clearly, it also illustrates the need not only to think about reversing the precipitous dismantling of U.S. defense capabilities, but to begin doing so fast. The costs of proceeding further down this reckless path will be measured in American lives and vital interests lost to the "radical entente."

Poor Sam Nunn. Shortly after Congress returns from its August recess, the chairman of the Senate Armed Services Committee will have the unenviable task of shepherding the annual Defense Department authorization bill safely through floor debate. Senate action on this legislation is generally a messy affair; this year it promises to be particularly so.

After all, even the Clinton administration now acknowledges that it has grossly underestimated what is actually required in fiscal 1994 to meet U.S. military commitments. Defense Secretary Les Aspin has reportedly told Georgia Democratic Sen. Nunn and other congressional leaders that the Pentagon will require an additional $20 billion this year, above and beyond what the administration had budgeted just seven months ago.

Unfortunately for Mr. Nunn and other legislators who have recognized for some time that President Clinton was overdoing his dismantling of key national security capabilities, however, a sizable number of senators - perhaps even a majority - are following the administration's previous guidance: Like the Clinton White House to date, such senators see the Pentagon budget as the government's last source of discretionary spending, an essentially cost-free way to underwrite otherwise unaffordable projects.

As a result, when the "world's greatest deliberative body" takes up Mr. Nunn's legislation, further raids are likely on Defense Department accounts that have already been ravaged by years of budget cuts. Worse yet, the effect of those cuts has been exacerbated by diversion of enormous resources to a host of activities tangential to the military's primary missions - such as "defense conversion," aid to Russia, peacekeeping operations and various environmental cleanups.

Consequently, like a lumbering supertanker whose sheer mass and forward momentum ensure that its course will be unaltered for miles after orders are given to change direction, Congress may well do still more violence to the nation's power projection capabilities, development of effective defenses against ballistic missile attack, readiness and defense industrial capacity - even though the need to undo the damage already done in these and other areas is becoming ever more apparent.

If the American military is to be kept off the shoals and prepared to deal with the burgeoning array of threats to U.S. security interests - from the catastrophe in the Balkans to North Korea's nuclear weapons program to Iran's intensifying malevolence to instability throughout the former Soviet Union – at least one of two conditions must apply: Either the Clinton administration must get its national security act together or congressional leadership must be asserted to fill the void.

There is, as yet, little ground for optimism on the first score. What positive signs exist - such as the appointment of Gen. John Shalikashvili as chairman of the Joint Chiefs of Staff, preparations for air strikes in Bosnia and reversal of earlier decisions to cut back the

Navy's inventory of aircraft carriers from 12 to 10 - are substantially confused, if not neutralized, by other administration actions.

For example, another Clinton personnel decision - involving the nomination of a certified leftist radical, Morton Halperin, to a top Defense Department job - threatens to overshadow the choice of a gutsy, well-qualified and independently minded individual to lead the nation's military. The Halperin confirmation hearings will be held by Mr. Nunn's committee; they could become the messiest in the foreign and defense policy arena since the 1977 bloodletting over President Carter's ill-advised appointment of Paul Warnke to the Arms Control and Disarmament Agency.

Similarly, the net effect of recent posturing about Serbian aggression in Bosnia may actually be to compound the perceived international devaluation of American will and power. After all, whatever progress the administration has finally made in getting NATO ready for strikes on Serbian positions has as a practical matter been negated by ceding a veto over such strikes to U.N. Secretary General Boutros Boutros-Ghali, an adamant opponent of Western military intervention. Worse yet, a dangerous precedent has been created by this subordination of NATO's action-taking authority to the United Nations.

Even the administration's laudable, albeit late-blooming, concern about military morale and retention has been contradicted by other actions. Indeed, the same factor that caused Mr. Aspin to reconsider his initial decision to save money by reducing the number of aircraft carriers - namely, the hardship on service personnel wrought by the sort of excessively long deployments that result when fewer assets are asked to do the same (or more) work – prompted Marine Corps Commandant Carl Mundy to take steps to discourage young recruits from marrying before signing up. Mr. Aspin, however, summarily rejected this desperate bid by the Marines to preserve good order and discipline in its junior enlisted ranks.

So it will probably fall to Sen. Nunn and Republicans like Sen. Trent Lott, Mississippi Republican, to forge a bipartisan coalition capable of providing the leadership on defense policy and budget issues that should come from the executive branch - but won't. Such a coalition was created by the late Sens. Henry M. "Scoop" Jackson, Washington Democrat, and John Tower, Texas Republican, some 15 years ago when Jimmy Carter was doing approximately the same thing to American security interests and capabilities as is now being perpetrated by the current occupant of the White House.

If the Democratic leadership of the Senate Foreign Relations Committee has its way, the next week will witness a wholesale retooling of the legislative history of the Cold War. If the Clinton administration has its way though, the committee's markup of bill H.R. 3000 will not only bring that "twilight struggle" to a formal end; the U.S. Code will actually be rewritten to make it look as though the Cold War never happened!

This is, as the Soviet communists used to say, "no accident, comrade." After all, President Boris Yeltsin and the Russian military-industrial complex and security apparatus to which he is increasingly beholden have repeatedly asserted that the repeal of U.S. statutes derided as the "legacy of the Cold War" is a litmus test of the American commitment to Russian reform. The Clinton team (many of whose members were vehemently opposed to these statutes even during the Cold War) is now only too happy to seize upon this excuse to press for their immediate elimination.

It says much about the dubious nature, indeed the superciliousness, of this exercise that H.R. 3000's official title is the act "For Reform In Emerging New Democracies and Support and Help for Improved Partnership with Russia, Ukraine and other new independent States." Leave it to the obsessive marketeers of the Clinton administration to go to such lengths to come up with an acronym that says it all: "F.R.I.E.N.D.S.H.I.P. 'R. U.S." If such silliness did not bespeak a possibly dangerous lack of strategic vision - to say nothing of prudence and common sense - it would be rather amusing.

Consider, however, the following, ill-advised changes in permanent U.S. law contemplated by H.R. 3000. The "FRIENDSHIP 'R US" act would:

- Eliminate statutory restrictions on communist activities in the United States.

- Eliminate prohibitions on Moscow's use of the controversial Mount Alto site for its Washington embassy - long believed to be ideally suited for electronic espionage – and the requirement that Moscow pay for the costs incurred by its past efforts to bug the new U.S. Embassy in the Russian capital.

- Eliminate the statutory provisions governing reciprocity in numbers of personnel and other aspects of diplomatic missions and limiting the employment of Soviet nationals in U.S. missions in the former Soviet Union.

- Effectively reinforce what is, at the moment at least, a quite controversial 1961 congressional statement of policy concerning the United Nations:

- "The Congress of the United States reaffirms the policy of the United States to achieve international peace and security through the United Nations so that armed force shall not be used except for individual or collective self-defense."

- And add impetus to the Clinton administration's reckless gutting of multilateral export controls on strategic technologies by eliminating prohibitions on the transfer of military research and development to Russia and by completely striking the congressional finding that:

"The acquisition of national security sensitive goods and technology by the Soviet Union and other countries the action or policies of which run counter to the national security interest of the United States, has led to the significant enhancement of Soviet bloc military-industrial capabilities. This enhancement poses a threat to the security of the United States, its allies and other friendly nations, and places additional demands on the defense budget of the United States."

Not surprisingly, the Clinton administration is anxious to avoid any congressional debate on this audacious legislative initiative. Accordingly, it has adopted procedural tactics reminiscent of recent administration efforts to effect a similar, wholesale and permanent dismantling of statutory restrictions concerning the Palestine Liberation Organization. In both cases, the administration has insisted that Congress act precipitously to effect sweeping changes in the law of the land. In both cases, the Congress has been asked - and has thus far agreed - to do so without hearings and with a view to "marking up" and scheduling floor action on the relevant legislative instruments in a manner that all but forecloses real deliberation.

Fortunately, the Congress declined to be railroaded on the PLO legislation. It acted, instead, to permit only limited and temporary relief from existing statutory restrictions. In so doing, the legislative branch has established both a basis upon which future concessions can be conditioned on the PLO's actual behavior - rather than merely its rhetoric - and a precedent for dealing with no less problematic partners in the former Soviet Union.

Hearings are now in order to establish, at a minimum, whether the demise of the Soviet Union has, in fact: eliminated the danger posed by communist subversion and the need for statutory protections against it; ended the need to safeguard U.S. secrets - both commercial and governmental - against the largely undiminished espionage operations of the KGB; or obviated concerns about the uses to which strategic Western technology might be put by the Russian military-industrial complex.

If the answer to such questions is, as I believe, "No," then significant changes to H.R. 3000 are urgently needed. Otherwise, the "FRIENDSHIP 'R US" act will simply contribute to a far worse setback for U.S. security interests than anything yet experienced in Somalia, Haiti and Bosnia - and do so in one of the few foreign policy areas where the Clinton administration has the cheek to assert that it is performing competently.

If President Clinton thinks the international debacles he has gotten himself into over Cuba, Haiti or Bosnia are vexing, imagine how he would feel if faced with one of the following scenarios:

- India decides pre-emptively to strike Pakistan with nuclear weapons delivered by ballistic missiles rather than allow Pakistan to go first, as threatened last week by a former Pakistani prime minister who formally declared that his country had nuclear arms.

- North Korea threatens to attack Japan with ballistic missile-delivered chemical, biological or nuclear weapons if, following the meltdown of diplomatic attempts to defuse the crisis over Pyongyang's "bomb," Tokyo permits American bases in the Japanese islands to be used as staging areas for U.S. reinforcement of or military action on the Korean Peninsula.

- When international sanctions against Iraq are lifted, Saddam Hussein displays Scud missiles he had successfully concealed from international inspectors, announces they are equipped with weapons of mass destruction and reiterates his intention to lay waste to Israel - only this time, he warns that any Arab nation making peace with the Jewish State will also be destroyed.

- Western nations are obliged once again to mount a coalition campaign to prevent a despotic regime - this time, Iran - from closing the Persian Gulf to vital oil shipments. But Tehran reveals that it has bought medium-range ballistic missiles from China or North Korea and serves notice that London, Paris and Bonn will be attacked if they allow such an operation to receive a U.N. mandate, to say nothing of participate in it. The United States is also warned that its forces on land and at sea will be subjected to lethal missile strikes.

Perhaps President Clinton, unlike most Americans, is aware there is essentially nothing the United States could do today in the event that any of these or other plausible scenarios involving theater ballistic missiles (that is, missiles of less than intercontinental range) comes to pass. Yes, given time and favorable circumstances, a few Patriot missiles might be dispatched to defend some of the possible targets. But, as was evident in Operation Desert Storm, these interceptors have exceedingly limited capability. They were not designed to defend cities or large areas; with luck, they might be able to defend themselves and hardened facilities nearby.

Ever keen to fob blame onto others, Mr. Clinton may argue that today's inadequacies are largely the fault of his predecessors. There is, unfortunately, truth to this contention. Ronald Reagan - who in 1983 sponsored for the first time in over a decade a serious re-examination of the contribution ballistic missile defenses might make to U.S. security - left office with the nation as completely vulnerable to missile attack as it was when he entered it. George Bush spent billions more on the problem but, with the exception of the software enhancements that gave Patriot its self-defense capability, fielded no anti-missile systems.

This is so even though the vulnerability of U.S. forces and allies overseas in circumstances like Saddam's Scud attacks in Desert Storm (not to mention those involved in the more dire contingencies described above) has prompted nearly every prominent American politician to profess a strong commitment to developing and fielding defenses against theater ballistic missiles. In 1991, Congress was actually moved to pass the Missile Defense Act that demanded early deployment of such defenses. Legislators from both parties - from Ron Dellums to Jesse Helms - have subsequently stressed the need for effective protection against shorter-range missiles.

The Clinton administration has been no less supportive of this objective, at least at the rhetorical level. President Clinton, Vice President Al Gore, Defense Secretary William Perry and Deputy Defense Secretary John Deutch, among others, have stressed development and deployment of these defenses as a critical component of the U.S. response to international proliferation of nuclear and other weapons of mass destruction.

It is, therefore, positively bizarre that Mr. Clinton and his national security team are taking steps that will lock the United States permanently into a posture of inadequate defenses against theater missile attack. The vehicle for doing so is a diplomatic initiative with the Russians aimed at expanding the prohibitions contained in the 1972 Anti-Ballistic Missile Treaty to cover most militarily and cost-effective options for theater missile defense.

For example, the option to develop and deploy space-based defenses against shorter- to medium-range ballistic missiles - which could defuse, if not deter, all of the aforementioned scenarios - has already been given up by the Clinton administration. Worse yet, it seems bent on finishing off every other option for defending large areas efficiently by the time of next month's summit meeting with Russian President Boris Yeltsin.

If so, Mr. Clinton will have no one but himself to blame when (not if) he finds himself unable to affect catastrophes around the world involving ballistic missile-based threats to our troops and friends. The rest of us, however, will be able to take small comfort from holding him responsible for the terrible and probably avoidable tragedies that will ensue.

Even before the polls open, the early returns are coming in on President Clinton's desperate bid for the political rehabilitation needed to stave off his expected, massive repudiation in balloting tomorrow. Across the board, Mr. Clinton's "string of foreign policy successes" is coming unraveled.

That it was bound to — given the short-term, expediency-driven nature of the president's "solutions" — is not news; that it is beginning to do so now, prior to the elections is remarkable. The question is: Will Mr. Clinton's disservice to American interests overseas be broadly enough perceived by the electorate to be added to the litany of grievances expressed tomorrow against the President and his friends?

A tour of the horizon offers powerful reasons why it should. Consider recent developments in each of the areas Mr. Clinton has been taking credit for:

- Iraq: While the Clinton administration did swiftly and credibly signal to Saddam Hussein that it would resist any further military threat to Kuwait from Iraq, the plausibility of that commitment is rapidly fraying. The idea of creating a heavy weapons exclusion zone in Southern Iraq as a means of precluding a renewed Iraqi buildup there was quashed by the French and Russians. Worse yet, this diplomatic debacle offered fresh evidence of the untenability of the international sanctions regime against Iraq.

  Then, during his photo op. in Kuwait week before last, Mr. Clinton signaled he expected to have the troops now stationed there home by Christmas. Unless he is planning to take out Saddam in the intervening eight weeks — and there is no basis for believing that is what the president has in mind — Mr. Clinton will either have to abandon his pre-election commitment or abandon the field yet again to the Iraqi despot.

- Haiti: The thousands of U.S. troops with responsibility for maintaining Jean-Bertrande Aristide in power were understandably angry at discovering that their military colleagues sent to deter Saddam well after operations began in Haiti would be repatriated first. The administration's pre-election response? Promise to pull out 9,000 of the roughly 17,000 now there before Christmas and fobbing the bulk of the nasty, protracted business of "nation-building" off onto multinational forces. Unfortunately, as the U.N. special envoy for Haiti noted last week, the island is not safe enough for international peacekeepers; he will not agree to put them in until the United States has further "pacified" the country. Here too, the writing is on the wall: There will either be more American troops in Haiti for longer than the Clinton administration has indicated or Mr. Aristide will have to be abandoned to his fate.

- North Korea: When the Clinton administration's deal with Pyongyang was first unveiled, it was obvious that the accord entailed immense U.S. concessions to one of the most dangerous communist regimes on Earth. Not the least of these were the untold billions of dollars for oil, reactors, nuclear fuel and upgrades to the North's power grid that will be entailed. To allay criticism somewhat, official American spokesmen maintained that these costs would be borne substantially, if not entirely, by others.

  The White House was obliged to acknowledge in recent days, however, that Mr. Clinton has sent the North Koreans a letter saying he will do everything in his power to ensure that the U.S. taxpayer assumes these costs if other nations cannot be induced to do so — something that seems increasingly probable. Congress and the public may well refuse to go along with this deal insofar as it amounts to what might be called "strategic rape." They certainly should if the president winds up adding insult to injuring by obliging the U.S. taxpayer to pay for it.

- Syria: President Clinton made a hastily arranged trip to Damascus — the capital of a nation that: sponsors international terrorism against Americans and their allies; promotes drug trafficking that destroys American lives; is acquiring weapons of mass destruction that may well be used in the future against a key U.S. ally, Israel; and engages in economic warfare against the United States by counterfeiting its currency. He did so in the hope of achieving a politically valuable pre-election "breakthrough" in peace negotiations between Israel and Syria. Although no such breakthrough occurred, the president nonetheless claimed that significant (albeit unspecified) "progress" was made.

  At present, it is unclear whether Mr. Clinton was merely contemptuously snubbed by the Syrian despot, Hafez Assad, or whether Mr. Assad has pocketed other, more substantive concessions than a symbolic presidential pilgrimage to Damascus. These might include not only committing U.S. troops to a dangerous deployment on the Golan Heights but also sweetheart deals for Syria concerning U.S. trade, technology and financial assistance. Either way, the trip was ill advised and counterproductive.

This list of prematurely declared "successes" is illustrative of the larger problem with the Clinton security policy record. In due course if not tomorrow, the critical swing group of voters – the Reagan Democrats — are going to vote against Clinton and Company. These voters will do so for the same reasons they rejected the last Southern Democratic president, Jimmy Carter: They have no use for leaders who squander America's prestige and reduce its power and who, in the process, embolden U.S. adversaries at the expense of our interests overseas.

Mr. President:

Sunday's New York Times reveals you have become personally seized with the nation's vulnerability to biological warfare. If that is the case, you have the potential to create a legacy that could be as profound and positive as any of your presidency. But to do so, you must take care to grasp the true magnitude of the problem and to avoid counterproductive actions.

According to the Times' report, your concerns about bioterrorism have been catalyzed by Richard Preston's novel "The Cobra Event" and by a recent, secret interagency exercise in which a bioterrorist attack was simulated. In both, terrorists use a genetically engineered virus to inflict mass casualties and to sow mayhem on American society.

You evidently were particularly, and properly, alarmed by the conclusion of the civilian "war-game." As the New York Times put it: "The United States, despite huge investments of time, money and effort in recent years, is still unprepared to respond to biological terror weapons." The game showed state, local and federal government representatives were quickly overwhelmed and found themselves at odds over how to deal with the resulting catastrophe - and whose responsibility it was to do so.

As a result, you are now said to be preparing two Presidential Decision Directives (PDDs) aimed: (1) at putting the country on a better footing to prevent biological, chemical or computer attacks on its people or infrastructure and (2) if all else fails and they occur, to mitigate their effects. To maximize the benefit of these PDDs, I would respectfully urge that you consider two points:

First, the problem with which you are now grappling - namely, the United States' dangerous susceptibility to biological weapons attack - is, of course, just one manifestation of a much larger problem. This is what might be called our posture of "assured vulnerability."

Ever since 1972, when President Nixon signed the Anti-Ballistic Missile Treaty with the Soviet Union, it has been the policy of the U.S. government to leave its people deliberately exposed to destruction by missile-delivered nuclear weapons. Having done so in a world in which the Soviet Union had a virtual monopoly on such a threat, the idea gradually took hold that it made no sense to invest the vast sums required to protect Americans against Soviet bomber-delivered weapons, either. If there would be no defenses against these delivery systems, it seemed unnecessary (not to say virtually impossible) to mitigate the effects on the population of the weapons they carried. So civil defense went over the side, as well.

Thus, the vulnerability you are now concerned with, is a direct by-product of the inexorable, if bizarre, logic that says keeping America at risk of assured destruction is a good thing and defenses that might prevent, or at least mitigate, such destruction are bad things. If you are committed meaningfully to rectifying our present posture, you must also correct its intellectual underpinnings.

Unfortunately, until now, your administration has adamantly insisted it is committed to perpetuating the ABM Treaty. If this policy were to persist, you would be seriously compromising your new PDDs by addressing attacks with biological weapons if they are made possible by suitcase bombs, aerosol trucks or Cessna crop-dusters, but not if they come via ballistic missile.

The folly of such an approach was laid bare in the course of testimony provided last week by Mr. Preston before a Senate hearing chaired by Sen. Jon Kyl, Arizona Republican. The best-selling author of "The Cobra Event" and "The Hot Zone" declared Russia may have as many as 800 intercontinental range ballistic missiles aimed at the United States and armed with smallpox or other viruses (including, perhaps, genetically engineered biological "cocktails").

Surely you appreciate that, even if the former Soviet Union's own missile and biological weapons programs were not cause for grave concern, missile, biological weapons and other WMD-relevant technology are turning up in other, potentially unfriendly hands. For example, yesterday, it was revealed that the Russians are assisting Indian efforts to develop a submarine-launched missile system. Saturday, it was disclosed that Russia nearly succeeded in smuggling specialty steel suitable for missile bodies to Iran. And China is known to have supplied missile technology to, among others, Pakistan, Iraq and North Korea.

Each of these countries is believed to have weapons of mass destruction programs. The absence of effective U.S. global missile defenses merely serves as an incentive to fit such weapons on missiles of ever-increasing capability, whether to threaten regional foes or Americans and their interests. It makes no sense to try to close the back door to bioterrorism while leaving the front door open.

In addition to including comprehensive missile defenses in your WMD vulnerability-reduction program - the fastest, simplest and cheapest way to do this is by adapting the Navy's AEGIS fleet air defense system to allow it to shoot down long- and shorter-range ballistic missiles, as well aircraft and cruise missiles - there is something you should not do:

Under no circumstances should the U.S. government endanger, if not preclude, the cooperation its efforts to counter the threat of biological weapons must enjoy with the biotech and related industries. Your first director of central intelligence, R. James Woolsey, warns that: "One way I think we could destroy the possibility of having that kind of partnership is to move toward some ineffective and very intrusive notion of how to verify the Biological Weapons Convention. Trying to have a verification regime that would on a routine basis go into pharmaceutical facilities and look at them would really only penalize the people who are... behaving themselves and staying within the law... You're not going to find what Hezbollah is doing with biological weapons that way or, for that matter, a Unabomber, who thinks about using biologicals instead of explosives in packages."

Mr. President, if you are serious about ending our nation's posture of assured vulnerability - which will be readily apparent if you promptly begin deploying effective antimissile systems and eschew counterproductive arms control ideas -you will enjoy the support, and enduring appreciation, of every American.

George W. Bush

The emerging conventional wisdom about President Bush is that he can be determinedly principled with respect to certain "big" issues and ruthlessly pragmatic when it comes to compromising about smaller ones. This explains, we are told, why he stood his ground on tax cuts but, for example, decided to bail out on military training at Vieques.

The question now urgently arising is: Will Mr. Bush's oft-stated pledge to deploy missile defenses prove to be one of the big issues, to which he will remain steadfastly committed? Or does he see it as one of those policy areas where he can safely agree to compromises that would effectively eviscerate his commitment to defend the American people, their forces overseas and allies "at the earliest possible time?"

This is hardly an academic question. If Mr. Bush sees missile defense as the moral equivalent of tax relief, he needs to start making at once no less concerted an effort for the former than he did for the latter.

After all, the battle lines are now being clearly drawn. This was particularly evident when Secretary of Defense Donald Rumsfeld was confronted during a hearing on June 21 before the Senate Armed Services Committee with the sort of disciplined Democratic opposition to missile defense last seen in 1998. In the run-up to that year's congressional elections, the then-minority caucus succeeded on three different occasions in sustaining exactly the 40 votes needed to filibuster legislation making it U.S. policy to deploy an effective, limited national missile defense as soon as technologically possible. (The next year, essentially the same bill passed both houses of Congress with overwhelming majorities and was signed into law by President Clinton.)

The committee's new chairman, Sen. Carl Levin, Michigan Democrat, ended Thursday's proceedings by pointedly warning Mr. Rumsfeld that "you may find some of your priorities... for little things like missile defense, changed" in favor of greater spending in areas like quality of life, morale, pay and benefits and retention."

For his part, Russian President Vladimir Putin, the man Mr. Bush concluded he could "trust" after their 90-minute meeting in Slovenia, is doing what he can to inflame opposition here and abroad to U.S. missile defense deployments. After their summit, he has repeated earlier warnings that Moscow would respond to such an initiative by retaining nuclear missiles that would otherwise be retired and/or by putting multiple warheads aboard new missiles that were supposed to carry just one. Such threats of an arms race, no matter how implausible (because of Russia's economic situation) or incredible (given the lack of any compelling strategic rationale for such behavior in the post-Cold War world), are having the predictable effect of emboldening the critics.

So, too, are indications that Mr. Bush is really seeking a deal with Mr. Putin. The latest indicator to that effect is a report published by Peggy Noonan in Monday's Wall Street Journal based on an interview with President Bush last week. This generally very astute observer observes, "One might infer – and perhaps should infer - from the president's comments that he will not attempt to tear the Anti-Ballistic Missile Treaty up, but instead will move for an amendment that would allow further missile testing." Could Ms. Noonan have completely misread Mr. Bush?

Or is she correctly discerning the migration of missile defense from a big issue to a compromisable small one?

The only problem with that idea is that, if Mr. Bush compromises on missile defense - whether by acquiescing to Senate Democrats' budget games, by quailing in the face of threats from Russia (or, for that matter, from China or North Korea) or by trying to negotiate amendments to the ABM Treaty with the likes of Mr. Putin - he can forget about actually deploying protection against ballistic missile attack. It won't happen on his watch, unless someplace we care about is destroyed by one.

Here's the rub: The ABM Treaty expressly required each of the two parties - the United States and the Soviet Union (a country that, by the way, ceased to exist a decade ago) - "not to deploy ABM systems for a defense of the territory of its country and not to provide a base for such a defense." To ensure that such a "base" was not established, the treaty also obliged each party "not to develop, test or deploy ABM systems or components which are sea-based, air-based, space-based, or mobile land-based."

Senators, Russians and allied leaders who insist that the United States must not depart from the ABM Treaty understand full well the practical effect of this arrangement. As long as the United States foreswears sea-, air- and space-based missile defenses in particular, it will be unable to develop, to say nothing of deploy, effective anti-missile systems. And it is impossible to "amend" a treaty whose sole purpose is to preclude national missile defenses so as to allow such defenses to be tested efficiently and deployed quickly – particularly if our Russian negotiating partners remain adamantly opposed to our doing so.

In short, Mr. Bush must establish at once where he stands on defending the United States, its forward deployed forces and allies. If Mr. Bush has not just been paying lip service to the need for missile defenses, and remains determined to deploy them, he has no choice but to get started. Only by displaying the kind of resolve he showed on tax cuts - refusing to take "No" for an answer, mobilizing his base and the country at large and not allowing himself to be stymied or slow-rolled - will he be able to begin to provide the needed protection, first from the sea.

If Mr. Bush does not take that course of action, however, all other things being equal - big issue or no - he is going soon to find himself utterly hamstrung by those who oppose him politically and strategically. What will be compromised as a result, however, will not be merely his credibility, but the security of his nation and its people.

In his syndicated column in yesterday's New York Times, William Safire offers an ominous assessment of Russian President Vladimir Putin and the signal successes he has achieved since President Bush started looking "into his soul" and declared that he "trusts" his Kremlin counterpart.

Unfortunately for Mr. Bush, as alarming as the Safire critique is now - concerning, for example, Russia's machinations, at U.S. and Western expense, on NATO, Chechnya, oil prices, weapons sales to Iraq and other state-sponsors of terrorism, etc. - the record could become even more damning if Secretary of State Powell has his way.

Bill Safire rightly worries that the "new relationship" being forged at President Bush's behest between Russia and the Atlantic Alliance will translate into Moscow having access to NATO's military secrets and an effective veto over its conduct of operations. He notes that Mr. Putin's ruthless repression of the Chechens has now been legitimated as just another front in the global war on Islamist terrorism.

Mr. Safire wonders about Russian double-dealing on oil prices, too. He notes that Moscow at first declined to go along with production cutbacks sought by OPEC, but has recently signaled a willingness to make more than token reductions in supply so as to jack up the price per barrel.

And he observes that, while the Kremlin was only too happy to have us attack its enemies in Afghanistan, Moscow will want no part of our doing the same in Iraq or other Russian client-states.

These concerns are hardly unjustified. If press reports are correct, however, the gravity of their implications may be greatly compounded by Secretary of State Colin Powell during his personal diplomatic mission to Moscow this week.

According to The Washington Post, Mr. Powell told reporters en route to Russia that "a deal between the United States and Russia to sharply reduce nuclear weapons is 'just about done,' and the two countries are now looking for ways to verify that they abide by the proposed limits."

Specifically, they are "focusing on how to apply verification measures included in the earlier START I and START II arms control treaties to the new limits proposed for offensive weapons."

In other words, President Bush risks having a unilateral decision to reduce American strategic nuclear forces by two-thirds over the next decade morphed by his secretary of state into a binding bilateral agreement, replete with verification mechanisms carried forward from earlier arms control treaties.

This would be a very bad idea on several grounds. First of all, the number of strategic arms President Bush has decided to retain a decade from now - 1,700-2,200 weapons - may prove inadequate to future targeting requirements. One of the distinct advantages of making that decision as a matter of unilateral U.S. discretion is that it could relatively easily be revised down the road. That is not the case with understandings formalized by accords (treaties, executive agreements, etc.) between countries.

Second, the START I and II verification measures are predicated on elaborate and artificial counting rules. For instance, a given long-range missile may have fewer warheads aboard it than the number it can carry but, in the interest of arms control monitoring, a larger number is automatically assigned to each missile of that type. Should such rules now be applied to the president's projected force levels - something explicitly rejected in their formulation and adoption - the practical effect would be that the United States could field still fewer weapons than even he thought necessary.

Finally, and most troubling, Mr. Powell's efforts to get a "deal" on strategic arms violates a fundamental principle of the president's approach to Russia: The Cold War is over. The State Department's preference for arms control agreements with the Kremlin - replete with arrangements for verifying each others' compliance with such accords - amounts to a direct repudiation of Mr. Bush's concept of a new post-Cold War era. The affront would only be compounded were Mr. Powell to sign onto another "deal" that would perpetuate the 1972 Anti-Ballistic Missile (ABM) Treaty but somehow allow the U.S. greater latitude to conduct missile defense tests it prohibits.

In the world President Bush has envisioned, massive American nuclear reductions are possible. U.S.-Russian cooperation on intelligence, counterterrorism, drug enforcement and maybe even missile defense are imaginable (if debatable). Who knows, in such an environment, it might actually be possible to "trust" Russia with access to NATO's innermost councils, to maintain stable energy prices, to end its dangerous ties with rogue states, etc.

If, on the other hand, what is really going on here is a State Department-abetted, Russian gambit to make the most of changed circumstances so as to pursue the Kremlin's abiding agenda - weakening the United States and improving Russia's relative power, then the indictment served up by Bill Safire will be but a foretaste of what is to come.

Mr. Bush can't have it both ways. Either his administration will put the Cold War - and its relics, like negotiated offensive arms control accords and the ABM Treaty - behind it and insist on a genuinely different relationship with Russia and, for that matter, a different Russia.

Or he will find himself getting the worst of both worlds: in effect rewarding his "friend," Vladimir Putin, for persisting in behavior antithetical to vital U.S. security and other interests.

President Bush has just put some expensive additional chips on an extraordinary gamble. With his visits over the past week to Moscow, St. Petersburg and Rome in the company of his Russian counterpart, Vladimir Putin, Mr. Bush has greatly expanded his bid to recast relations between Washington and the Kremlin from Cold War enemies to "partners."

For this gamble to pay the sorts of long-term returns the Bush administration hopes for, however, it must be rooted in hardheaded realism, based on transparency and practical measures. In particular, it must amount to more than another spasm of American enthusiasm for the Kremlin-leader du jour, the sort of "cult of personality" to which a succession of previous U.S. presidents have succumbed in the past.

Consider a few of the steps that have already been taken by Mr. Bush or his predecessors in the hope of encouraging a systemic and irreversible transformation of Russia, steps that have entailed the dismantling of many of the instruments upon which the United States and its Western allies relied to check or counter their Cold War foe:

- A new "Strategic Offensive Reductions" Treaty (SORT) has been signed, formalizing parallel, but unilateral, commitments by the Russian and American presidents to reduce their nuclear arsenals by roughly two-thirds – reflecting Mr. Bush's view that mutual deterrence no longer is the governing principle between the two countries.

- Russia has become a sort of guest member of the NATO alliance under an arrangement that will afford it considerable opportunity to influence that organization's deliberations but, in theory at least, no veto over decisions taken by the other, full-fledged members.

- Various Cold War impediments to Russian economic growth have already been removed or shortly will be. The multilateral regime governing exports of high-technology items with military applications, known as COCOM, is long gone. Obstacles to Western European dependence on Russian energy supplies have given way to a natural gas infrastructure that relies heavily on such sources. For its part, the United States is likely to import much more oil from Russia and the Caspian Basin in the years ahead.

- Mr. Bush has also promised to clear the way for permanent normal trade relations status for Russia by getting the 1974 Jackson-Vanik Amendment formally repealed and to use his influence to secure membership for a free-market Russian economy.

- Mr. Putin's refraining from strenuous objections to U.S. withdrawal from the 1972 Anti-Ballistic Missile Treaty appears likely to be rewarded with some sort of cooperative role in the American missile defense program. Like the sharing of sensitive intelligence in the interest of U.S-Russian collaboration in the war on terrorism, voluntarily affording Moscow access to such American secrets would have been most ill-advised, if not actually unthinkable, before now.

That brings us to the big question: Has Russia changed sufficiently to this point for these sorts of adjustments - most of which will be politically, if not technically, irreversible - to be in order?

In the course of a hearing last Thursday of the House Armed Services Committee, Rep. Roscoe Bartlett, Maryland Republican, offered a cautionary note. He called attention to a vast underground facility deeply buried beneath Mount Yamantau in the Urals, upon which some 20,000 workers continue to labor to this day.

According to Mr. Bartlett, one of the few legislators with real scientific credentials: "In recent years, the Russians have had a ramp-up in activity there - building soccer fields and accoutrements that they don't provide for anybody else in their society. This is more important to them than $200 million for the service module on the International Space Station. It's more important to them than paying the salaries of military personnel. It is as large underground as inside our Capital Beltway... And the only reasonable use of this sort of facility is either during or post-nuclear war. There's no other reason for a country as financially strapped as Russia that they should continue to pour enormous resources into an undertaking like Yamantau Mountain.

"Now what does this tell us about the Russian psyche and what caution should it give us about presuming what Russian actions would be in the future? They apparently believe - from this and other indications - that nuclear war is inevitable and winnable, and they're preparing to win that war... I would submit that this kind of activity by Russia - that we should be aware of that when making prognostications of what Russia may or may not do in any given circumstance."

Mount Yamantau is hardly the only worrisome indicator of Russian intentions. Others include the following: The Kremlin apparently is continuing covert manufacture of chemical and biological arms and has a "hot" production line for new nuclear weapons; the United States currently produces none of these. Mr. Putin's government continues to dissemble about the true nature of its supplier relationship - read, proliferation - to Iran's radical and terrorist-sponsoring Islamic regime. According to one of the most knowledgeable observers of the Soviet and Russian systems, Johns Hopkins' David Satter, Mr. Putin is also covering up the security services' complicity in apartment building bombings used to justify genocidal attacks in Chechnya. And Moscow is helping to arm China to the teeth, including with weapons expressly designed and built to kill Americans.

None of these is, in and of itself, necessarily an argument for abandoning altogether President Bush's Russian gamble. They do, however - particularly when taken together - argue for an insistence on transparency concerning Kremlin behavior and a disciplined approach on the part of the West to ensure that measures taken from here on that are aimed at bringing Russia into the fold are predicated on tangible changes in that behavior, not just wishful thinking or a blind-faith investment in the likes of Vladimir Putin.

Every once in a while a highly visible political gambit comes completely a cropper. Particularly when it involves - to say nothing of embarrasses – the president of the United States, it generally gets considerable public notice. Often the proverbial head rolls. At the very least, a course correction is usually quickly effected.

What are we to make, then, of the astonishing silence, the utter lack of accountability and the absence of any apparent shift in electoral strategy that has accompanied the meltdown of the one of the Bush political team's major initiatives: Its effort to recruit Muslim- and Arab-American voters [and donors] by pandering to foreign-funded organizations led by radical leftists and even pro-"Islamists" - despite the fact that most members of those communities neither are radical nor subscribe to the virulently intolerant, and often violently anti-American, tenets of those who promote Islamism.

This courting formally got under way back in 2000, when senior advisers to then-Gov. George Bush invited representatives of highly problematic groups like the Islamic Society of North America [ISNA], the American Muslim Council [AMC] and the Council on American-Islamic Relations [CAIR] to Austin.

On the presidential campaign trail that year, he met with and received support from an Islamist activist named Sami Al-Arian and embraced Mr. Al-Arian's personal pet project - the prohibition of the use of "secret evidence" by federal law enforcement.

After Mr. Bush gained the White House, ISNA, the AMC, CAIR and like-minded groups and individuals such as Sami Al-Arian were invited to the White House for meetings there with, among others, political guru Karl Rove. In fact, on September 11, 2001, a number of them were scheduled to hold a meeting in the presidential complex for the purpose of cashing in on the promised end to the use of secret evidence - one of law enforcement's few and most important pre-Patriot Act tools for protecting classified information while prosecuting suspected terrorists.

Incredible as it may seem, in the wake of the attacks that day, organizations with long records of support for radical Islam and sympathy for those who murder Americans and others in its name were afforded increased access to high-level administration officials and myriad federal agencies. Mr. Al-Arian's access only ended when he was indicted and held without bail on some 40 counts, including charges that he ran Palestinian Islamic Jihad for 10 years from his office at the University of South Florida.

CAIR's access has continued, even though three of its officials have been arrested in recent months on terrorism-related charges.

Such "outreach" to Muslims was routinely justified by a legitimate, even laudable, desire on Mr. Bush's part to demonstrate that the War on Terror was not a war on Islam. But for some around the president, it had a more crass political impetus: pandering for votes in 2002 and 2004.

Unfortunately, the pro-Islamists and their friends had a very different agenda. They sought to use the access thus afforded to White House officials, Cabinet and sub-Cabinet officers and the FBI to undermine counterterrorist techniques and initiatives on the grounds they were racially or ethnically motivated. Worse yet, they publicly exploited meetings with the president and his subordinates to shore up their dubious - and highly undesirable - claim to leadership both within and on behalf of their community.

Just how undesirable this phenomenon is became clear in an important hearing last Wednesday by the Judiciary Subcommittee on Terrorism headed by Sen. Jon Kyl, Arizona Republican. After establishing Saudi funding as a source of revenue for and influence over organizations like the Council on American-Islamic Relations, witnesses and senators on both sides of the aisle condemned CAIR for its "extreme" agenda and its support for terrorist organizations like Hamas.

If any further evidence were needed that the Bush administration's embrace of groups like CAIR was as politically unjustifiable as it is strategically dangerous, it was provided recently in Chicago. Two weeks ago, tens of thousands of immigrant and black Muslims met there in separate conventions. Their inability to assemble in a single venue or to agree on a common agenda offered clear evidence that their communities are hardly monolithic.

In fact, the only thing on which there was apparent accord was an announced determination on the part of the radical groups who sponsored these events that they would work to register 1 million Muslim voters to defeat George W. Bush in 2004.

It is clearly time for George Bush to reach out to moderate Muslims, not the radicals and Islamists his team has been romancing - to empower the former and to diminish, for both compelling strategic and political reasons, the influence of the latter. If any pandering is to be done from here on, let it be lavished on those - Muslim and non-Muslim alike - who are committed to strengthening this country against its enemies, instead of those who sympathize with them.

During a Camp David press conference with South Korean President Lee Myung-bak last Saturday, George W. Bush appealed for patience with respect to his administration's efforts to secure through negotiations North Korea's nuclear disarmament.

Ironically, the people most in need of such counsel are not Americans convinced by Pyongyang's past behavior that it will breach today's denuclearization accords as it has all previous ones. Rather, the folks who really need to heed the president's injunction against impatience are those in Foggy Bottom responsible for these negotiations: Secretary of State Condoleezza Rice and Assistant Secretary for East Asian and Pacific Affairs Christopher Hill. These diplomats are trying to achieve a fait accompli – accepting uncritically and immediately rewarding incomplete, unverified and surely fraudulent North Korean representations about their nuclear programs

Never mind that this latest, so-called " breakthrough " bears no resemblance to the total, verifiable and verified accounting we were promised as part of the deal Chris Hill struck with the North Koreans in February 2007. Those of us who believed Mr. Hill was just the latest of a string of ambitious interlocutors to be duped by the North Korean regime were not surprised when that accounting was not provided by the stipulated deadline of the end of last year.

Now, we are told Pyongyang will be allowed to make nothing more than unverified declarations about their plutonium program. Worse yet, they will not have to disclose anything about their covert enriched uranium activities and their proliferation of nuclear weapons technology to the likes of Iran and Syria.

In what passes for forceful American diplomacy these days, the North has been induced to do nothing more than acknowledge we believe they are engaged in such behavior and are "concerned " about it.

Of course, the State Department continues to dissemble about its acceptance of this proverbial pig-in-a-poke. Last Thursday, spokesman Sean McCormack said about this new deal: " Every aspect will be subject to verification and, if we detect that they have misled or attempted to mislead, there will be diplomatic consequences. " In other words, if we catch them lying to us again, Foggy Bottom will begin firing off demarches - the diplomats' missives that Richard Perle famously ridiculed as "demarshmellows. "

Even this laughable threat will prove empty if no real effort is expended to detect North Korean misrepresentations. The Rice-Hill team has systematically cut out the State Department's own verification professionals under Assistant Secretary Paula DeSutter. Instead, in a maneuver reminiscent of the notorious decision to send diplomat Joe Wilson to ferret out the truth about Saddam Hussein's alleged uranium purchases in Africa, Foreign Service officers are dispatched to go through the motions of "verifying " the latest deal.

The worst of it is that so little is being bought at such a high cost. Mr. Hill is determined to have North Korea removed from the State Department's state-sponsor of terrorism list and relevant provisions of the Trading with the Enemy act. He evidently seeks to do so the moment Pyongyang serves up its incomplete and unproven declaration, possibly as soon as Friday.

It is obvious why North Korean dictator Kim Jong-il is so keen on securing these U.S. concessions. He knows they will clear the way for infusions of foreign investment from companies anxious to exploit his nation's vast slave-labor work force - providing desperately needed life-support for a regime President Bush once rightly said he "loathed. "

What is less apparent is why is Foggy Bottom pushing so hard to dismantle, as a practical matter irreversibly, the most important sources of U.S. leverage on the North? It is not as though North Korea is out of the terrorism business; its ongoing help to the nuclear weapons programs of Iran and Syria constitutes the ultimate in state-sponsored terrorism. The former has repeatedly declared its intention to wipe Israel off the map and bring about a world without America. And the threat posed by the latter will finally be disclosed to Congress Thursday in a classified briefing on the September 2007 Israeli raid aimed at countering the Syrian-North Korean nuclear joint venture.

The easy explanation for Chris Hill's impatience is that he is a veritable poster child for the State Department affliction known as "clientitis. " He pushes for whatever the North Koreans demand, without regard for U.S. interests.

Another factor may be the progress now made to enable millions of Americans to invest " terror-free. " Thanks to recent steps by the Financial Times Stock Exchange, Conflict Securities Advisory Group and Northern Trust (among a rising number of other investment houses), such investors will soon be able easily to ensure their portfolios do not include publicly traded companies doing business with North Korea or other officially designated state sponsors of terror.

Kim Jong-il pitched a fit when the U.S. Treasury froze $25 million in one of his accounts in Macau two years ago. Imagine his upset if billion-dollar capital infusions he expects are threatened.

Mr. Bush was reportedly told last week by his Director of National Intelligence, Adm. Mike McConnell, that the U.S. intelligence community does not believe the regime in Pyongyang will denuclearize and that it will, instead, simply cheat on this deal as on all the previous ones. That being the case, it is all the more obvious that the president's call for patience should apply first and foremost to his State Department's efforts to give away what is left of the store - appropriate and needed designations of North Korea as a state-sponsor of terror and enemy of this country.

Barack Obama

How appropriate that Barack Obama featured Aretha Franklin in his inaugural festivities since her signature song is "Respect." Literally from the moment she finished belting out "My Country Tis of Thee" on January 20, the new President has been conveying his "respect" the Muslim world. Unfortunately, the way he practices it seems to be spelled S.U.B.M.I.S.S.I.O.N.

Several observers have noted in recent days that Mr. Obama's outreach to the Muslim world is not only defensive and apologetic. It explicitly embraces a narrative that is factually erroneous and deprecating to his own country.

For example, in his inaugural address, the President spoke of seeking "a new way forward [with the Muslim world], based on mutual interest and mutual respect." He amplified this idea during his first post-inaugural interview which was granted to a Saudi-owned network, al-Arabiya: He is determined to "restore" the "same respect and partnership America had with the Muslim world as recently as 20 or 30 years ago."

The problem with this formulation is that it misrepresents the more distant as well as the recent past, even as it panders to those (abroad and at home) who would blame the United States for the ills of the Muslim world. As Charles Krauthammer put it in his syndicated column last week, over the past 20 years, "America did not just respect Muslims, it bled for them....It is both false and injurious to this country to draw a historical line dividing America under Obama from a benighted past when Islam was supposedly disrespected and demonized."

The President also told al-Arabiya that: "My job is to communicate the fact that the United States has a stake in the well-being of the Muslim world, that the language we use has to be a language of respect. I have Muslim members of my family. I have lived in Muslim countries." Lest there be any doubt about the priority he attaches to this messaging, Mr. Obama repeated the point. "My job to the Muslim world is to communicate that the Americans are not your enemy. We sometimes make mistakes. We have not been perfect."

For good measure, the new President described America as a country of "Muslims, Christians, Jews" and others – a presumably intentional upgrading of adherents to the faith of his father, Islam, from the second place position he accorded them in his State of the Union address several days before. (The rankings of both orderings obviously reflect something other than demographics; there are far fewer Muslims than Christians in the United States and, according to independent estimates, only half as many – or less – than Jews.)

Mr. Obama has also seriously mischaracterized our enemy as "a far-reaching network of violence and hatred," averring "We cannot paint with a broad brush a faith as a consequence of the violence done in that faith's name." Such statements deliberately ignore the animating and unifying role in jihad of authoritative Islam's violent and hateful theo-political-legal program: Shariah.

What is really worrying is that Mr. Obama's actions and rhetoric are almost certainly being perceived by his target audience as evidence not of respect but of subservience – precisely what Islam (literally, "submission" in Arabic) requires of all of us, Muslims and non-Muslims, alike. Consider the following:

Mr. Obama has made no secret of his desire to cultivate improved relations with the mullahs of Iran, who have repressed their people and threatened ours for thirty years. It appears that he started to do so months before his election, as a senior campaign advisor, former Clinton Secretary of Defense William Perry, met repeatedly with a representative of Iran's genocide-supporting president, Mahmoud Ahamadinejad. In recent days, Obama special envoy for Afghan and Pakistan, Richard Holbrooke, hired as a senior advisor Professor Vali Reza Nasr – an Iranian expatriate with an appalling record of shilling for the Islamic Revolutionary Iranian regime.

According to GeostrategyDirect.com, a newsletter published by ace national security reporter Bill Gertz, "Diplomatic sources said Barack Obama has engaged several Arab intermediaries to relay messages to and from al Qaeda in the months before his elections as the 44th U.S. president. The sources said al Qaeda has offered what they termed a truce in exchange for a U.S. military withdrawal from Afghanistan. 'For the last few months, Obama has been receiving and sending feelers to those close to al Qaeda on whether the group would end its terrorist campaign against the United States,' a diplomatic source said. 'Obama sees this as helpful to his plans to essentially withdraw from Afghanistan and Iraq during his first term in office.'"

If surrender in Afghanistan, Iraq and Iran were not enough, upcoming opportunities for Mr. Obama to exhibit American submission to Islam include: ordering U.S. participation in the UN's "Durban II" conference – thereby legitimating its Iranian-dictated, rabidly anti-Israel, anti-American, Holocaust-denying and "Islamophobia"-banning agenda; adopting the program for undermining Israel promoted by longtime Friends-of-Barack Rashid Khalidi and Samantha Power (the latter just appointed a senior National Security Council official); and reversing the FBI's long-overdue decision to end its association with the Council on American Islamic Relations (CAIR), a prominent front organization of the Muslim Brotherhood (whose stated mission is "to destroy America from within.")

Whatever Barack Obama's intentions, the kind of "respect" he is exhibiting towards Shariah-adherent Muslims will surely be seen by them as submission. And that spells only one thing: D.I.S.A.S.T.E.R.

"We have met the enemy, and he is us." Increasingly, it appears Barack Obama feels the same way about America. Call it the PogObama worldview.

The president's first 100 days have been a blur of legislative initiatives, policy pronouncements and symbolic gestures that, taken together, constitute the most sweeping and fundamental makeover of U.S. domestic and foreign policies since at least World War II. Animating them all is a hostility toward this country's traditional values, institutions and conduct that is best described by Jeanne J. Kirkpatrick's phrase "blame America first."

To be sure, Mr. Obama has plenty of company in this camp, both at home and abroad. "San Francisco Democrats" (another Kirkpatrickism) like Speaker of the House Nancy Pelosi and tyrants like Venezuelan President Hugo Chavez (with whom the president did "high fives" over the weekend) and Saudi King Abdullah (to whom the president bowed two weeks ago) are of a mind: The United States owes the world myriad apologies for its arrogance, unilateralism, aggression and other sins. And it needs to make amends in various, substantial and ominously portentous ways, including the following:

Releasing the so-called "torture memos": The president pandered to the left last week by ignoring the advice of five past and present CIA directors and declassifying several top-secret legal memorandums. They lay out in excruciating detail what "enhanced interrogation techniques" could be used in extreme circumstances to secure information being withheld by al Qaeda and other high-value enemy operatives.

Though Mr. Obama says that those who followed these guidelines will not be prosecuted, he has, as a practical matter, invited their prosecution by others. Certainly, he left the door open, both here and overseas, to inquisitions of the memo-drafters and their superiors by Spanish judges, witch hunters in the U.S. Congress, prosecutors with the International Criminal Court, etc.

By effectively declaring "open season" on those in the Bush administration who helped secure this country in its time of need post-Sept. 11, Mr. Obama is not only wronging dedicated public servants who acted in good faith and prescribed techniques well short of torture. (As David Rivkin and Lee Casey point out in Monday's Wall Street Journal, thousands of American servicemen have been subjected to such methods for decades as part of their survival training.) He is also opening his own team to similar jeopardy, perhaps for killing innocent civilians with their Predator strikes in Pakistan or attacks said to be under discussion on putative Somali "terrorist camps."

Undermining U.S. sovereignty: Mr. Obama is embracing sovereignty-sapping treaties, theories of "universal jurisprudence" and individuals such as State Department legal adviser-designate Harold H. Koh who espouse them. The desired result evidently is a world governed by international norms and bureaucrats rather than one dominated - or even forcefully led - by bad old America.

Cutting America's power-projection capabilities: The defense budget reductions recently unveiled by Defense Secretary Robert M. Gates seem to have one thing in common: They will diminish the United States' ability to extend its global reach for the protection of this country and its interests around the world.

For example, Mr. Obama and Mr. Gates propose to cancel the C-17, America's indispensable airlifter; the F-22, the world's best fighter/attack aircraft; and the Army's Future Combat Systems program, a comprehensive and long-overdue modernization program for that service's armored forces. They would also truncate the purchase of F-18 E/Fs, the backbone of naval aviation, evidently as a precursor to reducing the number of operational aircraft carriers. Missile defense programs will be ravaged. There will be no modernization, ever, of the nation's nuclear deterrent. And the industrial base needed to support all of the above will be allowed to atrophy and/or be sold off to foreign powers keen to manufacture the superior weapon systems we no longer will.

Trying to appease America's adversaries: Mr. Obama is determined to normalize relations with literally every one of the world's bad actors - notably, Vladimir Putin's Russian kleptocracy, Iran's incipient nuclear mullahocracy, the Castro brothers' island gulag, the megalomaniacal Kim dynasty in North Korea, the spreading and virulently anti-American axis in our own hemisphere led by Mr. Chavez and the Muslim Brotherhood and other Shariah-adherent entities - without regard to their continuing, dangerous behavior or ambitions.

By associating himself with these hostile powers' critiques of the United States and by acquiescing to many, if not all, of their demands, Mr. Obama may temporarily cultivate the illusion of having improved bilateral relations and America's "image" internationally. Unfortunately, it is absolutely predictable that - in the absence of systemic changes in these and other despotic regimes the president is romancing - any "improvements" will come at the Free World's expense. And the image America ultimately will project will be of an emasculated, formerly great power, easy prey for those who seek not just to displace, but to destroy, it.

Under these circumstances, those of us who reject the PogObama view of the United States have our work cut out for us. Fortunately, most Americans do not see their country as "the enemy." It is time for legislators and other leaders who prize our sovereignty, who recognize the importance of preserving and wisely using our power and who understand that our true foes are numerous, elsewhere and being emboldened to enlist the public in challenging Team Obama's agenda before it brings us to grief.

During his White House years, William Jefferson Clinton -- someone Judge Sonia Sotomayor might call a "white male" -- was dubbed "America's first black president" by a black admirer. Applying the standard of identity politics and pandering to a special interest that earned Mr. Clinton that distinction, Barack Hussein Obama would have to be considered America's first Muslim president.

This is not to say, necessarily, that Mr. Obama actually is a Muslim any more than Mr. Clinton actually is black. After his five months in office, and most especially after his just-concluded visit to Saudi Arabia and Egypt, however, a stunning conclusion seems increasingly plausible: The man now happy to have his Islamic-rooted middle name featured prominently has engaged in the most consequential bait-and-switch since Adolf Hitler duped Neville Chamberlain over Czechoslovakia at Munich.

What little we know about Mr. Obama's youth certainly suggests that he not only had a Kenyan father who was Muslim, but spent his early, formative years as one in Indonesia. As the president likes to say, "much has been made" -- in this case by him and his campaign handlers -- of the fact that he became a Christian as an adult in Chicago, under the now-notorious Pastor Jeremiah A. Wright.

With Mr. Obama's unbelievably ballyhooed address in Cairo Thursday to what he calls "the Muslim world" (hereafter known as "the Speech"), there is mounting evidence that the president not only identifies with Muslims, but actually may still be one himself. Consider the following indicators:

- Mr. Obama referred four times in his speech to "the Holy Koran." Non-Muslims -- even pandering ones -- generally don't use that Islamic formulation.

- Mr. Obama established his firsthand knowledge of Islam (albeit without mentioning his reported upbringing in the faith) with the statement, "I have known Islam on three continents before coming to the region where it was first revealed." Again, "revealed" is a depiction Muslims use to reflect their conviction that the Koran is the word of God, as dictated to Muhammad.

- Then the president made a statement no believing Christian -- certainly not one versed, as he professes to be, in the ways of Islam -- would ever make. In the context of what he euphemistically called the "situation between Israelis, Palestinians and Arabs," Mr. Obama said he looked forward to the day ". . . when Jerusalem is a secure and lasting home for Jews and Christians and Muslims, and a place for all of the children of Abraham to mingle peacefully together as in the story of Isra, when Moses, Jesus and Muhammad (peace be upon them) joined in prayer."

Now, the term "peace be upon them" is invoked by Muslims as a way of blessing deceased holy men. According to Islam, that is what all three were - dead prophets. Of course, for Christians, Jesus is the living and immortal Son of God.

In the final analysis, it may be beside the point whether Mr. Obama actually is a Muslim. In the Speech and elsewhere, he has aligned himself with adherents to what authoritative Islam calls Shariah -- notably, the dangerous global movement known as the Muslim Brotherhood -- to a degree that makes Mr. Clinton's fabled affinity for blacks pale by comparison.

For example, Mr. Obama has -- from literally his inaugural address onward -- inflated the numbers and, in that way and others, exaggerated the contemporary and historical importance of Muslim-Americans in the United States. In the Speech, he used the Brotherhood's estimates of "nearly 7 million Muslims" in this country, at least twice the estimates from other, more reputable sources. (Who knows? By the time Mr. Obama's friends in the radical Association of Community Organizers for Reform Now (ACORN) perpetrate their trademark books-cooking as deputy 2010 census takers, the official count may well claim considerably morethan 7 million Muslims are living here.)

Even more troubling were the commitments the president made in Cairo to promote Islam in America. For instance, he declared: "I consider it part of my responsibility as president of the United States to fight against negative stereotypes of Islam wherever they appear." He vowed to ensure that women can cover their heads, including, presumably, when having their photographs taken for passports, driver's licenses or other identification purposes. He also pledged to enable Muslims to engage in zakat, their faith's requirement for tithing, even though four of the eight types of charity called for by Shariah can be associated with terrorism. Not surprisingly, a number of Islamic "charities" in this country have been convicted of providing material support for terrorism.

Particularly worrying is the realignment Mr. Obama has announced in U.S. policy toward Israel. While he pays lip service to the "unbreakable" bond between America and the Jewish state, the president has unmistakably signaled that he intends to compel the Israelis to make territorial and other strategic concessions to Palestinians to achieve the hallowed two-state solution. In doing so, he ignores the inconvenient fact that both the Brotherhood's Hamas and Abu Mazen's Fatah remain determined to achieve a one-state solution, whereby the Jews will be driven "into the sea."

Whether Mr. Obama actually is a Muslim or simply plays one in the presidency may, in the end, be irrelevant. What is alarming is that in aligning himself and his policies with those of Shariah-adherents such as the Muslim Brotherhood, the president will greatly intensify the already enormous pressure on peaceful, tolerant American Muslims to submit to such forces - and heighten expectations, here and abroad, that the rest of us will do so as well.

Sunday night, President Obama tried to allay concerns that his headlong rush to get a health care bill enacted defies the time-tested axiom that haste-makes-waste: "I intend to be president for a while and once this bill passes, I own it."

The comment may have been intended as just a colloquial way of describing the responsibility that the chief executive will have for making the new health system work. Against the backdrop of myriad other aspects of this presidency, however, a more literal - and worrying - interpretation seems in order.

Mr. Obama's remark prompted a pointed response by Weekly Standard editor William Kristol on the magazine's website: "No, Mr. President. It's not about you. If legislation passes, you don't own it. We all own it. Any health care bill will become part of the U.S. Code, not simply an item on the Obama White House web site. We will all feel its effects. We are all responsible for the future of our country. Here the people rule."

With those four words - "Here the people rule" - Mr. Kristol has identified what's most grievously wrong with President Obama's agenda. In myriad ways, some great, some small, the new administration seems increasingly to be supplanting the nation's fundamental constitutional arrangements and the institutions built upon them. The trajectory is unmistakably in the direction of certain people ruling, specifically the President.

Reduced to their essence, the endangered order can be defined as a government of, by and for all the people, one rooted in the principle that power must be exercised, pursuant to the rule of law, in representative and accountable ways. Thanks to these constitutional arrangements and institutions, the people's rule here has been assured for over two hundred years.

In the place of such quintessentially American principles and practices, however, we increasingly confront power over our economy and society being concentrated in the hands of faceless federal bureaucracies and - worse yet - those of appointed and generally unvetted "czars." [The more we learn about some of the latter, like the erstwhile "Green Jobs" czar (or, more aptly, "commissar") Van Jones, the more unsettling such a concentration of power becomes.]

The checks and balances on the executive built by the framers into the co-equal legislative branch have withered, particularly when the same political party controls both the White House and both chambers on Capitol Hill. Legislation is now routinely adopted without careful deliberation, let alone real debate. With increasing frequency, votes are taken without an opportunity afforded to lawmakers even to read the massive bills they are asked to approve. The only way one of the most controversial proposals ever considered by any Congress, namely Mr. Obama's "reform" of health care, will be approved is if the Senate disregards its own traditions and rules designed to protect the rights of the minority.

Perhaps even more worrying is the embrace by Team Obama of a still-greater affront to American sovereignty and self-governance: transnationalism. The notion that laws, regulations and rulings promulgated by foreign bureaucracies, organizations and courts should be considered to have equal standing, if not more, than those produced pursuant to the U.S. Constitution and Code further undermines the latter. Mr. Obama has begun to populate the executive and judicial branches with transnationalists like Harold Koh, Eric Holder and Sonya Sotomayor, making it increasingly probable that those unrepresentative of and unaccountable to Americans will be exercising ever-greater influence over our lives and fortunes.

Mr. Obama's characterization that he will "own" the "reformed" health care system speaks to another, more intangible but increasingly vexing factor in his presidency: the practice known in totalitarian systems as the "cult of personality" whereby, as Wikipedia puts it, "a country's leader uses mass media to create an idealized and heroic public image, often through unquestioning flattery and praise."

To be sure, all American presidents are the subject of intense press attention and public interest. Still, the extent to which the incumbent has received, with few exceptions, decidedly and sustained favorable treatment from the mass media is unprecedented. The effect is compounded by, for example, the phenomenon of what amount to Obama shrines in every airport bookstore, magazine racks full of periodicals with covers featuring one or more members of the First Family and Pepsi ads imitating the president's campaign posters and themes.

Perhaps the most dramatic example of the upending of the traditional relationship between Americans and their government is captured in the video released earlier this year that featured dozens of Hollywood celebrities led by actors Demi Moore and Ashton Kutcher. The participants urge us to join them as they "pledge to be a servant to our President and to all mankind."

Now, this can be chalked up to nothing more than ditsy folks in Tinsel Town enthusing about the arrival of an administration that shares their politics and deserves their unalloyed support. Still, the notion that these prominent figures are popularizing - namely, that the relationship between the President and the public should be one of the ruler and his servants - is wholly incompatible with the American Constitution and system of government it prescribes.

Worse yet, it seems consistent with the aforementioned affronts to the principle that "Here the people rule." If this pattern persists, the thousands of our disaffected countrymen and women who descended on Washington last week will be but a small foretaste of a rising determination to restore government truly of, by and for the people.

Attorney General Eric Holder's decision to bring self-professed 9/11 mastermind Khalid Shaikh Mohammed and four of his alleged co-conspirators to trial in New York City is a disaster. Barring a repetition in civilian court of an earlier confession, it is at least as likely that the terrorist known internationally by his initials, KSM, will be set free as it is that he will be executed for the murder of nearly 3,000 innocent Americans eight years ago.

As unlawful enemy combatants, Mohammed and his fellow jihadists are not entitled under the Geneva Convention to *any* judicial review. President Obama himself has said that there are scores of individuals being held at Guantanamo Bay - the so-called "worst of the worst" - who cannot be tried but must nonetheless be detained indefinitely. Such treatment should certainly be applied to a man who is arguably *the very worst* of the worst of the worst.

Mr. Holder's insistence that KSM and Company should come to the very heart of the city that is the biggest target for international terrorism is flawed on so many grounds that it is hard to escape the conclusion that the decision has more to do with President Obama's determination to close Gitmo than it does with ensuring justice is done. After all, if the most dangerous of our enemies can be safely brought to America soil, why can't the rest?

Consider just a few of the problems that seem likely seriously to complicate, if not preclude, the conviction of the 9/11 plotters:

- The moment they set foot in this country, all will be accorded constitutional rights to which they are not entitled - but from which they will extract considerable benefit. For example, they will have access to the best defense counsel, men and women determined to use civil liberties designed to protect the innocent to secure release of the guilty. Many of these lawyers comprise what is known as the "Guantanamo bar," including attorneys from Mr. Holder's former law firm and some of his senior subordinates now responsible for detainee policy at the Department of Justice.

- The attorneys will point out that, when apprehended, the accused were not read their Miranda rights. That was because, of course, they didn't have any. But that was then and this is now.

- The terrorists' lawyers will also try to exploit the government's reluctance to compromise intelligence sources and methods, in the hope of ensuring that the cost to the national security of prosecuting their clients will become excessive.

- The defense will work hard to reveal as much as possible of the enhanced interrogation techniques and other means used to extract information from hardened terrorists like KSM. In particular, they will endlessly trumpet the fact that Mohammed was subjected to one of those techniques - waterboarding - on over 180 occasions. (Never mind that afterwards he divulged invaluable information that prevented new attacks, made it possible to roll up al Qaeda operatives and saved American and others' lives.) My guess is that the defendants will ask Messrs. Obama and Holder to testify on why they consider such a practice to be "torture."

Then, there is the probability that the defense will successfully argue that they can't find an impartial jury in the city profoundly traumatized by the 9/11 attacks. The Washington Times reported Monday that Sen. Jack Reed, Democrat of Rhode Island, believes "'The people in New York who saw the towers fall' would be the ideal people to judge the September 11 terrorists." But will a federal judge agree? And if not, will the security arrangements in the alternative venue be as good as we are assured they are in New York?

Speaking of security, as with the various locations where Team Obama is trying to dump the rest of the Gitmo detainees (including most recently an Illinois prison 150 miles from Chicago), the problem is only partly one of ensuring the prisoners are unable to escape. The surrounding communities assuredly become higher-value, as well as inherently "soft" (read, easy), targets for further terrorist attacks.

Even if the likes of KSM can be safely confined in our prisons, that does not mean they pose no danger. FBI Director Robert Mueller has publicly warned that such rock stars of the Shariah-mandated jihadist movement constitute a grave threat in our penal system as they inspire, recruit and train other prisoners. This is not a hypothetical risk: Several recently uncovered terrorist plots in this country involved individuals who joined the jihad in American jails.

To be sure, if Khalid Shaikh Mohammed goes to trial in civilian court, he might again plead guilty. Even if he does not, he might be convicted. Years from now, he might even get the death penalty.

There are, however, real and unacceptably high risks associated with trying to secure such outcomes in U.S. federal court.

One thing is clear already: Neither American values, the families of those who lost loved ones on 9/11 nor rest of us are going to be well served by affording Mohammed and his co-conspirators a platform for waging lawfare and political warfare against us. The proper way to deal with such unrepentant psychopaths who justify their murderous actions by Shariah is to include them in the group Mr. Obama intends to lock up forever without trial - and to do so at the most secure prison in the world: Guantanamo Bay.

Even for a man known for his arrogance, Barack Obama's treatment of the Senate in connection with the New START Treaty is astounding. His demand that Senators approve this defective accord during the few days remaining in the lame-duck session amounts to contempt of Congress. It must not be tolerated, let alone rewarded.

To be sure, Mr. Obama is not the first chief executive to hold the legislative branch in low esteem. Still, his highhandedness when it comes to the constitutional responsibility of the Senate to play a real role in treaty making seems particularly contemptuous, and contemptible.

The Obama administration's insistence that Senators accede to his efforts to relegate them to rubber-stamps is without precedent. As a bipartisan group of fifteen former senators recently observed, never before in the history of the U.S. Senate has the deliberation and vote on an arms control agreement been truncated by their being conducted during a lame-duck session.

The effort to ram the treaty through before Christmas is no more justified than it is precedented. The claim being made by the administration and its surrogates that uncertainty about Russian activities necessitates such haste is laughable. President Obama himself is responsible for allowing previous verification arrangements to lapse. He did so over a year ago and seemed untroubled until now about there being no monitoring systems in place. And the insights this accord's limited inspection and monitoring arrangements will afford are hardly up to the job of detecting the Kremlin's inveterate cheating and other strategically ominous developments.

It turns out the real need for verification lies elsewhere - namely, in establishing what Team Obama has given away with respect to missile defense in course of negotiating New START, and in the months since that treaty was signed. Last week, the *Washington Times'* ace national security reporter, Bill Gertz, revealed that the administration had been caught lying to Senators concerned about yet another agreement now being developed with the Russians. Apparently, it would go beyond the undesirable limitations on U.S. anti-missile systems - both direct and indirect - that were incorporated into the present accord. (In a marvelous essay at National Review Online, former federal prosecutor Andy McCarthy demonstrates both the reality and undesirability of those limitations.)

The Obama administration has tried to allay concerns about any new negotiations by saying that they are simply building on talks the Bush administration had previously held with Moscow on missile defense cooperation. As former Deputy Assistant Secretary of Defense Keith Payne, who headed up the U.S. delegation to those talks, pointed out to a Capitol Hill audience last week, his explicit instructions were not to discuss (let alone agree to) limits of any kind on our anti-missile capabilities. It is hard to imagine a more different agenda than that of Mr. Obama - whose ideologically driven antipathy to such defenses seems about as deep-seated as his disdain for those in Congress who have sought to protect Americans against ballistic missile attack.

Such Senators have an obligation to understand what the administration has actually *agreed to* with respect to missile defense. Yet, as was made plain by the false official assurances Mr. Gertz uncovered, legislators cannot possibly do so unless they have access to the New START negotiating record - which chronicles the evolution of the treaty over the many months of parleys between the two sides.

This document would also reveal how the U.S. position on issue after issue unraveled in the face of Russian opposition and Mr. Obama's determination to get a deal, no matter how bad its terms. It would, in short, be an embarrassment as well as an impediment to ratification of the New START Treaty.

As a result, every request by Senators for the negotiating record has been spurned in what Secretary of State Hillary Clinton recently characterized as a "no-hit" game. Presumably, she is referring to the success her department and the rest of the administration have had in suppressing opposition witnesses, inconvenient questions and unhelpful information.

The question is: Will the Senate allow such contempt to be tolerated? If so, one thing is sure. There will be more where that comes from.

Senators are on notice that New START establishes a Bilateral Consultative Commission (BCC) that can, and surely will, make deals that affect the treaty's terms in material ways - and do so without the Senate's advice or consent. U.S. and Russian negotiators working on restricting our missile defenses and still further reductions in our nuclear deterrent forces will be emboldened, confident that their handiwork will not be subjected to serious quality-control.

And the administration will portray the Senate as on board with its agenda of denuclearizing the world, starting with the United States. It is absolutely predictable that any deal made to secure approval of New START that is at odds with that agenda (notably, Sen. Jon Kyl's laudable efforts to secure funding for modernization of the nuclear weapons complex) will soon be over the side.

In short, if the Senate ignores the President's contempt for it as a constitutionally mandated partner in treaty making, if it ignores the lack of precedent for lame-duck consideration of an arms control treaty, if it ignores the need to do due-diligence, if it ignores the request of eleven of those newly elected to serve in the Senate of the 112th Congress to hold off on New START until they are sworn in, Senators will not only get more contempt. They will have earned it.

Like ordinary folks, presidents of the United States are known by the company they keep. It is a test of their character. Often it shapes their policies. And, in the case of Barack Obama, it may blight his legacy and our nation's security interests.

Until now, one of the most egregious examples of the problem were the "Friends of Bill" who played prominent roles in William Jefferson Clinton's presidency. Those folks included a mix of unsavory political operatives, Chinese agents and convicted felons. [Their overnight stays in the Lincoln bedroom, legally challenged fundraising and eleventh-hour pardons raised serious questions not just about President Clinton's ethics, but his judgment.]

President Obama's trusted circle has been, if anything, even more problematic. For example, Mr. Obama has consorted with people who are revolutionaries, communists, liberation theologians and Islamists. Some have even been appointed "czars" in his administration.

At the moment, though, we must be concerned not only with who Barack Obama considers his friends, but with those who deem him to be one of theirs: The record suggests he must be seen as a "Friend of Shariah."

How else can we explain the seeming inconsistency between, on the one hand, the president's indifference to demonstrations in Iran last year that were vastly larger and more sustained than those to date in Egypt, and, on the other, his insistence after a week's worth of protests in the latter that there be nothing less than complete "regime change," starting immediately?

The only obvious common denominator is that, in both cases, Mr. Obama is pursuing policies favored by those who adhere to the repressive, supremacist and virulently anti-American Islamic political-military-legal program its adherents call shariah. In Iran, shariah is already the law of the land, ruthlessly enforced by the Shiite theocrats of Tehran. In Egypt, the Mubarak regime's failure faithfully to enforce shariah is one of the principal impetuses behind the Iranian mullahs' Sunni wannabe counterparts, the Muslim Brotherhood (MB or, in Arabic, Ikhwan).

Alas, President Obama's seeming affinity for shariah has not been confined to his ever more evident support for the Ikhwan taking power in a nation the United States has long seen (rightly or wrongly) as an indispensable and reliable regional ally. For instance:

In September 2009, the Obama administration co-sponsored a resolution introduced in the UN Human Rights Council by Egypt on behalf of a Muslim multinational entity known as the Organization of the Islamic Conference (OIC). The measure advanced the OIC's longstanding purpose, pursued in the name of the seemingly unobjectionable goal of preventing "defamation of religion," to impose worldwide what amount to shariah blasphemy laws.

Last August, President Obama used the occasion of a White House dinner breaking the Ramadan fast to endorse the construction of a controversial mosque close by the site of the former Twin Towers in Manhattan. This initiative became notorious as the American people learned that it is not merely a matter of "insensitivity" to put an "Islamic community center" on hallowed ground. Such a step fits a distinct pattern under shariah of symbolically using the construction of triumphalist mosques on the holiest sites of conquered peoples to make the latter, as the Koran puts it, "feel themselves subdued."

Mr. Obama nonetheless expressed his support for the Ground Zero mosque. He did so to the delight of those in his audience like Ingrid Mattson. At the time, she was the figurehead leader of the largest Muslim Brotherhood front organization in the United States, the Islamic Society of North America (ISNA).

Yes, that would be the same Muslim Brotherhood Mr. Obama is helping come to power in Egypt. And yes, ISNA was an unindicted co-conspirator in the biggest terrorism financing trial in U.S. history. Under the Obama administration, though, ISNA remains the vehicle of choice for official "outreach" to the Muslim-American community and the parent organization responsible for certifying chaplains for the U.S. military and prison system.

Then, there is the latest symptom of submissive behavior on the part of Mr. Obama and what appear to be other "friends of shariah" in his administration. As my colleagues, Patrick Poole and Christine Brim, have illuminated at BigPeace.com, we now have the Virginia Military Institute preparing to "celebrate" the 1300th anniversary of "Tariq ibn Ziyad's crossing of the Straits of Gibraltar" ushering in some 800 years of Moorish conquest and occupation of Spain and, in VMI's words, "setting into motion the fusion between two worlds."

It turns out that this new act of submission to Islamist triumphalism is a by-product of a transnationalist program funded by the Defense Department and known as "Project GO," in which GO stands for "Global Officers." It is administered for the Pentagon by the Institute for International Education which is, in turn, advised by "dedicated internationalists" from Saudi Arabia, the UAE and, as it happens, the Chinese Communist Politburo. It is obscene that such propagandizing is taking place at what has long been one of America's preeminent military academies. But it is, as the Politburo's Li Yuanchao might say, "no accident, comrade."

The foregoing are but a few of the manifestations of a deeply worrying trend involving acquiescence to and, in some cases it appears, outright embrace of the dictates of shariah under the Obama administration. The question occurs, with friends of shariah like Barack Obama, who needs enemies?

For some time, the outlines of an Obama Doctrine have been apparent. It can be summarized in nine damning words: Embolden our enemies. Undermine our friends. Diminish our country. These days, it is hard to avoid proof that these outcomes are not inadvertent, or attributable to sheer and sustained incompetence. Rather, they are a product of deliberate decisions approved, we must assume, by the President himself.

Consider last week's announcement by Secretary of State Hillary Clinton that the United States was going to "engage" the Muslim Brotherhood in Egypt. At one fell swoop, Team Obama hit its doctrinal trifecta:

America arguably has no more mortal enemy than the Muslim Brotherhood (MB or *Ikhwan*in Arabic). The MB's own documents - including a number of those introduced into evidence by the Justice Department in the largest terrorism financing trial in U.S. history, the Holy Land Foundation prosecution - make clear that this international Islamist organization seeks to impose its politico-military-legal doctrine of shariah on our country.

One such document describes a "phased plan" that calls for the *Ikhwan* assiduously and stealthily to pursue precisely this objective. Ultimately, the plan calls for the use of violence to take over our government, clearing the way for the triumph of Islam worldwide and the reestablishment of a global ruler, the Caliph, who will govern in accordance with shariah.

Sounds crazy, right? Or at least unachievable? It does - at least until you realize that the message being sent by the Obama administration is that, despite such ambitions, we are prepared to legitimate and deal with the Muslim Brothers who are animated by them.

Well, perhaps you say, just because we are recognizing that the Muslim Brotherhood is likely to be a big player (read, the winner) in the elections currently scheduled for later this year in Egypt does not mean we are going to facilitate their aspirations in this country. Unfortunately, that is exactly what it means.

By engaging the *Ikhwan* in its native land, the Obama administration is effectively eliminating any lingering impediment to the operations of its myriad front groups in this country. Even before Secretary Clinton's announcement, many of them have already been accorded unprecedented access to and influence in the U.S. government. In fact, it stands to reason that one of the factors prompting Team Obama to embrace the Muslim Brotherhood is the success of such influence operations within the United States.

In addition to emboldening our enemies by reinforcing their conviction that we are in decline, the Obama administration's MB initiative undermines our friends. That is most obviously the case with respect to Israel, a nation already reeling from the President's serial, gratuitous acts of enmity towards the Jewish State. Now, his embrace of the *Ikhwan* can only exacerbate the worsening strategic environment the Israelis have faced in the months since the United States pulled the plug on Mubarak.

For example, Israel has been seriously buffeted by actions taken to date by an Egyptian military clearly under the influence of the Muslim Brotherhood. These include steps taken to: restore relations with Hamas and Iran; broker the Palestinians' so-called "unity government; open the Raffa crossing into Gaza; afford a hero's welcome in Tahrir Square to one of the world's most virulent Islamist ideologues, Sheikh Yusef al-Qaradawi; and threaten to dispense with the peace treaty with Israel.

If both the Egyptian military and the Brotherhood conclude - as they reasonably could be expected to do - that there will be no costs associated with going beyond the unfriendly initiatives Cairo has already adopted, it is predictable that still worse behavior with respect to our interests and allies will be forthcoming. That conclusion will probably not be lost on one other important audience: whatever secular democrats there actually are in Egypt, who must be watching with horror the dissipation of any hope for support in keeping their country from becoming the next shariah-adherent Islamist stronghold.

It is hard to characterize all this as other than a further diminishing of America as a beacon of liberty and reliable friend to those who cherish freedom, or aspire to obtain it. If we are unable to counter even those who are explicitly hostile to our survival as a nation, we encourage the perception that this country is reduced to appeasing its enemies and selling out our friends. We will have many more of the former and far fewer of the latter.

A further impetus to the perception of a diminished America may come this week after Atlantis performs the planned final flight of a U.S. space shuttle. President Obama declined to keep the shuttles going, canceled the planned replacement platform for manned space flight and thereby condemned this country for the foreseeable future to reliance on Russian and perhaps, in due course, Chinese rockets to deliver our astronauts to the space station.

Lest we forget, this momentous dismantling of America's place as the world's preeminent space power fits the Obama Doctrine in one other way: It was just a year ago that the then-newly appointed NASA Administrator, Charles Bolden, recounted how President Obama had apprized him of his priority mission: "Perhaps foremost, he wanted me to find a way to reach out to the Muslim world and engage much more with dominantly Muslim nations to help them feel good about their historic contribution to science...and math and engineering."

Kind of hard to miss the pattern here.

"WANTED: A COMPETENT COMMANDER IN CHIEF" | APRIL 30, 2012

It turns out Team Obama suddenly wants the 2012 presidential campaign to be about foreign policy rather than the economy. Such a pivot might not be surprising given that by President Obama's own test, he has not cut unemployment to the point where he deserves to be re-elected.

The Democrats have - if anything - a weaker case for re-electing this president on national security grounds. The campaign ad they unveiled on Friday, timed to take credit for the liquidation of Osama bin Laden on the first anniversary of that achievement, is a case in point.

The video uses former President Bill Clinton to extol his successor's role in the mission - and selectively quotes Republican nominee Mitt Romney to suggest he would not have done the same thing.

It is an act of desperation and contempt for the American people that, of all people, Mr. Clinton would be used in such a role. Let's recall that during his presidency, he repeatedly declined to take out bin Laden. The former president is so sensitive about this sorry record that his operatives insisted in 2006 that ABC excise from "Path to 9/11" - an outstanding made-for-TV film by Cyrus Nowrasteh - a dramatized version of one such episode.

More telling still is an issue inadvertently showcased by this controversy. While the Clinton-Obama-Biden spot tries to make Mr. Romney sound as though he wouldn't have had the courage, or at least the vision, the president exhibited in a risky bid to take out bin Laden, what the presumptive Republican nominee actually said in 2007 in context illustrates a far better grasp than Mr. Obama has of the enemy we confront:

"I wouldn't want to over concentrate on bin Laden. He's one of many, many people who are involved in this global jihadist effort. He's by no means the only leader. It's a very diverse group - Hamas, Hezbollah, al Qaeda, Muslim Brotherhood and, of course, different names throughout the world. It's not worth moving heaven and earth and spending billions of dollars just trying to catch one person. It is worth fashioning and executing an effective strategy to defeat global, violent jihad, and I have a plan for doing that."

Mr. Obama, by contrast, would have us believe that the problem is al Qaeda and that threat is pretty much a thing of the past, thanks to bin Laden's elimination and the decimation, primarily by drone strikes, of others among its leadership and rank and file. An unnamed senior State Department official told the National Journal last week, "The war on terror is over" as Muslims embrace "legitimate Islamism."

Unfortunately, as Seth Jones observed in the Wall Street Journal on Monday, "Al Qaeda is far from dead. Acting as if it were will not make it so."

Even if al Qaeda actually had been defeated, however, we are – as Mitt Romney said five years ago - confronting a host of other jihadist enemies who seek the same goals as bin Laden's al Qaeda and its franchises: the triumph of the totalitarian, supremacist Islamic doctrine of Shariah and a global government, known as a caliphate, to govern accordingly.

Unfortunately, as demonstrated conclusively in a free, Web-based video course titled "Muslim Brotherhood in America: The Enemy Within," released last week by the Center for Security Policy (MuslimBrotherhoodinAmerica.com), far from understanding the danger posed by the rest of the jihadist enterprise, the Obama administration is actually making it stronger.

The evidence presented in this course suggests that that could be, at least in part, because of the six Muslim Brotherhood-associated individuals the center has identified who are either on the government's payroll, advising it or being used for outreach to the American Muslim community. (See Part 8 of the video course for details on the Obama Six.)

Whatever the motivation, consider how Team Obama has managed the three other groups Mr. Romney mentioned. The administration made no effort to impede the takeover of Lebanon by the Iranian foreign legion, the designated terrorist organization known as Hezbollah. It has actively helped bring to power, recognized and effectively turned over $1.5 billion to the Muslim Brotherhood in Egypt. Worse yet, it has, as noted above, embraced its operatives and front groups here. President Obama personally directed last week that $170 million in U.S. foreign aid be given to a Palestinian Authority "unity government," which includes another designated terrorist organization, Hamas - incredibly - on the grounds that "U.S. national security interests" required it.

Unfortunately for the Obama administration, fundamentally misconstruing the nature of the enemy is just part of this president's ominous legacy with respect to his commander-in-chief portfolio. The wrecking operation he is engaged in concerning our military's capability to project power, its unilateral cuts to the U.S. nuclear deterrent and weakening our missile defenses may not be fully evident between now and the election. But the impact will be felt for generations to come. That will be true in spades of the war on the culture of the armed forces being waged in pursuit of the radical left's efforts to make over American social norms and mores, starting with its most esteemed institution: the United States military.

Getting bin Laden isn't the issue. The issue is whether Mr. Obama is getting right the rest of his job as commander in chief. Regrettably, he is not.

HOW TO WAGE AND WIN THE WAR FOR THE FREE WORLD

Ronald Reagan famously observed first in 1961 that: "Freedom is never more than one generation away from extinction....It must be fought for, protected and handed on [to our children] to do the same. Or we will spend our sunset years telling our children...what it was like to live in the United States when men were free."

Over the past twenty-five years, that multi-generational struggle to preserve freedom from its enemies' determined efforts to extinguish it – a struggle that I believe is best described as the War for the Free World – has undergone a number of important changes.

We have seen various threats emerge (see Section 1). Some have seemed to take on less importance due to the rise of others. For instance, the apparent end of the Cold War and a promising transition from Soviet empire and misrule to the freeing of formerly enslaved nations with popularly elected governments for a time diminished concerns about the Kremlin and its nuclear forces.

In its place, concerns have inexorably – if altogether too slowly – grown over the dangers posed by what has been euphemistically described as "terrorism" or "violent extremism." While too many Americans are still unclear about the wellspring of this menace, namely the Islamic supremacist doctrine known as shariah and those who seek to impose it on all of us, awareness that we face a mortal peril from this jihadist quarter has grown inexorably.

Regrettably, resurgent challenges from Vladimir Putin's Russia, an increasingly aggressive China, a more-and-more capable North Korean military, an Iranian nuclear weapon (topics addressed in the first section of this volume) have been somewhat obscured by our growing preoccupation with the global jihad movement.

Matters are made worse by the lack in much of official Washington and the body politic more generally of what I call, for want of a better term, national security-mindedness. Too many among the American population at large and among their elected representatives have little, if any, idea about these threats – let alone what should be done about them.

That reality has moved me for the past twenty-five years to endeavor not only to identify the present dangers – and incipient ones. I have also striven to put forward in column after column ideas about what should be done to address them.

This section offers illustrative examples of such remedies grouped thematically. As is true with the organization of this volume more generally, some of these columns could as easily appear elsewhere. But their focus on prescriptions for action causes them to fit best in this section and, I believe, to be of continuing value as the threat environment continues to mutate and worsen, and the imperative for corrective measures grows accordingly.

Peace Through Strength

In the aftermath of the impeccably executed aerial attack that initiated the war with Iraq, the old saw that success has many fathers while failure is an orphan comes to mind.

Indeed, so feverish have become the recent paternity claims and counterclaims by former government officials over who deserves credit for the technological wizardry exhibited in Operation Desert Storm's opening hours that nothing short of genetic testing seems likely to resolve the matter.

The controversy seems to have been precipitated by partisans of the Reagan administration who have averred that the much-maligned military buildup of the early 1980s made it possible for the U.S.-led air strike to wreak so much destruction on the Iraqi military with virtually no loss of American lives and minimal collateral damage to the civilian population.

In response, officials of the Carter administration, notably former Defense Secretary Harold Brown, have observed somewhat testily that it was on his watch that the key decisions were made on technologies central to this brilliant military feat.

The truth of the matter is that no single presidency, nor either political party, can take exclusive credit for the success of Desert Storm. The capabilities utilized for the attack were the product of investments made by the Nixon, Ford, Carter, Reagan and Bush administrations. Indeed, given the extraordinarily long process involved in bringing modern weapon systems from the drawing board to operational status - typically more than 10 years in duration - responsibility for realizing a given technical achievement can almost always be reasonably claimed by more than one president and his team.

That said, it strikes me as patently misleading to suggest that the performance of the U.S. military in the opening days of the war with Iraq is other than a tribute to the dedicated and sustained program of force modernization, recruitment, training and maintenance of the armed forces accomplished during the Reagan years.

To be sure, the Carter administration initiated research and development on the F-117A Stealth fighter and the Tomahawk sea-launched cruise missiles – two of the weapon systems that starred in the early hours of the air campaign. That step represents, however, the relatively easy part of the torturous process of acquiring and fielding state-of-the-art military technologies.

Without for a minute deprecating Mr. Brown's vision in funding work on what were then largely "gleams in the eye" of their designers, the truly hard part comes not in the research and development phase but at the point where promising projects turn into multibillion dollar procurement programs. This is the point where, as the military puts it, "the rubber meets the road."

As a general rule, congressional oversight committees that are willing to support even expensive R&D initiatives become much more parsimonious when it comes to the decision to put a system into production. Capitol Hill, like the news media, relishes stories about the shortcomings of big-ticket weapon systems, their test failures, their cost overruns and the scheduled milestones they have missed. Virtually every U.S. weapon system employed in the Persian Gulf today - from the M1A1 Abrams main battle tank to the Bradley infantry fighting vehicle to the Apache attack helicopter to the Patriot missile system to the Aegis cruiser to the F-14 fighter to the low-altitude LANTIRN targeting system to the Global Positioning Navigational System - has been, at one point or another, the subject of controversy, vituperative criticism and nearly fatal legislative attack.

These weapons are operational in quantity today in the U.S. armed forces, instead of mere prototypes collecting dust in a museum of developmental also-rans, thanks to the policies and tenacity of President Reagan and his stalwart defense secretary, Cap Weinberger. Bedeviled though they were by distorted stories of defense procurement scandals - for example, the infamous

$700 toilet seats, $100 hammers and $7,000 coffee pots - these leaders never wavered in their determination to correct the cumulative effects of nearly a decade of post-Vietnam underfunding and deferred modernization for the Pentagon. Just as importantly, the Reagan team never lost sight of the critical importance of recruiting, training and retaining the highest-quality personnel to man these weapons. As a result of hard-won pay increases, re-enlistment incentives and significant improvements in the quality of military life, it was able to bequeath to its successor not the "hollow army" it inherited from the Carter administration but rather the finest fighting force on Earth.

Perhaps far more intangible, but no less significant, was the contribution Mr. Reagan made to restoring the American military to a position of prestige, respect and honor in our society. His utterly genuine and unabashed admiration and gratitude for those who served in uniform was infectious. Arguably, it did as much as did his successful use of force in liberating Grenada and in retaliating for Libyan terrorism to encourage the national psyche to discard the anti-military sentiments so much in evidence after Vietnam.

These then were the elements that underpinned the quintessentially Reagan strategy of Peace Through Strength. Taken together, they helped create conditions at home and abroad that contributed to the dawning of an era of unprecedentedly dramatic yet largely peaceful change in Europe and elsewhere. Taken together, they also were decisive in giving the United States the capability to engage militarily and effectively anywhere in the world – a capability on such stupendous display in the present war with Iraq.

In short, taken together, the Reagan contributions to American security made the difference between Desert Storm and Desert One, the patch of Iranian sand where Jimmy Carter's disastrous hostage rescue mission and his presidency were aborted.

A funny thing is happening on the defense budget's way to the chopping block: People are beginning to have serious second thoughts.

Interestingly, such people include not only the defense secretary and the chairman of the Joint Chiefs of Staff. To be sure, these senior defense officials have let it be known that the draconian reductions anticipated in fiscal 1992 and the remainder of the president's five-year plan may need to be reconsidered in light of the recent experience with Operation Desert Storm and rapidly unfolding events in the Soviet Union.

And yet, Defense Secretary Dick Cheney, Gen. Colin Powell and their senior subordinates have suggested that the data are not yet in hand to recommend changes from baseline presidential request for the Defense Department. Implicitly, if not explicitly, they seem to be saying that, in the meantime, the sensible thing to do is to proceed with the recommended defense cuts.

Amazingly enough, members of Congress - the body most insistent in recent years on gutting the defense budget - have also begun to challenge the advisability of the planned cuts in military spending. Administration witnesses have been pelted by questions from representatives of both sides of the political aisle with hard - and timely - questions about how prudent it is to be dismantling defense capabilities, the requirement for which has been so recently, and vividly, validated by the war with Iraq.

Some are inclined to dismiss such concerns as simply one more example of congressional desires to have it both ways - to cut the defense budget but not to accept the consequences of doing so as they translate into constituents' lost jobs. While this consideration is clearly a factor, the phenomenon now beginning to emerge from the annual authorization and appropriations hearings appears to transcend narrow pork-barrel politics and vested self-interests.

Instead, legitimate questions are being raised about the prudence of steps that would:

- Reduce the capacity of U.S. armed forces for rapid, distant deployment - a capacity sorely taxed by the Desert Shield exercise - by eliminating from the inventory valuable sea- and air-lift assets, shrinking the number of men and women under arms and scrapping carrier battle groups, air wings and army divisions.

- Terminate production of battle-tested tanks, aircraft, missiles and ships before follow-on systems have been proven - to say nothing of put into full-scale production, with incalculably adverse effects on the defense industrial base and wartime surge manufacturing capabilities.

- And cancel or stretch out necessary modernization programs needed to maintain the sort of qualitative, technological advantage on such brilliant display in the war with Iraq.

The cumulative effects of these and related, budgetarily driven Defense Department initiatives is not hard to discern: Simply put, if planned Pentagon cuts are fully implemented, by 1995 the United States would not be able to mount a Desert Storm operation as it did over the past seven months. With the memories of the need for such a campaign so fresh in congressional minds, this reality is unsettling in the extreme.

Unfortunately, Office of Management and Budget Director Richard Darman's determination to hold defense spending to the limits imposed by a budget summit largely agreed upon prior to the war with Iraq is compelling Mr. Cheney and company to suggest that needed upward revisions of the Pentagon budget will not be sought until after the lessons of Desert Storm have been fully digested and analyzed. Presumably, that means next year.

Of course, it makes no sense at all to proceed with cuts there is reason to believe should not be made this year in the expectation that they will be reversed in the next one. In some cases, there are prohibitive costs in rectifying mistakes like closing the production line for Airborne Warning and Control System (AWACS) aircraft and the MX missile; in others, the costs are simply unnecessary and exacerbate an already difficult budgetary problem.

The good news is that we need not wait for a year's worth of analyses and post-mortems on Desert Storm before arriving at judgments about the adequacy of the present five-year defense plan. Last summer, the Naval War College ran an extraordinarily sophisticated and valuable simulation of the performance of U.S. forces at decade's end in a range of projected scenarios - including a possible war in the Persian Gulf. This war game, "Global '90," can tell the Bush administration and the Congress all they need to know about the insufficiencies that will arise from the fiscal 1992 defense budget and its projected follow-ons.

Before the nation takes one more ride on the dizzying roller coaster of defense cutbacks that necessitate wasteful spending binges to correct for previous underfunding of the military, both the executive and legislative branches should be compelled to assess the available evidence that argues for preserving - and, if anything, improving - existing capabilities. "Global '90" would be good place to start.

"ABDICATION THERAPEUTICS; THE TARNOFF DOCTRINE" | JUNE 1, 1993

On May 25, Undersecretary of State for Political Affairs Peter Tarnoff dispelled any lingering doubts about the Clinton foreign policy. According to the "Tarnoff Doctrine," the United States neither has the resources nor the will any longer to be the leader of the international community - and "our friends" around the world had better get used to it.

In remarks made "on background" to the Overseas Writers Club in Washington, Mr. Tarnoff articulated the vision of an America in decline - preoccupied with domestic economic concerns and increasingly disengaged from international developments - that heretofore could only be inferred from Clinton policies:

"We simply don't have the leverage, we don't have the influence, we don't have the inclination to use force and we certainly don't have the money to bring to bear the kind of pressure that will produce positive results any time soon.

"[Our] approach is difficult for our friends to understand. It's not different by accident, it's different by design. . . . We're talking about new rules of engagement for the United States. There will have to be genuine power-sharing and responsibility-sharing."

The key ingredient in the "Tarnoff Doctrine" is its reliance upon "collective security." Put simply, this concept means that the United States will voluntarily decline to act - except in circumstances where U.S. interests are immediately at risk - unless multilateral consensus can be achieved. In Mr. Tarnoff's words:

"There may be occasions in the future where the United States acts unilaterally - if we perceive an imminent danger very close to home that can be defended and where the amount of resources that we expend are commensurate with what our interests are. But these will be exceptions."

The results of the first test of this strategy is on vivid display in Bosnia. Mr. Tarnoff tellingly lauded Secretary of State Warren Christopher's trip to discuss Bosnia options with key European allies and the Russian leadership as an example of a "form of leadership that's quite appropriate" in the post-Cold War world: "People were genuinely disarmed by the fact that he was there to consult. He did not have a blueprint in his back pocket. . . . He had some things we favored."

Never mind that Mr. Christopher's mission had been described at the time by President Clinton himself as intended to generate allied support for military action against the Bosnian Serbs. Never mind either that the people who were disarmed are not those who should be - the Serbian aggressors in this conflict. Regrettably, the Clinton-Tarnoff emphasis upon consultation, consensus and multilateralism simply had the effect of sealing the fate of the victims of that aggression.

In the process, the administration's abdication of leadership on Bosnia also served to underscore the yawning vacuum of power that is now emerging as the United States succumbs once more to the temptation to disregard and disengage from its overseas responsibilities. Unpunished Serb transgressions are inspiring other members of the "Radical Entente" - like Saddam Hussein, Kim Il-sung and the mullahs of Tehran - to pursue their respective, malevolent agendas.

As a result, more grief will flow from the "Tarnoff Doctrine" in the future. It embraces, after all, an approach Lady Margaret Thatcher has properly reviled as "leadership by consensus" - an oxymoronic concept doomed to fail. By adopting this strategy, the Clinton administration is poised to recreate the international conditions precipitated by the Carter administration (in which Peter Tarnoff also served as a senior State Department official): An environment in which America continues to have global interests but is perceived to lack the will, if not the resources, to safeguard them and inevitably finds those interests in jeopardy even from what Mr. Tarnoff calls "middleweight powers."

It is instructive that another former Carter hand, Secretary Christopher, chose not to repudiate Mr. Tarnoff or to disassociate himself from the Undersecretary's remarks. While Mr. Christopher did attempt a bit of damage-limitation by blithely telling reporters in the wake of Mr. Tarnoff's remarks that, "There is no derogation of our powers and our responsibility to lead," the Secretary of State on ABC New's "Nightline" subsequently affirmed the essence of the "Tarnoff Doctrine":

"We can't do it all. We have to measure our ability to act in the interests of the United States, but to save our power for those situations which threaten our deepest national interest, at the same time doing all we can where there's humanitarian concern."

In fact, the surest way to fritter away power and lose influence in the international arena is to try to husband political capital. It is only by routinely exercising leadership that one retains the ability to lead successfully in situations deemed to "threaten our deepest national interest."

The only people who could believe the United States will be better positioned to lead its allies in the wake of the Bosnian debacle and the enunciation of the "Tarnoff Doctrine" are probably the same people who think U.S. economic problems will prove more tractable as America's power and influence over Japan, Germany and other trading partners evaporates. It is a real tragedy - and may prove to be a very costly one - that such people hold high office in the U.S. government at this perilous moment.

Three simple words comprise the motto of the nation's newest and most powerful aircraft carrier, the USS Ronald Reagan: "Peace Through Strength." The choice of this phrase could scarcely be more appropriate, given that it captures both the purpose of the vessel and the most important legacy of the president whose name she proudly bears.

What is more, the philosophy that guided Ronald Reagan throughout his life and whose practice made the 40th presidency one of this country's greatest – the proposition that the competent exercise of U.S. power is essential to maintaining international security – remains a formula for guiding U.S. defense and foreign policy in our own time.

At a moment when the nation is in the throes of mourning and nostalgia for our fallen leader, it is easy to forget that this core Reagan principle was once considered wildly controversial. In fact, it took great fortitude and robust leadership to overcome the virulent opposition of those who railed against the costly military build-up and "aggressive" policies in Europe, Afghanistan and Central America.

The history of strenuous opposition to Mr. Reagan's application of the philosophy of peace through strength for the purpose of ending the "Evil Empire" and liberating its oppressed subjects offers important perspective on the present controversy: President Bush's determination that, among other things, the liberation of Iraq was required to achieve success against yet another global threat – the use of terrorism to advance political agendas.

One of the most important insights from the previous experience, however, is the importance of being clear about precisely who and what we are up against. Ronald Reagan appreciated that it was necessary – but not sufficient – for U.S. military strength to be rebuilt. He also understood the need to wage a "war of ideas" against the Soviet Union.

Specifically, Mr. Reagan explicitly and repeatedly addressed the odiousness and illegitimacy of Soviet communism, discrediting it in the world's eyes, demoralizing its proponents and emboldening those who longed to be free of that tyrannical ideology.

In today's conflict, clarity about our enemy is no less essential. Most of those wielding terrorism against us, our allies and interests adhere to an ideology every bit as dangerous as that of the Soviet Union. Some have described it as "Islamofascism"; others as communism with a god. While not all who threaten us are Islamists – the radical, intolerant and violently jihadist subsets [both Sunni and Shi'ite] of the Muslim faith – the latter tend to be the best organized, financed and disciplined. And the rest, like Saddam Hussein's regime, either actively cooperate with the Islamofascists [see Stephen Hayes' excellent new book, "The Connection: How al Qaeda's Collaboration with Saddam Hussein Has Endangered America"] or are, at the very least, supportive of their hostility toward us.

The need for a "war of ideas" has been much on the mind of the man charged with securing peace through strength through more obvious means, Secretary of Defense Donald Rumsfeld. For months, he has been warning that the Islamist recruitment and training pipeline is capable of generating jihadist cannon fodder faster than U.S. and allied forces can kill them.

According to the Associated Press, in remarks to an international security conference in Singapore on Saturday, he warned that "the United States and its allies are winning some battles in the war against terror but may be losing the broader struggle against Islamic extremism that is terrorism's source."

The Pentagon chief observed, "What you have is a civil war in [Islam] where a small minority are trying to hijack it."

Complicating matters further is the fact that Saudi Arabia - ostensibly one of our most important allies in the war on terrorism - is a significant part of the problem. A featured article in the New York Times, was headlined, "The Saudis fight terror, but not those who wage it." It reported that "the attempt by some [Saudis] to expose and uproot the ideological and theocratic influences used to justify [terrorist] attacks was suppressed by the religious establishment. ... Instead, the official line became that the terrorists were infected with an alien ideology, imported by those who fought in Afghanistan or Chechnya, and that the religion espoused by Saudis is a peaceful one. ...'The official religious establishment does not admit there is a problem inside Wahhabism [the state-approved fundamentalist version of Islam] itself," said ...a former radical turned reformer."

If President Bush is to succeed in defeating Islamofascism as Ronald Reagan defeated Soviet communism, he must not only rebuild and employ effectively U.S. military strength. He must also bring to bear, as Mr. Reagan did, reinvigorated U.S. intelligence capabilities and the panoply of economic, financial and technological assets at our disposal.

But arguably most importantly, he must emulate Mr. Reagan's war of ideas by countering the Islamist ideology that animates our enemy and powers its ambition to succeed in world domination where godless communism failed.

If the conventional wisdom is correct, today's presidential election will be tightly contested and ultimately decided by voters' concerns about winning the war against terrorists bent on our destruction. If the second indeed proves to be uppermost in American voters' minds, however, this should not be a close election at all.

In truth, John Kerry is woefully ill equipped to wage this war. To be sure, he served in the military in Vietnam. His experience as a junior officer 35 years ago would be more of a credential for the role of commander in chief had he not spent virtually every moment subsequently disqualifying himself – and doing so in ways directly relevant to today's struggle.

For example, upon leaving Vietnam, Mr. Kerry made himself a leader of the effort to divide and demoralize the American people, allowing the North Vietnamese to win on our home front what they could not achieve on the battlefield. To this day, museums in Communist Vietnam reportedly pay tribute to the contribution the future presidential candidate made to the North's victory.

Regrettably, Mr. Kerry's current political ambitions have caused him to reprise this antiwar role in his current bid for the White House. In doing so, he has fed expectations at home that, if elected, he will bring the troops home from "the wrong war" in Iraq. He has once again emboldened our adversaries to believe they will prevail over an America that lacks the moral convictions or will to vanquish them.

While Mr. Kerry and his running mate John Edwards glibly talk about how much they "support the troops" even as they demean their mission and leadership, such behavior can only have a negative effect on the armed forces' morale and performance. In a deeply moving - and nonpartisan - address to the Center for Security Policy last month, the vice chairman of the Joint Chiefs of Staff, Gen. Peter Pace, observed that the one thing the troops want to know as they put themselves in harm's way for their nation is: "Are the American people behind us?" Mr. Kerry must take no small responsibility for imparting the impression that nearly half the country is not.

Apart from an allusion now and then to his "35 years of foreign policy experience," John Kerry has been astonishingly taciturn about his 20-year record on defense programs, intelligence matters and foreign affairs in the U.S. Senate. This is because it is a virtually unbroken record on votes that mattered (as opposed to his willingness to join virtually everyone else in supporting final passage of defense spending bills) reflecting a left-wing ideology at odds with sensible Cold War strategies. Mr. Kerry's instincts are no better suited to the dangerous strategic environment that emerged in the wake of that previous, global struggle.

Based upon this record, a President Kerry's idea of a "smarter war" would be one in which, by his own admission, the "legitimacy" of America's self-defensive actions would be determined by a "global test" - the decisive votes evidently cast by countries suborned by commercial ties, strategic relations or corrupt connections with our enemies. It would be one in which primacy would be accorded to international organizations and treaties over American sovereignty and freedom of action. And, as in the Clinton years, America's foes like Iran and North Korea would be appeased and propped-up, not confronted.

Scarcely less comforting is the "new direction" Mr. Kerry would seemingly chart on the home front. Despite his mantra about making America "stronger at home," if elected, he seems determined actually to weaken the nation in at least three ways:

(1) He would seek to dismantle parts of the Patriot Act. Although he has been somewhat coy about exactly what he would change in this critical piece of counterterrorism legislation, his pandering to interests like the American Civil Liberties Union will likely jeopardize the national interest in monitoring and countering enemies at home.

(2) Mr. Kerry has embraced the idea of an amnesty for illegal aliens, which would only compound our present vulnerabilities at home by ensuring further influxes of undocumented foreign nationals, including terrorists.

(3) Mr. Kerry has been one of the most ideologically committed opponents of missile defense, a capability becoming more necessary every day that he will prevent from being fully realized if elected president.

In each area, the voters are being offered a real choice. Since September 11, 2001, George W. Bush has evidenced an unwavering determination to prosecute the war against America's terrorist foes with patience, determination and the necessary resources. He has appreciated that the terrorists' state-sponsors must also be neutralized, not just terror cells and networks. He has demonstrated to our combat forces that their country is behind them, proud of their accomplishments in Iraq, Afghanistan and elsewhere and convinced the sacrifice they and their families make is not only worthy but absolutely necessary.

The one choice we are offered today, however, is an end to the war on terror. Whoever is president will have to wage it for the foreseeable future. If that reality is properly understood by the voters, there is little doubt who will be our commander in chief for the next four years.

Last week, Republicans in the House of Representatives unveiled with much fanfare their "Pledge to America." It is intended by the GOP leadership to serve as both a campaign platform for winning a new majority and as a program for governing should they succeed.

The document transparently is designed to appeal to those Republicans, Tea Party activists, independents and conservative Democrats who are rallying to the defense of the U.S. Constitution at a moment when it is under assault, in the words of the congressional oath of office "from enemies, foreign and domestic."

Just as the framers saw the need for the immediate amendment of the original Constitution with the Bill of Rights, however, the Pledge to America cries out for a strengthened national security plank. Call it a "Bill of National Security Rights" or, better yet, "the Peace Through Strength Pledge."

As it stands, the House GOP's Pledge treats the Constitution's obligation to "provide common defense" as a kind of afterthought. Just 758 words - a little under two pages of the forty-five in its glossy blueprint for "a governing agenda" - are devoted to mostly hortatory statements about demanding policies, "getting all hands on deck" and passing "clean" troop-funding legislation.

The "Plan for National and Border Security" reads like focus group-tested themes embraced as a sort of issue box-checking exercise. What the times require, though, must be a key element of a defining - and differentiating - platform for a would-be governing party.

There are considerably more pictures in the Pledge booklet than there are substantive commitments on why we need a different approach to national security than has been the practice under Democratic control, and to what end.

A modest suggestion would be to flesh out the Pledge to America with a *real* national security platform - one that has the advantage of addressing more comprehensively and more definitively the choices facing the country in this critical election.

To this end, leaders of six preeminent national security-minded public policy institutions - including the Heritage Foundation, the Claremont Institute, the Foundation for Defense of Democracy and my own Center for Security Policy - came together earlier this year to define such an agenda. As it is rooted in the tradition and vision of Ronald Reagan, we call it the Peace through Strength Platform.

This 10-item Bill of National Security Rights includes the following commitments:

- **A robust defense posture** including: A safe, reliable effective nuclear deterrent, which requires its modernization and testing; the deployment of comprehensive defenses against missile attack; and national protection against unconventional forms of warfare - including biological, electro-magnetic pulse (EMP) and cyber attacks.

- **Preservation of U.S. sovereignty** against international treaties, judicial rulings and other measures that would have the effect of supplanting or otherwise diminishing the U.S. Constitution and the representative, accountable form of government it guarantees.

- **A nation free of Shariah**, the brutally repressive and anti-Constitutional totalitarian program that governs in Saudi Arabia, Iran and other Islamic states and that terrorists are fighting to impose worldwide.

- **Protection from unlawful enemy combatants.** Enemies who refuse to wear uniforms, use civilians as shields and employ terrorism as weapons are not entitled to U.S. constitutional rights or trials in our civilian courts. Those captured overseas should be incarcerated at Guantanamo Bay, which should remain open, or in other prisons outside the United States.

- **Energy security**, realized by exploiting to the fullest the natural resources and technologies available in this country. We Americans must reduce our dependence for energy upon - and transfers of national wealth to - enemies of this country.

- **Borders secure against penetration** by terrorists, narco-traffickers or others seeking to enter the United States illegally. Aliens who have violated immigration laws should not be rewarded with the privileges of citizenship.

- **High standards that protect the military culture essential to the All-Volunteer Force.** The Pentagon should implement sound priorities, policies and laws that strengthen recruiting, retention, and readiness.

- **A foreign policy that supports our allies and opposes our adversaries.** It should be clearly preferable to be a friend of the United States, not its enemy.

- **Judicial and educational institutions** that uphold the constitutional responsibility of elected officials to make policy for our military and convey to future generations accurate portrayals of American history, including the necessity of defending freedom.

Some of these points are touched on in the Pledge to America; others are not. But taken together, an amended and augmented Pledge would provide a far more firm basis for appealing to the American electorate. It would also ensure that those elected this Fall have a mandate for leadership in this most important of portfolios, one that promises to stand the country in far better stead during the difficult months and years ahead. One that would be worthy of broad-based political support - and likely to secure it.

To paraphrase President Reagan, if not we, who will offer the leadership necessary truly to meet the constitutional obligation to provide for the common defense? And, if not now, when?

Military Readiness

"BUSH'S GO-ALONG POLICY ON DEFENSE" | JANUARY 8, 1992

In an interview last week with David Frost, President Bush agreed in principle to re-open the 1990 budget summit agreement that currently prohibits raids on defense spending accounts to meet non-defense purposes. Subsequently, in the course of his Pacific rim tour, he even signaled a willingness to have defense reductions applied toward a tax cut for the "middle class." With these initiatives, Mr. Bush has once again sought to head off conflict with his Democratic critics by pre-emptively accommodating them.

Unfortunately, like the budget agreement itself - which, it will be recalled, was the vehicle for the president's abandonment of his "read-my-lips, no-new-taxes" pledge - this concession is a terrible idea, both in terms of the national interest and for Mr. Bush's more parochial concern with reelection.

First, it makes utterly problematic Defense Secretary Dick Cheney's already difficult effort to chart an orderly approach to effecting deep reductions in the defense budget. His present plan envisions a whopping 25 percent cut in Pentagon forces and funding.

Indeed, the issue has ceased to be one of whether more money can responsibly be re-moved from Defense's accounts in light of changing circumstances and if so how fast - issues worthy of serious reflection and debate. Now, it is simply a matter of how large the additional cuts will be.

One need look no further than the reaction of congressional Democrats to the presi-dent's statements to see the magnitude of the problem. Even as House Speaker Tom Foley and Senate Majority Leader George Mitchell were welcoming Mr. Bush's change of heart, Senate Budget Committee Chairman Jim Sasser was pronouncing his view that the planned cuts in defense spending could be increased by fully $100 billion more over the next few years without adversely affecting U.S. military capabilities. While that is an emi-nently rebuttable proposition, with the president committed to such cuts in the abstract, it is far from clear that the administration will be able to challenge - let alone defeat - this sort of irresponsible proposal.

How sharply this contrasts with the Pentagon budget fights of the mid-1980s, when Defense Secretary Caspar Weinberger - with the full support of the president he served - strenuously resisted congressional demands that the defense accounts be cut. While Cap Weinberger was never in any doubt that the Reagan proposals would be reduced in the end, his tenacity in arguing against pre-emptive concessions to those demanding reductions meant that the ultimate outcome was always closer to what he believed was needed. As a result, the United States made the defense investments that the Soviet empire could not afford to match, contributing directly to the latter's demise over the past two years. Similar-ly, the wherewithal needed to execute Desert Shield and Desert Storm was in hand at the critical moment - something that would surely not have been the case had congressional

Democrats had their way.

Of course, it is argued, the early 1990s are not the mid-1980s. With the collapse of the Warsaw Pact, the breakup of the Soviet Union and the emergence - or triumph - of democratic forces elsewhere around the globe, U.S. defense capabilities simply no longer need to be what they were. While this is unquestionably true, no one can say for certain just what our requirements will be in the new era.

For example, will the successors to the Soviet Union continue to mount a nuclear threat and, if so, of what kind? Will the proliferation of weapons of mass destruction and the absence of escalatory concerns that tended to hold regional crises in check during the Cold War give rise to serious new challenges to U.S. security interests around the world? Will the United States actually have an increased need for expensive power projection capabilities as it gives up bases in Europe, the Pacific and elsewhere? In short, the temptation to cash in the "peace dividend" before the answers to these and similar questions become clear could well jeopardize our security.

Even if Mr. Bush were not unduly concerned about the national security implications of buying into the Democrats' line on defense spending, one would think that he would at least be aware of the damage that could arise in the coming presidential election from a blurring of the differences between his policies and those of the opposition. Arguably, his claim to be a more reliable commander in chief than any of the prospective Democratic challengers is his single strongest asset in the 1992 campaign.

Ironically, a reminder of the importance of this factor in U.S. presidential politics emerged at the very moment that Mr. Bush was compromising his position on the defense budget. In a feature report on Vice President Dan Quayle, The Washington Post's reporters David Broder and Bob Woodward recounted how in the 1988 campaign then-Sen. Quayle argued with candidate George Bush for a presidential veto of the 1989 defense authorization bill as a device for highlighting the differences between Republicans and Democrats on national security.

Then, as now, Mr. Bush was inclined to go along with the Democrats; he and his principal advisers felt accommodation would be the more prudent and damage-limiting course. When, with Mr. Quayle's strong support - and that of others like Cap Weinberger and the late Sen. John Tower - Mr. Bush was persuaded to accept a Reagan veto of the defense bill, the stage was set for a focused debate in the area of Michael Dukakis' maximum vulnerability. According to Messrs. Broder and Woodward, the maneuver got Mr. Quayle his job; it certainly helped Mr. Bush secure his.

The president is unlikely to prevail if he permits the 1992 campaign to become a bidding war with the likes of Tom Harkin and Bob Kerrey over who will cut defense spending the most deeply while putting the money back in the pockets of the middle class. More importantly, the nation will be very badly served if the budgetary actions likely to flow from such demagogeruery result in a wholesale gutting of U.S. defense capabilities.

What a difference a few days make! Last month, Deputy Defense Secretary John Deutch dismissed concerns that the U.S. armed forces were being reduced to the "hollow military" of the late 1970s, claiming that readiness was actually better than it was at the start of Desert Storm in 1991.

Last week, however, in a letter to Members of Congress, Mr. Deutch's boss - Defense Secretary William Perry - was obliged to acknowledge something approximating the truth: Fully three out of 12 active duty Army divisions are rated as "C-3" or seriously unprepared for combat.

Mr. Deutch claims that he did not know about these statistics when he made his misleading statement. This strains credulity, however, since the position of deputy secretary of defense traditionally has responsibility for day-to-day management of the Pentagon, including oversight of such data as readiness ratings for the services and their key components. If, indeed, Mr. Deutch were unaware of the true condition of one-fourth of the U.S. Army's combat power until a few days ago -when Mr. Perry publicly confirmed the facts - one might be forgiven for wondering whether there are other aspects of his duties with which he may also be out-of-touch.

The "didn't-get-the-word" explanation seems all the more incredible since alarms have been raised repeatedly in recent months by senior military personnel, key legislators and the media concerning the plummeting readiness of the U.S. military. For example:

- A top Marine officer recently noted that the Corps was being asked to do missions on a scale commensurate not with the 175,000 troops and resources it currently has but with those at its disposal when it had 50,000 more Marines. Worse yet, it is being funded at a level of training, operations and investment appropriate to a Marine Corps of only 125,000 troops.

- Sen. John McCain, Arizona Republican, in September 1994 published a lengthy report chronicling on the basis of congressional testimony from members of senior military officers myriad, serious deficiencies in the readiness and sustainability of the nation's armed forces. And the ranking member – and incipient chairman - of the House Armed Services Committee, Rep. Floyd Spence, South Carolina Republican, has issued a series of press releases over the past few months highlighting a problem that he aptly summarized this week:

    "Wholesale categories of combat units are in a reduced state of readiness and those that are not are managing to preserve short-term readiness only through engaging in a desperate 'shell-game' with dwindling resources."

- On the eve of the invasion-turned-uncontested-occupation of Haiti, ABC News broadcast a stunning picture of a U.S. military whose personnel were going untrained, whose equipment was being cannibalized and going unmaintained and whose operating tempos were being stretched to the limit in order to perform - and pay for - the various peacekeeping and other noncombat operations in which the United States military is now engaged. To varying degrees, other news organizations have also documented the phenomenon Mr. Perry has now acknowledged:

"Any major contingency operation is not in the budget. And, therefore, if you conduct that, you either have to put in supplemental funds to pay for that, or you have to take away funds, which we have in the budget for the standard thing. ... And, therefore, you will degrade your readiness to conduct any operation."

It goes without saying that the serious shortfalls being experienced by the U.S. armed forces, shortfalls that go well beyond three divisions in a C-3 status, will only be exacerbated by increasing costs of the American military's open-ended constabulary mission in Haiti and those new ones associated with a Pentagon peacekeeping (or "peace-monitoring") assignment on the Golan Heights. The truth of the matter is that troops that have been reduced to performing police functions rapidly lose their capacity to perform more demanding military tasks.

A vivid example of this problem was the experience of Task Force Smith, a contingent of U.S. troops hastily diverted in July 1950 from occupation duties in postwar Japan to the Korean Peninsula in a desperate bid to counter Kim Il-sung's invasion of the South. They had only six anti-armor artillery rounds and were easily routed by the more combat-ready North Korean aggressors.

Clearly, the Congress has an obligation not only to take those steps necessary to undo the hollowing-out of the U.S. military that has occurred in recent years. It also must get to the bottom of the multibillion-dollar question: Was official confirmation by the Clinton Defense Department concerning this deplorable situation deliberately withheld from the public until after the November balloting, presumably in the hope of preventing an electoral outcome as dramatic as - or even more lopsided than - that which actually occurred? If so, who was responsible for this action and what will be the consequences for having engaged in it?

When the House Appropriations Committee voted last week to defer production of the Air Force's next generation fighter plane, the F-22, the image that came to mind was that of the cartoon character Pogo who once famously declared, "We have met the enemy and it is us." Unless the Republican-led Congress comes to grips with the central reality of the defense budget - namely, that its present and projected funding levels are woefully inadequate to meet America's future security needs - the GOP will become fully implicated in the Clinton administration's hollowing out of the U.S. military.

To be sure, critics of the F-22 cast this fight in narrower terms. They claim an aircraft with its characteristics - low-observability ("stealth"), supersonic cruise capability (that is, the ability to fly at supersonic speeds without having to utilize afterburners that consume huge quantities of fuel) and sophisticated avionics and weapon systems - is no longer needed to dominate the skies. They contend that, with the decline in the technical skills and productivity of the former Soviet military-industrial complex, the United States can safely make do with far less sophisticated and expensive warplanes.

Unfortunately, as the war in Kosovo reminds us, threats to U.S. pilots can come from the ground as well as the air. We owe it to those asked to fight the nation's future wars to ensure they are given platforms for doing so that are as immune as possible to the continuing improvements being made by potential adversaries in both air-to-air and terrestrial anti-aircraft weapons. As one retired Air Force general recently put it: "We don't want a fair fight. We want to win decisively."

Another source of the flak the F-22 is taking arises from the perennial temptation to forgo a near-term defense expenditure in favor of an outlay that is farther off. In recent years, Democratic critics of the Pentagon have made an art form of this gambit, promising to support the next program as long as the present one is terminated, only to oppose its successor when its turn comes. Even normally responsible Republicans are susceptible to this siren's song when, as has been the case with the F-22, the estimated production costs have inexorably grown as the various technical challenges associated with this extraordinary plane's development have been overcome.

The alternative some prefer is to skip the F-22 and procure instead another promising aircraft called the Joint Strike Fighter (JSF), now in the early stages of development. Estimates of the JSF's ultimate price tag and performance characteristics, however, are currently as soft as the F-22's used to be. If anything, the JSF may cost more than the F-22 when the former reaches the latter's level of programmatic maturity.

Others favor a two-step procurement strategy, involving the purchase first of up-to-date versions of the F-15 and F-16 as a stopgap awaiting the maturing of the JSF, which would then be purchased in quantity when it becomes available. Producing modernized F-15s and -16s is probably a good idea under all circumstances, but it would be a mistake to kill the F-22 to pay for it.

The painful truth is that the problem is far larger than the fate of the F-22, or even that of the Pentagon's aviation account more generally. This reality is evident in the fact that House appropriators found lots of areas into which to reallocate the roughly $1.5 billion sought by the Clinton administration for the purpose of producing the first six F-22s.

An impressive analysis conducted by Dr. Dan Goure of the Center for Strategic and International Studies and Jeffrey Ranney, a strategic planner at the defense consulting firm MSTI, quantifies this problem. According to these highly respected experts, there is a $376 billion deficit in the funding needed over the next five years to meet the Clinton Pentagon's own modernization goals as defined in its latest blueprint, the 1997 Quadrennial Defense Review (QDR). In fact, the Goure-Ranney study, titled "Averting the Coming Department of Defense Train Wreck," suggests the procurement shortfall in fiscal 2000 alone is $71 billion.

If the QDR projections prove unduly optimistic, moreover, even that staggering amount would actually be understated.

The good news is that the procurement "gap" - and similar, although less acute, shortfalls in the research and development, operations and maintenance and personnel pay accounts - would essentially disappear if the United States were willing for the foreseeable future to allocate 4 percent of its gross domestic product to defense, rather than today's less than 3 percent.

Such a proportion of GDP is well below the more than 5 percent to 6.7 percent that President Reagan dedicated during the 1980s to rebuilding our military after its last hollowing-out. And this percentage is a small fraction of the allocations the nation made to national security earlier on, notably during John F. Kennedy's administration.

The bad news is that, despite the surging U.S. economy and the attendant increase in tax revenues, Republicans in Congress find themselves opposing the sorts of defense spending increases that are clearly required if the American military is to be able to preserve its decisive qualitative edge via modernization of its inventory, without further reducing an already overstretched force structure and/or the global commitments it is being asked to fulfill. It is not that most Republicans are averse to additional funding for the armed forces. Rather, they fear that - were they to rupture the "caps" on Pentagon accounts agreed to in the 1997 budget deal with President Clinton – it would be impossible to maintain the constraints that deal imposed on the growth of spending on popular domestic programs.

As the F-22 episode makes clear, however, unless there is relief from the Pentagon caps, there is a defense "train wreck" coming. Military leaders know this to be true, as do their more responsible civilian counterparts.

The so-called "bow-wave" of deferred procurement, like compounded interest, is intensifying daily. The attendant risks of an inadequate defense posture are increasing concomitantly.

If the present Congress does not come to grips with this reality - not by cutting needed defense programs but by adding the funds necessary to buy them and to cover other Pentagon shortfalls - the next president will face an even more dangerous deficit in our national security capabilities, and an even more daunting price tag for correcting it. And the Republicans will lose one of their most important planks in their campaign for renewed control of the legislative branch, namely their ability to understand our vital interests and their willingness to provide the resources needed to safeguard them.

Finally, there is reason to believe that one of the most important challenges likely to confront the next president will actually become a focus for the 2000 elections: the present and future readiness of the U.S. military to fight the nation's wars.

In his acceptance speech on Thursday, Republican nominee George W. Bush put the issue squarely in the spotlight when he declared, "If called on by the commander in chief today, two entire divisions of the Army would have to report: "Not ready for duty, sir.' "

The next day, the Clinton Pentagon responded with interviews by its highly political press spokesman, Ken Bacon, and a statement by the chairman of the Joint Chiefs of Staff, Gen. Hugh Shelton, asserting that all of the Army's divisions are good-to-go. Of course, they could not deny that the two divisions of which Mr. Bush spoke -the 1st Infantry Division and the 10th Mountain Division - had been declared unready for war last fall because of the detachment of a brigade from each to peacekeeping duties in the Balkans. But that was then, reporters were told, and this is now. According to The Washington Times, Gen. Shelton declared that "the Army had 'jumped right on top of that' and brought both divisions back to combat readiness."

The problem for the Clinton-Gore administration is that, whatever the status of any given unit at any point in time, the overall trend for the armed forces is bad - and getting worse. This fact is so palpable that the Joint Chiefs chairman was compelled to acknowledge it, even as he carried out his assignment of rebutting Mr. Bush's specific point. As The Times reported, Gen. Shelton felt compelled to add, "That doesn't mean that everything is the way we would all like to have it." There are "some readiness shortfalls" that will not be fixed quickly. "Once readiness starts down, you don't just turn it around overnight."

To be sure, this is not the first time Gen. Shelton has warned about these "readiness shortfalls." In September 1998, he used an aeronautical metaphor to describe the situation the armed forces faced: "In my view, we have 'nosed over' and our readiness is descending. I believe that with the support of the administration and Congress, we should apply corrective action now. We must 'pull back on the stick' and begin to climb before we find ourselves in a nose dive that might cause irreparable damage to this great force we have created, a nose dive that will take years to pull out of."

Interestingly, just a month before, Under Secretary of Defense Jacques Gansler had declared that the military not only had already entered such a "nose dive." He opined that it was an irrecoverable one: "We are trapped in a 'death spiral.' The requirement to maintain our aging equipment is costing us more each year - in repair costs, down time and maintenance tempo. But we must keep this equipment in repair to maintain readiness. It drains our resources – resources we should be applying to modernization of the traditional systems and development and deployment of the new systems. So, we stretch out our replacement schedules to ridiculous lengths and reduce the quantities of the new equipment we purchase, raising their costs and still further delaying modernization."

In other words, the truth of the matter is far worse than Mr. Bush suggested. Not only is today's military facing severe shortfalls that are impinging upon its combat readiness. The fact that the armed services are obliged constantly to rob Peter (tomorrow's forces) to pay Paul (allowing today's barely to make do) means that future defense capabilities may be seriously inadequate. History suggests that the consequence of such a practice is a vacuum of power that hostile nations often feel invited to fill.

The magnitude of this double whammy is staggering. According to the most rigorous independent analysis done to date concerning the deplorable condition of the U.S. military - a study entitled "Averting the Defense Train Wreck in the New Millennium" published last year by Daniel Goure and Jeffrey Ranney: "A substantial defense strategy-resources mismatch . . . already exists. It is profound. It has been ongoing for sometime and will take years to overcome. It is reaching crisis proportions and requires immediate attention, involvement and action by the White House, Defense Department, Congress and the general public. It is of great national importance today because military spending levels now are too dangerously low in relation to current and future U.S. foreign policy and national security interests - which remain global and immense."

The irony is that, as Messrs. Goure and Ranney observe, the military is getting far less than even the Clinton-Gore administration believes it requires. In order to pay for the forces deemed needed by the Quadrennial Defense Review (QDR) performed by the Pentagon in 1997 would entail an allocation "equal to 3.9 percent of U.S. gross domestic product (GDP) in Fiscal Year 2001. Thereafter, to provide for continued modernization and replacement of military hardware, the QDR force will require slightly larger defense budgets. Based on the cost characteristics of the QDR force, the defense budget will need to equal 4.0 percent of the GDP in FY 2010 and, later, 4.3 percent of the GDP in FY 2020."

But as the commandant of the Marine Corps, Gen. James Jones, told Congress in February: "The percentage of our gross domestic product that we currently invest for the national security pillar upon which our superpower status maintains itself is about 3 percent -roughly 3 cents on the dollar. Over the last 60 years, the average has been 8 percent. Three cents on the dollar for global responsibilities and global leadership. My opinion is that if we do not sustain this turnaround that we will not sustain our role as a superpower, we will not be able to recapitalize and modernize at the rate that we require, and we will not sustain the all-recruited force, which we refer to as the all-volunteer force, that the nation deserves."

The prognosis for the future is worse yet. According to the Goure-Ranney analysis: "The February 1999 Office of Management and Budget (OMB) FY2000-2009 10-year

269

budget projection provided to the Senate Budget Committee projected that - while the defense budget will grow during this period at an average annual rate of 1 percent (from $270 billion in FY 2000 to $293 billion in FY 2009) -measured in terms of GDP, it will fall from 2.9 percent of GDP in FY 2000 to 2.4 percent of GDP in FY 2009. Thereafter, if defense budget levels continue to grow at an annual rate of 1 percent during FY 2010-2020, the Pentagon's share will gradually fall from 2.4 percent of GDP in FY 2010 to 2 percent of GDP in FY 2020."

A nation with a projected $1.9 trillion budget surplus can afford consistently to allocate a minimum of 4 percent of its GDP to ensure its security. Such an commitment of resources would assure the readiness of both today's armed forces and tomorrow's for many years to come, while allowing important new defense initiatives -like Mr. Bush's laudable pledge to protect the American people against ballistic missile attacks at the earliest possible time - to be fulfilled. We must not forget that the alternative has, in the past, often proven to be far more costly: unnecessary, avoidable wars whose price in blood and treasure dwarfs the savings achieved by pound-foolish "peace dividends."

This election is an opportunity not only to acquaint the American people with the full magnitude of the crisis facing our military but to seek a mandate from them for correcting it by adopting what might be called "the 4 percent solution. " If all candidates will pledge, as Mr. Bush did so eloquently last week, to "use these good times for great goals," there is surely no greater goal than assuring we have the freedom to pursue our other ones in peace and security.

The Bush-Cheney administration made a lot of its supporters very nervous last week when it signaled that there would be no immediate increase in defense study has shown the armed forces have been seriously underfunded and over utilized for the past decade and Mr. Bush had made a point during the campaign of pledging to fix what is known to ail the military.

By week's end, however, the administration was putting out the word that the promised help for the men and women in uniform was on the way, after all. The new team clarified that it would not only be seeking additional sums for pay, housing and re-enlistment incentives in next year's budget. It would also be willing to seek additional funding in the course of this fiscal year – if warranted by a fresh review of strategy and force structure that was ordered by Mr. Bush and expected to catalyze a wholesale transformation of the Defense Department.

Fortunately, the task of completing such a sweeping, yet expeditious review has been given to a man who has trained for most of the past 50 years for just this moment: Andrew Marshall, the Pentagon's legendary director of Net Assessment.

Mr. Marshall is one of the unsung heroes of the Cold War. Since he joined the Defense Department in the mid-1970s, and during his prior service at the Rand Corp., he has been the principal patron of outside-of-the-box thinking within the U.S. national security community. He has consistently challenged the conventional wisdom, often recognizing before the rest of the military establishment the declining utility of existing weapon systems and the need to develop and field new capabilities suited to a changing world.

Working almost entirely outside of public view, Andy Marshall has spawned not only creative ideas; he has been a mentor to a generation of first-rate strategic thinkers and sponsored some of the best security policy research at the nation's academic institutions. While the worst of the many defense secretaries under whom he has served have ignored him and, in one case at least, tried to get rid of him by banishing him from the Pentagon, the best – including the only man to hold the position twice, Donald Rumsfeld - have prized and benefited greatly from his counsel.

Now, the nation as a whole stands to be the beneficiary of Mr. Marshall's wisdom and unsurpassed corporate memory. These are among the points we must hope his strategic review will underscore:

- The threat from China: Few senior officials have better understood and done more to document the determination of the People's Republic of China to anticipate and prepare itself for conflict with the United States. He grasps the danger the Chinese might pose to U.S. interests in Asia and beyond – including outer space - and his recommendations about the sizing and equipping of America's military will surely reflect the need to be able to contend with the growing asymmetric and other threats from China.

- The need for urgent deployments of missile defenses: Andy Marshall has long appreciated the risks associated with America's present, absolute vulnerability to missile attack. He also understands, as Secretary Rumsfeld noted recently, that an anti-missile system need not be perfect to have strategic value. The new Marshall Plan should give urgent priority to beginning the deployment of a global missile defense, starting with the approach that promises to be the fastest, most flexible and least expensive: adaptation of the Navy's Aegis fleet air defense ships.

- The requirement for safe, reliable and effective nuclear forces: During his Rand years, Mr. Marshall was a specialist in nuclear weapons matters. Although it is not entirely clear at this writing whether the study President Bush has commissioned to determine the future size of the U.S. deterrent will fall within his mandate, Mr. Marshall certainly appreciates that the quantity of nuclear arms the nation needs is only part of the calculation. Quality also matters and the arsenal must be modernized and tested if it is to remain viable for the foreseeable future.

- Transformation cannot be accomplished on the cheap: President Bush clearly hopes to reconfigure the U.S. military so as to enable it to meet tomorrow's challenges. Andy Marshall assuredly will have many ideas for doing so - some of them brilliant, many of them heretical, all of them probably controversial. Still, he would be the first to acknowledge that, even if one envisions revolutionary changes in the weapons of the future (for example, an Army built around lighter, more mobile yet more lethal weapons than main battle tanks and tracked infantry fighting vehicles or a Navy weaned from large carriers in favor of arsenal ships and submarines), the military will have to maintain and operate the preponderance of what it has for at least the next decade or so.

  This is more than a matter of correcting current, egregious shortfalls in spare parts and other training- and combat-related gear. There will have to be some interim modernization since the generation of weapons Mr. Bush talked about skipping during the campaign was actually skipped during the last decade. Recapitalization of the armed forces must go forward apace to offset the effects of looming block obsolescence of much of the Pentagon's hardware.

All these steps, to say nothing of the research and development and procurement costs associated with the next generation of military hardware simply cannot be paid for within existing budget limitations. What is more, the increased funding needs to start right away. It will fall to Andy Marshall to help the new Bush-Cheney team and the nation appreciate these facts of life.

For most of the past half century, Andrew Marshall has been a man ahead of his time. Thanks to George W. Bush and Donald Rumsfeld, his time has come.

Presidents have discovered that the surest way to make history is by playing against type. The paradigmatic example occurred in 1972 when anti-communist Richard Nixon decided to go to Red China. Liberal Democrat Bill Clinton is remembered for helping to "end welfare as we know it" some two decades later.

We should all hope Barack Obama too will recognize the need for a role reversal by deciding early that - despite his campaign promises and past predilections - he must strengthen, not savage, our national security posture.

To be sure, this would be a breathtaking departure given the commitments Mr. Obama recently made on the hustings. For example, he undertook to reduce defense spending (inspiring one of his congressional allies, Rep. Barney Frank, to offer an opening bid of a 25 percent cut), abolish nuclear weapons, and end funding for "unproven" missile defenses. He also pledged to repeal the prohibition against homosexuals serving in the military. And he promised to withdraw U.S. forces from Iraq within 16 months, irrespective of conditions on the ground.

It is no exaggeration to say the cumulative effect of these commitments would be devastating to our security. The U.S. military has been waging two wars for most of the last seven years. Though the defense budget has grown dramatically over that period, necessary modernization of the armed services has been substantially deferred in favor of meeting the immediate requirements to fund combat and support operations and maintenance. Under these circumstances, even modest military spending cuts, let alone those contemplated by Mr. Frank, risk another "hollowing-out" of the armed forces of a kind not seen since another "progressive" Democrat, Jimmy Carter, occupied the White House in the late 1970s.

A failure to address the deteriorating condition of our nuclear deterrent and its supporting human and industrial infrastructure - to say nothing of pursuing a deliberate policy of eliminating these pillars of our national security posture - would be reckless. Like it or not, we live in a world in which all of the other declared nuclear powers (and a few undeclared ones) are busily upgrading their arsenals. The combination of such armaments with ever-expanding capabilities to deliver them via ballistic missiles makes U.S. anti-missile systems, even less-than-perfect ones, more needed than ever.

For the foregoing reasons, among others, the nation's all-volunteer military is already under considerable stress. Changing the basis on which those volunteers enlisted - namely, that they would not have to live and work in settings of forced intimacy with people of the same sex who might find them attractive - would have a traumatic effect on recruitment, retention and morale. In time of war, it would not be merely reckless but the height of folly to jeopardize the good order and discipline of the armed forces.

Speaking of war, we are in the process of winning the one in Iraq. In the years to come, Mr. Obama may be able to withdraw U.S. forces from there in a way that does not imperil that victory. But to do so, he will, as a practical matter, have to be flexible and guided by conditions on the ground - not an artificial timetable. The repercussions of getting the Iraqi end game wrong will extend far beyond that nation, Iran and the rest of the Middle East. Potential adversaries from Russia and China to North Korea and Hugo Chavez's Venezuela will become emboldened and more dangerous should we be defeated in Iraq, especially if that defeat is seen as part of a more comprehensive collapse of American power and will.

As it happens, there is another compelling reason for investing in a stronger defense posture, rather than weakening it. As a former chairman of the Council of Economic Advisers under President Reagan, Martin Feldstein, noted in the Wall Street Journal last week, government spending through the national and homeland security agencies can contribute powerfully to economic revitalization. He estimates that, for example, an increase of $20 billion in defense procurement and research and of $10 billion in operations and maintenance could translate into an additional 300,000 jobs.

I have long believed it is a mistake to use the defense budget as a jobs program. We should buy military hardware because it is needed for our security, not to boost employment. That said, where increased employment follows from making necessary investments in our armed forces' capabilities to fight today's wars - and, no less important, tomorrow's - it would be absurd not to include the Pentagon in an economic stimulus package. The same basic principle should apply to the homeland security and intelligence organizations, as well.

During the campaign, Vice President-elect Joe Biden warned that the world would test his running mate early in his presidency. That is almost certainly true, even though we cannot be sure what form that test will take or from which quarter. Mr. Obama is far more likely to pass that test - on his own behalf, and ours - if he confounds expectations by "going to Defense" as Nixon went to China: Resetting the force with necessary modernizations, as well as maintenance; increasing the robustness of our nuclear deterrent and missile defenses; preserving the good order and discipline of the military; and winning in Iraq.

"HOW CONGRESS WAS DUPED INTO REPEALING MILITARY GAY BAN" | JUNE 27, 2011

One of the more sordid moments in recent congressional history came during last December's lame-duck session. Democratic majorities on both sides of Capitol Hill rammed through a controversial repeal of the 1993 statute (wrongly described as "Don't Ask, Don't Tell"), which prohibited avowed homosexuals from serving in the armed forces.

The Senate and House leadership did so with scarcely any hearings and extremely limited opportunity for debate. This action amounted to a raw abuse of power, a last gasp by an Obama administration able and determined to appease gay activists - a key political constituency - before the setbacks of November's elections made doing so vastly more difficult.

We now know, however, that it was a gambit made possible by deliberate efforts by senior executive branch officials to mislead the Congress into taking a step that the administration's own surveys had established would be deeply injurious to the U.S. military. Thanks to the release of a previously undisclosed Defense Department Inspector General investigation report, recently analyzed by the invaluable Center for Military Readiness (CMR), legislators now have the proverbial "smoking gun" revealing politically motivated misconduct at the highest levels of government.

Evidently, this misconduct was deemed necessary because, even with control of both the House and Senate unfriendly hands, President Obama required Republican votes in the upper chamber to secure passage of his repeal initiative. In order to garner the support of swing GOP senators, they would have to be given political cover on a key question: How would the military respond to such a dramatic change in its traditions, culture and code of conduct?

The IG report makes clear that a skewed response was manufactured and leaked to friendly journalists by top Pentagon and White House officials. Specifically, an executive summary of a Defense Department survey was written by the department's General Counsel, Jeh Johnson, before the survey was even begun on July 7, 2010. It prompted one reviewer - a "former news anchor" whom Johnson allowed to see his draft over the July 4th weekend - to tell the IG he was "struck by how many members of the United States Armed Services thought this was just fine."

The situation intensified further in November 2010 after Jeh Johnson briefed five top White House officials about the findings of the so-called Comprehensive Review Working Group (CRWG) - a Pentagon task force on the gays-in-the-military issue that he co-chaired. The CRWG had, in the interval, conducted the survey of some 400,000 servicemen and women, held scores of town hall style meetings around the world and compiled a 300-plus-page report.

Among the five presidential aides identified but not interviewed by the Inspector General was James Messina. At the time, Messina was Mr. Obama's Deputy Chief of Staff, and his portfolio included serving as "liaison" to gay activists and their community. Interestingly, one prominent homosexual group leader has described Messina as an "unsung hero" in the campaign to repeal the 1993 law.

The Inspector General's report nonetheless suggested that "the primary source of the information was someone who had a strongly emotional attachment to the issue" and "carefully disclosed specific survey data to support a pro-repeal agenda." Specifically, that source provided to sympathetic journalists at the Washington Post a finding that seventy percent of those in uniform thought it would be no problem to have avowed homosexuals in the ranks. Importantly, the IG report noted how percentages in this finding could have been presented to support the opposite conclusion.

The IG went on to say: "We consider it likely that the primary source disclosed content from the draft Report with the intent to shape a pro-repeal perception of the draft Report prior to its release to gain momentum in support of a legislative change during the 'lame duck' session of Congress following the November 2, 2010, elections."

In other words, legislators were misled by this selective - and endlessly repeated - distortion of the Working Group's findings into ignoring some of its other, unpublicized and deeply troubling conclusions. These included a single sentence buried on page 49 of the CRWG report: "Our sense is that the majority of views expressed were against repeal."

Moreover, as CMR's Elaine Donnelly points out, the Working Group also found that "Nearly 60% of respondents in the Marine Corps and in Army combat arms said they believed there would be a negative impact on their unit's effectiveness in this context; among Marine combat arms the number was 67%." Tables that could only be found on the CRWG survey website also suggested that many in these vital elements would leave sooner than planned - perhaps as many as 36% in the Army and 48% in the Marines.

As Mrs. Donnelly puts it in an analysis of the Inspector General's report, "The gradual loss of even half as many combat troops and what the report described as 'only 12%' of families likely to decline re-enlistment could put remaining troops in greater danger, and eventually break the All-Volunteer Force."

Even before the IG-supplied smoking gun, legislators in the current Congress - including members of the House Armed Services Committee led by its Chairman Buck McKeon and Reps. Duncan Hunter and Joe Wilson - have been warning that the U.S. military is simply not ready to have the gay activists' social experiment imposed upon it. Certifications to the contrary by the outgoing Secretary of Defense, soon-to-depart Chairman of the Joint Chiefs and President would compound the travesty of last December's abuse of power and must not happen, especially now that the true character of that outrageous gambit is public knowledge.

As with his commitment to the newly minted Air Force officers, in the immortal words of Ira Gershwin, this narrative "ain't necessarily so."

Let's start with the promise of military superiority. Only someone completely oblivious - or indifferent - to what it takes to achieve and maintain superiority could make such a statement under present and foreseeable circumstances. The fact of the matter is that the nearly $800 billion already excised from the Pentagon budgets over the next 10 years has caused the evisceration of virtually every military modernization program previously on the books. Research and development accounts crucial to the next generation of weapons are being similarly savaged.

As a result, we will be lucky to be competitive with adversaries who are busily upgrading their forces, often in ways specifically designed to counter advantages we have. "Superiority" will, in important respects, likely be out of the question.

That is especially true if the defense budget is beset with yet the next $500 billion in cuts ordered by existing statute starting in January 2013. You might not know this train wreck is upon us from the lack of disclosure about the impact of such reductions in Defense Department planning documents. You can get a sense of the effects, however, from the Center for Security Policy's Defense Breakdown Reports. The Pentagon understandably worries about disclosing in advance ways in which this magnitude of harm would be accommodated lest a blueprint for making it so is provided.

As of this writing, unless some deus ex machina materializes like in a Greek drama too complicated to be resolved by mere mortals, the armed forces will not be spared from what the Joint Chiefs' chairman has called a "catastrophe."

Sadly, it seems increasingly unlikely that a consensus will be found during a contentious lame-duck session of Congress to negate the effects on our national security of the "sequestration" mechanism - a legislative device Secretary of Defense Leon E. Panetta has called a "doomsday machine" since it failed to compel Congress to find other ways of reducing the deficit. To be sure, leading Republicans, including House Budget Committee Chairman Paul Ryan, House Armed Services Committee Chairman Howard "Buck" McKeon and Senate Minority Whip Jon Kyl, have developed means of staving off this debacle for our armed forces. But neither Mr. Obama nor Senate Majority Leader Harry Reid want any part of them.

Some would have us take comfort in the fact that even at these reduced levels, the United States will spend more on defense than do our potential adversaries combined. Set aside uncertainties about exactly how much the Chinese and Russians are actually investing in amassing new weapons designed to kill Americans. (For example, does anyone really know how much China has spent to build 3,000 miles of hardened underground tunnels in which are concealed heavens only knows how many nuclear missiles?)

As with domestic law enforcement, the outlays involved in preserving the peace always vastly exceed the sums spent by those intent on disturbing it. Typically, the more decisively the former is resourced relative to the latter, the more likely it is that hostile parties will be dissuaded from threatening us or our interests. President Reagan dubbed this axiom "peace through strength."

History teaches that the alternative - the deliberate, systematic and sustained diminishing of our defense capabilities - only invites adversaries, who might otherwise be deterred, to act aggressively. Unfortunately, the present crop of such adversaries don't need any encouragement.

Consider just one example: Russia under Vladimir Putin. The Kremlin claims it will spend on the order of $700 billion to modernize its nuclear and conventional forces. At the same time, Mr. Obama is actively considering eliminating up to 80 percent of our deterrent and ensuring that little, if anything, is done to ensure that the remaining force remains viable, let alone superior, to new generations of Russian nuclear arms.

Mr. Obama is clearly proceeding under the influence of his favorite general, former Joint Chiefs Vice Chairman James "Hoss" Cartwright, who in a paper released on May 16 proclaimed that he believes we can safely eliminate one leg of our strategic triad and "de-alert" or shelve the weapons that would be left. Such notions are being promoted in the name of achieving "global zero" - a world without nuclear weapons. In practice, it will result in a world with many more such arms, including in all the wrong places, as friends and allies alike adjust to a denuclearizing America and the folding of its deterrent "umbrella."

Last week, one of our nation's most storied warriors, nonagenarian Maj. Gen. John Singlaub addressed a Center for Security Policy event in New York City. He spoke forcefully of the need for leadership and urged all of us to settle for nothing less. We require the real deal, now more than ever, with respect to our national security. We literally can accept no substitutes.

In "Lone Survivor," a chilling firsthand account of the loss of 11 members of the Navy's elite Sea, Air, Land (SEAL) Team and eight Army aviators, Petty Officer Marcus Luttrell describes the fateful decision that led to disaster for him and death for his comrades. It came down to a judgment call about whether to risk prosecution and jail time for doing whatever it took to complete their mission, or to allow three Afghan goatherds to rat out his unit to the Taliban.

Petty Officer Luttrell cast the deciding vote to turn loose the farmers who had stumbled upon him and three other SEALs shortly after they had been dropped behind enemy lines to take down a particularly dangerous Taliban leader. He describes the thought process:

"If we kill these guys, we have to be straight about it. Report what we did. We can't sneak around this. ... Their bodies will be found, the Taliban will use it to the max. They'll get it in the papers, and the U.S. liberal media will attack us without mercy. We'll almost certainly be charged with murder."

Such concerns prompted Petty Officer Luttrell to make the call to release the goatherds, setting in motion calamity for his buddies and 16 others dispatched to rescue them from the massive Taliban assault that ensued. It turns out those concerns were well founded, as was demonstrated most recently in a case before the U.S. Military Court of Appeals. By a 3-2 vote, the judges outrageously determined that an Army Ranger, 1st Lt. Michael Behenna, had no right to self-defense when he killed an Iraqi prisoner he was interrogating after the man threw a concrete block at him and tried to seize his firearm. Unless he is pardoned, Lt. Behenna will remain incarcerated for the next 12 years.

Unfortunately, under President Obama, service members' rising fears of being prosecuted for acting to protect themselves and their missions are among many ways in which the military is being "fundamentally transformed," to use Mr. Obama's now-infamous turn of phrase. Consider a few examples:

- Losing wars: Few things can have a more corrosive effect on the morale and esprit de corps of the armed forces than being ordered to participate in and sacrifice - not least by risking life and limb - in protracted conflicts, only to have political authorities throw in the towel. Add in the repeated combat tours pulled by many service members, with all that entails for both them and their families, and you have a formula for disaster for the U.S. military.

- Budget cuts: Matters are made much worse by the sense that the military is being asked to pay more than its fair share of the burden associated with deficit reduction. Even though defense-spending accounts for approximately 20 percent of the budget, the Pentagon has been required to absorb roughly 50 percent of the cuts, while entitlements have been spared.

The roughly $800 billion already excised or in the works to be cut is denying our troops in uniform the modern, properly maintained and qualitatively superior equipment they need to wage war safely and successfully on our behalf. The next $500 billion in reductions - which, all other things being equal, are to go into effect in January - will have, in the words of Joint Chiefs Chairman Gen. Martin E. Dempsey, a "catastrophic" effect.

- A defective counterinsurgency (COIN) strategy: As documented in Part 9 of the Center for Security Policy's online curriculum, "The Muslim Brotherhood in America: The Enemy Within," the effort to win hearts and minds in places like Iraq and Afghanistan has exposed our troops unnecessarily to danger. They are being obliged not to wear protective eyewear and body armor, at risk literally to life and limb. They are ordered to honor their hosts in visits with local elders by consuming foods offered, despite the fact that doing so can subject them to life-long affliction by parasites and diseases. They must observe rules of engagement that restrict use of their firearms and deny them air cover and artillery support in circumstances where it can mean the difference between living and dying.

  Worse yet, our troops are seen by the enemy in these and other ways to be submitting to the latter's doctrine of Shariah. According to that supremacist code, its adherents are compelled, when confronted with evidence they are winning, to redouble their efforts to make us feel subdued. This generally translates into more violence against our troops and us, not less.

- Assault on the culture of the military: Last, but not least, President Obama's use of the military as a vehicle for advancing the radical homosexual agenda in the larger society has demonstrated for many in uniform civilian indifference to the unique attributes of the armed forces. That message can only have been reinforced by the Supreme Court's ruling allowing fraudulent claims to military decorations as protected free speech.

Unfortunately, these sorts of assaults on the U.S. military are likely to "fundamentally transform" it, all right. Perhaps that transformation will manifest itself, among other ways, by precipitating the collapse of the all-volunteer force, as many of those who are serving decline to do so and fewer and fewer new, high-quality recruits enlist. We can ill afford such an Obama legacy in an increasingly dangerous world.

Nuclear Deterrence

Russian President Boris Yeltsin visit last week had a most ironic effect. Despite the hoopla attending his initialing with President Bush of the most dramatic arms reduction agreement of all time, the disinterest most Americans feel toward such initiatives was palpable. Indeed, the vast majority of Americans seemed far more interested in the details of Mr. Yeltsin's comments about U.S. POWs than in his undertakings about nuclear weapons.

And why, some might ask, should it be otherwise? After all, the Cold War is said to be over, the erstwhile enemy converted into a friend. Even under more frightening circumstances than these, most Americans chose not to dwell upon the arcane terminology and incomprehensible destructive potential involved in the superpowers' nuclear standoff and related arms control agreements.

The danger is that such inattention on the part of the public at large tends to encourage inadequate oversight of the arms control process - and quality control of its products - by the people's elected representatives in Congress. The consequent prospect that the Senate, in particular, will fail to play its constitutional function as a real check-and-balance on executive treaty-making power has a predictable and insidious effect: If senators are not going to pay attention to the details of arms accords that determine the equitability and verifiability of such agreements, why should senior executive officials?

A case in point is the Strategic Arms Reduction Treaty (START) that was the subject of testimony yesterday by Secretary of State James Baker before the Senate Foreign Relations Committee. This agreement was signed nearly a year ago by Mr. Bush and then-Soviet President Mikhail Gorbachev after Mr. Baker engineered "breakthroughs" on a number of issues that were outstanding when the Reagan administration left office. It is a matter of record that in virtually every one of these issues, the Baker "breakthroughs" came when the U.S. capitulated.

Such concessions will enable the former Soviet Union, among other things, legally to: field mobile intercontinental ballistic missiles; flight test and modernize a large force of heavy ICBMs; retain unlimited numbers of non-deployed missiles (except those associated with mobile systems); avoid on-site inspections at a large number of facilities that might be suspected of treaty violations; eschew "tagging" of missiles and monitoring of their final assembly to assist in verification; and ascribe far fewer weapons to their missile forces than are known to be deployed aboard them.

These and other Baker "breakthroughs" helped to make the START Treaty substantially less equitable and vastly more un-verifiable than the Reagan administration was prepared to accept. In fact, "breakout" - not breakthrough - should be the watchword of this agreement; under its terms the former Soviet Union could retain the capacity to field weapons that were quantitatively and qualitatively far more formidable than is advertised by the START salesmen.

Has the demise of the Soviet Union subsequent to the START Treaty's signature or the initialing last week of yet another agreement - entailing far more draconian reductions - made these concerns moot? Regrettably, no.

The wholesale transformation of the old Soviet empire along democratic and free market lines - with an attendant dismantling of its residual, vastly overbuilt military-industrial complex - would assuredly greatly reduce the possibility that we would face a renewed threat from that quarter any time soon. In fact, such a transformation would offer a much more reliable protection than START or even more effective arms control accords.

Unfortunately, Mr. Yeltsin is far from consolidating that sort of overhaul of the former Soviet system. If anything, the military and industrial support system once again seem ascendant in the ongoing contest for power in Russia.

Notably, its spokesmen have recently obtained a number of important positions in the Yeltsin Cabinet. They are indulging in increasingly bellicose statements about Russia's nationalist destiny and the dangers of structural reform. The incursion against Moldova is ominous; the rationale used to justify it - defense of ethnic Russians - can be deployed at will to legitimize violence against the Baltic States, Ukraine and other former Soviet republics.

START and other arms control agreements will only serve to modulate the risks posed to the United States by a resurgent Russian military to the extent that such accords are effective, verifiable and enforceable. It is irresponsible self-delusion to believe that an inequitable, unverifiable and unenforceable treaty like START will "lock in" such a military force to anything other than more Soviet-style cheating and circumventions of agreed limitations.

Similarly, the outline of a new treaty - offering roughly to halve the nominal forces permitted under START - initialed last week by Presidents Bush and Yeltsin does not vitiate the present treaty's shortcomings. It will be months, perhaps years before there is a formal treaty to sign; it will be years, perhaps a full decade before the cuts it is supposed to entail (for example, in Russian heavy missiles and multiple warhead ICBMs) go into effect.

Still more worrisome is the prospect that START's deficient counting rules, inadequate verification procedures and loophole-riddled limitations will be carried forward into the new treaty. Inevitably, using agreed formulations would greatly simplify the task of cobbling together a START II agreement relatively quickly and set the stage for still further half-Bakered "breakthroughs."

In short, the American people have a substantial stake in START. If they do not pay attention to the content of this agreement - and demand that their elected representatives do likewise, including where necessary insisting upon significant amendments to the treaty - they will deserve the fatally flawed accord they get.

A decade ago, George Bush served in an administration that successfully resisted the demands of a vocal minority determined to destroy what was then, and remains, the ultimate guarantor of American security - nuclear deterrence. With his decision last week to sign legislation halting nuclear testing, however, Mr. Bush today presides over an administration that has effectively put into place every important element of the discredited "nuclear freeze" campaign.

If we are lucky, history will record this 180-degree change in the direction of official policy as but one of many instances of Reagan decisions being undone by his handpicked successor. If we are not, the Bush administration's wholesale adoption of the nuclear freeze platform will have done irreparable harm to this country's defense posture: At a time when more and more nations are getting into the nuclear weapons business, this country is getting out of it.

Worse yet, thanks to decisions taken by Energy Secretary James Watkins and White House Chief of Staff James Baker, it is not clear whether the United States will be able to reverse course if - or rather, when - the need to do so becomes apparent. Consider the following:

- The Bush administration has essentially shut down the infrastructure of reactors, laboratories, manufacturing plants and other facilities known as the Energy Department's "nuclear weapons complex." While cannibalizing older weapons will permit the United States to maintain a substantially smaller nuclear arsenal for a time, it cannot be relied upon indefinitely. The natural decaying of one critical ingredient - the radioactive gas tritium, the atrophying of inactive and obsolescing facilities and the attrition of skilled workers will ensure at some point (probably early in the next century) that even this improbable arrangement for underpinning the linchpin of the national defense posture will become unsustainable.

- The manner in which the Bush administration has suspended operations at a number of the weapons complex's most critical sites effectively precludes them from ever being put on-line again. Once such facilities have been turned off for safety, environmental or other reasons, they cannot be put returned to operational status without meeting exceedingly stringent EPA standards.

As a practical matter, thanks to decades of inattention to environmental concerns and deferred modernization, most of these Energy Department facilities will never be able to pass muster. While tens of thousands of people can be employed and billions of dollars spent cleaning up such sites, it is unlikely that they will ever again be available to produce nuclear weapons and their components.

- This problem is being aggravated by the Bush administration's inaction on longer-range programs needed to replace such troubled and aging production facilities. The most glaring example is the decision to defer, effectively indefinitely, construction of a new reactor capable of producing tritium. This is a double tragedy: Not only will the nation's long-term needs for this essential defense commodity go unmet as a result, but the leading design for this reactor could have also served as the prototype for a next generation of safer commercial nuclear power plants. Instead of obtaining in this manner a real "peace dividend," the American people are likely to find themselves in the future without either a credible deterrent or real independence from foreign sources of energy.

- Most recently, President Bush's political handlers - read, Jim Baker - have put political expediency before the national security concerning nuclear testing. As recently as last month, administration spokesmen (including then-Secretary of State Baker) were denouncing congressional efforts to curtail this activity. At the time, they correctly observed that modest numbers of underground tests were essential to preserving a safe, reliable and credible nuclear deterrent.

Unfortunately, congressional opponents of such testing - many of them among the original proponents of the nuclear freeze - shrewdly packaged a moratorium on testing with legislation funding an $8 billion supercollider to be built in Texas. This immense chunk of "pork" is deemed by the White House to be an essential element in the president's re-election bid. According to undisputed press reports, Mr. Baker "decided that the supercollider was going to take precedence" over the concerns of National Security Adviser Brent Scowcroft and Defense Secretary Dick Cheney.

In other words, in keeping with President Bush's announced intention to do "anything necessary" to get re-elected, his administration has agreed to a "temporary" ban on testing. It is absolutely predictable, however, that – like temporary housing - this ban is virtually certain to become permanent.

The Bush administration, in abandoning the policy set by its predecessor with respect to the nuclear freeze, has not - as some contend – responded properly to changed world conditions. The collapse of the Soviet Union has not been accompanied by a slackening of Russian efforts to produce nuclear weapons and associated special materials. What is more, it has exponentially increased the prospect that formerly Soviet nuclear weapons will find their way into the hands of others perhaps even more likely to use them.

Mr. Bush may come to regret the role he has played in implementing the nuclear freeze as it significantly undercuts his election claim to exclusive trustworthiness with regard to safeguarding the national security. In any event, the American people will likely have cause to regret that role as they face a world of increasing nuclear threats without either a reliable in-kind deterrent or the protection afforded by deployed strategic defenses.

"FATE OF THE B-2 AND DEFENSE ENTWINED: CRITICAL SECURITY DECISION" | JUNE 13, 1995

This afternoon, the House of Representatives is expected to make a critical national security decision - whether to continue production of the world's most advanced and militarily capable manned bomber, the B-2. The case for doing so is compelling on both strategic and fiscal grounds.

A bipartisan group of seven former defense secretaries - Melvin Laird, James Schlesinger, Donald Rumsfeld, Harold Brown, Caspar Weinberger, Frank Carlucci and Dick Cheney - made that case succinctly in a joint letter to President Clinton in January:

"[The B-2] remains the most cost-effective means of rapidly projecting force over great distances. Its range will enable it to reach any point on Earth within hours after launch while being deployed at only three secure bases around the world. Its payload and array of munitions will permit it to destroy numerous time-sensitive targets in a single sortie. And perhaps most importantly, its low-observable characteristics will allow it to reach intended targets without fear of interception."

Just how important the combination of low-observability or "stealthiness" and precision munitions can be to successful military operations is evident from the air war in Operation Desert Storm. During the first day of that conflict, 36 F-117 stealth fighters flew just 2 percent of the sorties, but successfully attacked almost 31 percent of the targets. What is more, because of their stealthiness, these planes were able to operate without the armadas of escort and defense suppression aircraft that have traditionally had to accompany strike planes. Each sortie by the stealthy F-117 proved to be worth approximately eight non-stealth sorties.

The B-2, however, has something that neither the F-117 nor any other aircraft in the world has: a formidable combination of stealthiness, large precision munitions-carriage, all-weather delivery capability and extraordinary range. For example, the B-2 has lower observability signatures than the F-117, even though it is a substantially larger aircraft. Its payload is roughly eight times that of the F-117. It can deliver its ordnance despite clouds or smoke that would stymie F-117 missions.

And, perhaps most importantly, the B-2 does not have to operate from bases close to the theater of operation. Thanks to a range that is six times that of the F-117, it can be rapidly brought to bear anywhere on the planet, irrespective of whether foreign governments give their permission (something that was a chronic problem in Desert Storm) or have surviving bases (something that happily was not a factor in the war with Iraq, but almost certainly will be the next time around).

By contrast, the case for the alternative that the House will be asked to adopt - halting B-2 production at just 20 aircraft - has very little to commend it. For one thing, it would leave the United States with far too few modern, long-range, manned bombers. The Clinton administration's own "Bottom-Up Review," which was used to determine the size of the U.S. military's inventory in the post-Cold War world, concluded that 100 bombers would be required in the event the nation had to fight and win two nearly simultaneous conflicts. These aircraft would be thrown into battle rapidly to help defeat hostile forces in the first contingency. They would then be rapidly shifted to interdict the enemy and set the stage for victory in the second one. To maintain such capability, the Defense Department determined that a total inventory of some 184 aircraft would be required.

Unfortunately, the Clinton administration has not budgeted sufficient funds to allow this full force to be retained in the active inventory. That is due, in part, to the fact that maintaining 40-year-old B-52 aircraft is an expensive proposition. When the costs associated with the fleet of aircraft that are required to allow these extremely unstealthy planes to perform their mission are factored in, they prove to be prohibitive.

To justify fielding far fewer bombers than its own planning blueprint called for, the Pentagon recently produced a "Heavy Bomber Force Study" performed by the Institute for Defense Analysis (IDA). This study proves that even the most preposterous conclusions can be justified if one is willing to make absurd assumptions. Take, for example, IDA's assumption that, even if two major regional conflicts (MRC) were to happen nearly simultaneously, the United States will have 14 days of warning before the initiation of hostilities by the aggressor in the first MRC. In theory, this would afford the United States two weeks to move tactical aircraft and ground forces into the theater of battle.

In the real world, of course, it is imprudent to expect either that timely or unambiguous warning will be forthcoming. Indeed, history is replete with examples in which such warning as was available was accompanied by conflicting signals. The mixed indicators tend to discourage steps requiring the expensive, disruptive mobilization and deployment of U.S. forces. This is doubly true when, as is usually the case, concerns abound that such steps will be seen as provocative - if not escalatory.

The truth of the matter is that we are going to need more manned bombers, and the B-2 is the only one in production or development. Consequently, were Congress to fail to preserve the capability to produce additional B-2s, it would be doing far more harm than simply foregoing the option to buy the most flexible, potent aircraft ever built. It would also effectively sound the death knell for the U.S. manned bomber force. After all, once the B-2 production line is closed, it will, as a practical matter, become impossible to replace the remaining, aging bombers.

There has been a lot of loose talk lately about isolationist tendencies in Congress. The reality is that the United States is increasingly withdrawing from the overseas bases upon which it has long relied to protect American interests and fulfill our alliance commitments. Whether one views this development as good or bad, a function of isolationism or simply a reflection of budgetary realities, it places a premium on systems that can efficiently project power worldwide from U.S. bases. Committed internationalists and isolationists alike should appreciate that a large and flexible B-2 force is essential if we are to meet the nation's abiding defense needs largely from the continental United States.

It has become fashionable of late to mourn the passing from public life of large numbers of experienced legislators who have decided to call it quits. Generally, their departure is taken as evidence of the decline of Congress and the civil, deliberative debate it is supposed to foster. Worse yet, we are often told, the absence of these individuals -many of them self-styled "moderates" reputed to disdain ideology and partisanship - can only exacerbate this trend.

Perhaps it's the nature of the season. Perhaps it's the depressing performance turned in by a bipartisan gaggle of retiring U.S. senators on a "60 Minutes" segment last Sunday. Or perhaps it's the legislative record of this and recent past Congresses. But I find myself thinking of what might be called "the ghosts of Senates past."

Specifically, I am reminded of the contribution made by now-departed legislators of the stature of Henry "Scoop" Jackson and John Tower, men whose principled positions and vast knowledge used to dominate the Senate's work on national security matters. In their day, the institution served as the Framers of the Constitution intended it to - namely, as a real check-and-balance on the executive branch's management of the defense budget and its conduct with respect to international treaties affecting vital U.S. interests.

In particular, under Sens. Jackson and Tower, the Senate and its Armed Services Committee (on which they long served) played pivotal roles in arms control matters. They saw to it that rigorous hearings were held concerning complex and potentially risky treaties affecting, for example, U.S. strategic offensive and defensive forces. Such hearings routinely featured both advocates and critics of pending agreements. Before the Senate considered these treaties, it would generally have the benefit of a substantive analysis prepared, debated over and voted on by the Armed Services Committee. (The committee's critical report on SALT I actually had the effect of killing that "fatally flawed" accord). And extended debate typically occurred on the Senate floor.

If Scoop Jackson and John Tower were in the Senate today, it seems inconceivable that the institution would be in its present position: As noted in this space last week, senators are obliged to take up the START II Treaty - arguably, the most risk-laden arms control agreement ever to come before the Senate - before the end of the present session (presumably before Christmas recess). If this happens, senators will have to act without benefit of a hearing record that adequately reflects informed criticism, as well as endorsements. They will have to vote in the absence of a carefully deliberated Armed Services Committee analysis of the treaty and without an opportunity for thorough debate.

As a result, senators may vote on START II unaware that it will probably not produce the hoped-for strategic stability at far lower levels of strategic nuclear forces. To be sure, the attraction of START II -which was hastily signed in the closing moments of the

Bush administration - is that it is supposed to make large reductions in Russia's stockpile of strategic nuclear weapons. In particular, it calls for the elimination of Moscow's fearsome inventory of multiple warhead (or "MIRVed") land-based missiles.

In the politically foreshortened negotiating end game, however, the United States agreed to incorporate inherently unverifiable "downloading" and "conversion" provisions in START II. These provisions afford Moscow an option to retain the capability rapidly and covertly to re-MIRV many of its missiles. If this option is exercised, a remilitarizing Russia could break out massively and on short-notice.

Sens. Jackson and Tower would almost certainly view that prospect as dangerously increased by the victory of the Communists and Vladimir Zhironovsky's ultra-nationalist/xenophobic party in Sunday's Russian parliamentary elections. They would certainly understand that - although the United States in theory retains a re-MIRVing option - as a practical matter, budgetary, programmatic and nuclear stockpile considerations assure a strategically significant asymmetry in this area.

Worse yet, serving senators are being asked to accept a linkage explicitly rejected by President Bush, but asserted by Moscow and the Clinton administration: In order to obtain the strategic benefits of START II, it is now said that the United States must effectively foreclose its right to withdraw from the ABM Treaty. This implies that the U.S. will have to remain absolutely undefended against emerging ballistic missile threats from other quarters (for example, China, North Korea, Iran, Libya or Iraq, which was recently caught trying to acquire long-range missile components).

Let's be clear: If the 3,500 START II-accountable thermonuclear weapons Russia could retain under the treaty were to be unleashed on the United States, the devastation would likely be so vast that few would appreciate the difference between such an attack and one involving substantially larger numbers of "incomings." On the other hand, if - as the price for achieving what amounts to an inconsequential draw-down in Russian forces - America must remain unable to stop even one nuclear missile fired at it by, say, Iraq or North Korea, most citizens would probably view that as a very bad deal.

It is somewhat ironic that the preeminent spokesman in the Senate today for such a dubious proposition is retiring "moderate" Sen. Sam Nunn, a longtime colleague of Sens. Jackson and Tower on the Armed Services Committee and a successor to the latter as its chairman. In this connection, the Georgia Democrat has announced his intention to try today to defeat the long-awaited conference report on the Fiscal Year 1996 Defense Department authorization bill, H.R. 1530. He opposes this legislation's requirement that the entire United States be protected against ballistic missile attack by the year 2003 on the grounds that it amounts to an "anticipatory breach" of the ABM Treaty and jeopardizes Russian ratification of START II.

Fortunately, there remain a few legislators who recognize the folly of this approach. Notably, a group of senators led by Republicans Robert Smith of New Hampshire and Jon Kyl of Arizona are trying - in the absence of an inclusive hearing record and a rigorous analysis of the START II Treaty from the Armed Services Committee and in the face of opposition from "moderates" like Sen. Sam Nunn -to fend off pressure to complete action on START II before Christmas. They understand that to accede to that pressure would be tantamount to rubber-stamping this risky accord. Members of "the Senate future" like Messrs. Smith, Kyl and Company are to be commended for their efforts to live up to the best traditions and constitutional responsibilities of the institution. With a little luck, the "ghosts of Senates past" like Scoop Jackson and John Tower will inspire their colleagues to follow suit.

For seven years, the West has been an unwilling participant in a variation on the fabled game of "Russian Roulette." Call it "Iraqi Roulette." The difference is that, the Russian version involves a player spinning the cylinder of a revolver loaded with just one bullet, holding it to his own head and pulling the trigger. In the Iraqi version, it is Saddam Hussein who holds the gun; the head in question is ours.

Time after time, year after year, Saddam has tested the resolve and cohesiveness of the U.S.-led coalition that defeated him in Operation Desert Storm. He has flouted the protection we afforded his opponents in northern and southern Iraq and engaged in genocidal attacks upon them. He has threatened to shoot down our aircraft. He has made threatening military moves towards Kuwait. He has interfered with the inspectors charged with ferreting out his concealed stock of weapons of mass destruction (WMD) and the ballistic missiles that could deliver them. Now, he has gotten rid (at least temporarily) of the United Nations inspectors altogether, and tampered with the cameras left behind to keep an electronic eye on things while they were gone.

Thanks to Saddam's latest gambit, it must be assumed that his covert chemical, biological, nuclear and missile programs are once again up and running. Consequently, the stakes involved in Iraqi Roulette are becoming higher then ever.

As discussed in this space last week, the threat posed by these weapons can only be permanently addressed by toppling the Iraqi despot and his clique. In the meantime, serious thought needs to be given to the ways in which Saddam can be dissuaded from pulling the WMD trigger.

The Bush administration apparently succeeded in deterring Saddam from using the chemical or biological weapons he had at the time of the Gulf War with the credible threat of nuclear retaliation. This threat remains the ultimate trump card today - both with respect to the Butcher of Baghdad and vis a vis other bad actors emerging as challenges to our security in the increasingly untidy "post-Cold War" world.

This would seem, therefore, to be an inopportune moment to be considering, to say nothing of implementing, changes in our nuclear posture that degrade its credibility and, therefore, that could reduce its deterrent value. There is, nonetheless, a vocal chorus of erstwhile government officials - notably, former CIA director Stansfield Turner, former Strategic Commander Gen. Lee Butler and former White House scientific aide Frank von Hippel - and anti-nuclear activists that is urging just such a course. "De-posture" our forces, they urge, claiming that the world will be a safer place if all of our ballistic missiles are incapable of being launched without days or months of corrective actions.

Surely such steps would be matched by corresponding Russian measures, the de-posturers argue, thus rectifying the danger of an accidental launch by an arsenal the Kremlin has under increasingly uncertain command and control. Unaddressed is the larger point: Even if Moscow were actually to eliminate its entire nuclear arsenal, the United States would still require effective deterrents to post-Cold War threats posed by others, like Saddam Hussein's Iraq.

Unfortunately, the idea of unilaterally dismantling the U.S. nuclear deterrent is not a notion advanced only by radical disarmers outside the government. The following are illustrative examples of steps the Clinton administration has taken that have the effect of eroding the robustness, credibility and effectiveness of American deterrence:

- The United States no longer produces nuclear weapons. In fact, its nuclear weapons production complex is almost entirely shut down. The trained personnel responsible for the development, testing and reliability of the stockpile have been hemorrhaging from its national laboratories. It has not conducted a nuclear test in over five years and has pledged never to do so again. And there is no program to design or procure replacements for the United States' aging missiles, long-range bombers and strategic submarines.

- As one of its first acts, the Clinton administration dismantled programs associated with U.S. efforts to ensure the survival of constitutional, representative government in the event Washington is attacked with a weapon of mass destruction. Few things could do more to weaken deterrence, if not actually serve to invite attack, than the prospect that the U.S. military could be paralyzed by "decapitation" of its command structure.

- This problem is compounded by the fact that the administration operates today only one-quarter of the survivable airborne command-and-control aircraft fielded during the Cold War. Worse yet, those that remain are kept at reduced readiness and are, therefore, less able to provide an assured ability to formulate and communicate orders in the event of a chemical, biological or nuclear strike on Washington.

- The Clinton administration has also significantly eroded the nation's early warning systems, deferring maintenance and suspending operations of some of the assets that would provide critical data should a missile or bomber attack be launched on the United States. For example, the two large, phased-array missile warning radars covering the southeastern and southwestern approaches to the continental U.S. have been quietly shut down and cannibalized for parts.

Bear in mind, none of the United States' prospective adversaries are emulating these actions. For example, the Russians, Chinese, North Koreans and Iraqis, among others, are investing heavily in deeply buried underground shelters to ensure the survival of their respective regimes and the success of their war-fighting strategies. They are either still producing nuclear weapons in quantity or are aggressively trying to do so.

Unfortunately, sources in the Pentagon report that the Clinton administration is actively seeking still further measures that could be taken in response to the radical disarmers' pressure to "de-alert" and "de-posture" the U.S. nuclear arsenal. These prospective initiatives, like those already taken, can only be described as the reckless abandonment of our nuclear posture – a policy that threatens to undermine America's capability to deter the likes of Saddam Hussein at the very moment that the need to do so is becoming ever more apparent.

Tomorrow, President Clinton, Vice President Al Gore and a host of Cabinet officers, military leaders, Nobel Prize winners, scientists and others will gather at the White House for a pep rally in support of the Comprehensive Test Ban Treaty (CTBT).

If, as expected, a sufficient number of U.S. senators next week reject this fatally flawed treaty on the grounds it is inconsistent with U.S. national security, many of the participants in this extravaganza who would be expected to recognize that reality are likely to find their authority seriously diminished in the future.

In the event 34 or more senators decline to consent to the CTBT's ratification, one reason seems likely to prove overriding: Not one of those participating in the White House pep rally - not the administration's luminati, not the former chairmen of the Joint Chiefs of Staff, not the directors of the nation's nuclear laboratories or other scientists - can honestly say the U.S. nuclear deterrent can be maintained in a safe, reliable and credible condition for the indefinite future without at least low-yield, periodic underground nuclear testing.

To be sure, there will be a lot of talk tomorrow about how "confident" these assembled worthies are that that will be the case. The president and his cheerleaders can be expected to reiterate some variation on the line Mr. Clinton pronounced on Aug. 14, 1995 - the day he revealed he would agree to a treaty banning even undetectable, low-yield nuclear tests: "I consider the maintenance of a safe and reliable nuclear stockpile to be a supreme national interest of the United States." Clinton and Company will assert their confidence that the nation's supreme interest in preserving such a stockpile will in the future (actually 10 years or so in the future) be satisfied by sophisticated computer modeling, not actual testing.

Unfortunately, being "confident" is not the same thing as being certain. And no one can be certain that our arsenal of aging nuclear weapons will be viable in the future if we are unable to use the tool that every president from Harry Truman on - until, that is, Bill Clinton - understood was necessary for that purpose: realistic nuclear testing.

Indeed, there is already reason to be less than confident that today's U.S. arsenal meets the exacting standards for safety and reliability that have heretofore been observed. After all, we have not tested any nuclear weapons since 1992 - the longest such moratorium since the dawn of the nuclear age. Importantly, up until the time we suspended testing seven years ago, we were routinely finding problems with our arsenal.

In fact, according to Robert Barker, a physicist and thermonuclear weapons designer who served as the Pentagon's top expert on atomic energy matters under three secretaries of defense, he was obliged to recommend taking U.S. nuclear arms off alert (known as "redlining") five times during the six years before U.S. testing was halted. No weapons have been redlined since then. It strains credulity this is due to their condition actually being perfect. More likely, we simply do not know what our weapons' defects are since, without testing, they are not apparent.

Some of the military leaders and scientific experts whose authority and credibility the president will be shamelessly exploiting in the hope of selling the CTBT to the requisite 67 senators by the time the vote is held on Oct. 12 may be willing to overlook this natty reality on the basis of what is known as "Safeguard F." The treaty's proponents want legislators and the public to believe there is an escape hatch in case our "supreme interests" are jeopardized by an unexpected lack of confidence in our nuclear stockpile: Pursuant to Safeguard F, they aver, we can always resume nuclear testing.

To appreciate what a fraud this assurance is, one only need read the convoluted, characteristically hedged language the president used in describing in August 1995 the nature of his commitment to resume testing, should the need arise:

"In the event that I were informed by the secretary of defense and secretary of energy, advised by the Nuclear Weapons Council, the directors of the Energy Department's nuclear weapons labs and the commander of U.S. Strategic Command that a high level of confidence in the safety or reliability of a nuclear weapons type which the two secretaries considered to be critical to our nuclear deterrent could no longer be certified, I would be prepared, in consultation with Congress, to exercise our supreme national interest rights under the CTB in order to conduct whatever testing might be required."

Let us count the weasel words: Everybody having anything to do with nuclear weapons has to agree that a "high level of confidence" (a most subjective standard) is no longer certifiable (another subjective judgment) with regard to a weapon that is "critical" to America's deterrent posture (a third). If all that happens, the president would "consult" with Congress. Assuming that goes swimmingly, he would be - what? - "prepared" to conduct whatever testing might be necessary.

In short, this so-called "safeguard" is pure Clintonian sophistry. Set aside the fact that the administration is allowing the ability to resume testing to erode seriously, making it hard to do so even if the go-ahead were given. If concerns about the safety and reliability of U.S. nuclear weapons arise, it is far more likely that such weapons will be retired from the arsenal on the grounds that the specified, subjective thresholds for resuming testing have not been crossed. This is especially true since it will surely be argued at the time that the effect of the United States returning to testing will be to precipitate the wholesale abrogation of the CTBT by others and a huge upsurge in nuclear proliferation.

Fortunately, Senate Majority Leader Trent Lott and more than 33 of his colleagues have broken the code on the Comprehensive Test Ban Treaty. They understand that, no matter how many respected former military officers, Nobel Prize winners, Hollywood celebrities and Cabinet officers endorse this accord, it is a formula for unilateral U.S. nuclear disarmament. This is precisely why it has been a prime objective of every anti-nuclear crusade and the cherished goal of the administration's high-ranking "denuclearizers."

Far from "locking in America's technological superiority," this unverifiable agreement will lock out the technological tools upon which the U.S. deterrent uniquely relies. We already have evidence that other nations (notably, Russia and China) are exploiting the CIA's acknowledged inability to monitor low-yield testing - a problem that will be aggravated, not corrected, by the ambiguous information likely to be generated from the multilateral seismic system being set up under this treaty. In any event, since the CTBT does not define what constitutes a prohibited "nuclear test explosion," we will be unable to hold others to the same stringent standard of zero tests to which this country surely will adhere.

Defeating the Comprehensive Test Ban Treaty will not be sufficient to ensure the future safety and reliability of America's nuclear deterrent that President Clinton professes to be a supreme interest of the United States. But it will be an important and indispensable step in the right direction.

During her travels in Wonderland, Alice found herself embroiled in a kangaroo-style trial in which the judge famously announced, "Sentence first, verdict afterward," followed by the pronouncement "Off with her head."

Regrettably, a similar approach appears to have guided the Bush administration in preparing the Nuclear Posture Review (NPR) it is releasing this week. This review is intended to guide the future size and composition of the U.S. nuclear arsenal for the early years of the 21st century. Yet its most prominent feature - a reduction by roughly two-thirds in the number of deployed nuclear weapons - was effectively pre-determined by a pledge Candidate Bush made on May 23, 2000:

"As president, I will ask the secretary of defense to conduct an assessment of our nuclear force posture and determine how best to meet our security needs. While the exact number of weapons can come only from such an assessment, I will pursue the lowest possible number consistent with our national security. It should be possible to reduce the number of American nuclear weapons significantly further than what has been already agreed to under START II without compromising our security in any way."

During his summit meeting last November in Crawford, Texas with Russian President Vladimir Putin, President Bush announced the sentence: By 10 years from now, the United States will have cut its nuclear arsenal from the present roughly 6,500 weapons, past the 3,500 allowed under START II, to no more than 1,700-2,200 deployed nuclear arms. Now comes the verdict - a Nuclear Posture Review that tries to explain how such unprecedented and draconian reductions in the U.S. deterrent force can be made "without compromising our security in any way."

With the NPR not yet released, one can only guess at how this feat of prestidigitation is accomplished. Whether it turns out, in fact, to be a blueprint for a strategic deterrent force with which we can safely live - or a prescription for the wholesale denuclearization of the United States – will depend on several questions that cannot be answered at this writing:

- Will the levels of forces envisioned by the NPR be compatible with the maintenance of our strategic "Triad" - weapons deployed on land-based ballistic missiles, on submarines and aboard airborne platforms (bombs and cruise missiles)? Historically, the complementary strengths of these various systems have been seen as essential to maintaining a credible deterrent by offsetting their respective shortcomings. Unless costly new programs are undertaken to replace aging missiles and bombers, the small numbers of weapons allowed will greatly exacerbate the temptation simply to dispense with one or another "leg" of the Triad.

- Will the residual force be deployed in a manner that renders it unduly susceptible to preemptive attack? This could, for example, be the effect of concentrating a large percentage of the deployed stockpile at a small number of vulnerable bomber bases. Bad idea.

- Perhaps most importantly, will the president authorize the steps needed to ensure that whatever nuclear deterrent is retained remains safe, reliable and credible? If so, he must swiftly authorize the resumption of periodic underground nuclear testing.

To date, Mr. Bush has tried to straddle this issue. On the one hand, he courageously and correctly rejected the Comprehensive Test Ban Treaty (CTBT), with its permanent ban on all nuclear testing. On the other hand, he has perpetuated a moratorium on this activity - an initiative first imposed upon his father in 1992 by congressional Democrats who favored U.S. denuclearization, something subsequently and explicitly embraced by Bill Clinton and his first energy secretary, Hazel O'Leary. The CTBT's proponents understood that without actual nuclear testing, it would ineluctably become impossible to maintain, let alone to modernize, our arsenal.

As it happens, the moment of truth has arrived, just as the NPR is being released. The Washington Post reported on Jan. 3 that the Energy Department's inspector general recently unveiled a dirty little secret: There are "growing problems associated with the safety and reliability of the nation's nuclear weapons, which without nuclear testing, have become a 'most serious challenge area.' "

Of particular concern are mounting backlogs in the nonnuclear testing program upon which the U.S. has relied exclusively to monitor the safety and reliability of the stockpile since 1992. Energy's I.G., Gregory Friedman, concluded: "If these delays continue, the department may not be in a position to unconditionally certify the aging nuclear weapons stockpile." In fact, even if they don't, the absence of realistic underground tests will likely make such certification little more than educated guesswork.

To his credit, President Bush has created conditions that may provide a safety net for the sorts of nuclear disarmament he wants to undertake. By withdrawing from the 1972 Anti-Ballistic Missile Treaty, he has cleared the way for the deployment of effective, global missile defenses that can reduce somewhat the requirement for nuclear weapons-based deterrence.

To realize his goals for a secure and properly defended 21st century America, however, Mr. Bush must take several concrete actions:

(1) Ensure that missile defenses are actually deployed as soon as possible (within days of his ABM Treaty decision the Pentagon and/or Congress had killed or dramatically slowed no fewer than three important anti-missile programs).

(2) Resist State Department efforts to mutate his unilateral (and, thereby, revisable) decision on nuclear cuts into an ill-advised, binding treaty with Russia,

(3) And direct the resumption of nuclear testing needed to ensure the continued viability of the nuclear forces the United States must retain for the uncertain, and probably quite dangerous, decades ahead.

Ever since North Korea's dictator, Kim Jong-Il, broke bad – acknowledging cheating on his promises to forgo nuclear weapons and then doing so openly and in earnest - government officials and others have been speculating about how fast the "Dear Leader" will be able to build up his stockpile. If he has two weapons now, will he have five or 10 by this time next year? Some think Kim might be able to build as many as 50 over the next few years.

Lost in the discussion to date is a dirty little secret: Whatever the number Pyongyang's weaponeers can churn out in the months ahead, it will almost certainly be larger than the number of nuclear weapons the United States could build during a similar period. The truth is that the U.S. cannot produce any new weapons at the moment, having shut down some years ago its only facility for manufacturing the heart of such weapons: plutonium "pits."

Now, the argument will be made that the United States has thousands of nuclear weapons and does not need to produce additional ones just because North Korea does. Still, it is an extraordinary thing that the world's sole superpower lacks the capability to augment its arsenal - a capability that not only North Korea but every one of the other declared nuclear powers [Britain, France, Russia, China, India and Pakistan] has maintained.

This situation may prove to be far more than a bizarre anomaly, however. What if it turns out that the weapons currently in the U.S. inventory [most of which were designed 20 or 30 years ago with a very different strategic environment in mind] are not only obsolescent, but are of very limited or no utility - and, therefore, incredible as deterrents - in the present environment? For example, is it acceptable that no weapon in the stockpile today can reliably hold at risk the sorts of deeply buried and assiduously hardened command centers and weapons bunkers in which Saddam Hussein and Kim Jong-Il have invested heavily?

Worse yet, America's present inability to manufacture new nuclear weapons in any quantity is but a symptom of a far larger problem: the dismal state of the industrial and technological infrastructure that the Department of Energy is charged with maintaining to support the U.S. deterrent.

This state of affairs is the predictable, and intended, product of a decade of neglect - or worse - of this nuclear weapons complex. The House Armed Services Committee once described the combination of policies and spending aimed during this period at hobbling, undermining and ultimately dismantling the complex as "erosion by design."

Thanks largely to this legacy, we not only lack the ability to replace or modernize the nuclear weapons currently in the U.S. stockpile.

There is also growing uncertainty about their safety and reliability.

Today, we cannot address those uncertainties in the only proven and most cost-effective manner, since we are unable at the moment to conduct underground nuclear tests. None of the other, as yet unvalidated and much more expensive technologies that have been held out as substitutes for testing will be available for years to come; some may never pan out technically or be funded to fruition.

If anything, the problems may be even more acute on the personnel side of the complex. Last week's resignations by the top two officials of the Los Alamos National Laboratory is but the latest evidence of the difficulties confronting the national labs. Their people, who are absolutely critical to the technical excellence and operation of the nation's nuclear weapons infrastructure, have for much of the past 10 years been poorly led, demoralized and, in many cases, profoundly alienated by their treatment from higher-ups in Washington.

As a result, there has been an acute brain drain from the labs.

This is particularly true among the small cadre of physicists who have actually had firsthand experience with the extremely esoteric business of designing, testing and maintaining the nuclear weapons in our stockpile today - arguably, the most complex pieces of equipment ever produced by man.

The good news is that President Bush and his national security team have brought the sort of fresh and more responsible perspective to these matters that has been so sorely needed. Their 2002 Nuclear Posture Review [NPR] for the first time gave equal importance to the nuclear stockpile and the infrastructure necessary to sustain it.

It is not enough, of course, simply to recognize the problem. Real leadership must be brought to bear to take corrective action. An opportunity to provide such leadership now looms, thanks to the reassignment of Gen. John Gordon, who previously ran the Nuclear National Security Administration, the openings at Los Alamos and the possibility of competing the contract to run that laboratory – a job that has, from the lab's founding, been the exclusive responsibility of the University of California.

In particular, a key test will be the administration's replacement for Gen. Gordon. Clearly needed is a leader with: a demonstrated ability to manage large, technically sophisticated government organizations and industrial facilities; firsthand familiarity with the weapons complex yet, ideally, independence from it; and an established commitment to the president's ambitious agenda of ensuring the long-term viability of the U.S. nuclear deterrent.

With the help of such an individual, Mr. Bush and Energy Secretary Spence Abraham have a chance to halt and reverse the meltdown of America's nuclear weapons infrastructure, and the self-inflicted "erosion by design" that is all the more ill-advised in light of proliferation in North Korea and elsewhere.

Wednesday marks the 63rd anniversary of the destruction of Hiroshima by an American atomic bomb. For most of us, if we think of that occasion at all, it will be a passing thought - a distant historical fact, probably noted with sympathy for those killed or wounded in the attack. Perhaps we will recollect - as we should - that the unprecedented destruction wrought by a single weapon helped bring World War II quickly to a close, obviating the need for an invasion of the Japanese home islands that would have been infinitely more destructive, for both the inhabitants and for our forces.

Others intend to observe that anniversary very differently. The event and its victims will be exploited as props in an international anti-nuclear weapons campaign. Ironically, under present and foreseeable circumstances, those who seek to "ban the bomb" would likely clear the way for the next terrible global conflagration.

Apparently, the Japanese television network NHK has enlisted in this campaign, whose stated goal is to achieve the worldwide abolition of nuclear weapons. A case in point was the propaganda-fest filmed by NHK for broadcast in Japan on August 6, in which I recently found myself featured.

For three hours on a Saturday evening last month, 16 other Americans and I and 17 residents of Hiroshima were asked to discuss how to rid the world of nuclear arms. Most of the American participants and all of those beamed in from Japan (including a resident American anti-nuclear activist) hoped it would be possible to ban such weapons.

It fell to me and a handful of my commonsensical countrymen to make the case that it was impossible to create a nuclear-free world. I argued it would actually be ill advised even to seek such a goal.

For one thing, the proverbial nuclear genie is out of the bottle. The technology for making crude atomic weapons at least as destructive as the ones dropped 63 years ago, first on Hiroshima and subsequently on Nagasaki, is widely available. That is due not only to the likes of Pakistan's A.Q. Khan and his North Korean clients - the world's "Nukes-R-Us."

Unfortunately, the dissemination of nuclear weapons-relevant technology has been the result of an international agreement meant to prevent it: the Nuclear Non-Proliferation Treaty (NPT). The NPT offered non-nuclear weapon states all the know-how and most of the materials they needed to become nuclear-armed, if only they promised not to do so.

Secondly, as that experience suggests, there is no basis for believing all nuclear weapon states would abide by a new undertaking to abolish their nuclear arsenals. The Russians and Chinese - inveterate cheaters on their international obligations - are busily modernizing their nuclear forces. Pakistan and North Korea are among the problematic lesser nuclear powers expanding theirs, while still others - notably, Iran - are covertly trying to acquire the Bomb. A number of these states have ties to terrorists that could result in the latter "going nuclear," too.

Thirdly, even if a global ban on nuclear weapons were universally embraced and, somehow, were honored verifiably, where would that leave us? History suggests that, in the absence of nuclear deterrence, the world would eventually be plunged yet again into the sort of cataclysm that twice scarred the 20th century. Making the world safe for conventional war should not be either our goal or an acceptable outcome.

Sadly, as the NHK program made clear, the campaign to eliminate nuclear weapons - heretofore a hobbyhorse of the radical left and its Soviet handlers - has now taken on a unprecedented degree of respectability. Prominently featured in the taping was a clip lionizing former Secretary of State Henry Kissinger. Thanks to two op-ed articles he co-authored in the Wall Street Journal urging a nuclear-free world, Mr. Kissinger has been transformed in the eyes of the anti-nuke crowd from a "war criminal" into a sage and inspiration.

As a result, many who do - or certainly should - know better, have begun to embrace the idea that we can safely and responsibly effect the global elimination of nuclear weapons. Some, like Barack Obama, appear intent on doing so forthwith. In what passes for prudence, John McCain says it is a long-term goal.

Like it or not, the truth is that we cannot rid the world of nuclear arms. But we can eliminate ours. And the dirty little secret is that we are well on the way to doing just that - unbeknownst to most Americans who would rightly be appalled at the prospect.

Thanks to 16 years of inattention, purposeful neglect and willful unilateral disarmament measures under both Republican and Democratic administrations, the United States' nuclear arsenal is steadily obsolescing, becoming evermore problematic to maintain and increasingly losing its deterrent credibility. We alone among nuclear powers - declared and undeclared - are going out of the business by failing properly to preserve, let alone modernize, our aging stockpile.

The 63rd anniversary of the destruction of Hiroshima should serve as an opportunity for urgent stocktaking. We can persist in the pretense that our inexorable, solo denuclearization is of no strategic consequence by pretending to rid the world of all nuclear arms.

Or we can recognize reality: A world without effective, safe, reliable and credible U.S. nuclear weapons will not be one in which there will be no more Hiroshimas. It will, instead, be one in which others can continue to inflict such destruction on us. And the contribution our deterrent has made to world peace - to say nothing of the security and freedom of this country and its allies (including post-war Japan) - will be no more.

North Korea celebrated Memorial Day with an underground test of a nuclear weapon reportedly the size of the bomb that destroyed Hiroshima.

With that and a series of missile launches that day and subsequently, the regime in Pyongyang has sent an unmistakable signal: The Hermit Kingdom has nothing but contempt for the so-called "international community" and the empty rhetoric and diplomatic posturing that usually precede new rewards for the North's bad behavior. The seismic waves from the latest detonation seem likely to rattle more than the windows and members of the U.N. Security Council. Even as that body huffs and puffs about Kim Jong-il's belligerence, Japan and South Korea are coming to grips with an unhappy reality: They increasingly are on their own in contending with a nuclear-armed North Korea.

Until now, both countries have nestled under the U.S. nuclear umbrella. This posture has been made possible by what is known in the national-security community as "extended deterrence." Thanks to the credibility of U.S. security guarantees backed by America's massive arsenal, both countries have been able safely to forgo the option their respective nuclear-power programs long afforded them, namely becoming nuclear-weapon states in their own right.

A bipartisan blue-ribbon panel recently warned the Obama administration that extended deterrence cannot be taken for granted. In its final report, the Congressional Commission on the Strategic Posture of the United States unanimously concluded: "Our military capabilities, both nuclear and conventional, underwrite U.S. security guarantees to our allies, without which many of them would feel enormous pressures to create their own nuclear arsenals. ... The U.S. deterrent must be both visible and credible, not only to our possible adversaries, but to our allies as well."

Unfortunately, the Obama administration is moving in exactly the opposite direction. Far from taking the myriad steps needed to assure both the visibility and credibility of the U.S. deterrent, Mr. Obama has embraced the idea of eliminating that arsenal as part of a bid for "a nuclear-free world."

The practical effect of such a policy direction is to eschew the steps called for by the Strategic Posture Commission and, indeed, the recommendations of Defense Secretary Robert M. Gates; Gen. Kevin P. Chilton, the commander of U.S. Strategic Command; and Thomas D'Agostino, director of the National Nuclear Security Administration. Each has recognized the need for modernization of the U.S. nuclear stockpile, enhanced "stewardship" of the obsolescent weapons that likely will continue to make up the bulk of the arsenal for years to come, and sustained investment in the infrastructure - both human and industrial - needed to perform such tasks.

The Obama administration is, nonetheless, seeking no funds for replacing existing weapons with designs that include modern safety features, let alone ones more suited to the deterrent missions of today - against states such as North Korea and Iran rather than the hardened silos of the Soviet Union. It is allowing the steady atrophying of the work force and facilities of the Department of Energy's nuclear-weapons complex.

Arguably worst of all, Team Obama is pursuing an arms-control agenda that risks making matters substantially worse. Using the pretext of the year's-end expiration of the U.S.-Soviet Strategic Arms Reduction Treaty (START), the president has dispatched an inveterate denuclearizer, Assistant Secretary of State Rose Gottemoeller, to negotiate in haste a new bilateral agreement with the Russians. By all accounts, she is seeking a deal that would: reduce by perhaps as much as a third what is left of our arsenal (leaving as few as 1,500 nuclear weapons), preserve the Kremlin's unilateral and vast advantage in modern tactical and theater nuclear weapons, and limit U.S. ballistic missile defenses.

The administration is equally fixated on another non-solution to today's threats: ratification of the Comprehensive Test Ban Treaty (CTBT), rejected by a majority of the U.S. Senate a decade ago. That accord would permanently preclude this country from assuring the viability of its arsenal through the one means absolutely proven to be effective - underground nuclear testing. Meanwhile, nonparty North Korea and its partner in nuclear crime, Iran (which has signed but not ratified the treaty), would not be hindered from developing their arsenals. In addition, Republican members of the Strategic Posture Commission, who all opposed CTBT ratification, think the Russians are continuing to do valuable underground testing as well.

The Obama agenda will not make the United States safer. If anything, it will increase international perceptions of an America that is ever less willing to provide for its own security. States such as Russia and China that are actual or prospective "peer competitors" are building up their nuclear arsenals. They and even smaller powers such as North Korea and Iran increasingly feel they can assert themselves with impunity.

In such a strategic environment, America's allies will go their own way. Some may seek a more independent stance or try to strike a separate peace with emerging powers such as China. Others may exercise their option to "go nuclear," contributing to regional arms buildups and proliferation.

If Mr. Obama wishes to avoid such outcomes, he would be well advised to heed the advice of the Strategic Posture Commission: "The conditions that might make the elimination of nuclear weapons possible are not present today and establishing such conditions would require a fundamental transformation of the world political order." Until then, we had better do all that is needed to maintain a safe, reliable, effective and, yes, extended deterrent.

Amidst the late night machinations and parliamentary skullduggery that now passes for legislative process in what was once rightly known as "The World's Greatest Deliberative Body," a potentially decisive blow for freedom has been struck by forty-one Senators.

No, sadly I am not talking about a setback to the defective health care "reform" bill now trundling towards enactment. Rather, I am referring to an effort that suggests a critical block of Senators are determined to exercise quality control with respect to another of President Obama's alarming agenda items: denuclearization of this country as a lubricant to his oft-stated goal of "ridding the world of nuclear weapons."

As first reported by Bill Gertz, the Washington Times' ace national security correspondent, every member of the Senate's Republican caucus and Independent Joe Lieberman signed a strongly worded letter to Mr. Obama last week regarding the so-called "Strategic Arms Reduction Treaty (START) follow-on agreement." The latter is an agreement the administration has been frantically trying to negotiate with the Kremlin, not simply to extend the now-expired, original START accord, but to replace it with a treaty making further, dramatic and controversial cuts in U.S. and Russian strategic forces.

In their missive, the signatories have thrown down the gauntlet, aligning themselves with an approach to nuclear deterrence fundamentally at odds with that of Team Obama. They flatly declared "...We don't believe further reductions can be in the national security interest of the U.S. in the absence of a significant program to modernize our nuclear deterrent."

In other words, the Senators reject the President's apparent belief that a smaller nuclear arsenal can be maintained indefinitely absent a comprehensive effort to replace existing, obsolescing weapons and the industrial infrastructure required by such new arms. The Senators' assessment is shared by a bipartisan, blue-ribbon commission chaired by former Secretaries of Defense William Perry and James Schlesinger - a fact prominently featured in the letter: "The members of this commission were unanimously alarmed by the serious disrepair and neglect they found [in the nuclear arsenal and its weapons complex], and they made a series of recommendations to reverse this highly concerning situation."

What might be called the "Gang of Forty-One" went on to declare that they "believe [the Commission's recommendations] constitute the minimum necessary to permit further nuclear force reductions." The Senators wrote that such "modernization should, at a minimum, include" the following four initiatives:

- "Full and timely life-extension upgrades" to the aging B61 bomb and the Navy's W76 submarine-launched ballistic missile warheads.

- "Funding for a modern warhead" that would be designed to remain in the inventory for extended periods of time.

- "Full funding for nuclear stockpile surveillance [the process whereby the safety, reliability and effectiveness of the deterrent is supposed to be assured] through the nuclear weapons complex, as well as the science and engineering campaigns at the nation's [nuclear] laboratories." And,
- "Full funding for the timely replacement of the Los Alamos plutonium research and development and analytical chemistry facility, the uranium facilities at the Oak Ridge (Tennessee) Y-12 plant and a modern pit facility."

These are the sorts of steps that have been needed for years but been stymied, first by a single, imperious House appropriations subcommittee and now by the Obama administration. As Mr. Gertz reported, "The Senators made clear to the President their view that the nuclear-modernization plan should be fully funded beginning with the fiscal 2011 budget and that the new treaty should be sent to the Senate for ratification with the plan."

The signers concluded their letter with another, vitally important shot-across-the bow: They warned that the administration risked violating the law if it made the grave error of allowing - as the Russians and at least some U.S. negotiators desire - the START follow-on treaty to "limit U.S. missile defenses, space capabilities, or advanced conventional modernization, such as non-nuclear global strike capability."

What makes these points so consequential is the unique math of the United States Senate. Under the Constitution, it only takes 34 votes to prevent the ratification of a treaty. And, as we all now know, thanks to the civics lesson to which the country has been treated in the weeks since the health care debate began in earnest, 41 Senators can preclude consideration of legislation - including treaties.

In short, President Obama's determination to pursue deep reductions in the U.S. arsenal en route to global denuclearization has just met its first serious obstacle. Even before the full details are known about a START accord that appears problematically set, among other things, to compel America to abandon the robust strategic "triad" that has underpinned deterrence for fifty years this month, this treaty is in trouble.

Vice President Joe Biden reportedly dismissed the prospects of such Senate opposition and felt confident that he could ram through not only a START follow-on but the previously rejected Comprehensive Test Ban Treaty (CTBT), all without addressing the serious problems identified by the Perry-Schlesinger Commission and now by a decisive faction in the Senate.

The Obama administration must chose: Will it commit to measures to ensure the future viability of America's deterrent, or risk defeat of its arms control agenda at the hands of forty-one Senators who understand that nothing less is acceptable?

President Obama announced last Thursday that he had concluded a follow-on to the 1989 Strategic Arms Reduction Treaty (START) with Russia. He characterized the cuts that it would make in the two nations' nuclear arsenals as a major step towards his goal of ridding the world of nuclear weapons. In practice, however, the so-called "New START" accord will contribute primarily to the denuclearization of the United States and to making the world a more dangerous place. Accordingly, it would be more accurate to call it "False START."

The first thing to note about the Obama treaty is that it confers real advantages on the Russians. For starters, the Kremlin will have to make essentially no cuts in the numbers of its deployed strategic launchers, whereas the United States will have to destroy several hundred of ours.

It is unclear at this writing whether such reductions by the U.S. will, as a practical matter, make it difficult – if not impossible – for America to preserve its strategic "Triad" of land- and sea-based ballistic missiles and long-range bombers. If so, there could be serious implications for strategic stability as the confidence of friends and foes alike in the robustness of our deterrent declines markedly.

What is clear, though, is that we will be obliged to cut back our arsenal to match the lower levels that the Russians can afford to maintain at the moment. The advisability of such a step would be debatable even if it produced a genuine equality between the two parties.

Unfortunately, the seeming equality thus established is deceptive in at least three respects:

- First, the Russians are aggressively modernizing their strategic forces with both new missiles and warheads. They claim that by 2015 roughly 80% of their long-range arsenal will have been upgraded – an activity we are subsidizing by paying to dismantle their old weapon systems, freeing up funds for Moscow's modernization programs.

   By contrast, the United States has not introduced a new nuclear weapon in over fifteen years. Its missiles, submarines and bombers are, by and large, even older, with some dating back to the 1950s and '60s. Today, the nation has no capability to produce new nuclear weapons and could not manufacture them in quantity for many years – the only nuclear power of whom that can be said.

- Second, the Russians are reintroducing multiple, independently targetable reentry vehicles (MIRVs) on their land-based ballistic missiles. This step could enable a break-out capacity that would allow Moscow rapidly to deploy far more weapons than its forces are allowed to have under the new START treaty. By contrast, the United States decided back in the 1980s that such a capability was "destabilizing";

it has systematically de-MIRVed its underground silo-launched intercontinental-range ballistic missiles ever since.

- Third, the newly unveiled START accord fails to take into account or otherwise limit several thousand Russian "tactical" nuclear weapons. The Kremlin has focused for twenty years on such low-yield devices; some with the explosive power of the Hiroshima weapon and fitted on submarine-launched cruise missiles are deployed off our coasts today. While the administration says such armaments could be the subject of a future, bilateral treaty that makes still deeper reductions in U.S. and Russian nuclear stocks, don't count on it. In any event, they will constitute a real, asymmetric advantage for Russia for many years to come. [This is a particularly worrisome prospect to American allies in Europe who have long relied on America's "extended deterrence" to counteract such threatening Kremlin capabilities.

Then, there is the matter of missile defense. The Obama administration tried to finesse Russian insistence on including in the new accord language that would capture American defenses against missile attack by confining to the preamble an acknowledgement of a "relationship" between such systems and offensive forces. The United States claims that, by its nature, such preambular language is not binding. Yet, a Kremlin spokesman has already served notice that Moscow will feel free to abrogate the START follow-on treaty if it believes that U.S. missile defenses in Europe are a threat to its deterrent.

The biggest problem of all with the New START treaty, however, is that it is a product of President Obama's fixation with "devaluing nuclear weapons" and ridding the world of them. On these grounds, he refuses to take the steps necessary to modernize America's deterrent. Even though he professes that a nuclear-free globe will not be realized any time soon, he is condemning the nation to unilateral disarmament by allowing the steady and unavoidable obsolescence of the U.S. stockpile, and the dissipation of the workforce and infrastructure needed to maintain it, to continue unabated.

The acuteness of this obsolescence has reached a point where the directors of the nation's nuclear laboratories have felt compelled to express strong concerns about the continued reliability of the arsenal. Even before they did so, forty-one U.S. Senators wrote President Obama warning him that they would not support ratification of a follow-on START accord unless his budget explicitly funded a modernization program for our deterrent forces. That number is more than enough to preclude the Senate advice and consent required by the Constitution.

Taken together, these factors ensure that the New START treaty will contribute to U.S. nuclear disarmament alright, but do nothing to advance the ostensible purpose of the exercise – namely, enhancing the security of this country or the world. A False START indeed, and one that should be rejected by at least thirty-four United States Senators.

Sovereignty

The U.S. Senate's decision last April to ratify a multilateral treaty with the admirable, but totally unachievable, objective of effecting a worldwide ban on poison gas has had the predictable - and predicted - result of encouraging proponents of other, utopian arms control delusions.

Pre-eminent among these is the proposal now being massively promoted by a former British queen-in-waiting, the Red Cross, an assortment of generally left-of-center organizations (including the Vietnam Veterans of America), and a number of U.S. legislators led by Sen. Patrick Leahy, Vermont Democrat: A ban on the production, stockpiling or use of anti-personnel landmines (APLs).

At risk of being altogether lost in the frenzy of hype, do-goodism and political correctness associated with the effort to prohibit these weapons - devices routinely portrayed as inhumane and relentlessly exacting a toll on innocent civilians - are a few inconvenient facts:

- The U.S. military uses certain types of anti-personnel landmines in a responsible manner in order to save American lives. Its active inventory consists entirely of mines designed to self-destruct after a short period (four hours to 15 days) - in contrast to "dumb" mines that remain deadly for decades. These self-destructing APLs are laid down in marked areas to protect U.S. forces especially in circumstances where they are outnumbered, as is the case in many combat and peacekeeping situations (notably, at the entry of forces into a theater of operations).

  In fact, recent studies by the Army indicate that American casualties would increase by as much as 35 percent if U.S. land forces are obliged to fight without the use of landmines. As a result, the images of maimed children endlessly conjured up by proponents of the APL ban are not the only ones to be borne in mind; the practical effect of such a ban will probably be to create a great many more American flag-draped coffins and body-bags in future conflicts.

- U.S. anti-personnel mines are particularly important as a means of preventing tampering with or breaching of anti-tank mines, a weapon system that would ostensibly not be covered by the proposed ban. In fact, even retired Gen. Norman Schwarzkopf, who has in the past expressed support for a ban on anti-personnel landmines, has noted that "anti-tank mines...[are] undeniably militarily useful weapons."

  The International Committee of the Red Cross (ICRC) - an organization spending millions of dollars (at least some of them apparently U.S. government contributions) promoting bans on landmines and various other weapons - wants, however, to prohibit "dual-purpose mines which can destroy, for example, either a vehicle or a person." The Leahy bill would make no distinction between self-destructing and "dumb" landmines; in fact, its broadly worded definition of the term "landmine" would cover a host of other non-mine weapon systems essential to U.S. war plans.

- While banning the use of anti-personnel landmines by the United States and other Western states that employ them responsibly will have a deleterious effect on those nations' military operations, such a ban will do nothing to address the problem with which its proponents claim to be concerned. For one thing, a treaty cannot prohibit the many millions of landmines already in the ground in a handful of developing nations scarred by past or ongoing conflicts (e.g., Cambodia, Afghanistan and Bosnia). For another, there is no reason to believe that other nations - notably, China, Russia and Vietnam -whose use or widespread sale of anti-personnel landmines has done much to create the present humanitarian problem - will join or comply with a treaty banning APLs.

Under these circumstances, as an unnamed Army officer recently put it: "The decision to take landmines away from U.S. forces is like taking firearms away from policemen because a criminal has used one for an illegal purpose." This sort of moral equivalence is all too evident among those who might be called "abolitionists" - people who argue, in the words of one, that "If we cannot prevent war, we will make it impossible to fight."

Of course, banning landmines, lasers, poison gas or even bullets from the arsenals of the United States and other law-abiding nations will not make it impossible to fight wars, just difficult - if not impossible - for such nations to win them at the lowest possible cost. Put differently, so-called "international norms" may make some feel better, but surely not those who will bear with their lives the price of such wishful thinking.

These considerations have prompted an unprecedented outpouring of opposition by serving and retired military leaders to the idea of banning self-destructing anti-personnel landmines or otherwise precluding their responsible use by the nation's armed forces. In an unprecedented appeal to Congress, all six members of the Joint Chiefs of Staff and all 10 of the regional commanders-in-chief warned on July 10 that such a ban "will unnecessarily endanger U.S. military forces and significantly restrict the ability to conduct combat operations successfully."

Then yesterday, 24 four-star generals who are among the United States' most respected former top soldiers and Marines wrote President Clinton strongly urging that he reject "all efforts to impose a moratorium on the future use of self-destructing anti-personnel landmines by combat forces of the United States." They believe this county's "responsible use of APLs is not only consistent with the nation's humanitarian responsibili-

315

ties; it is indispensable to the safety of our troops in many combat and peacekeeping situations."

These active duty and retired military leaders are to be commended for placing the welfare, safety and combat effectiveness of their troops above political correctness and/or political expediency. Those troops deserve no less from civilians in the legislative and executive branches of the U.S. government, in the media and among well-meaning, but seriously misguided, anti-landmine activists.

Last Friday, the lower house of the Russian Duma agreed to the ratification of the Chemical Weapons Convention (CWC). This step, coming six months after the treaty entered into force, is being trumpeted by the treaty's proponents as a major step forward toward realization of its goal of globally banning the production and stockpiling of chemical weaponry.

In fact, assuming that the Duma's upper house goes along, Russia's accession to the treaty will simply move it from one category (a non-party) to another (a party that will violate the CWC). I am not making this up: Even as it ratified the accord, the legislature actually formally announced Russia cannot afford to comply with the accord's weapons dismantling requirements.

Unacknowledged, but far more ominous, is the certainty the Kremlin also will violate the CWC by continuing its vast chemical weapons modernization program - including the manufacture of new classes of "binary" weapons that are far more toxic than anything known in the West and specifically designed to circumvent the CWC's inspection regime.

Clearly, the Russians calculate that the United States and its allies can be induced to defray the costs of such complying as the Kremlin does, namely those associated with eliminating Moscow's huge stocks of obsolete chemical arms. And the Clinton administration seems quite willing to go along.

Unfortunately, such a dunning of the U.S. taxpayer was not only predictable; it was predicted. In this respect, as in so many others, those of us who opposed this treaty can say, to be sure more in sorrow than in anger, "We told you so."

Here are a few of the other areas in which the passage of six months' time appears to have vindicated the Chemical Weapons Convention's critics:

- As predicted, the CWC is going to facilitate economic espionage. This problem is already a serious one for the United States, entailing by some estimates losses on the order of $2 billion per year with the U.S. chemical industry a prime target.

  Last spring, the treaty's proponents blithely dismissed fears that its intrusive inspection regime would assist foreign operatives in gaining access to and ripping off American businesses' proprietary information. No one made this case more forcefully than the Chemical Manufacturers Association (CMA) - a trade group whose membership of 192 large companies with a well-heeled political action committee assured them deference in Congress when they claimed (erroneously) to speak for all of American industry.

  With its recent publication of a 38-page report, however, the CMA seems to have adopted a much more realistic, and dire, view of the threat. In "Economic

Espionage: The Looting of America's Economic Security in the Information Age," the trade association cites examples where even limited access to American facilities was exploited by both friendly nations and unfriendly ones to try to steal U.S. competitive business information.

To make matters worse, key jobs at the new international bureaucracy created to implement the Chemical Weapons Convention have gone to nationals hailing from two of the most inveterate practitioners of economic espionage: France and Japan. A retired French major general got the job of director of Verification; the director of the organization's Inspectorate is a former senior official in Japan's Self-Defense Force.

- As predicted by its opponents, the CWC is actually going to have the absurd effect of contributing to proliferation, and to protecting those who engage in it. It is now evident the CWC's notorious Article 11 - a section that obliges states parties to facilitate the fullest possible transfer of non-military chemical manufacturing technology and know-how to other parties - will provide cover for those seeking to acquire for military purposes what are, inherently, dual-use capabilities.

A case in point was revealed last Thursday by this newspaper's crack national security reporter, Bill Gertz. Mr. Gertz reported that U.S. intelligence believes that in June China completed the transfer to Iran of a factory for manufacturing glass-lined equipment. Such a plant is assessed to be "capable of producing chemical warfare equipment as well as equipment for producing civilian chemicals like detergents."

As long as the Chinese and Iranians stick to their cover story, other CWC parties are supposed to refrain from impeding this "cooperation." If they do so, one can safely anticipate it will be a model for other covert chemical proliferation operations.

- Finally, as critics of the CWC warned last spring, the Convention's verification regime - while the most intrusive ever negotiated in an arms control agreement - is wholly inadequate to the job of detecting and proving the existence of covert chemical weapons production and stockpiling by nations determined to persist in such activities. For proof, one need look no further than Saddam Hussein's success in thwarting the work of the U.N. Special Commission (UNSCOM) inspectors who have, at least until now, been able to use a far more intrusive and effective regime to search for concealed Iraqi arms. (Reportedly, Iraq will receive a three-member U.N. team in Baghdad in an effort to defuse the crisis.)

As one U.N. official put it a few months ago: "UNSCOM has shown that it is very, very easy to conceal this sort of thing. We've been here six years and have a very intrusive mandate. We can . . . go anywhere and take anything away. But we still can't confirm we know everything. It raises questions about what other countries can get away with." This is true in spades of the relatively weak inspection mandate that is supposed to underpin the CWC.

Last April, the Clinton administration euchred the U.S. Senate into agreeing to ratification of the Chemical Weapons Convention, relying heavily on the argument that the United States would otherwise be unrepresented and have no influence as the treaty's implementation went forward. Like so many of the other claims for the CWC, this one proved unfounded - as the Russians' six-month demurral demonstrated.

The real reason for such haste is now apparent for all to see: It was required in order to prevent the passage of time from further validating the opponents' critique. The nation has been badly served by this flim-flam – and by those in the executive branch and in the Senate who brought it about. One further prediction: The price for having foolishly done so will only grow in the years ahead.

Today, there are no fewer than three different inquiries under way aimed at assessing shortfalls in what the military calls "force protection" that led to the death and wounding of scores of American sailors and the near loss of their ship, the USS Cole. When all is said and done, heads will likely roll, as otherwise unblemished records of service and command are destroyed over the failure to provide adequately for the security of our uniformed personnel as they went into harm's way in service to their country.

This tragic reminder of the vulnerability of the men and women in uniform and the solemn responsibility their leaders - civilian and military - have to ensure they are not unnecessarily put at risk comes to mind as one considers a letter sent to President Clinton on Oct. 5 by more than 90 members of Congress. In this missive, the predominantly liberal Democratic signatories called on Mr. Clinton before leaving office to deny ground-based American troops one of the most tested and dependable means of force protection ever invented: anti-personnel landmines (APL).

Specifically, this group led by Reps. Lane Evans, Illinois Democrat, and Jack Quinn, New York Republican, appeal to the president "before leaving office" to take such steps as: "announcing a permanent ban, or at least a moratorium, on the production of APLs and their components"; "deciding not to produce the RADAM mixed mine system which employs anti-personnel devices to prevent the rapid neutralizing of accompanying anti-vehicle landmines "; and "placing in inactive status" existing APLs immediately, "with the intent to destroy as soon as possible."

To be sure, most - if not all - of these members of Congress are motivated by the plight of the thousands of innocent civilians all over the world who are harmed each year by so-called "dumb," long-duration APLs. Frequently, they are terribly maimed, rather than killed outright, by landmines left behind from wars long past. These victims become burdens on their usually impoverished families and communities, and are vivid reminders of obscene efforts by earlier combatants to "cleanse" contested territory of rival ethnic, religious or other communities.

Unfortunately, such legislators - and most of those whose heartstrings are similarly pulled by the ongoing blight APLs represent in places like Afghanistan, Cambodia, Bosnia, Angola and Nicaragua - fail to appreciate a basic reality: Banning the responsible use by the American military of short-duration, self-destructing anti-personnel landmines will not contribute in any way to the enormous humanitarian challenge of finding and destroying what are estimated to be many millions of APLs already in the ground around the world. The only exception to the ban would be the Korean Demilitarized Zone, where "dumb" APLs are deployed in a no-man's land barred to civilians and are critical to deterring any renewed North Korean aggression against the South.

A ban - whether imposed unilaterally or via U.S. enrollment in the 1997 Ottawa Convention that prohibits the "use, stockpiling, production and transfer of APLs - would, however, ensure that American troops forward-deployed in dangerous parts of the world would be denied a tool understood by them and their military commanders to be absolutely essential to force protection. In fact, it was the unprecedented unanimous and forceful opposition in 1997 of every member of the Joint Chiefs of Staff and every regional commander in chief to the Ottawa Convention that dissuaded President Clinton from signing on. This was all the more remarkable since he had been, as noted in the legislators' letter, "The very first world leader to call for the eventual elimination of all landmines in his 1994 address before the United Nations General Assembly."

As it happens, the congressional correspondence unintentionally underscores how irrelevant the U.S. armed forces' retention of the ability to employ APLs for force protection and in support of combat operations is to the problem at hand. The legislators note, notwithstanding American refusal to join the Ottawa ban, that: "Exports of APLs have slowed to a trickle. The number of new mine victims is decreasing in heavily infested nations. . . . Global funding for mine clearance programs has increased greatly, and funding for victim assistance programs is also on the rise, although at a slower pace than demand requires."

In other words, things that can make a difference vis-a-vis the humanitarian problem are going forward. That said, it is not clear the progress is quite as great as claimed (particularly with respect to exports of landmines, an activity that can be - and almost certainly is being - pursued covertly by countries like China that profit greatly from manufacturing "dumb" landmines for a dollar or so apiece).

It would have been appropriate, if out of character for most of the congressional signatories, to note that much of the progress that is being made is a function of very substantial efforts on the part of the American military. The latter's help with demining and the development of new technologies holds promise that the effectiveness of such efforts will continue to increase, while the inherent risks are greatly reduced. (On the latter front there has been a possible breakthrough, thanks to the private development of a technology dubbed the ELF system now being tested in the field in Croatia and Cambodia.)

Regrettably, the zealots bent on banning landmines are not swayed by such inconvenient facts. They are typically indifferent to force protection considerations or assert blithely that they can be addressed by some new, as-yet-unidentified technology. They subscribe to the "disarm the one you're with" school; America must adhere to the "international norm" they believe they are creating, irrespective of whether it is real, verifiable or responsible for the U.S. do so.

The pressure is on now, as they fear a President George W. Bush would sensibly want no part of a landmine ban opposed by his armed forces and likely to cost them dearly in unnecessary loss of life and perhaps successful missions in future overseas operations. The question is: Will the lame duck Bill Clinton try with respect to APLs to do what he is working on in so many other areas - from normalizing relations with rogue states like North Korea and Cuba, to euchring Israel into a phony and highly dangerous peace deal with the Palestinians, to giving the Chinese renewed access to American missile-related technology - namely, pre-empting his successor?

If Mr. Clinton gets away with it on landmines, the inquiries into the failure of force protection that are sure to arise down the road will be obliged to hold him, and his congressional correspondents, responsible.

Most Americans have come – correctly, if reluctantly – to the conclusion that the United Nations has been a failure. Sixty years ago, the UN's founders envisioned it as an engine of freedom, an international mechanism in which sovereign nations would come together to protect liberty and to facilitate its spread throughout the world.

Instead, for most of its life, the "world body" has been dominated by the unfree. Under their influence, the UN has morphed into a protection racket for the world's despots and, effectively, an abettor of those who would supplant liberty with corrupt authoritarianism, or worse.

In recent months, evidence of how far the United Nations has strayed from its original purpose has steadily leached into plain sight. The staggering Iraq Oil-for-Food scandal has implicated senior members of the UN leadership including, it would appear, Secretary General Kofi Annan. Others in the Secretariat have engaged in embarrassing personal and official misconduct. The bureaucracy is notoriously bloated and inefficient. The agenda remains dominated by anti-Israel and anti-American initiatives. And the reputation of UN peacekeeping operations around the world has been sullied as some of the foreign troops assigned to them have turned into rape squads and sex-traffickers.

Against this backdrop, even the United Nation's most assiduous supporters have been obliged to pronounce that they favor "reform" of the organization. It would appear that what most have in mind, however, is little more than a reshuffling of the proverbial deck chairs.

For example, under proposals advanced to date by Mr. Annan, the fundamental problems arising from the preeminence enjoyed by nations hostile to the United States and/or freedom and the malfeasance, if not malevolence, of the UN's largely unaccountable staff will be perpetuated.

History shows that there is only one way to effect constructive change at the United Nations: By the United States exercising the power of the purse .

Each year, the U.S. is obliged to pony up nearly a quarter of the United Nation's roughly $2 billion annual budget – far more than any other member state. This represents, by the way, just the contribution for which America gets credit. In addition, we provide untold billions worth of support (notably, that given by the U.S. military for logistical and other assistance to UN peacekeepers) which is neither acknowledged nor reflected in calculations of what we "owe" the organization.

In light of past experience and present problems with the United Nations, the U.S. House of Representatives recently endorsed by a wide margin the recommendation of the distinguished chairman of its International Relations Committee, Rep. Henry Hyde, Republican of Illinois. It makes future American payments to the "world body" contingent upon a set of sensible and wide-ranging reforms being adopted by the United Nations.

The UN is determined to deny the United States such leverage and to insulate itself from further American pressure for systemic change. On September 14-16, the UN General Assembly is scheduled to hold a high-level plenary meeting to consider the implementation of "Millennium Development Goals" contained in the report of the UN's 2002 International Conference on Financing for Development. According to this so-called "Monterrey Consensus," the United States and other developed nations are obliged to provide 0.7 percent of their gross national income in foreign aid (also known as Official Development Assistance or ODA).

Secretary General Annan's special advisor, Dr. Jeffrey Sachs, contends that the United States has only provided 0.15 percent of its GNI. Sachs and his friends at the United Nations maintain we therefore "owe" the international community $65 billion each year from 2002 to the target year of 2015, for a total of $845 billion in additional foreign aid.

Since no one in their right mind expects either this President or any other – let alone any foreseeable U.S. Congress, to provide these vast amounts in notoriously ill-spent foreign aid, the UN types have come up with an alternative means of making Americans pay their huge "debt" to the undeveloped world: international taxation (hereafter known as "globotaxes").

Incredible as it may seem, a Bush Administration viscerally opposed to raising taxes has not shown the sort of vehement resistance to this initiative that it should. In fact, Annex II of the Gleneagles G-8 communiqu? (entitled "Financing Commitments"), reveals that the United States agreed to create a working group proposed by France, Germany, Italy and Great Britain to consider implementation of "innovative financing mechanisms" that can "help deliver and bring forward the financing needed to achieve the Millennium Development Goals."

Among the "financing mechanisms" to be considered is a "solidarity contribution on [international] plane tickets." French President Jacques Chirac has declared that he believes this "small levy" would bring – presumably into UN coffers – at least $3 billion.

If the United States goes along with this arrangement come September, it will allow a precedent to be established for taxation without representation that would send the Founders' bodies spinning in their graves. It can forget about the modest constraint its ability to withhold "dues" has exercised on UN behavior. It can be sure real reform of the UN will not be in the cards. And it can expect that other globotaxes will shortly be proposed.

The mother of all globotaxes is an idea that has been kicking around the East River for some time and named after the Yale Nobel Laureate who first proposed it, Dr. James Tobin. The "Tobin tax" would theoretically raise an estimated $13 trillion – yes, trillion – from a small levy on international currency transactions. Imagine what the one-worlders and UN bureaucrats could do to our sovereignty and interests with that kind of wherewithal.

If the Bush Administration is unable or unwilling to resist such globotaxes, it will fall to the Congress to do so. With the August recess looming and the UN's fundraiser coming right after Labor Day, there is no time to waste.

Since it seems the only news fit to print (or air) these days has to do with Hurricane Katrina and its aftermath, finding a related angle to call needed public and leadership attention to something else requires a little ingenuity.

But since the stakes associated with another, largely unremarked story - involving a drama that will reach its denouement at United Nations headquarters this week - may be nothing less than the future sovereignty and character of the United States, a way must be found.

As it happens, the answer lies in the toxic liquid now being pumped out of New Orleans into waterways that will, inexorably, contaminate the international reaches of Gulf of Mexico, and perhaps beyond. The United States unilaterally determined this potentially huge environmental damage is justified by the need to recover and restore a major American city, its population and economy.

Interestingly, shortly before Katrina precipitated this crisis, a gaggle of former senior government officials wrote Senate Majority Leader Bill Frist demanding he swiftly effect ratification of the controversial Law of the Sea Treaty (or LOST) accord. The authors dismissed concerns of conservatives that LOST would impinge upon U.S. sovereignty and vital interests.

If the United States were a party to the Law of the Sea Treaty today though, it is very likely America would be enjoined from dumping New Orleans' toxic stew into Lake Pontchartrain and the Mississippi River. For one thing, this would violate the Treaty's environmental obligations to protect marine life and its habitats, obligations whose sweep makes those of the Kyoto Treaty seem modest by comparison.

For another, the Law of the Sea Tribunal - the sort of multilateral legal institution whose tendency for politicization and anti-American actions has prompted the Bush administration to reject the International Criminal Court - has already established a relevant precedent. In a case brought by Ireland against Great Britain, the Tribunal established its jurisdiction extends to activities on sovereign member states' soil that can arguably affect international waters.

Unfortunately, since Ronald Reagan's day, U.S. governments have tended to pay too little attention to sovereignty-sapping treaties and institutional power-grabs by the U.N. and other multilateral organizations. To his credit, Mr. Reagan recognized the Law of the Sea Treaty for what it was intended to be by the World Federalists and so-called nonaligned movement types who had a significant hand in shaping its supranational International Seabed Authority and related entities: a highly precedential, and undesirable, vehicle for establishing world-government controls of the "international commons" (in this case, the oceans) at the expense of sovereign states.

President Reagan refused to agree to LOST's ratification in part because he regarded as anathema the idea of empowering an international organization to raise its own revenues through what amount to taxes on seabed mining and energy exploitation. Regrettably, the Bush administration has so far chosen to overlook this and other adverse treaty implications for U.S. sovereignty, and supports LOST's ratification.

The good news is President Bush seems in no mood to go along with the logical extrapolation of the Law of the Sea Treaty - the so-called "Draft Outcome Document" for the U.N. General Assembly meeting Sept 14-16. The document has been the focus of intense negotiations since Mr. Bush got his representative, John Bolton, in place at Turtle Bay. Despite fresh evidence from former Federal Reserve Chairman Paul Volcker that the U.N. is scandal-ridden, corrupt, poorly organized and managed and incompetently led, Secretary General Kofi Annan wants American and other world leaders to ratify this week what amounts to his wish-list.

As of this writing, however, Mr. Bolton has registered strong U.S. objections to language that would bind America to actions that, under this president, it has firmly opposed: ratification of the Kyoto Protocol and the Comprehensive Test Ban Treaty; negotiations on space arms control; creating what amounts to a standing U.N. army; and forgoing systemic in favor of cosmetic U.N. reforms.

Of arguably greatest importance is the U.S. refusal to empower the United Nations to levy taxes - a step that would, as with the Law of the Sea Treaty, advance the organization's ambitions to promote world government. Globotaxes would also eviscerate any remaining U.S. leverage to effect real U.N. reform and punish its misbehavior. It is estimated one proposed tax on international currency transactions alone could generate a staggering $13 trillion in revenue.

Just as Hurricane Katrina ruptured the levees protecting New Orleans, the concerted U.N. assault on the barriers to further erosion of American sovereignty threatens to swamp our freedom of action and our Founding principle of "no taxation without representation." It behooves President Bush to reject any Outcome Document that leaves the door open to globotaxes, let alone one that endorses them outright.

Rather than lend his authority to such an exercise, he should be willing to refuse to attend the U.N. summit this week that Mr. Annan hoped would be the biggest fund-raiser in world history.

For millions of Americans, the spectacle of buffoonery and bombast served up last week in New York by the U.N. General Assembly in particular, the appearances there of despots like Venezuelan dictator Hugo Chavez and Iranian President Mahmoud Ahmadinejad raised anew questions about the legitimacy and utility of the United Nations. Incredibly, despite this performance and the U.N.'s rampant corruption, scandals and virulent hostility toward the Free World, the organization has taken a major step toward becoming a supranational government, unaccountable to and ever more routinely at odds with the United States.

The occasion was the seemingly innocuous launching on Sept. 19 of a new International Drug Purchasing Facility, dubbed UNITAID, to combat HIV/AIDS, malaria and tuberculosis. UNITAID will, for the first time, rely for its institutional funding on what the U.N. euphemistically calls an "innovative financing mechanism." Another word for it is "globotaxes" levies imposed on international transactions, in this case, airline tickets.

As Secretary-General Kofi Annan noted on the occasion of UNITAID's launching, the French, Chilean, Norwegian, Brazilian and British governments have been responsible for this initiative. He also credited them with "advancing similar innovative financing mechanisms" that "can help us reach the Millennium Development Goals" for reducing poverty, disease and other blights on humanity.

That is U.N.-speak for commitment-developed nations like the United States undertook in 2002 to commit 0.7 percent of their gross domestic product to Official Development Assistance (ODA, also known as foreign aid). The Bush administration claims to have a different interpretation of this commitment. But U.N. types like Jeffrey Sachs, Mr. Annan's point man on the Millennium Development Goals, assert that since the United States only gives 0.15 percent of GDP in official (as opposed to private) foreign aid this country "owes" some $845 billion between now and 2015 in ODA.

Since there is no likelihood any Congress, whether controlled by Republicans or Democrats, will approve that kind of money for foreign aid, the alternative idea of generating such funds instead through new, international taxes has gained traction. That is, in part, due to the vested interest former President Bill Clinton has in such an idea.

As Kofi Annan noted in his Sept. 19 statement welcoming UNITAID: "I am pleased that . . . the Clinton Foundation will be actively involved" in this initiative. In fact, under the leadership of Hillary Clinton's controversial former health care guru, Ira Magaziner, the Clinton Foundation will be responsible for negotiating bulk purchases of drugs for UNITAID. Mr. Magaziner enthused about the power of such a private sector-U.N. partnership last week: "Through this initiative we'll have a sustainable way to assure a supply of drugs and tests for the long term."

What is particularly worrying is that UNITAID's seemingly unobjectionable disease-relief program will simply be the first of many purposes to which the U.N. hopes to apply globotaxes. For example, U.N. types have already begun discussing levies on energy purchases, carbon emissions, international corporate activity and currency transactions. The last of these alone is estimated to be capable of generating a mind-boggling $13 trillion per year.

The purposes towards which such funds might be applied include development assistance, humanitarian relief, peacekeeping operations, raising and maintaining a U.N. army, and underwriting for the international institutions that will be charged with administering these funds. Some advocates even explicitly propose international taxes as a means of redistributing wealth from the developed to the developing world.

The cause of promoting "innovative financing mechanisms" on U.S. taxpayers has become a focus of, among others, the Clinton Global Initiative. This is the former president's vehicle for promoting international good works with respect to climate change, poverty alleviation and mitigating religious and ethnic conflict, along with global health.

Under the rubric of public-spiritedness, Mr. Clinton has enlisted the help of a number of major corporations, Democratic Party operatives and policy wonks and public figures, including First Lady Laura Bush. Of particular concern, however, are the political implications of the immense amount of money and personal prestige being put in the service of the U.N.-Clinton agenda by such philanthropists as Bill Gates, Warren Buffet, George Soros, Ted Turner and Richard Branson.

With the resources and influence of such deep-pocketed friends, it seems likely that the traditional mantra of Democratic class warfare "soak the rich" will be turned on its head. All other things being equal, the precedent created by an international airline levy-funded UNITAID for fighting disease will likely result in a determined campaign aimed at imposing a variety of globotaxes whereby Bill Clinton's rich friends will help soak the American taxpayer.

A United Nations that becomes, thanks to globotaxes, increasingly independent of its member states' contributions is a U.N. that will become even more unaccountable, non-transparent and, in all likelihood, even more corrupt and virulently anti-American. Such an organization will inevitably also seek to sap this country's sovereignty as it strives to build a supranational government attuned to the sentiments of its so-called "non-aligned" majority that is increasingly brazen in its hostility towards the United States.

Legislation sponsored by Sens. Jim Inhofe, Oklahoma Republican, and Ben Nelson, Nebraska Democrat, and Republican Reps. Roy Blunt of Missouri and Ron Paul of Texas is pending in Congress that would block U.N. taxation of Americans without representation. Our forefathers fought a revolution to prevent just such an infringement on our sovereignty and rights. We must resist the present danger no less vociferously.

Any minute now, President Bush is going to make a fateful mistake. He will announce that his administration will make a concerted effort to secure the prompt ratification of a deeply flawed multilateral accord universally known by its acronym - LOST, as in the Law of the Sea Treaty.

When it comes to LOST, of course, prompt is a relative thing. It was first opened to signature and ratification in the early 1980s, but Ronald Reagan rejected it. In the mid-1990s, Bill Clinton resuscitated and negotiated a side-deal designed to fix, or at least obscure, what Mr. Reagan found objectionable.

Then, in 2004, the Bush administration decided to embrace the Law of the Sea Treaty. The argument seemed principally to be that, in the aftermath of the bruising fight over Iraq, doing so would demonstrate that the United States could still play well with its allies and other nations. Most were parties to LOST and are slavishly devoted to this and other treaties on the agenda of the Transnational Progressives (or Transies, for short).

Fortunately, a happy correlation of forces kept the Transies at bay temporarily. Despite an effort to secure Senate advice and consent to LOST in the parliamentary equivalent of the dark of night, a broad coalition of largely conservative and libertarian organizations came together in adamant opposition. Then-Senate Majority Leader Bill Frist, who had presidential ambitions, recognized the inadvisability of bucking such forces. To his credit, he also came to see how substantively problematic LOST would be and kept the treaty bottled up.

There things might have rested - with the United States continuing to do what it has done since President Reagan's day: remain a non-party to the Law of the Sea Treaty, observing its unobjectionable provisions concerning navigation and transit rights, while not subjecting itself to the accord's myriad supranational institutions. The latter purport to govern the international sea beds and, according to some, the oceans and even the airspace above them.

Regrettably, a new correlation of forces is operating in Washington. The Bush administration is now under the influence of American Transnational Progressives - notably, foreign service officers like Undersecretary of State Nicholas Burns and his nominal superior, Deputy Secretary John Negroponte. Thanks to Secretary of State Condoleezza Rice's virtual domination of the international affairs portfolio, the Transie agenda is largely supplanting what once was the Bush 43 version of Reagan's exceptionalist program for peace through American strength.

To be sure, the leading edge of the sales campaign for LOST will not be the foreign service or, for that matter, its allies among various environmental and commercial special interests. (Don't ask how both the Greens and the deep-sea oil and gas industry can believe that the Law of the Sea Treaty will advance their programs; one of them is surely wrong.)

Rather, the administration is trotting out lawyers and other officials of the armed forces to make the case for LOST. In particular, the Navy, the Marine Corps and the Coast Guard are on record as favoring the treaty. Their argument has a certain superficial appeal: The treaty establishes rules of the road for littoral waters that are better than might otherwise apply and, if we are a party to LOST, we can ensure they stay that way. The alternative, we are told, is that the Navy will have to take risks to assert our rights to untrammeled innocent passage. And, frankly, we no longer have sufficient naval vessels or the political will required to undertake such potentially risky operations wherever necessary.

Sadly, being party to the Law of the Sea Treaty is not going to keep our foes from using it against us. Like those of virtually every other international organization, LOST's institutions (executive, legislative and judicial, if you please) are rigged-games. The United States will be routinely outvoted or otherwise unable to prevent infringements on its sovereignty and, yes, in all likelihood over time even its military operations.

Some earnest officers insist that should the latter happen, America can always withdraw from the treaty. Don't count on it. The only instance in memory when such a step occurred was the 1972 Anti-Ballistic Missile Treaty - and that took 20 years to accomplish. Moreover, it could only have occurred because the very survival of the nation could plausibly be argued to require it.

Even if the Navy and its sister sea-services were right about the value of the treaty from their parochial perspectives, roughly 60 percent of LOST's provisions have to do with the supranational management of two-thirds of the world's surface and its resources. The argument about whether such arrangements will prove to be in the long-term interest of the nation as a whole should be considered on their merits, not subordinated - let alone ignored - out of misplaced deference to some in the military.

The push President Bush intends to make for the Law of the Sea Treaty will win him few friends among his enemies. It will, however, cost him dearly among those who have steadfastly supported him, but are dead-set against the Transnational Progressives and their agenda. One would think that a man with an approval rating below 30 percent would not be so cavalier with what remains of his base, especially on behalf of so dubious an enterprise as ratification of LOST.

War of Ideas

When Defense Secretary Donald Rumsfeld's internal memorandum to top subordinates leaked last week, most press attention and political commentary focused on his observation that the conflicts in Afghanistan and Iraq were likely to be a "long, hard slog."

Many cast this assessment as new or at least evidence of a private view at odds with the Pentagon chief's public emphasis on the real progress being made in the war on terror. The secretary forcefully denied saying, or even intending to imply, any such thing.

Unfortunately, the controversy obscured another of Mr. Rumsfeld's insights - arguably a much more important one: He questioned whether the United States government is effectively waging "the war of ideas."

The good news is that, if others are still not sufficiently attentive to this important front in the war on terror, our two-time defense secretary is clearly seized with it. In fact, after his memo was leaked, he specifically addressed this topic in an interview last Thursday with The Washington Times and an op-ed column in the Sunday editions of The Washington Post.

In the former, he noted that, "[Our] ideas are important and they need to be marshaled, and they need to be communicated in ways that are persuasive to the listeners. "In the latter, he emphasized what is at stake: "To win the war on terror, we must also win the war of ideas - the battle for the minds of those who are being recruited by terrorist networks across the globe. The task is to stop terrorists before they can terrorize. And even better, we must lean forward and stop them from becoming terrorists in the first place."

The magnitude of this challenge will be on display at a hearing of the Senate Governmental Affairs Committee tomorrow. Itamar Marcus, director of an outstanding Jerusalem-based organization called Palestinian Media Watch, will present evidence of the relentless effort Yasser Arafat's Palestinian Authority makes to brainwash its people - and most especially their children - to hate not just Israel but also its ally, America.

The leitmotif running throughout innumerable newspaper articles, cartoons, crossword puzzles, TV news items, "educational" broadcasts and music videos is a systematic glorification of those who die while destroying these "enemies." Such a perversion of the Islamic tradition of sacrifice for the faith known as Shahada into a cult of death is a hallmark of the radical, usually violent Muslim sects that have come to be called Islamists.

In the Palestinian community, Islamist ideas have been so pervasively, seductively and, evidently, effectively cultivated that, according to a new poll supervised by Frank Luntz, there would appear to be little hope for peace - irrespective of the concessions Israel might make.

This phenomenon is hardly confined to the Palestinians. Thanks largely to Saudi and Iranian bankrolling, state-owned media in much of the Muslim world, "independent" satellite television networks like Al Jazeera and countless Islamist schools known as madrassas are cultivating similar ideas near and far. Indeed, inroads are being made by Islamists in the United States as well, as suggested by the arrests in recent months of several prominent figures in the Arab-American and Muslim-American communities [notably, Abdurahman Alamoudi] in connection with terrorist organizations and/or state-sponsors of terrorism.

As readers of this column know, the Islamists here have not only sought to shape the minds of their co-religionists. They have also worked to disarm the United States in the war of ideas. One of their most successful gambits to date has been the promotion of the notion at the highest levels of the U.S. government that "Islam is a religion of peace."

To be sure, as practiced by hundreds of millions of Muslims the world over, there is no conflict between adherence to Mohammed's teachings on the one hand and the leading of peaceful, tolerant and constructive lives on the other. This is not true of Islamists, however, who misconstrue or selectively embrace Koranic passages to justify the use of violence against non-Muslims and even fellow Muslims who refuse to join them. Unless the U.S. government recognizes this reality, it will be unable effectively to resist, let alone to counter, the war of ideas being waged by Islamists to dominate us all.

If the Bush administration is finally getting serious about waging the war of ideas, it will not only have to differentiate between those wielding them against us and those who fundamentally share, or at least are not fundamentally hostile to, our values. No less importantly, the president will also have to engage the services of people who understand and can conduct this war effectively.

Toward that end, Mr. Rumsfeld should once again retain the services of Air Force Brig. Gen. Simon "Pete" Worden, an able and inventive officer who was charged early on in the war on terror with conducting strategic information operations, but was then cut loose at a time when the importance of the war of ideas was less well appreciated.

Success in the war of ideas - and, therefore, in the war on terror – will require having both better ideas and the warriors like Gen. Worden who are prepared to advance them competently and aggressively.

In recent weeks, senior Bush administration officials have begun talking about a heretofore largely neglected, and arguably decisive, front in the War on Terror: the battlefield of "ideas." Unfortunately, as a powerful cover story in this week's U.S. News & World Report makes clear, the United States has for years remained essentially disarmed in this arena.

By contrast, its enemies - notably an array of Saudi princes, charities, businessmen and front organizations - have been spending some $70 billion to recruit, train and arm adherents around the world in the name of the central idea being wielded against us, namely jihad or "holy war."

This U.S. News article was reported by one of the magazine's most highly regarded investigative reporters, David Kaplan. Titled, "The Saudi connection: How billions in oil money spawned a global terror network," Mr. Kaplan's article documents the extent to which successive American administrations turned blind eyes toward mounting evidence of Saudi involvement in Osama bin Laden's al Qaeda terror organization and its counterparts.

According to Mr. Kaplan, "U.S. officials now say that key [Saudi government and affiliated] charities became the pipelines of cash that helped transform ragtag bands of insurgents and jihadists into a sophisticated, interlocking movement with global ambitions. Many of those spreading the Wahhabist doctrine abroad, it turned out, were among the most radical believers in holy war, and they poured vast sums into the emerging al Qaeda network."

Mr. Kaplan quotes my colleague, Alex Alexiev, as saying, "The Saudi funding program is 'the largest worldwide propaganda campaign ever mounted' – dwarfing the Soviets' propaganda efforts at the height of the Cold War."

If Saudi Arabia's investment in the weaponry and infrastructure of the war of ideas has been staggering, so have its results. Mr. Kaplan cites the Saudi weekly Ain al-Yaqeen as saying the funds produced "some 1,500 mosques, 210 Islamic centers, 202 colleges, and nearly 2,000 schools in non-Islamic countries."

Unfortunately, many of these Saudi-bankrolled institutions are in the United States. The kingdom's investments in this country have produced the base for radical, intolerant and violent Muslims - known as Islamists - to mount a Fifth Column threat from within.

Last week, a new example of the potentially devastating gravity of this threat was revealed by the Wall Street Journal. It has previously been reported that Abdurahman Alamoudi, a prominent Washington-based activist who made no secret of his pro-Islamist sympathies, was able to secure the right for his own and a like-minded institution to train at least nine of 14 Muslim chaplains for the U.S. military.

The Journal discovered that Alamoudi - who is currently in jail on charges of laundering $340,000 in Libyan terrorist-related funding - was able to secure a similar arrangement for between 75 and 100 so-called "Islamic lay leaders." Their job was to minister to Muslims in the armed forces when the chaplains were unavailable. The institutions used to train chaplains received Saudi funds. The lay leaders got their training from an Institute for Islamic and Arabic Studies described by the Journal as "an arm of the Saudi government." All these organizations appear to have engaged in Islamist indoctrination.

Mr. Kaplan's article suggests the Saudi government is now cracking down on the monster its ideas and funds have created around the world. They may indeed be doing so at home, for reasons that have more to do with preserving the House of Saud's hold on power than with any real conversion about the unacceptability of the Islamofascism that they have enabled elsewhere.

Apart from ostensibly disowning the Institute for Islamic and Arabic Studies after the Journal story ran, however, there is not much evidence they have abandoned the war of ideas they and their clients have been waging elsewhere.

Meanwhile, the United States government remains woefully ill equipped to fight back in the war of ideas. Shortly after September 11, Defense Secretary Donald Rumsfeld - who has understood the importance of this front from the get-go of the War on Terror - tried to give the Pentagon a focal point for such efforts. Regrettably, the Office of Strategic Influence was taken down within months by unfounded rumors it would disseminate false news stories to promote American objectives.

Last week, the newspaper that gave currency and international attention to such fraudulent claims, the New York Times, breathlessly reported that an attempt to do the same thing was being quietly done through a contract with a consulting firm, SAIC. The Times was affronted by the wording of the Sept. 17, 2003, contract for a $300,000 study:

"Our inability to seize the initiative in the 'War of Ideas' with al Qaeda is perhaps our most significant shortcoming so far in the war against terrorism. We do not fully understand al Qaeda and its relationship to supportive communities in the Islamic world, and so are not yet able to develop an effective strategy for countering its propaganda in those communities, let alone for winning the information campaign in the war against terrorism."

Far from being embarrassed by or opposed to this exceedingly modest initiative - as the Times suggested several Defense Department officials were when confronted with the SAIC contract - the U.S. government should be mobilizing every available resource to alter the damning ideas about us being assiduously promoted by the Saudis and their proxies around the world.

If we do otherwise, we are unlikely to be able to hold our own in the War on Terror, let alone win it.

The report issued last week with much fanfare by the congressionally mandated September 11 commission is a stunningly comprehensive litany of recommendations aimed at reducing America's still-acute vulnerability to terror.

Commission members, victims' families and legislators warn failure to act quickly on these prescriptions will result in unnecessary risk of attack and grave political repercussions.

As nothing less than the nation's security is on the line, such warnings should be given every consideration. Unfortunately, the sheer volume, ambition and costs associated with the panel's recommendations dictate, as a practical matter, some will receive more urgent attention than others.

Some are sensible but difficult. For example, securing the country's borders is a vast, if absolutely necessary, undertaking. Others, like the eminently desirable consolidation of congressional terrorism-related oversight functions, have proven exceedingly resistant to previous reformers' efforts.

Then most publicized commission recommendation is a new "intelligence czar." This seems a classic Washington response to a real problem - throw additional bureaucracy at it.

At best, creating a director of national intelligence, with new staff and budgetary authority to manage the entire intelligence community, is likely to be disruptive during a time of war. At worst, it may actually prove counterproductive, leading either to new layers of officialdom that impede the efficient flow of information to policymakers, or the sort of streamlining that precludes competitive collection and analysis of intelligence needed to counter "group-think."

Fortunately, there is a commission recommendation that is both eminently doable and urgently needed.

The September 11 panel recognized what we are fighting is not "terrorism" but a hostile ideology - the radical, intolerant, jihadist faction of the Muslim faith known as Islamism - that uses terror as a political instrument. They concluded:

"The United States has to help defeat an ideology, not just a group of people, and we must do so under difficult circumstances. The U.S. government must define what the message is, what it stands for. We should offer an example of moral leadership in the world, committed to treat people humanely, abide by the rule of law, and be generous and caring to our neighbors. America and Muslim friends can agree on respect for human dignity and opportunity. To Muslim parents, terrorists like [Osama] bin Laden have nothing to offer their children but visions of violence and death. America and its friends have a crucial advantage - we can offer these parents a vision that might give their children a better future.

"Just as we did in the Cold War, we need to defend our ideals abroad vigorously. If

338

the United States does not act aggressively to define itself in the Islamic world, the extremists will gladly do the job for us. Recognizing that Arab and Muslim audiences rely on satellite television and radio, the government has begun some promising initiatives in television and radio broadcasting to the Arab world, Iran, and Afghanistan. These efforts are beginning to reach large audiences. The Broadcasting Board of Governors has asked for much larger resources. It should get them."

The need to augment the instruments of ideological warfare is especially acute in Muslim nations where the cancer of Islamism is metastasizing. For example, the U.S. effort to define itself for critical Iranian audiences is limited to a half-hour of television news and information. The U.S. government now has no television service to one of the most pivotal of Muslim nations, Turkey. Its Voice of America radio broadcasts to Pakistan are hampered by obsolescent transmitters in Tajikistan and it has no TV broadcasts in Urdu or other native dialects.

Meanwhile, the America government has no satellite television beamed into Afghanistan, where - as with much of the rest of the developing world - satellite dishes are sprouting like mushrooms after a rain. Its TV and radio are only available in Indonesia four hours daily. And Arabic-speaking Muslims in Europe are unable to receive programming on one of the few new U.S. government-sponsored international broadcasting initiatives: the Alhurra television network.

Meanwhile enemy propaganda instruments, like al-Jazeera and hostile state media pump out anti-American indoctrination in myriad languages around the world and around the clock.

The money required to expand access to the American ideology of freedom, respect for human rights and the rule of law to these and other critically important target nations of Asia and the Far East - and to restore coverage cut off in recent years to the still-emerging democracies of the former Soviet bloc since additional funding was not provided to meet the pressing need for ramped-up Arabic-language broadcasting - are relatively modest. The one-day costs of military operations in Iraq would go a long way toward paying for an entire year's worth of high-quality U.S. government and "surrogate" broadcasting everywhere we need to be.

While the White House and Congress wrestle over which of the other September 11 commission recommendations to implement, and exactly how to do so, they should come together promptly on at least one: Rearming the U.S. government with the broadcast vehicles and other instruments needed to wage a war of ideas against an enemy that must be fought 24/7 at the ideological, as well as tactical, levels.

It is generally accepted that the conflict we are in is as much a war of ideas as a military one. Sadly, the United States has largely failed to wage this ideological struggle against adversaries who both understand its vital importance to the outcome and who often, like most ideologues, are very skilled in its ways.

This is bad enough overseas, where adherents to one strain or another of the ideology best described as Islamofascism use various organizations, media and educational institutions to recruit and indoctrinate young people. The failure to recognize the danger such activities represent, let alone to counter them effectively, is among the most serious shortfalls in the Free World's response to our Islamist enemies.

Even more alarming is accumulating evidence we are also failing to appreciate the inroads being made by those promoting a similar agenda on this war's homefront - here in the United States. In fact, Islamists have been assiduously waging the war of ideas for decades, in American mosques and prisons, on military bases and college campuses across the country and, increasingly, in the public square. The infrastructure that has made possible such ideological inroads has largely been built by various Saudi institutions, charities, princes and businesses. The Islamofascists' success in these areas owes as much to our indifference, political correctness and cognitive dissonance as to their zeal.

A case in point is a new school that New York City seeks to initiate this autumn with public funding. The so-called Khalil Gibran International Academy (KGIA) will start small - a single sixth-grade class lodged temporarily inside an existing public school in Brooklyn. According to Garth Harries, an official in the city's Department of Education, the KGIA's purpose will be to "offer a challenging multicultural curriculum ... [that] integrates intensive Arabic language instruction and the study of Middle Eastern history and historical figures to enliven learning across all subject areas."

There are a number of grounds for concern that what is billed as "multiculturalism" will actually be Islamist indoctrination - at taxpayer expense:

- For starters, the curriculum for classes supposed to start in little more than a month has not been made available to parents of prospective students or concerned citizens. Even assuming the best of intentions on the part of New York educators - notably, Public Schools Chancellor Joel Kline has promised to "shut [the school] down" if it assumes a religious, political or national character inconsistent with a public school - it is a serious error to rush into an educational experiment fraught with peril without the closest scrutiny by parents and independent experts.

That is especially so since the KGIA's principal-designate, Dabah (a k a "Debbie") Almontaser told a reporter in May: "What will be different [is that] we will be able to infuse historical information into math and science and literature...

340

With any foreign language you engage in, you need to learn the history, culture and customs of the people in order to navigate the language effectively and not offend anyone."

- If such a curriculum sounds like a vehicle for injecting the Islamists' slanted view of Middle East history and promoting the culture of victimhood that is a staple of much of their proselytizing and indoctrination, it probably is, given Ms. Almontaser's views and associations. In January 2002, she told an interviewer: "The American people believe that everything is all right and that the U.S.A. lives by its ideals of democracy, individual freedom and the American dream out there as well. So did I, until September 11, 2001... Earlier you could be arrested for being black and driving a car, now it has become a crime to fly when you are brown. I believe a lot of Arab-Americans have realized that we are in the same boat as the black Americans; we must learn from their experiences and struggle against racism. I have realized that our foreign policy is racist; in the 'war against terror' people of color are the target."

- The deck has been further stacked in the direction of creating a publicly funded madrassa (or fundamentalist Muslim religious school) by putting Islamist organizations and individuals on its planning and advisory committees. For example, the latter include 12 religious figures - a striking departure from the principle of separating church and state. The three Muslim clerics are, respectively, the director of Jamaica Muslim Center Koranic Memorization School in Queens, the deputy emir (leader) of Majlis Ash Shura (a group that advocates the repressive theocratic code known as Shariah law) and New York University's imam, who forced the New York University administration not to display the Danish editorial cartoons of Muhammad that Islamofascists used to foment violence around the world.

A group of parents and concerned citizens calling itself the "Stop the Madrassa Coalition" (www.stopthemadrassa.wordpress.com) has just written New York's Mayor Michael Bloomberg and the state's governor, Eliot Spitzer, urging that the opening of the Khalil Gibran International Academy be postponed until satisfactory answers are provided to a host of questions.

Among other things, these concern: the character of the curriculum; the competence and agenda of the teaching staff; and "the amount of politicization and Shariah-tainted indoctrination our children are exposed to before Mr. Klein will 'shut it down.' "

If we hope to defeat the Islamists' in the war of ideas they are waging against us, we had better deny them a beachhead in Brooklyn - and a precedent and model for publicly funded madrassas across America.

Finally, justice has been done to one of the most important, yet heretofore truly un-sung, heroes of our time: William P. Clark. In "The Judge: Ronald Reagan's Top Hand," Paul Kengor and Patricia Clark Doerner provide the back story to the making and the success of the Reagan presidency - and the indispensable role played in both by an individual universally known simply as "the Judge."

This telling of Judge Clark's remarkable story is like the man himself – and perhaps as unique in the history of Washington as is its subject: Unfailingly honest, unpretentious, self-effacing, scrupulously fair and plain-spoken. Unlike most Washington memoirs or biographies, this book is not about settling scores. Rather, it is about laying out the facts. In so doing, it makes a compelling case that - despite the modesty that has caused him throughout his life to eschew the limelight and to give credit to others, Bill Clark was one of the most consequential public servants in our nation's history.

To be sure, many people deserve credit for Ronald Reagan becoming president and for his extraordinary service and accomplishments in that capacity. As "The Judge" makes clear, however, it is fair to say that, without Bill Clark's role as Gov. Reagan's chief of staff at a critical time in Sacramento, it is unlikely Mr. Reagan would have had a record on which to run successfully for higher office. And certainly, without Judge Clark's leadership for nearly two pivotal years as President Reagan's national security adviser, the Reagan presidency would not be remembered for having won the Cold War.

The latter is of particular relevance, not just as an historical insight but as a factor in contemporary public policy. During his tenure at the National Security Council from January 1982 to October 1983, the Judge assembled arguably the finest team of security policy practitioners since that institution's founding. Bill Clark's quiet competence, his skill as an effective administrator and the absolute confidence of his boss allowed the national security adviser to lead that team in developing, articulating and executing the strategy for destroying the Soviet Union.

This strategy was formalized and implemented in many of the 100 National Security Decision Directives promulgated under Judge Clark. They are remarkable both for their clarity about the repressive and threatening nature of Soviet totalitarianism and for the confident portrayal of the opportunity and the necessity for freedom to triumph over what President Reagan correctly called "the Evil Empire."

The bad news is that Judge Clark's time as national security adviser was cut short due to divisions within the Reagan team - largely (but not entirely) drawn along the lines of those who had been with the governor in California and who were politically aligned with his principled conservatism, on the one hand, and, on the other, those professional Washington insiders who opportunistically insinuated themselves into the administration once

Mr. Reagan came to power.

A stunning example of the intensity of this division - and the disloyalty by the latter group to the president the Judge served so faithfully - can be found in Mr. Kengor and Miss Doerner's revelation that then-White House Chief of Staff James Baker and his subordinates "began many inner-staff meetings by asking 'How can we roll Clark today?' "

The good news is that, while Bill Clark resigned his post in late 1983 (accepting at Mr. Reagan's insistence the position of interior secretary), the effect of the policies he promoted - aimed at restoring American strength as the most reliable instrument to promote peace, protecting U.S. sovereignty and interests around the world and taking down the Soviet Union - persisted, despite concerted efforts by his detractors to counteract them. The rest, as they say, is history.

Interestingly, however, the disagreements between the true Reaganauts and those who worked against them from within the Reagan administration persist to this day.

In recent months, Jim Baker and Reagan Secretary of State George Shultz wrote an op-ed in the Wall Street Journal brandishing their credentials with the former president to argue for ratification of the controversial Law of the Sea Treaty (LOST).

Bill Clark and the only other surviving senior California Reagan aide, Ed Meese, took it upon themselves to author a response (also published in the Journal explaining why Mr. Reagan rejected that defective accord in 1982 – and why he would continue to find it unacceptable today.

For this and all his many previous, inestimably important contributions to the national security, Bill Clark has earned a distinction this column confers each year: the "Horatius at the Bridge" Award. Like the Roman hero who legend has it singlehandedly staved off an enemy army bent on sacking his beloved city, Judge Clark was indispensable to sparing his nation - and many millions of other, freedom-loving peoples - the yoke of communist totalitarianism. Thanks to the efforts of Mr. Kengor and Miss Doerner, he will be remembered for a lifetime of extraordinary service to God and country, which happily continues to this day despite his affliction by debilitating illness.

Today, a new generation of would-be presidents is clamoring for the support of the American people. Whoever wins will face another form of totalitarian ideology - Islamofascism. We can only pray that, in so doing, they will be able to find and rely upon so steady a top hand as Ronald Reagan had in the Judge.

Try a little thought experiment. What would have happened in this country during the Cold War if the Soviet Union successfully neutralized anti-communists opposed to the Kremlin's plans for world domination?

Of course, Moscow strove to discredit those in America and elsewhere who opposed its totalitarian agenda - especially after Sen. Joseph McCarthy's excesses made it fashionable to vilify patriots by accusing them of believing communists were "under every bed."

But what if the U.S.S.R. and its ideological soul-mates in places like China, North Korea, Cuba, Eastern Europe and parts of Africa had been able to criminalize efforts to oppose their quest for the triumph of world communism? What if it had been an internationally prosecutable offense even to talk about the dangers inherent in communist rule and the need to resist it?

The short answer is that history might very well have come out differently. Had courageous anti-communists been unable accurately and forcefully to describe the nature of that time's enemy - and to work against the danger posed by its repressive, seditious program, the Cold War might well have been lost.

Flash forward to today. At the moment, another totalitarian ideology characterized by techniques and global ambitions strikingly similar to those of yesteryear's communists is on the march. It goes by varying names: "Islamofascism," "Islamism," "jihadism" or "radical," "extremist" or "political Islam." Unlike the communists, however, adherents to this ideology are making extraordinary strides in Western societies toward criminalizing those who dare oppose the Islamist end-state - imposition of brutal Shariah Law on Muslims and non-Muslims alike.

Consider but a few indicators of this ominous progress:

- In March, the 57 Muslim-state Organization of the Islamic Conference (OIC) prevailed upon the United Nations Human Rights Council to adopt a resolution requiring the effective evisceration of the Universal Declaration of Human Rights. Henceforth, the guaranteed right of free expression will not extend to any criticism of Islam, on the grounds that it amounts to an abusive act of religious discrimination. A U.N. Special Rapporteur on Freedom of Expression has been charged with documenting instances in which individuals and media organizations engage in what the Islamists call "Islamophobia." [Not to be outdone, the OIC has its own "10-year program of action" which will monitor closely all Islamophobic incidents and defamatory statements around the world.]

- Monitoring is just the first step. Jordan's prosecutor general has recently brought charges against Dutch Parliamentarian Geert Wilders. According to a lawsuit, "Fitna" - Wilders' short documentary film that ties certain Koranic passages to

Islamist terrorism - is said to have slandered and insulted the Prophet Mohammed, demeaned Islam and offended the feelings of Muslims in violation of the Jordanian penal code. Mr. Wilders has been summoned to Amman to stand trial and, if he fails to appear voluntarily, international warrants for his arrest will be issued.

Zakaria Al-Sheikh, head of the "Messenger of Allah Unites Us Campaign" which is the plaintiff in the Jordanian suit, reportedly has "confirmed that the [prosecutor's action] is the first step towards setting in place an international law criminalizing anyone who insults Islam and the Prophet Mohammed." In the meantime, his campaign is trying to penalize the nations that have spawned "Islamophobes" like Mr. Wilders and the Danish cartoonists by boycotting their exports - unless the producers publicly denounce the perpetrators both in Jordan and in their home media.

- Unfortunately, it is not just some companies that are submitting to this sort of coercion - a status known in Islam as "dhimmitude." Western officials and governmental entities appear increasingly disposed to go along with such efforts to mutate warnings about Shariah law and its adherents from "politically incorrect" to "criminally punishable" activity.

  For example, in Britain, Canada and even the United States, the authorities are declining to describe the true threat posed by Shariah Law and are using various techniques to discourage - and in some cases, prosecute - those who do. We are witnessing the spectacle of authors' books being burned, ministers prosecuted, documentary film-makers investigated and journalists hauled before so-called "Human Rights Councils" on charges of offending Muslims, slandering Islam or other "Islamophobic" conduct. Jurists on both sides of the Atlantic are acceding to the insinuation of Shariah law in their courts. And Wall Street is increasingly joining other Western capital markets in succumbing to the seductive Trojan Horse of "Shariah-Compliant Finance."

Let's be clear: The Islamists are trying to establish a kind of Catch-22: If you point out that they seek to impose a barbaric, repressive and seditious Shariah Law, you are insulting their faith and engaging in unwarranted, racist and bigoted fear-mongering. On the other hand, pursuant to Shariah, you must submit to that theo-political-legal program. If you don't, you can legitimately be killed. It is not an irrational fear to find that prospect unappealing. And it is not racist or bigoted to decry and oppose Islamist efforts to bring it about - ask the anti-Islamist Muslims who are frequently accused of being Islamophobes!

If we go along with our enemies' demands to criminalize Islamophobia, we will mutate Western laws, traditions, values and societies beyond recognition. Ultimately, today's totalitarian ideologues will triumph where their predecessors were defeated.

To avoid such a fate, those who love freedom must oppose the seditious program the Islamists call Shariah - and all efforts to impose its First Amendment-violating blasphemy, slander and libel laws on us in the guise of preventing Western Islamophobia.

Missile Defense

"BEGINNING OF THE END OF VULNERABILITY" | AUGUST 7, 1991

July 31, 1991, will live in history as a day when the United States took the first, momentous step toward genuine strategic security. That step was not, however, as the White House and the press would have you believe, a result of the signing of the Strategic Arms Reduction Treaty in Moscow.

Instead, it was the product of two important roll-call votes taken in the course of many hours of impassioned debate on the floor of the U.S. Senate. The upshot of those votes was an emphatic rejection of the posture of absolute American vulnerability to ballistic missile attack - a parlous state in which the United States has remained for nearly 20 years in the wake of the 1972 Anti-Ballistic Missile Treaty.

Starting with its repudiation (39-60) of an amendment offered by Sen. Albert Gore, Tennessee Democrat, the Senate signaled that it, at least, had learned one of the most important lessons of the Gulf war: It is better to be defended, even imperfectly, against ballistic missile attack than to be defenseless against it.

The Senate voted to stick with the recommendations of its Armed Services Committee, which had, after considerable wrangling behind closed doors, fashioned legislation as part of the fiscal 1992 Defense Authorization bill that would finally get the United States started on building strategic defenses against ballistic missile attack. As with most such things, the committee cobbled together a compromise that was not entirely satisfactory to even its supporters.

For example, it focuses on ground-based interceptor systems, weapons far less militarily efficient and cost-effective in defending vast stretches of territory than would be space-based missiles. It also emphasizes, at least initially, fealty to the 1972 ABM Treaty - an outdated arms control treaty that precludes the United States from fielding effective territorial defenses against ballistic missile attack.

Still, the Armed Services Committee did say the present posture of absolute vulnerability to such attack was no longer acceptable. It provided substantial sums for continuing necessary research and development on the space-based Brilliant Pebbles interceptors, leading to a future deployment decision. It also authorized a crash program for bringing on-line by 1996 one ground-based missile defense site, and clearly left the door open to the establishment of additional sites in due course.

Of incalculable significance is the timing of the Senate decision to uphold this recommendation to begin an active defense of the United States. The Senate took this step on the very day that the new START Treaty was signed and in the face of Moscow's explicit threat - one repeatedly underscored and seconded by Mr. Gore and his co-sponsors - to withdraw from that accord should the Untied States deviate from the ABM Treaty.

Clearly, the boogey-man that an American move to end its total vulnerability to ballistic missile attack would trigger an even more massive Soviet offensive weapons buildup than that which has occurred under the ABM Treaty - an argument which for too long has been cited to justify such a U.S. posture in perpetuity - is, in the face of Moscow's economic collapse, no longer plausible to senators.

Equally important, a substantial majority of the Senate concurred with its Armed Services Committee's judgment: The world we will face in the future requires an "adequate" territorial defense against the burgeoning danger of accidental or purposeful, small-scale attacks involving ballistic missiles. The Senate's votes suggest that allegiance to what President Bush has called "an abstract theory of deterrence" will no longer blind this nation's leaders to emerging threats unanticipated and unaffected by the codification of that theory - the ABM Treaty.

Especially noteworthy was the defeat by a vote of 43-56 of an amendment offered by Sen. Jeff Bingaman, New Mexico Democrat, that he described as having three objectives. It would have confined the Armed Services Committee's deployment initiative: (1) to an approach that would enhance "strategic stability;" (2) to a single, ground-based site; and (3) to an ABM Treaty-compliant system. By rejecting these amendments, and a raft of others offered the next day that would have slashed funding for some or all of the Strategic Defense Initiative program, the Senate has signally clarified its intent in endorsing the committee recommendations.

In so doing, we must hope, it has also made clear that the conference committee - which will shortly have to reconcile the Senate version with counterpart legislation recently adopted by the House of Representatives that would grossly underfund strategic defense and that essentially would terminate the Brilliant Pebbles program - must produce an outcome that reflects the Senate's position.

The days of perpetual, absolute American vulnerability to ballistic missile threats are clearly coming to an end. Even the adoption by a vote of 99-0 of an amendment offered by Sen. Carl Levin, Michigan Democrat, making clear that the Armed Services Committee's initiative was compatible with the ABM Treaty cannot alter or conceal reality: With or without that treaty, the people of the United States will shortly be able to expect from their government no less protection than it recently extended to the grateful people of Tel Aviv and Riyadh.

Two events last weekend may be seen, in hindsight, as ironic historical bookends marking the end of the Cold War and the beginning of a new adversarial period in relations between Washington and Moscow.

The first was a conference convened in New Jersey by Princeton University's Woodrow Wilson School of Public and International Affairs. It was an occasion for such figures as former Secretary of State George Shultz, former Defense Secretary Frank Carlucci and former Soviet Foreign Minister Alexander Bessmertnykh to meet and congratulate each other for the roles they played in winding down the four-decade-long conflict between the two nations.

Press reports suggest that much of the conversation revolved around the spirit of detente and the successes of the arms control process engendered by the evolving personal relationship between President Ronald Reagan and then-Soviet leader Mikhail Gorbachev. This is hardly surprising; many of the individuals present were, after all, prime movers behind the negotiations, summits and diplomatic "breakthroughs" that they would have us believe ended the Cold War.

What actually ended the Cold War, of course, was not the arms control process. Rather, it was a function of the collapse of the Soviet Union and its extended "Evil Empire." If anything this stunning achievement was realized despite the arms control process - not because of it. In fact, the U.S. and Soviet leaders shared a common interest in preserving the U.S.S.R., if only to ensure the continued sovereignty and legitimacy of the United States' negotiating partner. Toward this end, the process served as a vehicle for justifying substantial political and financial support for the communist regime in Moscow.

Interestingly, the participating former Soviet officials confirmed what many U.S. conservatives have long believed: Ronald Reagan's Strategic Defense Initiative (SDI) had a decisive effect on Soviet political and economic calculations. As Reuter's reported Feb. 26, these "officials said . . . Gorbachev was convinced any attempt to match Reagan's SDI, which was launched in 1983 to build a space-based defense against missiles, would do irreparable harm to the Soviet economy."

According to a CIA estimate produced in February 1983 and declassified at the Princeton conference, all other things being equal, the Soviet Union would have increased its strategic land- and sea-based ballistic missile forces by between 13 percent and 25 percent by the early 1990s. Mr. Reagan's technological trump, however, made it prohibitively expensive for Moscow to realize such a massive accretion of relative military power - and helped to seal the fate of the bankrupt Soviet empire.

No less striking than the former Soviet officials' acknowledgement of the importance of the SDI in changing the "correlation of forces" was the admission by their U.S. counterparts of considerable skepticism at the time about the value of SDI. Former National Security Adviser and Defense Secretary Frank Carlucci, for example, revealed that "I never believed in it."

Mr. Carlucci's successors in the Clinton administration should be encouraged not to make the same mistake. The technological and economic leverage inherent in effective space-based defenses against missile attack still can have a therapeutic effect upon the calculations of potential adversaries. Unfortunately, the other episode this weekend raises questions as to whether such adversaries might once again include the old Soviet Union.

In a Sunday address to Civic Union, the increasingly assertive political arm of the former Soviet military-industrial complex, Boris Yeltsin announced: "I think the moment has come when responsible international organizations, including the United Nations, should grant Russia special powers as a guarantor of peace and stability in the region of the former [Soviet] Union." This declaration must have been music to the ears of those represented by Civic Union and other nationalist/fascist organizations bent on re-establishing the Soviet empire and its aggressive foreign policies.

It should, however, also be a warning to the West. The increasingly ominous situation in Moscow (and elsewhere in the former Soviet Union) argues for prudence and vigilance, not just Western accommodation and largess in a blind effort to support President Yeltsin wherever he may lead. Now as before, the United States should be pursuing effective strategic defenses - both as an insurance policy against a renewed Soviet threat and as a continuing incentive to economic and political reform in Russia and beyond.

Unfortunately, the Clinton administration seems intent on both dismantling the Strategic Defense Initiative - at least its space-based elements – and undertaking what appears to be a massive and virtually unconditioned aid program described by officials as a "social safety net" for Russia. We can only hope that a future conference will not have occasion to date a renewal of the Cold War from these misbegotten decisions.

In March 1983, President Reagan shocked the political elite with an heretical suggestion: Might the United States not be better off defending its people against nuclear-armed
ballistic missile attack rather than avenging their deaths after one occurs? The fact that this
manifestly commonsensical proposition was viewed at the time as radical, dangerous heresy
spoke volumes about the mind-numbing grip of the 1972 Anti-Ballistic Missile Treaty - a
treaty that effectively prohibits the American government from fielding missile defenses
which could provide such protection to its population.

Indeed, although Mr. Reagan's address spawned a research program that became
known as the Strategic Defense Initiative (SDI) - into which tens of billions of dollars have
been poured over the past 14 years, the ABM Treaty remains the "supreme law of the
land." As a consequence, the United States continues to fail what has been called "the one-
missile test": No defenses are in place today to prevent even a single long-range ballistic
missile from delivering nuclear, chemical or biological warheads anywhere in the country.

This is all the more extraordinary since Republicans and like-minded conservatives
have generally recognized that such a posture has become not just dangerous but reckless in
the post-Cold War world where Russia no longer has a monopoly on threatening ballistic
missiles and weapons of mass destruction. In fact, one of the few commitments of the
"Contract With America" that remains unfulfilled was arguably among its most important
- namely, its promise to defend the American people against ballistic missile attack. Successive legislative attempts to correct this breach-of-contract have all foundered for essentially
two reasons.

First, most Republicans have shied away from a fight over the ABM Treaty. Some
deluded themselves into believing that the opportunity afforded by the Treaty to deploy
100 ground-based anti-missile interceptors in silos at a single site in Grand Forks, N.D.,
would allow the United States to get started on defenses. Even though such a deployment
would neither make strategic sense (it would not cover the entire United States from even a
limited attack) nor be justifiable from a budgetary point of view (while estimates vary widely, costs of this minimal system could be well more than $10 billion), some missile defense
proponents rationalized their support for it by claiming that the anti-defense crowd would
not object to this "treaty-compliant" deployment and that it would be better than nothing.
To date, however, all these "camel's-nose-under-the-tent" schemes have come to naught.

Second, while Republicans (and many Democrats) have been quite willing to spend
upward of $3 billion per year on SDI-related research, opponents of missile defenses have
skillfully exploited many legislators' fears of the large, budget-busting price-tags said to be
associated with more comprehensive missile defense schemes. The prospect of being pillo-
ried for adding to the deficit to buy unproven "star wars" technology in violation of a major

U.S.-Soviet arms control agreement was generally enough to dissuade all but the most visionary and courageous of political figures from pressing for prompt deployment of effective anti-missile systems.

Developments on both the treaty and technology fronts, however, suggest that the time has finally come when Ronald Reagan's vision can be accomplished and America defended - a vision made all the more compelling by the proliferation of ballistic missiles and deadly weapons of mass destruction far beyond the control of the Kremlin. The Clinton administration last Friday signed agreements that create new parties to the ABM Treaty (in the stead of the long-gone Soviet Union would be Belarus, Kazakhstan, Russia and Ukraine) and that expand the treaty's scope. Instead of dealing exclusively with defenses against long-range missiles, the ABM Treaty would get new limitations on so-called "theater" anti-missile systems designed to deal with shorter-range threats.

Clearly, a fight over the ABM Treaty now can no longer be avoided. The administration is expressly stating its intention to breathe new life into this accord by making it more difficult to amend and more comprehensive in its impediments to U.S. missile defenses. The Republican Congress now has no choice but to explicate the risks associated with a posture of defenseless, and to take corrective action. This will entail defeating Mr. Clinton's proposed amendments; if 34 senators reject the multilateralization of the ABM Treaty, there will be no other party to it and the treaty should die a natural death.

Fortunately, the United States also has near-term missile defense options that would allow it quickly to field global, militarily effective anti-missile defenses at relatively low cost. All that is required would be to adapt the infrastructure that is already in place - thanks to the Navy's $50 billion investment over the past few decades in its AEGIS fleet air defense system - giving it the capability to shoot down both shorter- and longer-range ballistic missiles. Such a system would create a basis for addressing near-term missile threats and complement space-based assets that may be needed in the future. The only problem is that the ABM Treaty prohibits such an affordable, formidable sea-borne defensive system.

As it happens, the opening salvos in what may be the end game of the ABM Treaty fight were sounded this weekend at the first International Conservative Congress (dubbed by one participant "the Conintern"). One pre-eminent leader after another - including House Speaker Newt Gingrich, former British Prime Minister Margaret Thatcher, once-and-future presidential candidate Steve Forbes, former U.N. Ambassador Jeane Kirkpatrick, Sen. Jon Kyl and columnist Charles Krauthammer - denounced the idea of making it still harder to defend our people against ballistic missile attack. Several, notably Mr. Kyl and Mr. Forbes, have explicitly endorsed the AEGIS option to begin performing that task.

With such leadership, there now looms a distinct possibility that the American people can finally be acquainted with the ominous reality of their vulnerability and empowered to demand corrective actions. Thanks to the Clinton ABM amendments and the new technical options for defending America, we have both the vehicle for getting out from under an accord that was obsolete even in Ronald Reagan's day and the means for making good and cost-effective use of the freedom that will flow from doing so.

Over the past 10 days, the Clinton administration has signaled its intention to make the most significant sea change in U.S. security policy since March 1983, when President Ronald Reagan surprised the world by unveiling his Strategic Defense Initiative. The question is: Is this a real change or is it but one more in a series of Clintonian "triangulations" - the term coined by Dick Morris for a bait-and-switch maneuver that robs the political opposition of its most politically potent issues, often at a cost of little more than lip-service to the need for action.

Announcements made first by Defense Secretary William Cohen and then by Mr. Clinton himself suggest that the United States is now finally poised to abandon the posture of "assured vulnerability" that it adopted in the wake of the 1972 Anti-Ballistic Missile Treaty. In accordance with that treaty, the U.S. government formally renounced any interest in defending the nation against ballistic missiles. And, having decided not to protect its people against that most palpable of threats from the missile-wielding Soviet Union, it came to embrace as a practical matter the idea that there was no sense expending huge sums to protect them against other threats, either.

As a result, today, Americans are exposed to blackmail or mass destruction by missile-delivered chemical, biological or nuclear weapons in the hands not only of an increasingly hostile Russian government. Nations from China to North Korea to Iran and Libya either already have or shortly will acquire the means credibly to threaten this country with one or more of these devices. As long as the United States allows its defense policies and programs to be governed by the restrictions of the ABM Treaty, we will be unable to prevent even a single missile from these or other rogue states from reaching our shores with devastating effect.

The notion that American vulnerability was actually desirable gave rise to a combination of decades of inattention to and lack of investment in programs that would mitigate the danger posed by weapons of mass destruction – whether delivered by crop-dusters, tramp steamers or suitcases. The nation accordingly now finds itself without the means to assure control of its airspace, the infrastructure to provide effective civil defenses or even the capability to assure the continuity of the U.S. government in the event of such attacks.

In recent years, as our society and defenses have become ever more dependent upon computers and information technology (IT), a new threat has emerged: a growing likelihood that enemies ranging from individual thrill-seeking hackers to terrorists to hostile nations will engage in deliberate attacks aimed at disrupting or destroying critical IT networks. Concerns about the so-called "Millennium Bug" have provided insights into the myriad ways in which the security of both the nation and its citizens could be severely harmed by even temporary disruptions in power grids, financial markets and systems, the telecommunications infrastructure, vital government functions, etc.

The Clinton administration has, in recent months, begun to evince a growing sensibility to these risks. Until very recently, however, it has seemingly confined itself to understated public hand-wringing and those favorite government activities - reorganizations, meetings and studies.

Then came nearly back-to-back announcements by the defense secretary and the president. On Jan. 20, Mr. Cohen ended six years of administration prevarication by acknowledging there is a growing threat of missile attack against the United States - and that we would have to deploy a limited national missile defense to protect the American people against it. Then, two days later, the president himself delivered a speech warning that: "The enemies of peace realize they cannot defeat us with traditional military means. So they are working on two new forms of assault . . . cyber attacks on our critical computer systems, and attacks with weapons of mass destruction - chemical, biological, potentially even nuclear weapons."

In connection with the former, Secretary Cohen declared that the administration would be setting aside $6.6 billion for deployment of ground-based missile defenses. While Mr. Cohen stressed that the decision to make such a deployment would not be made for another 16 months (the money is, therefore, all in the often-fictitious "out-year" budgets) - and, indeed, the initial operational capability for the proposed system has slipped by two years to 2005 - he took pains to make clear the nation would be defended against rogue state missile threats.

For his part, Mr. Clinton announced his budget would include $10 billion "to address terrorism and terrorist-emerging tools . . . including nearly $1.4 billion to protect citizens against chemical and biological terror - more than double what we spent on such programs only two years ago - and $1.46 billion to protect critical systems from cyber and other attacks."

Perhaps most important of all these announcements was Mr. Cohen's suggestion that the new-found determination to address America's ever-more-reckless posture of vulnerability would not be precluded by the Anti-Ballistic Missile Treaty or Russian opposition. Such a stance would clear the way not only for the limited, relatively ineffective and expensive ground-based system the administration fancies, but for the much more flexible, capable and cost-effective sea-based approach favored by many experts as the best way to begin providing near-term U.S. missile defense.

Unfortunately, within hours of the defense secretary's press conference, administration spokesmen were clarifying what the secretary meant to say - namely, that the U.S. actually had no intention of abandoning the ABM Treaty or even of pursuing limited defenses without Russian assent. This point was evidently reinforced by Secretary of State

Madeleine Albright in her just-completed talks in Moscow. And her deputy, Strobe Tal-bott, a lifelong devotee of this and other arms control treaties, will be dispatched to Moscow next month to continue these discussions. It is hard to imagine that the result will be an actual, early end to the American posture of assured vulnerability.

The good news is that a new, rigorous legal analysis by former Deputy Assistant Secretary of Defense Douglas Feith and George Miron has conclusively demonstrated that there is no ABM Treaty. Under international legal precedent and practice, it lapsed when the Soviet Union became extinct. So, members of Congress should feel free - indeed, feel compelled - to direct the executive branch to effect the deployment of missile defenses as soon as technologically possible and pursue aggressively other means of reducing the Nation's vulnerability to the various emerging non-missile threats.

The administration's response to such an initiative will be edifying. Should it persist in opposing efforts to defend America, the recent high-level expressions of a commitment to do just that will add to, not reduce, our insecurity - and to the indictment against this most cynical of presidents.

An important anniversary will be marked on Thursday with a Capitol Hill press conference. On March 23, 1983, President Ronald Reagan first committed his administration and the nation to the development and deployment of anti-missile defenses that would permit American lives to be "saved, rather than avenged."

Tragically, the participants -who are expected to include a number of influential legislators, senior former officials and military officers as well as technologists and public policy activists - will be obliged to observe that, 17 years after the Strategic Defense Initiative was launched, the United States still fails the "one-missile test": There are no systems deployed today that could stop even a single ballistic missile fired at this country from reaching its target.

This is a particularly chilling reality in light of the recent threats made by Communist China to use nuclear weapons to attack the United States in the event the man just elected by the people of Taiwan came to power and the PRC retaliated with force. By all accounts, Russia is about to install a career KGB officer who nostalgically recalls the Soviet Union and seems bent on restoring to their former power its instruments of state terror and influence. Vladimir Putin's stated determination to modernize and wield the nuclear arsenal bequeathed by the U.S.S.R. may or may not mean a deliberate renewal of the menace to the United States from that quarter. Most experts agree, however, that there is a non-trivial danger of an accidental or unauthorized missile launch from Russia.

Meanwhile, North Korea is believed to have acquired - or shortly will do so - the long-range missile it needs to hold American targets at risk. The present U.S. inability to thwart such a danger has made such technology a cash crop for Pyongyang and, for that matter, Beijing and Moscow, allowing them to secure hard currency and influence around the world by proliferating missiles and/or the deadly weapons of mass destruction they might deliver.

The fact that the United States remains undefended against these emerging threats is, of course, most immediately the fault of the Clinton-Gore administration. One of its first acts upon coming to office was to dismantle the Strategic Defense Initiative program. It has insisted, contrary to international legal practice and common sense, that the prohibition of any territorial missile defense of the United States contained in the Anti-Ballistic Missile (ABM) Treaty - an accord signed in 1972 under very different strategic circumstances with a country, the Soviet Union, that went out of business nine years ago - remains not only in force, but the sacrosanct "cornerstone of strategic stability."

Perhaps most pernicious of all is the fact the Clinton-Gore team has delayed by years the availability of robust anti-missile defenses with budgetary shenanigans and bureaucratic skulduggery. As a result, it contends, 2005 is the earliest the United States could have even a very limited defensive capability deployed at a site in Alaska. In other words, all other things being equal, Americans will remain vulnerable to missile attack sometime into the term of the person who will be elected after the man who wins next November's balloting.

Clearly, all other things cannot and must not remain equal. As the participants in Thursday's press conference sponsored by the newly formed Coalition to Protect Americans Now will emphasize, it is simply unacceptable to leave the people and territory of this country vulnerable to missile blackmail or attack for the next five years. The same can be said for our inability to provide anti-missile protection for our forces and allies overseas.

Should this situation be allowed to persist, it seems not only possible but likely that someone, somewhere, will decide to take advantage of this vulnerability. In the event someplace we care about -either in this country, or perhaps Taipei, Tokyo or Tel Aviv - is attacked, it is predictable that a crash program will be mounted at once to deploy whatever anti-missile defenses we can. At that point, nattering nabobs of scientific negativism will no longer be given the time of day. Cost will be no object. And the status of the ABM Treaty's constraints will no longer be of even academic interest.

The first thing we will do is the first thing we can do: Task the U.S. Navy immediately to adapt elements of its Aegis fleet air defense system so as to enable these existing cruisers and destroyers to shoot down long-range ballistic missiles. By taking advantage of the availability of more than $50 billion worth of sea-going mobile platforms, launchers, missiles, sensors, communications systems and the people that operate them, a near-term defensive capability system could be jury-rigged in short order and at relatively negligible cost.

Of course, such a system will not constitute a leak-proof "astrodome" defense, certainly not in the short-term. Its effectiveness will inevitably be improved with upgrades and modifications over time. And it will provide the greatest protection if it is complemented with ground-, air- and/or space-based defenses that will take somewhat longer to acquire and that should be brought on-line as fast as possible.

If a sea-based anti-missile system is what we would surely do after we have been attacked, it must be asked: Why wouldn't we do it now, before that dreadful event occurs - and, perhaps, thereby prevent it from happening?

Incredible as it may seem, the Clinton-Gore administration has done everything imaginable to prevent such an obvious action from being taken. It has consistently denied funds needed to give the Aegis program even limited defensive capabilities against longer-range ballistic missiles. It has adamantly rejected any role for Aegis ships in a National Missile Defense (NMD) program in deference to the ABM Treaty's prohibition on sea-based strategic anti-missile systems. Most recently, officials in the Office of the Secretary of

Defense have intervened to prevent the submission to Congress on March 15 - as required by law - of a report that confirms the valuable contribution missile defense-capable ships could make to NMD.

One of the things Republican presidential candidates Gov. George W. Bush and Sen. John McCain agree most strongly about is the need to give Aegis ships anti-missile capabilities. The case for doing so is now sufficiently apparent that even the Democrats' leader on arms control matters in the Senate, Sen. Joseph Biden of Delaware, expressed support on March 8 for "an Aegis sea-based system with missiles based off the North Korean coast that would let the United States intercept the North Korean missiles in their ascents." (Presumably, he would want them to be able to intercept such missiles whether they are going to Seoul or San Francisco.)

We cannot afford to bet that another anniversary of President Reagan's SDI speech can be safely observed without a deployed anti-missile system. Americans need to be protected now, and they can be - by an emergency effort to put to "gap-filling" capabilities to sea, a step that may just permit us to have defenses in place before we need them, rather than after.

During the inaugural European trip of his presidency this week, George W. Bush will receive a baptism of fire on his top national security priority - missile defense. It will come in a succession of group and bilateral meetings with allied leaders and subsequently with Russia's Vladimir Putin.

As the president sets off for these sessions, the first thing he should remember is that he is traveling in the capacity of leader of what continues to be the Free World - not, as most of his interlocutors would prefer, as the representative of a country that is merely first among equals.

It follows from the fact that the United States is, indeed, the world's only superpower that it has certain unique responsibilities. Among these, the most important is to lead with respect to matters that bear on its security and that of friends who rely upon American strength and resolve to provide for the common defense.

This leadership role requires the United States to take steps that are sometimes opposed by others - even, ironically on occasion, its closest friends. In the past, for example, America has deemed it necessary to challenge communist aggression in Europe, Africa, Asia, Cuba and Central America. For many years, it has deployed missiles, carrier battle groups and ground forces all around the world, and even gone to war when it believed the dangers posed by enemies of freedom demanded it. In the process, successive U.S. administrations have had to brook often intense criticism, including from time to time that served up by people on whose behalf it was taking such expensive and daunting steps.

By and large, though, America's actions have been proven by history to have been justified. The world is a far freer place than it would have been had U.S. presidents listened to those who caviled against our maintenance and projection of power worldwide, who urged that negotiations with adversaries - and, by implication, trusting them - was a surer way of securing not only our own interests, but those of our friends and allies. It's called leadership.

Unfortunately, for most of the past decade, U.S. security policy has largely been made by individuals who were leery of, if not actually embarrassed by and opposed to, forceful American leadership in international affairs. In particular, the Clinton administration tended to embrace the agenda of those who wanted to reduce the United States to the status of just another nation. It reflexively subordinated U.S. forces and sovereignty to the dictates of multilateral organizations and agreements; it recoiled from pursuing policies defined by national interests in favor of the lowest-common-denominator arrangements usually dictated by those in the United Nations, NATO or foreign capitals least friendly to this country.

The new American president is clearly being encouraged to follow suit – by allies led by left-wing activists, who pride themselves on their past anti-American agitation; by the former KGB operative who runs the Kremlin; and by congressional Democrats who cut their teeth opposing U.S. Cold War security policies. He is also under pressure to perpetuate Clintonesque policies from some within his administration, the latter reportedly being abetted at least occasionally by Mr. Bush's father. Still, it would be a singular mistake to accede to such urgings and, thereby, to perpetuate our present vulnerability to ballistic missile attack.

To Donald Rumsfeld's credit, during his own trip to Europe last week, the defense secretary set the stage for Mr. Bush to lead in a very different direction on missile defense. In meetings with NATO allies in Brussels, the Pentagon chief reinforced a message he had first imparted during a visit to Munich last February: The United States has decided to deploy missile defenses. He made clear that the obsolete, Soviet/Russian-violated and legally defunct 1972 Anti-Ballistic Missile (ABM) Treaty "stands in the way of . . . deployment of a defense that can deny others the power to hold our populations hostage to nuclear blackmail." According to the New York Times, he also signaled that "the U.S. is likely to deploy certain anti-ballistic missile systems before testing on them is completed."

It now falls to President Bush to make clear that this approach enjoys his strong support, and to explain why. Here are some of the points he should make:

The United States believes there is a serious and growing danger that places it cares about - for example, Taipei, Rome, Seoul, Tokyo or Paris and, in due course, American cities - may be subjected to attack by ballistic missile-borne weapons of mass destruction. If such a terrible thing should happen, the U.S. would certainly do everything humanly possible to put into place anti-missile capabilities to ensure that it could not happen again.

This sort of effort would, inevitably, involve starting with weapons already in hand. Specifically, the skippers of the U.S. Navy's Aegis ships would be immediately authorized to use their sophisticated air defense system to provide early, if necessarily very limited, anti-missile capabilities. That system would be modified and improved as quickly as possible and complemented by other air-, land- and space-based defenses. In the wake of a missile-delivered disaster, few complaints would be heard about the cost or lack of testing or incompatibility of such activities with the ABM Treaty.

Mr. Bush can then point out that, if this is what we would do after a devastating attack has occurred, why would we not do it now - especially if, by taking that step, we might prevent the missile strike from taking place in the first instance?

In this fashion, the president can underscore both his commitment to defend this country, its forces and allies overseas and to doing so at the earliest possible moment. He can make clear this is a missile defense program that will be as good as we can make it. But, as is true of any emergency deployment, the system need not - and, indeed, cannot - wait until it is certifiably perfected before it is brought to bear.

Most importantly, Mr. Bush can establish the leadership that will command support at home and abroad. In the words of an unnamed NATO official quoted in last Friday's New York Times: "When you know that they are going to build it no matter what, is it really worth the fight? I don't think so."

The U.S. president meets in an unusual location with his Kremlin counterpart. Amidst high expectations of a summit breakthrough, the latter offers the former a totally transformed relationship between their two countries, prominently featuring massive reductions in offensive nuclear arms. There is only one catch: The American leader must abandon his commitment to defend his people against the threat of ballistic missile attack.

Of course, the date was October 1986, not November 2001; the venue, Reykjavik, Iceland, not Crawford, Texas. The American president was Ronald Reagan, not George W. Bush. And the man from Moscow was Mikhail Gorbachev, not Vladimir Putin.

Yet, if press reports informed by State Department leaks are to be believed, basically the same play is going to be run by the Kremlin team in the upcoming summit at President Bush's Texas ranch as Mr. Reagan confronted 15 years ago in Iceland.

Now, as then, the diplomats of Foggy Bottom are encouraging the president to believe he has a historic opportunity to secure a breakthrough with the old Cold War enemy. Echoed by an international press corps and foreign policy elite that have always viewed with alarm the idea that the United States might actually depart from the 1972 Anti-Ballistic Missile (ABM) Treaty in order to have missile defenses prohibited by that accord, the State Department is pressing Mr. Bush to make a deal.

Under the terms of this deal, Mr. Bush would presumably have to dispense, for the time being at least, with any further talk about the ABM Treaty being "outdated, antiquated and useless" - let alone "dangerous."

Despite his repeated assertions that the United States has to "move beyond" that accord in order to deploy effective anti-missile systems "at the earliest possible time," he would have to agree not to deploy any missile defenses for some period and to leave intact the ABM Treaty's prohibitions on such deployments.

In exchange, the Russians would agree somehow to modify or at least to ignore other provisions of the ABM Treaty that also prohibit development and testing of promising U.S. defensive technologies - notably, sea-, air- and space-based anti-missile weapons and sensors. The Kremlin would also throw in an agreement to cut their strategic offensive forces to around 1,500 weapons, provided the U.S. undertook to do roughly the same.

Now, it is far from clear just how this would work. Of course, the Russians - and the Soviets before them - have been adept at ignoring provisions of treaties that prove inconvenient. (In fact, such a practice has allowed the former U.S.S.R. to deploy a full-up territorial anti-missile defense prohibited by the ABM Treaty). But, as Defense Secretary Donald Rumsfeld has made clear, Americans don't violate treaties.

Changing the treaty to eliminate its constraints on development and testing, however, sounds a lot like the sort of line-in, line-out amending process that National Security Adviser Condoleezza Rice has correctly, and repeatedly, said could not be used with the

ABM Treaty. If, instead of adopting the new "strategic framework" that dispenses with the ABM Treaty altogether sought by the new administration since it came to office, the Bush team winds up effectively amending it, the unamended parts will continue to constitute unacceptable impediments to the actual realization of protection against missile attack.

It is predictable, moreover, that such changes to an existing treaty will be seen by the Democratic Senate as requiring its advice and consent.

Under that body's present leadership, such an exercise would surely translate into an affirmation of the prohibitions on deployment that would be left intact - hardly a legislative history a president committed to defending his people would welcome.

In addition, preserving any part of the ABM Treaty would have the effect of establishing unequivocally that the Russians are a party to that accord. This would give them legal standing they do not currently enjoy (the 1972 accord having been signed with the U.S.S.R., not Russia).

It would also confer legitimacy on the Kremlin's future efforts to veto U.S. deployments of which they do not approve. At the very least, such an arrangement flies in the face of all President Bush's exhortations that the "Cold War is over" and that bilateral arms control treaties (whether governing defensive or offensive forces) are not appropriate in light of the changed nature of the Russo-American relationship.

The rejection by Ronald Reagan of Mr. Gorbachev's offer to ban all nuclear weapons if only the Gipper would give up on his Strategic Defense Initiative not only defined Mr. Reagan's presidency. Despite the Bronx cheers Mr. Reagan got from critics at home and abroad for having missed the opportunity Reykjavik presented for "peace in our time," even Soviet leaders subsequently acknowledged that his determination to stay the course on missile defense helped catalyze the unraveling of the Evil Empire.

Today, George W. Bush faces an eerily similar test of leadership.

To be sure, there will be those at the editorial boards of the New York Times and The Washington Post, in the salons of Cambridge and in allied capitals who will revile him for rejecting Mr. Putin's deal - even though it would ineluctably have the effect of perpetuating America's vulnerability to missile attack, rather than move us in the direction of ensuring it is ended once and for all.

Still, protecting the American people against ballistic missile threats is what Mr. Bush said he would do when he ran for office. It is what he has said since his election he was committed to accomplishing. And it is what he has forcefully declared is even more necessary in the wake of the September 11 attacks.

This is President Bush's Reykjavik moment. And as with that of his predecessor, a lot more is riding on the decision about missile defense than simply the credibility of the president's word.

Two amazing things happened in the aftermath of President Bush's visionary and courageous decision to withdraw from 1972 Anti-Ballistic Missile (ABM) Treaty.

First, contrary to the confident predictions of many so-called experts, the sky remained in its place. Russian President Vladimir Putin called the Bush action a mistake, but did not launch nuclear Armageddon or otherwise respond aggressively. In fact, he observed that it would not threaten Russia's security and that U.S.-Russian relations should continue "at the same level."

For its part, China mildly groused, but there was no talk of breaking off diplomatic - let alone commercial - relations with the United States. As for our allies, the worst of their reaction was confined to mild tut-tutting.

In other words, the concerted and sustained campaign to intimidate the United States into remaining within a treaty that prohibited the development and deployment of effective anti-missile defenses is now seen for what it always was: a flim-flam operation whose fraudulent character should have been exposed and rejected years ago. The upshot of our having failed to do that before now is that this country has been left vulnerable to the real and growing danger of ballistic-missile-backed blackmail and/or attack.

The Kremlin's exceedingly muted reaction has left the few congressional Democrats who have publicly assailed Mr. Bush (notably, Senate Majority Leader Tom Daschle of South Dakota, Joseph R. Biden Jr. of Delaware and Carl Levin of Michigan) in the unhappy position of being holier than the pope – professing more concern about how badly the Russians would take this than the Russians themselves were actually taking it. The foolishness of this stance may be why so few of the senators' colleagues are publicly following their lead. In fact, after the withdrawal notification was announced, Congress authorized full funding for the president's missile defense budget.

In short, Mr. Bush has now succeeded in creating legal, diplomatic and political conditions that give him essentially complete latitude in pursuing and putting into place the missile defenses he has so clearly recognized are needed now.

This makes all the more amazing the second thing that happened after Mr. Bush withdrew from the ABM Treaty on Thursday. On Friday, a small coterie of civilian Pentagon officials decided to cancel the Navy's short-range Area Missile Defense program. As a result, the Navy will be sent back to the drawing board, postponing - perhaps by years - the day when forward-deployed U.S. amphibious forces and naval battle groups will have any protection against the danger currently posed to them by widely proliferated ballistic missiles and weapons of mass destruction.

Predictably, missile defense critics - reeling from the body blow delivered by the president's disposing of their cherished "cornerstone of strategic stability" - were euphoric.

They chided the Defense Department, saying if it could not do something as relatively easy as building short-range anti-missile systems, it certainly couldn't build more complex defenses against longer-range ballistic missiles. And they claimed vindication in asserting that the president had not needed to abandon the ABM Treaty at this juncture since no developing missile defenses were ready to bump up against the treaty's limitations.

Regrettably, giving comfort to the president's political opponents is the least of the reasons why it was a mistake to terminate the Navy Area Missile Defense at this juncture. While this short-range anti-missile system has experienced both considerable cost growth and schedule slippage, it was described just last August by the now-chairman of the Joint Chiefs of Staff, Gen. Richard Myers, as "essential to national security." He declared that "a robust, sea-based, lower-tier theater ballistic missile defense capability, found in the Navy Area Missile Defense Program, is critical to reducing operational risk to the warfighter." Of particular relevance to the Friday decision, Gen. Myers' letter stated that, "there are no alternatives to this program that would provide equal or greater military capability at less cost."

This assessment was foreshadowed in a letter sent to the Joint Chiefs chairman in January by the chief of naval operations and Marine Corps commandant. They emphasized "the critical importance of early deployment of Navy Area Missile Defense capability. Navy Area is the number one priority of the Navy and Marine Corps among the different Theater Missile Defense systems."

The chairman was urged to "ensure that Navy Area capability is available to the Joint Force Commander at the earliest possible moment" and pledged that "we will do all in our power to ensure its effective deployment."

Unfortunately, these strong arguments for proceeding with the Navy system were not persuasive to the small group of civilian officials led by Under Secretary of Defense E.C. "Pete" Aldridge. Perhaps that is because these senior military officers were not given an opportunity to make their case when the decision was being made. Indeed, they seemed to have been as surprised - and appalled - by the decision as was the president's National Security Council staff.

Instead, the cancellation seems to have been largely driven by the recommendations of Lt. Gen. Ronald Kadish, who heads the Ballistic Missile Defense Organization. Gen. Kadish has gone out of his way under both the Clinton and Bush administrations to delay, dumb down and otherwise impede the most promising options for near-term missile defense: short- and long-range anti-missile systems based on the Navy's existing $60 billion Aegis fleet air defense infrastructure.

To his great credit, Mr. Bush has now created the opportunity for the U.S. military to finish the development and begin the deployment of effective missile defenses. If that opportunity is to be fully exploited, however, he will need to direct the Pentagon to test the Navy area system as planned in February, press vigorously ahead with other, more capable sea-based anti-missile systems and entrust the management of such programs to those who will deploy – not cancel - the defenses we need.

Tonight, President Bush has a chance to make not only a memorable speech, but a historic one. Thanks to an extraordinary event last Friday, Mr. Bush will have in his first State of the Union address the kind of opportunity John F. Kennedy seized so momentously four decades ago, challenging his countrymen to put a man on the moon in 10 years' time and setting in train the national effort needed to translate that epic vision into reality.

On Jan. 25, the USS Lake Erie - a Navy cruiser equipped with the Aegis fleet air defense system - made history in its own right. It conducted the first flight test of an SM-3 missile, an interceptor rocket that successfully intercepted and destroyed a mock ballistic missile warhead high over the Pacific Ocean.

With this test, the promise of sea-based missile defenses has begun to be realized. If, as is now apparent, the existing Aegis infrastructure – comprised of some 61 ships in the fleet today and another 25 abuilding - can be utilized to defeat ballistic missiles, the United States can relatively rapidly acquire a global anti-missile system. What is more, thanks to the roughly $60 billion already invested by the Navy in the Aegis program, it can do so at a fraction of the cost of other options for defending U.S. forces and allies overseas and the American people here at home against the present, and growing, danger of ballistic missile attack.

Mr. Bush will doubtless speak to that danger tonight, as he has on so many previous occasions. He has all the more reason to do so since a team of UN experts announced last week that the Taliban had as many as 100 Scud B ballistic missiles whose whereabouts today are unknown.

If such short-range missiles were fitted with weapons of mass destruction and launched from a ship off our coast - a danger identified in 1998 as real by the blue-ribbon Missile Threat Commission chaired by our present Defense Secretary Donald Rumsfeld - most of the nation's population centers could be at risk of devastating attack.

President Bush has previously and correctly observed that if terrorists have such a capability, they will doubtless try to use it. They and/or their state-sponsors clearly have the ballistic missiles. And they have, or have access to, ships that might be suitable for launching such missiles – for example, those suspected of helping al Qaeda operatives flee Southwest Asia, the one bearing Iranian arms to the Palestinian Authority and countless others flying flags of convenience.

The only near-term means of cost-effectively defending the American homeland and other potential targets against this threat is the widespread deployment of the SM-3 aboard Aegis ships. When combined with upgrades in these ships' radars, fire control and communications systems, their interceptor missiles will provide a degree of protection that we can no longer afford to be without. The introduction of such capabilities will facilitate, moreover, the further evolution and improvement of each subsystem so as to create ever better defenses against longer-range ballistic missiles.

Accordingly, President Bush should boldly use tonight's address to make a Kennedyesque commitment: We will begin defending the American people against ballistic missile attack by the end of this year.

The president should acknowledge that the earliest deployments of sea-based anti-missile systems will inevitably be of somewhat limited capability, while pledging to improve them as rapidly as possible. By pointing to and building aggressively upon the success of the Jan. 25 test, however, he can offer the public a practical, prudent approach to acquiring something that has, until now, been little more than a gleam in the eye - and that, until he withdrew last month from the 1972 Anti-Ballistic Missile Treaty, was actually prohibited: a missile defense for the United States of America.

As with Kennedy's moon program, a Bush missile defense challenge will not be realized if a business-as-usual approach is followed by those charged with its implementation. The authority and responsibility for a streamlined acquisition effort must be given to individuals who fully share the president's commitment and who respect the legal requirement to defend the American people "as soon as is technologically possible." It cannot be entrusted to those who have, at least until last Friday, deprecated, dumbed-down or otherwise impeded the development of sea-based missile defenses. (A particularly egregious example of such obstructionism was the unexpected decision one day after Mr. Bush withdrew from the ABM Treaty to terminate a shorter-range version of ship-borne defenses, known as the Navy Area Missile Defense program - even though $2 billion had been invested in bringing it to fruition and only six weeks remained before its own flight-testing was to begin.)

George W. Bush is committed to defending our country and its citizens against the array of dangers we confront in the war on terrorism.

He deserves our strong support in this effort. And, as JFK did with his challenge 40 years ago, this president will get the best of American ingenuity, innovation and achievement if he calls on the people of this great nation to start putting into place by year's end the missile defense we all so urgently require.

On June 14, the United States will complete its withdrawal from the 1972 Anti-Ballistic Missile Treaty, clearing the way for the expeditious development and deployment of effective U.S. missile defense systems.

Unless, that is, Sen. Carl Levin of Michigan and a few other congressional Democrats have their way.

The problem arises from the fact that Mr. Levin is no longer simply one of the most liberal defense critics in his caucus. Today, he happens also to be the chairman of the Senate Armed Services Committee.

Each spring, that committee and its House counterpart go through what is called the "mark-up" of legislation that authorizes appropriations for the Pentagon during the next fiscal year. Even during peacetime, the defense authorization bills that emerge from the Congress (usually late in the year) largely reflect the president's request and priorities. This is even more true during wartime periods, such as that in which we have found ourselves since September 11.

And so it was last year, when Mr. Levin initially sought to cut more than $1 billion from the budget George W. Bush had proposed to ready for deployment of a limited national missile defense. The senator seemed determined to do so, even after the attacks of September 11 validated the central point of Mr. Bush's argument for such a defense: There are people in the world determined to kill a great many Americans. Some of them are getting their hands on weapons (whether designed for the purpose or otherwise) capable of destroying thousands of us at a time - including the most efficient means of doing that, ballistic missiles equipped with weapons of mass destruction. It is, therefore, a matter of time before we are at the receiving end of such a deadly attack.

As an ideologically committed opponent of missile defense, Carl Levin remained unpersuaded by this logic. The senator nonetheless appreciated that he would have been soundly defeated had he brought to the Senate floor a bill mandating such deep cuts and chose to fight another day over funding for missile defense.

In the same way, and for the same pragmatic political reasons, a still-more-insidious Levin initiative died aborning after September 11: The Armed Services Committee's chairman decided not to pursue a plan to impose – via new legislative language - impediments calculated to preclude near-term deployments of effective anti-missile systems.

If President Bush and Defense Secretary Donald Rumsfeld do not act quickly and decisively, however, such obstructionism may yet emerge from the Committee mark-up Mr. Levin will conduct over the next few days.

For example, Mr. Levin has suggested that each of the armed services be required to certify that expenditures by the Pentagon's independent Missile Defense Agency enjoy their full support and are more important than their own, individual priorities. This transparent divide-and-conquer stratagem would directly, and perhaps mortally, erode the defense secretary's ability to establish and execute programs for the Defense Department as a whole.

Chairman Levin has also expressed an interest in denying President Bush the ability to streamline and greatly accelerate the development and acquisition of missile defenses. Toward this end, he would like to subject this priority effort to the same unbelievably sclerotic bureaucratic arrangements – featuring numerous, ponderous program reviews known as "milestones" - that typically keep new weapon systems from coming on line in less than 12 to 15 years.

Even more obnoxious is Mr. Levin's reported interest in requiring the Pentagon to get prior congressional approval before missile defense programs are allowed to undergo such "milestone" reviews. Then, after defense officials have performed their review, he thinks Congress ought to have the right to second-guess the department's decision.

Such micromanagement is a sure-fire way to prevent anything useful from coming out of the billions of dollars President Bush is allocating to end our increasingly dangerous vulnerability to missile attack. It would also go a long ways toward frustrating the intended effect of withdrawing from the ABM Treaty. The combined impact would be to position Mr. Levin and others on the left to rail disingenuously in the future as they have in the past - namely, that there is not much to show for the money spent on missile defense, that the technology is not ready to deploy, that the costs and risks of doing so are too great, etc., etc.

Since Mr. Bush came to office, he has exhibited impressive steadfastness and the courage of his convictions with respect to missile defense. He made the case for getting out of the ABM Treaty. He worked skillfully to create conditions that all but eliminated any international turmoil when last December he actually exercised the United States' right to do so. And he has wisely rejected appeals from the Russians and the American left to enter into a new agreement with the Kremlin aimed at limiting missile defenses in some fashion.

The historic and strategic significance of all of this may be substantially eroded, however, if he were now to allow determined congressional opponents like Carl Levin to strangle the missile defense program in unwarranted, counterproductive and politically/ideologically motivated red tape. To avoid this, Messrs. Bush and Rumsfeld should put the Congress on notice forthwith: Any effort to continue the garroting effect of the restrictive ABM Treaty via legislatively mandated congressional micro-management will precipitate a presidential veto of the defense authorization bill.

A new front has recently been opened in the attack on President Bush's defense and foreign policies and in particular, on the stewardship of his national security adviser, Condoleezza Rice.

One of Miss Rice's former subordinates, Richard Clarke, has made news [and presumably millions of dollars] contending the Bush team failed to comprehend - and do enough - about the threat posed by Osama bin Laden's al Qaeda terrorist network.

Now the president's critics claim he compounded that error by squandering time, energy and money pursuing defenses against a far more distant threat from ballistic missiles.

For example, The Washington Post reported breathlessly last week that in a speech prepared for delivery [but not given] on September 11, 2001, Miss Rice had planned to discuss the danger the country faced from missiles equipped with weapons of mass destruction. Here, it seemed, was proof ideologues in the Bush national security apparatus had their eye firmly and exclusively on the wrong ball, leaving the nation ill-prepared to deal with more prosaic threats – like hijacked, fuel-laden passenger planes flying into buildings.

Wait a minute. In fact, the undelivered Rice speech makes clear the Bush administration was quite concerned about the threat of terrorism in the United States and around the world. As she put it: "We need to worry about the suitcase bomb, the car bomb and the vial of sarin released in the subway."

From their earliest days in office, Mr. Bush and his subordinates pursued initiatives carried over from the Clinton administration, including improved security against truck bombs, shipborne weapons of mass destruction [WMD] and bioterrorist threats. In addition, the National Security Council's Mr. Clarke was laudably beavering away at another grave danger: the possibility of cyber-strikes aimed at the computers that enable America's critical infrastructure.

What Condoleezza Rice argued, however, was it made no sense to "put deadbolt locks on your doors and stock up on cans of Mace and then decide to leave your windows open" to enemy attack. That, she correctly contended, would be essentially the effect if the Bush administration were to perpetuate its predecessors' practice of leaving the country undefended against missile-delivered WMD.

In the years following September 11, President Bush has, to his lasting credit, provided the leadership, resources and latitude necessary to put into place at least limited anti-missile protection. Most importantly, he withdrew the United States from the 1972 Anti-Ballistic Missile Treaty, an archaic Cold War document that some [notably, Sen. John Kerry] foolishly considered the "cornerstone of strategic stability" even a decade after the other party – the Soviet Union - had ceased to exist. Without the myriad impediments posed by the ABM Treaty to developing and deploying competent missile defenses, getting them put into place became a relatively straightforward matter of time and technology.

Indeed, the Bush team now is poised to begin fielding, for the first time since 1974, anti-missile defenses for the American people. A relatively rudimentary capability will be brought on-line in coming months as a small number of interceptor rockets become operational at a site in Alaska.

Unfortunately, the urgency the Bush administration properly attaches to getting at least some protection against the one form of terror for which we currently have no defense is now the object of most intense criticism. A left-wing organization, the Council for a Livable World, circulated an open letter signed by former Joint Chiefs Chairman Adm. William Crowe and 48 other retired flag officers denouncing the deployment of anti-missile defenses in Alaska without more testing. The signatories claim that the money could be better spent on other anti terror priorities.

Meanwhile in the Congress, anti-antimissile-defense legislators led by the Armed Services Committee's ranking Democrat, Sen. Carl Levin of Michigan, insist on more "realistic tests" before defenses are put into place. According to press accounts, Mr. Levin is determined to go after some $500 million in the defense budget associated with deployment of future anti-missile interceptors.

The reality is that, as Condi Rice intended to say on September 11, 2001, we cannot afford to leave any avenue of attack open to our enemies. The threat of missile strikes could come not only in the future from places like North Korea, or for that matter China, armed with long-range, WMD-equipped ballistic missiles. It could arise at any time from a terrorist group that has managed to strap a short-range SCUD-type missile launcher onto a ship and sail it undetected within a hundred miles or so of an American coastal city.

If fault is to be found with the Bush administration, it is not that it is doing too much, too fast on missile defense. It is not doing nearly enough to bring quickly to bear other seagoing, airborne and most especially space-based anti-missile systems. Such a diversified approach would not only provide the most robust protection possible against various kinds of missile attack. It would also minimize the danger a President Kerry will be able easily to replicate an ill-advised action led 30 years ago by his most prominent supporter, Sen. Ted Kennedy, who succeeded in shutting down what was at the time America's single ground-based missile defense site in North Dakota.

Neville Chamberlain once called the nation of which this city was the capital in 1938, "a faraway country" with "people of whom we know nothing." With those words, he reneged on Britain's alliance with Czechoslovakia, abandoning it to Adolf Hitler's quest for "breathing room" for the German people and the rest, as they say, is history.

In recent months, the United States has undertaken important new security commitments with the Czech Republic and Poland in the face of emerging threats to those countries, the rest of Europe and indeed the Free World more generally from a regime whose aspirations are arguably even more ominous than those of the Nazis: the Islamic Republic of Iran.

After all, the mullahocracy of Iran seeks, in the words of its front man, President Mahmoud Ahmadinejad, to bring about the return of the 12th Imam, a messianic figure known in Shi'ite Iran as the Mahdi. The trouble is, according to the ayatollahs, the precondition to the Mahdi's ushering in of the golden age of Islam is something that sounds a lot like the apocalypse.

As a result, it is advisable to take seriously threats issuing forth with great regularity from Tehran to the effect that Israel will be "wiped off the map" and that it is "desirable and achievable" to bring about "a world without America." Iranian ballistic missiles have demonstrated the ability to reach distant targets like Tel Aviv, parts of the European Continent and, if launched from ships, the United States.

If used to detonate nuclear weapons in space over targeted nations, such missiles could unleash electromagnetic pulse (EMP) attacks, resulting in widespread destruction of electrical grids and what a congressional commission has described as the "catastrophic" disruption of civilizations reliant upon them. A world without America could be the practical result of such a strategic EMP attack here, as the United States is reduced to a pre-industrial society.

Against such a threat, the Bush administration has begun to put into place modest anti-missile defenses. Deployed ashore in Alaska and California and aboard a growing number of naval vessels, these systems afford some protection against certain ballistic missile-delivered attacks on the United States.

The United States has also concluded agreements with the governments of Poland and the Czech Republic that will allow the fielding of 10 land-based interceptors and an X-band radar, respectively, in the two nations. These systems will extend very limited missile defenses to our allies in Europe and permit some additional capability to intercept future intercontinental-range Iranian missiles aimed at the United States.

These benefits will accrue, however, only if the Congress agrees to fund such deployments and the associated military construction. As of this writing, Democrats in the House of Representatives have declined to do so. Thankfully, a Republican member of the House Appropriations Committee, Rep. Mark Kirk of Illinois, will offer Tuesday an amendment designed to honor America's commitment to its European allies and provide the protection they and we need at an absolute minimum.

The Kirk amendment has taken on greater urgency in the aftermath of Russia's recent, devastating invasion of another "faraway country" - the sovereign, democratic and pro-Western republic of Georgia. Even though the Polish-based interceptors and the radar in the Czech Republic represent no threat to Moscow's ability to destroy Europe should it choose to do so, Vladimir Putin is determined to try to stop their deployment.

The Kremlin has gone so far as to threaten nuclear attacks on the basing countries if they proceed with their efforts to defend themselves and others from the menace posed by Moscow's ally, Iran.

It appears Mr. Putin hopes to engineer a "re-do" of the 1983 deployment of U.S. ground-launched cruise missiles and Pershing II ballistic missiles in five West European countries. Back then, the NATO alliance held firm in the face of an all-out Soviet campaign to block the basing of such weapons and destabilize the governments involved. The failure of that campaign marked the beginning of the end of the Soviet Union, an event Mr. Putin mourns as the "greatest geopolitical catastrophe of the 20th century" and one he evidently seeks to reverse.

It would be unconscionable for the Congress now to give Mr. Putin - fresh from his rape of Georgia - a new and far more strategic victory by denying the funds needed to implement the missile defense agreements with Poland and the Czech Republic. Not only would doing so assure that Europe remained vulnerable to nuclear blackmail, or worse, from Iran. Not only would it deny the United States additional protection from Iranian missiles intended to bring about a world with this country.

A refusal to take the corrective action proposed by Mark Kirk would signal that the West, once again, views with indifference the security concerns of our allies. It will encourage the belief in Moscow and elsewhere that our time's most powerful democracy will, like its predecessor 70 years ago, abandon its friends to the appetites of their rapacious neighbors.

The vote in the Appropriations Committee Tuesday is an opportunity to demonstrate instead to our friends here in Prague, to America's allies around the world and to our actual and prospective foes that, despite the intense partisanship of this election season, Democrats and Republicans alike will honor our national commitments and stand together in defense of freedom.

Israel

The announcement last week by Secretary of State James A. Baker III that the third "phase" of the Middle East peace process would get under way in Moscow on Jan. 28-29 is merely the latest sign that a "sanity check" is urgently needed concerning the premises and objectives that animate the Bush administration's policy toward this process.

If - having personally witnessed the collapse of the Soviet Union - Mr. Baker still believes that the Soviet state (or its successors) remains central to the negotiation of peace between Israel and the Arabs, it could just be that he is equally deluded about some of the other aspects of this diplomatic initiative.

In fact, with the rapid unravelling of the Soviet Union, the administration's strenuous attempts to perpetuate the fiction that Moscow has actually been an equal cosponsor with the United States of the peace process has been more droll than dangerous. The same cannot be said of some of its other notions. Consider the following:

- The administration has, at least until the recent dramatic developments in the former Soviet Union, seemed to regard resolution of the Arab-Israeli conflict as being more important than any other contemporary international issue. The high-level attention and political capital invested in the first two phases of the peace talks came at the direct expense of U.S. capacity to address such immediate problems as: The unravelling of the U.S.S.R.; the intensifying warfare in Yugoslavia; the unfinished business of Saddam Hussein's misrule in Iraq.

  This is not to say that the tensions between Israel and her neighbors are inconsequential. It is simply to suggest that the administration has mistakenly given priority to its efforts to bring this long-simmering conflict to an end.

- This misinvestment of U.S. prestige and political capital is, in turn, a reflection of a more fundamental misconception: Namely that Arab-Israeli hostility is amenable to resolution if only Israel will give back land it occupied in the 1967 Six-Day war. That notion - which underpins the proposal that the Israelis exchange "land for peace" - bespeaks a contempt for history that is unworthy of the United States. The fact is that Arabs made war with the Jews long before the "occupied territories" were acquired by Israel, usually on the ground that Israel's pre-1967 boundaries also represented illegally occupied land.

  Unfortunately, there is at present no reason to believe that Syria and the Palestinian Arabs who lay claim to the Golan Heights and to the West Bank and Gaza Strip, respectively, would be any more willing to live in peace with an Israel reduced to its pre-1967 boundaries than they were in the past. To the contrary, their behavior with respect to the negotiations suggests they view the peace process not as a vehicle to create a durable end to hostilities with Israel but as a continuation by other, diplomatic means of a conflict they have thus far lost decisively.

The upcoming Moscow conference is a case in point: At the Arab's insistence, it will involve members of the European Community, Japan and the European Free Trade Area in what are ostensibly talks on such regional issues as water-sharing and arms control in the Middle East. By accommodating the Arab desire to dilute these potentially important talks between the parties to the Arab-Israeli conflict, the United States has seriously reduced the prospect that they will produce useful results.

- The administration has adopted a strategy of "evenhandedness." Such a strategy implies moral equivalence between those bent on the destruction of a sovereign state - one that is, moreover, democratic, pro-Western and an ally - and their intended victim. It is scarcely less implausible than would have been a U.S. effort to equate Iraq and Kuwait 16 months ago.

- The corollary to the Bush administration's conclusion that Israel can safely give up the West Bank and Golan Heights in exchange for peace is its view that the Jewish state no longer requires the strategic depth they afford. Senior U.S. government officials from President Bush on down have argued that the Persian Gulf War demonstrated the irrelevance of strategic depth in the age of ballistic missiles.

In fact, the difference between Kuwait's experience in the war with Iraq and that of Saudi Arabia was not that the former was vulnerable to ballistic missile attack and the latter was not. The fact that Kuwait was raped by Saddam's forces while Saudi Arabia escaped that fate was a function of strategic depth; the former did not have it, the latter did. As a practical matter, Saddam had to move his massed armored forces through Kuwait to occupy and destroy the Saudi oil fields, port facilities and airfields. Without the warning - and the time to mobilize and obtain U.S. help - that strategic depth afforded, the Saudi experience would likely have been quite different.

Similarly, the United States and its Western European partners have in recent months come to view the Continent as more secure than at any time since World War II. Until the collapse of the Soviet empire, this was due not to an appreciable diminution of the size or power of the Soviet ballistic missile threat. Rather, it was attributable to events in Eastern Europe that conspired to replace a forward-deployed, heavily armed Warsaw Pact with - you guessed it - strategic depth.

In short, strategic depth still matters to other people in an age of ballistic missile threats. If anything, it must matter even more to a tiny state like Israel, surrounded by well-armed and relentlessly hostile neighbors. Without the additional warning time, impediments to armored attack and ability to deny commanding heights to enemy gunners that go with Israel's retention of the Golan Heights and the West Bank, defense of the Jewish state would be utterly problematic.

U.S. efforts to compel Israel to return to such a posture on the basis of what amounts to an arms-control agreement will expose a vital ally to undue danger and oblige us to assume responsibilities for her defense that we are unlikely to be able to fulfill. The duration of Desert Shield bore out Golda Meir's famous response to an earlier suggestion that Israel rely on U.S. security guarantees: "By the time you get here, we won't be here."

In short, it is time for the United States to rethink its present policy toward the Middle East peace process. Only by doing so can we avoid participating in the diplomatic equivalent of the Moscow circus and, far more importantly, dooming the very peace we hope to promote in this troubled region.

As part of its search for a "comprehensive" peace, Israel is negotiating an agreement with Syria that is expected to entail Israeli withdrawal from the Golan Heights and possibly, over time, the complete return of the Heights to Syria. Relinquishment of this territory is a sensitive military and political issue not just in Israel but also in the United States, because Israel expects that compensatory security arrangements will include the deployment of American troops to the Golan as monitors or peacekeepers.

This study evaluates the benefits and costs to the United States of such a Golan mission for the U.S. armed forces. The benefits - that is, the rationale for such a deployment - divide into three categories: monitoring, deterrence, and support for a Syrian-Israeli peace.

Monitoring: A monitoring mission might focus either on (a) the monitoring of military activity for purposes of early warning and military intelligence or (b) monitoring the parties' compliance with the peace agreement.

Neither Israel nor Syria would in fact look to U.S. monitors or those of a multinational force to provide early warning of the other side's significant military activities. That kind of military intelligence collection and analysis is an essential national security function. Although a country might, under certain circumstances, choose to rely to some extent on another country for military intelligence, this is less likely to be the case when the second country is doing its monitoring not as an ally, but as an impartial or neutral observer, as would be the status of any U.S. forces deployed on the Golan under an Israeli-Syrian agreement.

U.S. troops could help perform the function of monitoring the parties' respective compliance with an agreement. This is a realistic function of some value. But it can be performed effectively without the permanent stationing of U.S. troops on the Heights, with all the attendant costs and risks of such a deployment. If a compliance issue arises and a party wants American personnel to serve as "honest brokers" to mediate the issue or monitor specific treaty conditions, that party could invite those personnel in on a case-by-case basis.

Deterrence: Some commentators suggest that U.S. forces on the Golan could help deter Syria from violating a peace agreement and attacking Israel militarily in the future. How might the U.S. forces fulfill this function? Are they to serve as a deterrent on the military level - i.e., the forces themselves would be a military factor in the calculations of a Syrian military commander - or are they to serve simply as a contribution to deterrence on the political level?

There are two ways the forces could function as a military deterrent: either (1) the U.S. deployment would be large enough to serve as an effective military barrier to a future

Syrian military offensive or (2) the U.S. deployment would serve as a "tripwire" to ensure that such a Syrian offensive would trigger a large American military intervention to oppose it.

First, no one has suggested that the United States deploy to the Golan a force with the numbers and types of men and equipment that would allow it to serve as military barrier against Syria's large armored forces. Much of the talk in press and policy circles has been of a [small] deployment -perhaps as few as 800 lightly armed troops.

Second, some commentators have spoken of the contemplated U.S. deployment as a "tripwire" -that is, a device to ensure that a future Syrian aggression would more or less automatically trigger a substantial U.S. military intervention to defend Israel. This is an idea of enormous strategic importance. It is the concept most likely to affect Israeli public opinion about the security risks of territorial withdrawals in favor of Syria. The concept deserves the most intense scrutiny, for it represents the gravest danger to U.S. interests.

A tripwire arrangement would create, in essence, a mutual defense alliance between Israel and the United States. Such an alliance, however, cannot be built on a trilateral peacekeeping agreement including Syria. It would require a formal defense treaty between Israel and the United States, duly ratified with the approval of the U.S. Senate. It would be reckless for Americans or Israelis to suppose that U.S. forces on the Golan could in fact function as a tripwire in the absence of such a formal treaty commitment.

The United States has an interest in discouraging its Israeli friends from harboring unrealistic expectations. Israel should not count on a peacekeeping force functioning as a mechanism that can be relied upon to engage the United States deeply on Israel's behalf in the event of another war with Syria. Were a future Syrian attack to injure or kill U.S. peacekeeping forces on the Golan, the U.S. government may decide to remove the peacekeeping force altogether rather than reinforce the troops.

Even if U.S. troops on the Golan do not contribute to military deterrence - as a tripwire or otherwise - might they not be justified as a contribution to deterrence at the political level? In the event (1) Israel and Syria sign a peace agreement, (2) Israel withdraws from the Golan under that agreement and (3) Syria, at some point in the future, decides to launch an attack on Israel to capitalize on that Israeli withdrawal, Syria would know that its aggression will antagonize the United States whether or not U.S. troops are stationed on the Golan. At most, such troops could serve as a marginal factor in Syria's calculations.

The real political deterrent to Syrian aggression is not U.S. troops on the Golan, but the strength of U.S. ties to Israel and the certainty of U.S. support for a swift and effective Israeli response to such aggression. This deterrent requires no U.S. troops on the Golan.

Moreover, such troops would be more likely to deter Israeli military action - action required for the defense of common U.S. and Israeli interests - than Syrian military aggression. The presence of U.S. troops on the Golan would increase the likelihood of U.S. opposition to pre-emptive military action by Israel, no matter how urgent or well-advised. The standard American tendency to disapprove military action would be reinforced powerfully by solicitude for the U.S. peacekeepers. Hence, the effect of the U.S. deployment might be the opposite of that intended: It could reduce fear of Israeli pre-emption among potential Arab aggressors. By tending to embolden rather than deter those contemplating renewed aggression against Israel, this would tend to undermine any Syrian-Israeli peace agreement, decrease regional stability and increase the risks of war.

Support for an Israeli-Syrian Accord: As a general proposition, it is not sensible for the United States to make a commitment of indefinite duration to put U.S. troops on the Golan for symbolic purposes, when the necessary symbolism can (and undoubtedly will) be supplied amply by other means. Such a commitment would not be sensible even if the troops were to be stationed in a stable and safe environment. Given the dangers of terrorism in the region, and the political instabilities and risks of war, it would be very irresponsible to deploy those troops as symbols.

Conclusion: There is no mission or rationale for a U.S. peacekeeping force on the Golan that would justify the resulting costs and risks. Indeed, the net effect could be negative for Israel's security and regional stability, while the consequences could include the loss of U.S. lives and, possibly, a credibility-damaging retreat of the U.S. forces under terrorist fire. In any event, such a deployment would increase the danger of direct U.S. involvement in a future Middle East war and undermine Israel's standing with the U.S. public as a self-reliant ally.

A U.S. deployment on the Golan Heights deserves immediate, serious consideration by U.S. policy-makers, legislators and the public. If such consideration is delayed until all the details are set - until after the United States is committed formally as part of an Israeli-Syrian peace agreement - U.S. options will be severely constrained. On the other hand, if the subject is now debated and Congress and the executive branch decide to oppose a deployment of U.S. troops on the Golan, Israel and Syria could take this into account in their negotiations and devise alternative security arrangements accordingly. Such a decision would be far less disruptive if made now than if deferred until after a Syrian-Israeli deal is concluded.

There was a clear winner following last week's Middle East summit in Washington: It was the interest the United States shares with Israel - and, one would hope, with the entire civilized world - in upholding the principle that Palestinian Arab violence will not be condoned, let alone rewarded.

Regrettably, it fell virtually exclusively to Israeli Prime Minister Benjamin Netanyahu to produce that result. Mr. Netanyahu's courage and determination were sorely tried as not only the Palestine Liberation Organization's Yasser Arafat and Jordan's King Hussein but also President Clinton hammered Israel's premier to make concessions on one or more fronts in the name of appeasing Palestinian Arab nationalists.

Particularly appalling was Mr. Clinton's failure to use the summit as a bully pulpit for establishing that Mr. Arafat's incitement of rock-throwing and automatic weapons fire was utterly unacceptable. Even inviting Mr. Arafat to the White House under the circumstances can reasonably be interpreted as a success of sorts for what Charles Krauthammer has called the PLO chairman's "war card" strategy. If the Palestinian Arabs opt to resume mob action and lethal attacks against Israelis, a contributing factor may be the belief that such steps will, at a minimum, entitle Mr. Arafat to the international attention and influence that goes along with obtaining a practically immediate audience with the President of the United States.

This danger is only compounded by the fact that Mr. Clinton apparently did not make clear to Mr. Arafat that, hereafter, Palestinian Arab demands can only be addressed through negotiations, that further violence in the future would preclude relations between the United States and the Palestinian leader – with implications for future aid flows, official visits to Washington, etc.

To the contrary, Mr. Clinton decided to abstain rather than veto a U.N. Security Council resolution that was, in its sympathetic treatment of the PLO's grievances, all too reminiscent of that organization's rabidly anti-Israeli past. He also declined to use his post summit press conference to condemn the practice of violence as a negotiating technique. Instead, he offered the appearance of moral equivalence between the parties, a posture that may or may not be conducive to mediation but that surely signals an American indifference toward the security needs of a key ally, which can only invite new efforts to divide the United States and Israel.

In this regard, it is instructive to consider the message sent by Egypt's refusal to participate in the Washington summit meeting. Egypt is, after all, a country that receives some $2 billion per year in U.S. taxpayer funds. This affront joins a long list of other invidious Egyptian actions - notably, the virulently anti-Netanyahu propaganda issued in recent weeks by Egypt's state-controlled media; Cairo's pursuit of improving relations with

Moammar Gadhafi's Libya (including its apologizing for the Libyan chemical weapons program); and Egypt's importing of Scud missiles, threatening military movements and efforts to sabotage U.S.-led efforts to extend the Nuclear Non-Proliferation Treaty. Since none of these appear to have had any effect on Washington's attitude of moral equivalence between Israel and Egypt or otherwise entail any costs for Cairo, more such behavior must be expected.

To be sure, Mr. Clinton did not engage in the sort of Israel-bashing that character- ized the Carter and Bush administrations' policy toward the Jewish State. Mr. Clinton and his subordinates reserved their pressure on Israel for private sessions; although the backbit- ing back grounding has begun, the president's refusal to find public fault with Mr. Netan- yahu's stance was refreshing. Unfortunately, it is unclear whether this relatively supportive conduct will survive the U.S. presidential election season.

In the final analysis, it is Prime Minister Netanyahu who must be credited with thwarting demands that Yasser Arafat be appeased. He conducted himself at the Washing- ton summit in a statesmanlike manner that puts his government in a strong position to deal with the turmoil that lies ahead. It can only be hoped that Mr. Netanyahu's own statements about the summit having "increased the degree of mutual trust" between himself and Mr. Arafat and his description of the latter as his "partner and friend" will not come back to haunt him as the PLO chairman is shown yet again to be utterly untrustworthy, a most unreliable partner and no friend of Israel.

It now behooves the United States to use the negotiations that began in Erez on Sunday to communicate the message Mr. Clinton failed to convey in Washington. If Mr. Arafat and his followers harbor any illusions that these negotiations will be made more productive or can be circumvented by renewed armed action against Israel, the talks are certain to prove futile at best. At worst, they will advance the very "peace"-without- security-for-Israel agenda that has come to characterize the so-called "peace process" and that Benjamin Netanyahu so ably resisted in Washington. These outcomes would be in neither America's interest nor Israel's; they must henceforth be discouraged every bit as much by Mr. Clinton as by Mr. Netanyahu.

In 1992, American Jews and others committed to the security of the state of Israel were among the most enthusiastic and generous supporters of the Clinton-Gore ticket - and with good reason. The government of George Bush and Jim Baker was arguably the most anti-Israel U.S. administration since the founding of the Jewish State.

To friends of Israel, the prospect of Bush-Baker's displacement by Messrs. Clinton and Gore, two men who made much of their commitment to Israel's security, seemed a heaven-sent two-fer: First, the American election afforded an opportunity through public repudiation at the polls to punish Mr. Bush for the harm he had inflicted on relations between the two countries. And second, it would permit the "special relationship" between the United States and the West's only democratic outpost in the Middle East to be restored to its traditional pre-eminence.

Yet today, slightly more than five years after Mr. Bush was sent packing, President Clinton is engaged in behavior toward the Israeli government of Benjamin Netanyahu eerily reminiscent of Bush-Baker's animosity toward an earlier government in Israel, that of Yitzhak Shamir.

Where Mr. Baker contemptuously announced that Mr. Shamir should "call us when you are serious about peace," Mr. Clinton refuses to see Prime Minister Netanyahu when he is visiting this country. Lest anyone take at face value the White House explanation that this insulting treatment was simply a function of scheduling problems, the president found plenty of time during Mr. Netanyahu's visit to entertain two of the latter's most virulent critics - Leah Rabin and Shimon Peres.

Even more ominous are the parallels between the Bush and Clinton administrations' characterization of Israeli government policy as the impediment to peace in the Middle East. Bush-Baker demanded that the Jewish State cease the construction of settlements in the West Bank and Gaza Strip. It went so far as to try to blackmail the Shamir government into doing so by withholding loan guarantees - even though these were intended to help Israel fulfill its mandate as a refuge for the world's Jews by accommodating a huge influx of Russian immigrants.

Now, the Clinton team sees the Netanyahu government's unwillingness to cede what the shuttling Madeleine Albright defines as "credible, substantial" territory to the Palestinian Arabs as a showstopper for the so-called "peace process." The U.S. administration has even suggested the breakdown in Israeli-Palestinian negotiations precipitated by Mr. Netanyahu's alleged intransigence is responsible for the lack of support American initiatives vis-a-vis Saddam Hussein now enjoy in the Arab world. It seems only a matter of time before Washington threatens to curtail flows of financial or other forms of assistance to Israel - if such threats have not already been intimated.

The truth is, as Robert Satloff, the executive director of the Washington Institute for Near East Policy, put it in a splendid op-ed in The Washington Post last week:

"Blaming the peace process impasse [diplo-speak for blaming Israeli Prime Minister Benjamin Netanyahu] for the weakening of the anti-Saddam coalition sidesteps the crass greed that motivates some, such as the French and the Russians, while it avoids facing up to America's own inadequacies that have turned off many others in the Arab world. One thing is certain -for both Western and Arab allies -the state of the peace process has almost never been a determinant of their willingness to follow America's lead vis-a-vis Iraq."

Notwithstanding this critical analysis of U.S. policy, Dr. Satloff feels constrained to attest to Bill Clinton's pro-Israel bona fides. He maintains the president has "earned the title of the most Israel-friendly chief executive in history." Closer examination of the record, however, shows that Mr. Clinton is not really pro-Israel; he is pro-Labor Party.

During the period of Labor rule - when even such rabidly anti-Israeli critics as Rowland Evans and Robert Novak were singing the praises of the Rabin-Peres governments (mostly for abandoning time-tested policies pursued previously by both Labor- and Likud-led coalitions), Mr. Clinton's support for Israel's official program could reasonably be construed as support for Israel.

When the people of Israel exercised their prerogative to reject the Labor program (despite Mr. Clinton's repeated personal interference aimed at dissuading them from doing so) and elected a government committed to a different line, however, President Clinton showed where his loyalties actually lie. Like George Bush before him, Bill Clinton is determined to undercut and, if possible, bring down a Likud-led coalition pursuing policies with which he does not agree.

Mr. Clinton's brazen and cynical disregard for the fundamentals of democracy - whether at home or abroad - are, of course, nothing new. Such behavior in this instance, though, could have particularly far-reaching repercussions. What is in prospect today as a result of Bill Clinton's broken campaign promises and interference in the internal affairs of a friendly country is nothing short of a wholesale undermining of Israel's political and physical well being.

Insult is added to injury by the fact Mr. Clinton's Bush-like policy toward the current Israeli government is unlikely even to advance his stated, mechanistic purpose of "moving the peace process forward." After all, there is little chance of "progress" toward a real peace as long as the Palestinian Arabs believe the Americans will apply further pressure on Israel so long as the Arabs declare its offerings to be unsatisfactory. To the contrary, such a dynamic simply encourages Israel's Arab interlocutors to hold out for more concessions.

In the absence of a genuine commitment on the part of the Arabs to peaceful coexistence with Israel -a commitment evident nowhere, apart from the empty rhetoric intended for Western consumption -the sorts of concessions now being demanded of Israel by the Clinton-Gore administration are at least as ominous for Israel's security as those previously sought by the Bush-Baker team. Those Jews and non-Jews alike, who appreciate better than either of these American administrations the peril confronting Israel today and the folly of forcing it to take still greater risks, must once again mobilize to achieve changes in U.S. policy through effective political action.

With Yasser Arafat's heated pronouncement following last weekend's Arab League summit that Israeli Prime Minister Ehud Barak should "go to hell," chances seem better than ever that Mr. Arafat will be responsible for taking the whole region there. He has announced he will proceed with the unilateral declaration of a Palestinian state, to which the Arab leaders pledged $800 million. That step will surely lead to a conflict with Israel of far greater proportions and lethality than the low-intensity struggle that Mr. Arafat oxymoronically calls the "peace intifada" now playing out in the streets of Gaza, the West Bank and Jerusalem.

What makes these prospects so tragic is not merely the enormous cost that will be associated with a renewed war between the Jewish State and her neighbors. It is that such an outcome was absolutely predictable given the way the Clinton-Gore administration pursued the so-called "peace process."

The truth of the matter is that this "process" was doomed from its inception, given the actual nature of Israel's purported "partner for peace" and his agenda. After all, Mr. Arafat's Palestine Liberation Organization has since 1974 formally subscribed to what it has called a "Plan of Phases."

This plan was adopted in the aftermath of the Arabs' crushing defeat by Israel in the 1973 Yom Kippur War. It effectively acknowledged an unpleasant fact of life for the Palestinians and other, sworn enemies of Israel: So long as Israel enjoyed the secure and defensible borders it obtained in the course of the penultimate Six-Day War in 1967, the Arab option of destroying the "Zionist entity" in their midst was effectively foreclosed.

Hence the Plan of Phases. Phase One would focus on the acquisition from Israel - through terrorism, coercion, international pressure and diplomacy – of territory that would be placed under the control of the Palestinians. This would change Israel's borders and in other ways diminish the Jewish State's self-defense capabilities (for example, by complicating the mobilization of Israel Defense Forces and confining their ground movements to easily interdicted roads).

Such territory would, thereafter, be used not only to create an independent Palestinian state but as the base from which Phase Two would be mounted: the ultimate liquidation of the State of Israel.

To its lasting shame and Israel's potentially mortal peril, the Clinton-Gore administration studiously ignored Arafat's abiding commitment to the Plan of Phases. It did not insist he renounce this stratagem as a price for the international legitimacy, financial assistance, armaments and other benefits (including the Nobel Peace Prize) that came the way of this unreconstructed terrorist thug by dint of his inclusion in the peace process. (Lest there be any doubt what effect such help translates into for desperate dictators, remember how the Clinton-Gore-Holbrooke decision to make Slobodan Milosevic a "partner for peace" at Dayton enabled that war criminal to stave off popular demands for his resignation for some five years, at huge expense to his own people, the Balkans and Western nations ultimately obliged to dislodge him from Kosovo?)

Worse yet, Messrs. Clinton and Gore, and a succession of like-minded Israeli leaders, have insisted in the name of the "peace process" on discounting Mr. Arafat's incessant affirmation in Arabic to his own people that the Plan of Phases remains their guiding document. They have made excuses for his calls to "jihad" or holy war. They have downplayed the clear implications of his use for official and other purposes, including in schoolchildren's textbooks, of maps showing a "Palestine" that includes all of pre-1967 Israel.

Now, Yasser Arafat is making his intentions known not just to Arabs but to all the world. As the Jerusalem Post put it in an editorial on Monday:

"Arafat told the Arab summit that the Palestinian goal is the 'establishment of our independent state on the blessed land of Palestine with holy Jerusalem as its capital, and the return of refugees based on international legitimacy resolutions, especially Resolutions 181 and 194.' These two U.N. resolutions, passed in November 1947 and December 1948, respectively, provide for an Israel even more truncated than the pre-1967 lines, and for the 'right of return' of millions of descendants of Palestinian refugees to Israel proper. These demands are in marked contrast to the 1967 and 1973 U.N. Security Council resolutions 242 and 338, which require that all states have 'secure and recognized borders' and which have been the basis of all subsequent peace agreements."

The great danger is that Mr. Arafat's increasingly brazen demands betray a conviction on the part not only of the Palestinians, but their Arab allies as well, that Phase One is now sufficiently complete to move directly to Phase Two - a renewed war of extermination against the Jewish State. There are press reports that Iraq has put four to five armored divisions in proximity to its borders with Syria and Jordan. And, despite what is being described as the triumph of the "moderate" Arab regimes during the weekend summit reaffirming, as the Jerusalem Post put it, their "strategic decision for peace, in practice . . . the summit backed Arafat's collapsing of the cycle of violence and the cycle of peace into a single process, a 'peace intifada' fought not with stones but machine guns and lynchings."

Now is the time for the U.S. government to end the ambiguity that has helped foster this phony peace process and the cycle of violence that it had to spawn - ambiguity about its support for Israel whenever that conflicts with the role of "honest broker" it has been pursuing to appease the Arabs; ambiguity about the acceptability of Mr. Arafat's Plan of Phases. Things may have already have deteriorated to the point where another war is unavoidable. By making clear our solidarity with Israel, however, we can maximize the disincentives to the Arabs contemplating the war option and the chances that Israel will prevail should her enemies once again try to destroy the Jewish State.

The plight of Israelis today calls to mind the tongue-in-cheek prayer of Tevye, the hero of "Fiddler on the Roof" who, in light of his people's suffering, asks the Almighty if someone else could be the chosen people for a while.

For years, the people of Israel have voted for leaders who promised to protect them against Arab neighbors bent on destroying the Jewish state and to eschew wooly-headed "peace processes" that advance their enemies' goal. Yet, in turn Yitzhak Rabin, Benjamin Netanyahu and Ehud Barak made a succession of concessions - most notably, legitimation of Yasser Arafat and his fellow terrorists as "partners for peace" that was at the core of the Oslo "process" - that have emboldened those who believe Israel will ultimately be dismantled and increased international demands for still more Israeli concessions.

Such pressure takes many forms. Foes like Egypt, Iran, Saudi Arabia, Libya and Syria disregard their obligations under U.N. Security Council Resolution 242, which, all too few remember, requires "termination of all claims or states of belligerency and respect for and acknowledgement of the sovereignty, territorial integrity and political independence of every state in the area and their right to live in peace within secure and recognized boundaries free from threats or acts of force."

As Shoshana Bryen of the Jewish Institute for National Security Affairs noted recently, the Arabs and Iranians instead cynically insist that Israel must first find - and pay - a price acceptable to the Palestinians. They do so knowing full well that none among the latter could make peace with the Jewish state, even if they wanted to, so long as the region's principal nations refuse to do so. These nations' totalitarian regimes offer the same excuse to justify staving off domestic and foreign calls to engage in long-overdue political and economic liberalization.

The Europeans are no less insistent the responsibility for peace rests first and foremost with Israel. To be sure, leaders like Britain's Tony Blair pay lip service to the need for an end to terrorism from the Palestinian quarter. Still, Europe seems determined to construe continued terrorism against Israel as an argument for demanding Israel swiftly resume negotiations with the Palestinians and concede the substantive points necessary to move them forward, rather than as legitimate grounds for refusing to re-enter the fraudulent "peace process."

Then there is the United Nations. The organization's domination by states hostile to Israel has made it a hotbed of agitation against the Jewish state from the get-go. While Zionism is no longer officially equated with racism by the United Nations, that sentiment remains much in evidence as Israel has been subjected to far more criticism and condemnatory resolutions than any other member state. Israel alone is ineligible for membership on the Security Council.

And an organ of the "world body," the International Court of Justice, has even ruled the Jewish state may not legally take measures to defend itself with a security barrier separating Israel and parts of the disputed West Bank where Jews live from terrorists bent on murder and destruction of property.

To their credit, President Bush and his administration have, to date, generally refrained from adding U.S. pressure on Israel to that emanating from other quarters. That may change, however. Mr. Blair is determined to be repaid for his loyalty on Iraq in the currency of "progress" toward peace in the Mideast. Best-selling author and former CIA official Michael Scheuer is among those pushing the line that U.S. support for Israel is the reason al Qaeda and other Islamofascist terrorists want to attack us. And last Sunday, former National Security Advisers Brent Scowcroft and Zbigniew Brezinzski jointly declared that the opportunity created by Arafat's death must be seized by the United States "imposing" a peace deal on Israel and the Palestinians – ignoring Winston Churchill's sound advice against weakening a strategic ally.

Washington may not have to take such a misbegotten step, however, if - as has been the case to date - the present Israeli government decides to make concessions on its own. For some time, Prime Minister Ariel Sharon has seemed more concerned with his place in history than in fulfilling the robust campaign security promises that won him the premiership.

Today, Mr. Sharon is rooting his claim to power in an embrace of Shimon Peres' Labor Party, the principal apologist for the myriad failures of Oslo and other peace processes. He is unilaterally withdrawing from the Gaza Strip, a superficially appealing and politically popular cut-your-losses move that will, unfortunately, give rise to a new haven for terrorists there (witness Sunday's attack). It will also compound the signal sent by Ehud Barak's earlier, precipitous withdrawal from Lebanon, namely that Israel's piecemeal destruction is inevitable. And Mr. Sharon is releasing terrorists and promising to pull Israeli forces from Palestinian communities as gestures to its electorate.

All this adds up to a grim forecast for the people of Israel. Their foes are implacable and being emboldened. Their "friends" at best encourage strategically dubious peace initiatives like the ill-conceived "road map"; at worst, they are part of the problem. And their leaders, both of the recent past and the present, seem intent on repeating, and compounding, past errors. Lovers of freedom can only hope all this does not add up to Tevye's prayer being answered in the worst possible way.

This is a lousy time to have a president in the White House who is, apparently, contemptuous of Winston Churchill. At this writing, President Obama was poised to meet with Israeli Prime Minister Benjamin Netanyahu on Monday, the latest in a series of efforts aimed at weakening Israel and otherwise bending it to the U.S. administration's will - a practice against which an historian/statesman like Churchill would have strenuously warned.

In his extraordinary memoir, "The Gathering Storm," the future British prime minister recalled how he had publicly pronounced in the run-up to World War II that he could not "imagine a more dangerous policy" than one then being practiced by the British government. It involved trying to appease Adolf Hitler by encouraging Britain's principal continental ally, France, to disarm - even as Nazi Germany was remilitarizing in increasingly offensive ways.

This practice was subsequently applied by both the British and French as they compelled another powerful ally, Czechoslovakia, to surrender its formidable Western defenses and military-industrial capabilities to the Nazis. The results of these misbegotten initiatives produced not peace, but an unprecedented conflagration. Extreme care should be exercised to avoid a repetition of this tragic history.

Yet, every indication is that Mr. Obama is determined to weaken Israel, America's most important and reliable ally in the Middle East, by forcing the Jewish state to surrender territory and make other strategic concessions in order to create a Palestinian state. As in the past, this weaken-your-friend approach to achieving the so-called two-state solution will not work. It will encourage, not eliminate, the abiding ambition of other nations in the region and their terrorist proxies to "wipe Israel off the map." It will actually exacerbate regional instability, not alleviate it.

Fortunately, another thoughtful student of history and accomplished statesman has come forth in Churchill's footsteps (and follows his example) by laying out a markedly different approach to the idea of creating a second state out of the 22 percent of the original mandate Palestine west of the Jordan River that was not given to the Arabs in 1922. (The other 78 percent became "Transjordan," known today simply as Jordan.)

At a Washington dinner hosted on May 6 by the Endowment for Middle East Truth, R. James Woolsey was recognized as a "speaker of the truth." In his brief acceptance address, a man who has served presidents of both parties as undersecretary of the Navy, conventional arms control negotiator and director of central intelligence laid out preconditions that must apply before there is any likelihood of a Palestinian polity with which Israel might actually be able to live "side by side in peace."

Mr. Woolsey's analysis is informed by the status Israeli Arabs enjoy in the Jewish state today. They make up roughly one-fifth of the population of Israel. They are able to have their own places of worship and schools. They are free to own and publish their own newspapers.

Israel's Arab citizens are also entitled to vote for real representation in a real legislature. Currently, they have 10 of the 120 seats in the Israeli Knesset. There is an Arab justice on the Israeli Supreme Court. And an ethnically Arab Druze holds a seat in Mr. Netanyahu's Cabinet.

Most importantly, as Mr. Woolsey notes, law-abiding Arab citizens of Israel "can go to sleep at night without having to worry that their door will be kicked down and they will be killed" by agents of the Israeli government or others among the majority Jewish population. In short, they enjoy real security as well as opportunities in a society in which Israeli Arabs are a distinct minority.

Regrettably, as Mr. Woolsey notes, the world has a tendency to "define deviancy down for non-Jews." As a result, governments around the world, including the Obama administration, never even mention the possibility that Jews should be able to enjoy the same rights and privileges in any future Palestinian polity that Israeli Arabs exercise today in the Jewish state.

So, instead of what amounts to a Hitlerian program of Judenrein in any prospective Palestinian state - meaning, as a practical matter, if not a de jure one, that no Jews can reside or work there - there could be about twice the number of Israeli Jews as currently reside in so-called settlements on the West Bank. They should be free to build synagogues and Jewish schools. And newspapers that serve the Jewish population in any future state of "Palestine" should be permitted to flourish there.

Jews should also have a chance to elect representatives to a future Palestinian legislature. They should be able to expect to be represented as well in other governing institutions, like the executive and judicial branches.

In order for the foregoing to operate, Jews in the Palestinian state must be able to live without fearing every day for their lives. In Mr. Woolsey's view, "Once Palestinians are behaving that way, they deserve a state."

By establishing full reciprocity as the prerequisite basis for a two-state solution Mr. Obama might just be able to make useful progress toward peace in the Middle East. If, however, he persists in distancing the United States from Israel and otherwise weakening the Jewish state, he will likely get war, not a durable end to hostilities. As Churchill and Mr. Woolsey might attest, no good will come of Mr. Obama ignoring history and his efforts to euchre Israel into doing the same.

From this vantage point, two events this week appear to be ominous straws in the wind, warnings of a "man-caused" maelstrom that inexorably may plunge the Middle East into another, potentially cataclysmic war.

The first is that Israel feels obliged to undertake an unprecedented, countrywide civil defense exercise this week. At one point, every man, woman and child in the Jewish state is supposed to seek shelter from a simulated attack of the kind Iran may shortly be able to execute against it.

The second is President Obama's latest effort to reach out to the Muslim world, on Thursday from one of its most important capitals, Cairo. There, he is expected to make a speech reiterating his previous statements on the subject - which, unfortunately, can only have been interpreted by his intended audience as acts of submission.

If the past is prelude, the president of the United States will: apologize yet again for purported offenses against Muslims by his country; promise to be respectful of Islam, including those who adhere to its authoritative, if virulent, theo-political-legal program known as Shariah; and enunciate diplomatic priorities and initiatives designed to reach out to America's enemies in the region while putting excruciating pressure on its most reliable ally there, Israel.

This pressure has become more palpable by the day. It has taken various forms, including: U.S. stances adopted at the United Nations that will isolate Israel; blank political and even financial checks for Palestinian thugs such as Mahmoud Abbas; diminishing U.S.-Israeli cooperation on intelligence and military matters; and the withholding from Israel of helicopters (and perhaps other weaponry) being provided to Arab states.

Perhaps the most chilling example of this coercive pressure so far, however, was reported originally in the Israeli paper Yediot Aharonot and given international prominence by my esteemed colleague and Jerusalem Post columnist Caroline Glick. According to these accounts, in a recent lecture in Washington, U.S. Army Lt. Gen. Keith Dayton, the American officer charged with training Palestinian military forces in Jordan, made a shocking declaration.

In Ms. Glick's words, Gen. Dayton "indicated that if Israel does not surrender Judea and Samaria within two years, the Palestinian forces he and his fellow American officers are now training at a cost of more than $300 million could begin killing Israelis." She noted that neither the general nor the Obama administration seemed to find this prospect grounds for rethinking the wisdom of such a training-and-arming program. In fact, her column observed that Defense Secretary Robert M. Gates "just extended Dayton's tour of duty for an additional two years and gave him the added responsibility of serving as

Obama's Middle East mediator George Mitchell's deputy."

Taken together with the U.S. administration's refusal to come to grips with what truly is the most serious threat to peace in the Middle East - Iran's rising power and growing aggressiveness, reflecting in part its incipient nuclear-weapons capabilities - the stage inexorably is being set for the next, and perhaps most devastating, regional conflict.

Whether the signals Mr. Obama is sending are intended to communicate such a message or not, they will be read by Israel's enemies as evidence of a profound rift between the United States and the Jewish state. In this part of the world, that amounts to an invitation to an open season on Israel.

It is hard to believe the Obama Middle East agenda enjoys the support of the American people or their elected representatives in Congress. Historically, the public and strong bipartisan majorities on Capitol Hill have appreciated that an Israel that shares our values, that is governed democratically and that is in the cross hairs of the same people who seek our destruction is an important ally. Quite apart from a sense of moral and religious affinity for the Jewish people's struggle to survive in their ancient homeland, most of us recognize it is in the United States' strategic interest to stand with Israel.

It is worrisome in the extreme that Mr. Obama does not appear to share this appreciation. To those who worried about his affinity for the Saudi king and Islam more generally and his long-standing ties to virulent critics of Israel such as Columbia University professor Rashid Khalidi and former Harvard professor-turned-National Security Council staffer Samantha Power, the president's attitude is not exactly a surprise.

His administration's posture may have been further reinforced by Arab-American pollster John Zogby's recent Forbes magazine article arguing that friends of Israel made up John McCain's constituency, not Mr. Obama's. (This raises an interesting question about the sentiments toward Israel of the 78 percent of American Jews who voted for the latter in 2008.)

My guess, however, is that, as the implications of Mr. Obama's Middle East policies - for the United States as well as Israel - become clearer, he will find himself facing the sort of popular and congressional revolt that has confronted him in recent weeks on Guantanamo Bay. The question is: Will such a reaffirmation of American solidarity with and support for Israel come in time to prevent the winds of war being whipped up by Mr. Obama's posturing and rhetoric - and driving Israelis into bomb shelters - from wreaking havoc in the Middle East, and perhaps far beyond?

A solemn vow has animated the people of the State of Israel and their admirers for over sixty years: "Never again." Those two words have captured a shared, steely determination to prevent another Holocaust - the genocide waged against the Jews by Nazi Germany. Today, alas, there is growing reason to fear that the operative phrase is becoming instead: "One more time."

Consider a few illustrative examples of the gathering storm that is developing in the Middle East and elsewhere, to the grave detriment of the Jewish State - and to America's vital interests:

The so-called "international community" as represented by the United Nations and its various subsidiaries has institutionalized anti-Zionism and, in the process, increasingly legitimated anti-Semitism. Israel is the target of the vast majority of UN investigations of human rights abuses and condemnatory resolutions. No other nation even comes close to the "world body's" sustained and vicious assault on one of the planet's most liberal democracies and freest societies.

The latest of such UN travesties is the denunciation of Israel produced by Sir Richard Goldstone, a South African jurist (who happens to be Jewish). The "Goldstone Report" he authored purports to be an objective analysis of the conduct of the Israelis and Palestinians when the former retaliated at last against the latter after years of rocket fire on Israel from the Gaza Strip. This odious document largely ignores the responsibility of Hamas for what happened, accuses the Jewish State of using excessive force and has encouraged international prosecution of Israelis on specious war crimes charges.

Barack Obama has had a longstanding enmity towards Israel. Under the influence of his one-time fellow University of Chicago professor Rashid Khalidi, the future president honed a sympathy for the Palestinian cause assiduously promoted by his colleague. Indeed, as far back as 2004, Mr. Obama was letting it be known that he had to subordinate public expression of his anti-Israel sentiments in order to advance politically. In a report published in March 2008, a similarly minded pro-Arab activist in Chicago, Ali Abunimah, quoted the then-Senate candidate as saying four years before, "Hey, I'm sorry I haven't said more about Palestine right now, but we are in a tough primary race. I'm hoping when things calm down I can be more up front."

Since entering the White House, Mr. Obama has been more "up front" - at least in his actions. He has pressed Israel relentlessly for territorial, political and strategic concessions to the Palestinians. He has reportedly denied Israel access to weapons, including bunker-busting bombs, even as sales of advanced arms to others in the Middle East - all of whom have tried to destroy Israel in the past - continue apace. The effect is to diminish the qualitative edge so vital to the survival of the outnumbered Jews and their state.

Most recently, President Obama seized upon an ill-timed bureaucratic announcement regarding planned housing construction within Jerusalem's city limits as a pretext for having his administration serially denounce Israel. In the name of promoting the peace process, he has thereby encouraged the Palestinians (who remain un-reconciled to a true peace with the Jewish State) to wait for him to extract concessions from the Israelis. The net result: For the first time in many years, public professions by Vice President Joe Biden to the contrary notwithstanding, there is perceptible daylight between the United States and Israel.

Nowhere is the gap between the two strategic partners more pronounced than with respect to Iran. Israel rightly perceives in the repeated threats by the regime in Tehran to "wipe Israel off the map" - and its imminent acquisition of the nuclear weapons and ballistic missiles with which to accomplish that goal - an existential threat.

President Obama claims to be determined to prevent Iran from getting "the Bomb," yet his team still seems focused primarily on "engaging" the Iranians. He has no interest in tougher domestic sanctions approved overwhelmingly by Congress and seems content to have adoption of their international counterparts blocked by the Chinese. The practical effect is to abet the mullahs in running the clock out, leaving America with no option but to try to "contain" a nuclear Iran - and Israel no prospect other than a new, genocidal attack at a time of its avowed enemy's choosing.

Even in the absence of such an attack by Iran, there is a real risk that the perceived shifts in the "correlation of forces" in the Mideast may conduce once again to the sort of threat of conventional war to "drive the Jews into the sea" that has not been seen since 1973 (perhaps this time accompanied by the use of devastating unconventional weapons).

Add to the mix published reports that General David Petraeus - one of America's most prominent military officers as the four-star commander of Central Command and a leading architect of the Iraq surge - sees the lack of progress in the Israeli-Palestinian "peace process" as a threat to American servicemen and women in his area of responsibility. Vice President Biden and other U.S. officials have seized on this analysis to claim that "Israel's intransigence could cost American lives."

In other words, Israel is a liability, not an asset. More daylight, more danger for Israel. And more evidence that it is better to be America's enemy than its friend, which is not good for our security, either.

Then there is this: Washington Post columnist Jackson Diehl disclosed on March 22 an open secret here: "Behind Obama's deliberate fight with Netanyahu last week [over Israel's Jerusalem housing decision] seemed to lie a calculation that a peace settlement will require the United States to bend or break Israel's current government." Will Israel's enemies interpret such contempt for the democratically leader of an ally as anything other than evidence it is open season on Israel?

Now is the time for all friends of freedom to give real meaning to "Never again" - before we witness a holocaust of the Jews, one more time.

In hindsight, it will probably be obvious that the missteps of the Obama administration vis a vis Israel were critical catalysts to a war that today seems ever more likely to engulf the Middle East, and perhaps the world more generally. Assuming such an outcome is neither the intention of the President and his team, nor desired by them, American course corrections must be urgently taken.

To be sure, as is often the case in the moment, a different narrative is operating. The rising tensions in the region are widely seen as the fault of the Jewish State. Most recently, Israel is being portrayed as the villain of the bloody interception of a "humanitarian flotilla" bringing relief aid to the Gaza Strip.

Before that, the Jewish State has been serially excoriated for: engaging in: "illegal" construction of homes in Jerusalem; exercising "disproportionate force" in military action in Gaza, including by some accounts "war crimes"; and being intransigent with respect to the sorts of territorial, strategic and political concessions needed to advance the "peace process" with the Palestinians.

In each case, the Obama administration has either strongly endorsed these memes or acted fecklessly to challenge them. Throughout their seventeen months in office, the President and his senior subordinates have been at pains to demonstrate a more even-handed approach to the Israeli-Palestinian conflict and to "engage" the Muslim "world."

The practical effect, however, has been to excuse, empower and embolden those hostile not just to Israel but to the United States, as well. Consider just a few ominous examples:

- The Iranian regime has understood that the Obama administration will do nothing to defeat the realization of Tehran's longstanding ambitions to acquire nuclear weapons. Instead, the United States is now focused on how it will "live with" a nuclear-armed Iran by trying to "contain" it. Meantime, the UN's International Atomic Energy Agency says Tehran has enough enriched uranium to make two atomic weapons. If true, it will be a matter of a relatively short time before such material is sufficiently processed to be ready for that purpose.

- The Syrians have, presumably at Iran's direction and with its help, transferred dangerous Scud missiles to the mullah's re-armed terrorist proxy, Hezbollah. Particularly if equipped with chemical or biological weapons (which the Syrians and Iranians have in abundance), such missiles would pose a mortal threat to Israel and her people.

- Egypt has recently conducted offensively oriented war games in the Sinai Peninsula. Their clear purpose: Honing the Egyptian military's capabilities for renewed attacks on Israel. The government of Hosni Mubarak has also failed to halt the massive network of smuggling tunnels into Gaza that are supplying another of

Iran's terrorist surrogates, Hamas, with an array of ever-more-deadly weapons in preparation for when (not if) hostilities are resumed with Israel.

- Even before last weekend's conflict over the blockade running "aid flotilla," Turkish Prime Minister Recep Tayyip Erdogan had effectively terminated the close ties Israel once had with his country. Erdogan's accelerating Islamicization of the once-secular Turkey has been accompanied by his intensifying rapprochement with Iran and Syria.

  Notably, the Turks recently joined Brazil for the transparent purpose of running interference for Tehran's nuclear weapons program. It remains to be seen whether these three nations will succeed in sabotaging Team Obama's latest bid to secure a new UN sanctions resolution against the mullahs.

- Last week, a powerful new weapon in the campaign to delegitimize the Jewish State was spawned by the Nuclear Non-Proliferation Treaty Review Conference. It mandated negotiations to start in 2012 with the aim of ridding the Middle East of nuclear weapons. Israel was the only nation named. It would also likely be the only one disarmed if the transnationalists (both the secular UN types and Shariah-adherent ones) have their way.

These developments have two things in common: First, particularly when taken together, they constitute the greatest existential threat to Israel since 1973. And second, they reflect-- and powerfully reinforce-- a growing perception that the United States has cut Israel loose.

Israel's many friends in this country - particularly a number of American Jews critical to Democratic electoral prospects this fall - finally seem to have awakened to these realities. Hence, Team Obama's feverish effort last week to have the President seen with Israeli Prime Minister Benjamin Netanyahu, a man it had humiliatingly spurned and publicly upbraided just a few months ago. (Mr. Netanyahu's decision to head home to deal with the Flotilla crisis spared both men the obvious PR challenges associated with the former making a Washington visit at this juncture.)

Unfortunately, matters have reached the point where such calculated exercises in Potemkin political rehabilitation will not suffice. Ditto rhetorical pledges of unseverable bilateral ties.

Unless and until President Obama gives comprehensive and tangible expression to America's commitment to Israel-- in terms of reliable military assistance, unstinting diplomatic support and wide latitude to act in its self-defense-- the forces that have been unleashed by him and others will assuredly translate in due course into war. It is certainly harder to do such prophylactic things today than it would have been at the outset of the Obama presidency. But such costs are nothing compared to those that will be incurred by freedom-loving people in the Middle East and elsewhere, including here, if he fails to undertake these necessary course-corrections.

In one of Team Obama's trademark Friday afternoon specials, Secretary of State John Kerry announced last week that his six rounds of shuttle diplomacy had resulted in an agreement to reconvene Israeli-Palestinian peace negotiations. As usual, the timing was appropriate for an initiative designed to garner favorable headlines, but that doesn't stand up to scrutiny.

It appears that Kerry has bought this "breakthrough" by bullying Israel into making further concessions to its Palestinian enemies, even before the talks begin. In exchange for nothing more than the Palestinians' agreement-in-principle to resume them, the Israelis will release some number of additional convicted terrorists. Never mind that the ones left in Israeli jails after numerous previous releases are, by and large, those who have most successfully and murderously attacked innocent civilians in the Jewish State.

If the Israelis once again pay this price, they must expect the same results as before: More hardened criminals unleashed to wage jihad against Israel – and against any Palestinians that might actually wish to make peace with her.

The rapturous public welcome routinely accorded these terrorists makes clear that it is such warmongers, not the peacemakers, who are blessed in the radicalized West Bank. That is even more true in Gaza, where few defy the despotic and virulently anti-Israel dictates of the Muslim Brotherhood's Palestinian franchise: the designated terrorist organization, Hamas.

For that reason, among many others, notwithstanding Kerry's ego-driven pursuit of negotiations, his purported "breakthrough" cannot produce real progress towards a genuine peace. And inevitably, pressure will begin to mount all over again for further Israeli concessions.

This pattern was evident in the immediate aftermath of the latest Friday afternoon special. Unidentified Palestinian officials promptly put out the word that Secretary Kerry had, as *The Blaze* reported, given "Palestinian Authority President Mahmoud Abbas a letter guaranteeing that new peace negotiations with Israel will be based on pre-1967 borders."

Israeli officials, including prominent politicians in Prime Minister Benjamin Netanyahu's ruling coalition, have responded sharply. They deny any agreement to use as the basis for these talks a return to the indefensible territorial boundaries that have aptly been called "Auschwitz borders." So, the new negotiations may founder before they begin.

But let's engage in a thought-experiment. Just for the purpose of discussion, consider what would happen if Israel *did* agree to surrender territory on the West Bank and Golan Heights that provides a modicum of strategic depth to the otherwise incredibly vulnerable Jewish State?

One need look no further than the emerging correlation of forces arrayed against Israel. The unmistakable reality is that it is facing the prospect for the first time in a generation of actual or prospective enemies on every side, including potentially devastating attacks from the sea.

- The most populous Arab state, Egypt, is convulsed by domestic unrest and a volatile confrontation between Islamists sworn to destroy Israel and a military that, in the past, has repeatedly tried to do so. The two nations' cold peace, enforced for decades by a demilitarized Sinai, is jeopardized as that desert peninsula is increasingly populated by al Qaeda and other jihadists itching to attack Israelis.

- Syria is wracked by civil war in which the ultimate victory of either Iranian/Hezbollah-backed Bashir Assad or the Muslim Brotherhood-al Qaeda alliance is likely to pose new threats to the long quiet, but now restive, Golan Heights. U.S. arming of the so-called "rebels" may or may not assure their triumph. But it will surely increase the danger that faction poses to Israel.

- Jordan, Lebanon and Iraq are in various stages of destabilization at the hands of Islamists of assorted stripes. Turkey is in the hands of a particularly dangerous one, Recep Tayyep Erdogan, who makes no secret of his hostility towards Israel and solidarity with its enemies. And the Islamic Republic of Iran is continuing to build the capacity to deliver an existential nuclear threat to Israel.

- As the brilliant strategic analyst and author Mark Helprin pointed out in the *Wall Street Journal* last weekend Israel can no longer take comfort in the "qualitative edge" in conventional armaments that previously enabled it to contend with numerically superior enemies: "Saudi Arabia's air force (soon 380 combat aircraft, primarily F-15s) is rapidly gaining on Israel (441 combat aircraft) in quantity and quality. Were the Saudis to take a Muslim-solidarity time-out with Iran and join Egypt, Syria and perhaps even Turkey to defeat Israel in an air war, it would mean Israel's death."

In short, this is no time for the U.S. government to be demanding that its most important, self-reliant and reliable ally in the Middle East make territorial concessions that will render it more vulnerable to attack from one, or more, of the aforementioned quarters. That is especially so given that such concessions have *no* prospect of translating into an enduring peace with all, or even most, of the Palestinians.

It is neither in the Israelis' interest nor our own that they weaken themselves further in the face of the region's burgeoning shariah-driven religio-politico-cultural dynamic, one that is feeding their enemies' unrequited ambition to "drive the Jews into the sea."

John Kerry's vainglorious diplomacy has thus far done nothing to mitigate that dynamic. If anything, his sympathies and those of President Obama towards the Muslim Brotherhood are feeding it. We must not permit such folly to continue to intensify Israel's peril, and our own.

Energy Security

The past 10 day's events made one thing, as Richard Nixon used to say, perfectly clear: The "Great Game" is on once again in the strategically critical and increasingly turbulent Caspian Sea Basin.

In previous eras, that term has been used to describe the periodic struggles in this region between great powers competing for territory, resources and influence. The stakes are today higher then ever before. By some estimates, the Caspian Basin is the locus of between 100 billion and 200 billion barrels of oil and natural gas deposits that could total more than those of the North Sea and Alaska's North Slope combined. Figured conservatively at today's prices, this equates to between $2 trillion and $4 trillion worth of exploitable hydrocarbon assets - a figure that does not include the tens of billions of dollars that will ultimately be invested in the region for the infrastructure needed to extract and transport these resources.

Until very recently, official Washington has been on the sidelines of the momentous contest taking place to shape, if not control, the destiny of the Caspian Basin. In its absence, Russia, China and Iran have been jockeying for position. Russia, in particular, has been employing every tool at its disposal -from financial incentives (including bribes) to violent intimidation (notably, via the arming of proxy forces to destabilize or coerce those in the region) to realize Moscow's goal of dominating the exploitation of Caspian oil.

Perhaps the most egregious example of the latter has been the assistance Russia has provided to Armenian military operations against neighboring Azerbaijan and the contested Azerbaijani enclave of Nagorno-Karabakh. Thanks to copious quantities of everything from Russian-made small arms to deadly missiles, Armenia has wrested substantial territory from Azerbaijan while imposing enormous economic hardship on a nation ill-equipped to contend with the needs of hundreds of thousands of refugees.

These actions have afforded Russia leverage on the one oil-rich nation in the Caspian Basin intent on pursuing a pro-Western course. Azerbaijan has made clear its desire to do business with American petroleum firms and has sought repeatedly to develop cordial diplomatic and military ties with the United States. Here too Russia's machinations in Armenia have proved helpful to the Kremlin: Citing the conflict between Azerbaijan and Armenia, the politically well-connected Armenian-American community has prevailed on successive U.S. Congresses to bar the provision even of direct humanitarian assistance to Baku - something for which a pariah state like North Korea is eligible.

The Clinton administration's reflexive deference to Moscow has only slowly begun to give way to an appreciation that an economically successful, pro-Western and secular Muslim state in Azerbaijan is in the U.S. interest, even if it is not in the Kremlin's. As a result, none other than the chief architect of Mr. Clinton's Russo-centric policy, Deputy Secretary of State Strobe Talbott, was heard last week emphasizing the importance of improved American ties with Azerbaijan, calling for the repeal of the legislation (Section 907 of the Freedom Support Act of 1992) that effectively makes impossible any direct U.S. involvement with Azerbaijan and warning Russia against "infringement on the independence of its neighbors."

Mr. Talbott's speech was only one of the indications that Washington is finally awakening to what is at stake in the Transcaucasus and Caspian Basin. Sen. Sam Brownback, chairman of the Foreign Relations Mideast subcommittee recently traveled to Baku and returned determined to recast U.S.-Azerbaijan relations. Within the past few days, the senator: introduced a Sense of the Senate resolution calling for a more balanced American policy toward the Southern Caucasus and Central Asia; made a major address of his own on the subject at the Heritage Foundation; and convened important hearings into U.S. geopolitical, strategic and economic interests in the region. Forceful testimony taken from, among others, former Defense Secretary Caspar Weinberger, is expected shortly to result in further legislative recommendations for corrective action.

Perhaps most importantly, the administration has finally seen its way clear to invite President Aliyev to make an official visit to Washington, complete with luncheon with Mr. Clinton. It can only be hoped that this occasion will mark the beginning of what Humphrey Bogart once called "a beautiful friendship" - replete with more active U.S. leadership in ending the Armenian-Azerbaijani conflict, alleviating its counterproductive repercussions for relations between this country and Azerbaijan and introducing a new, and far more engaged, American policy in the region.

Such a policy is all the more necessary in the wake of the Clinton administration's deplorable announcement on Monday that it would have no objection to the construction of a $1.6 billion pipeline to carry natural gas from Turkmenistan to Turkey via Iran. This step will not only unmistakably signal an American willingness to ease Iran's international isolation under circumstances in which that is still most ill-advised. It also will serve to facilitate Tehran's ambition to penetrate and exercise influence over the Caspian Sea Basin.

The United States needs to bend every effort to finding the means to bring the oil and gas resources of the Caspian Sea Basin to market through routes that will not enrich the Iranians, or, for that matter, the Russians or Chinese, and that are not subject to possible coercive manipulation by such powers. The obvious place to start is by forging a strong strategic partnership with Azerbaijan - the best hope that an independent, pro-Western state will survive the current, deadly iteration of the Great Game - and nurturing regional arrangements that will permit its hydrocarbon assets to transit safely to Turkey's Mediterranean coast, via Georgia.

Winston Churchill once wrote "safety and certainty in oil lies in variety and variety alone." The gasoline crisis after Hurricane Katrina vividly demonstrated the U.S. transportation energy sector's major structural flaw: lack of variety.

With 96 percent of our transportation energy petroleum-based, every time our oil supply is severed or a refinery goes off-line, there is nothing to stop gasoline, diesel and jet fuel prices from going through the ceiling. For a country that offers choice in every aspect of our life, the absence at the pump of anything to fuel our cars other than petroleum speaks volumes about how deeply dependent the nation depends on one energy source: oil.

For decades, advocates of energy independence have called for Detroit to produce fuel-efficient vehicles so less gasoline is used. For various political and economic reasons, this approach has failed. There are, however, ways for the U.S. to insulate its economy from future supply shocks without forcing Detroit to "reinvent the wheel" - or obliging the country to adopt costly infrastructure changes.

If we want to insulate ourselves better from oil supply disruptions – which have thus far precipitated every recession since World War II - we should seek simpler and faster ways to introduce variety in the types of fuel the transportation sector can utilize.

One such way is clear: Since 1996, America's auto manufacturers have produced and sold roughly 4 million flexible fuel vehicles (FFV) designed to burn gasoline, alcohol (ethanol and methanol) or any mixture of the two. Yet, outside the Midwest - where ethanol is widely available - many people who drive FFVs are not even aware of their cars' ability to use something other than gasoline. For an auto manufacturer adding fuel flexibility to a new vehicle costs as little as $150 per car, less than the price of a CD player. All it takes is a different fuel sensor and corrosion-resistant fuel line.

Were every new car sold in the U.S. a flexible fuel vehicle, within a decade half of our fleet could run on fuels other than gasoline. This doesn't mean drivers would have to utilize those other fuels if oil prices declined. But if oil prices continue soaring, as many predict, blending increasingly higher ratios of alcohol would be our best option when supply falters.

The model of a fuel choice economy already exists in Brazil, a nation with vast sugar cane resources and, therefore, the capacity to produce ethanol efficiently and inexpensively. Since the 1973 oil embargo, Brazil has built an impressive fleet of FFVs. By 2008, almost all new cars sold in Brazil will be flexible fuel vehicles. Even now, most Brazilian cars use at least 25 percent ethanol and many as much as 100 percent ethanol.

Bringing hydrocarbons and carbohydrates to coexist in the same fuel tank has insulated the Brazilian economy from the harmful effect of the current spike in oil prices.

Unfortunately, the American corn-based ethanol market is too small to supply the entire nation's fleet with such high blends. Matters are worsened by a congressionally imposed stiff tariff of 54 cents per gallon on imported ethanol to protect domestic corn growers, sugar producers and ethanol refiners. During a war and energy emergency, we must open the ethanol market to foreign imports and remove the tariff.

Brazil, the Saudi Arabia of sugar, already exports a half-billion gallons of ethanol a year. It could supply the United States upon request with relatively cheap ethanol. In addition, the economies of our Caribbean neighbors – all low-cost sugar producers - and our own would benefit if we encouraged them to turn their sugar into ethanol.

The answer to our energy woes is manifestly not increased reliance on the Saudis and other members of the Organization of Petroleum Exporting Countries. Rather, it is to diversify our sources of transportation fuels. In addition to relying on neighbors for help with manufacturing ethanol, we have the capacity to produce large quantities of methanol here at home from coal, agricultural waste and natural gas and to make diesel fuel from coal, agricultural and animal waste products. For that matter, electricity, which unlike 30 years ago the U.S. essentially no longer generates from petroleum, can also be made an important and cost-effective transportation fuel. Expanding our fuel choice to include such fuels will help protect our economy and security the next time Mother Nature or terrorists strike.

While the recently passed energy bill did little to encourage ramping up production of such alternative fuels or the vehicles that can utilize them, the current crisis gives Congress both an opportunity and an obligation to act. Now is the time to introduce simple, yet effective, policy solutions offering fuel choice at relatively low cost.

A new Oil and National Security Caucus will be inaugurated next week in the House to advance such initiatives. Taking such steps now - for starters, by making flexible fuel designs an industry standard, just like seatbelts and airbags - we can provide the American people with a valuable insurance policy to deal with oil shocks certain to occur in our future.

Meltdown in the financial sector. Recent spikes in oil prices. Democratic electoral gains throughout Washington, made possible in part by the political muscle of organized labor. Add it all up, what have you got? A perfect storm that will surely translate into an infusion of billions more in taxpayer life-support for the seriously - possibly terminally - ill U.S. carmakers.

Such an outcome may not happen during this week's lame duck session of the expiring 110th Congress. In fact, the smart money says enough Republican legislators will find offensive the idea of throwing good money after bad that they will preclude passage in the Senate this year of any bailout for Detroit that the Democrats manage to cobble together.

Even so, the increased numbers of Democratic legislators who will make up the 111th Congress and the evident support of the incoming Obama administration essentially assures there will be a rescue package for Ford, General Motors and Chrysler, known collectively as "the autos." The only question is what are its terms - how much money, how few strings and how long it will stave off the inevitable: the restructuring, downsizing and retooling of what used to be known as the "Big Three"?

At this writing, it seems likely that, come next year, economic conditions in general and those of the U.S. automakers (not to be confused with American-based manufacturing operations of their foreign competitors) will translate into relief for Detroit. "Too big to fail," too many jobs at stake, too much of the nation's manufacturing capability at risk are among the considerations that will justify government intervention on a massive scale.

The effect will probably be to perpetuate, rather than alleviate - let alone eliminate, the myriad problems that afflict Ford, GM and Chrysler. Until the effects of this bailout diminish, management changes may or may not be made. Inefficient facilities may or may not be shuttered. Turning the Big Three into the not-so-Big Two will or won't happen.

Unless the costs associated with producing American vehicles in union shops are dramatically reduced and there is a turnaround in the appeal of such cars and trucks to consumers buying fewer of them from anybody, the writing is on the wall: No amount of largess at the taxpayer's expense will stave off the autos' inevitable downsizing, job loss and economic dislocation.

One thing might make a difference in alleviating these bleak prospects and, if integrated into the coming rescue package for Detroit, even justify such an intervention: Tie the bailout to the adoption of a new "Open Fuel Standard" (OFS) that would have the effect of giving U.S. automakers a distinct, near-term competitive advantage, while making a giant leap on one of our most important national security challenges - energy security.

The idea is straightforward. The Big Three have produced approximately 6 million vehicles now on America's highways that are equipped with what is known as a Flexible

Fuel Vehicle (FFV) capability. FFVs can be configured to run on ethanol or methanol - fuels that can be manufactured from a variety of sources that we have here in abundance - or on gasoline, or some combination of the three.

The American auto manufacturers have also produced many more such vehicles for the Brazilian market where an OFS is effectively the law of the land, ensuring that all new cars offer consumers "fuel choice."

Brazil's experience is instructive. Where fuel competition is afforded and the monopoly gasoline currently enjoys in the United States is broken, the costs of powering the transportation sector are dramatically reduced. What's more important, billions of dollars that might otherwise go to purchase oil from sources that are unstable at best and unfriendly at worst can be kept at home.

During the recent presidential campaign, both Barack Obama and John McCain endorsed the concept of an Open Fuel Standard. Legislation that would institute it has been introduced on a bipartisan basis in both the House and Senate (H.R. 6559 and S. 3303, respectively).

By incorporating the bills' requirement that, by 2012, 50 percent of all new cars sold in this country be Flexible Fuel Vehicles - which Detroit's auto companies have already committed and are planning to do - we can begin weaning America off of our cars' current, absolute addiction to oil. The legislation would require that by 2015, a further 30 percent of these fleets be equipped with FFV technology, something that today costs less than $100 per car.

Imagine President Obama as one of his first initiatives formally embracing the Open Fuel Standard, rewarding Detroit for taking a step that is highly desirable from both an environmental and national security perspective with a bailout tied to the imposition of such a standard on both domestic and foreign cars. The new chief executive could inspire his people and advance his stated agenda of achieving energy independence by calling on the American people to purchase a vehicle with FFV capability. Until foreign manufacturers retool and conform to the Open Fuel Standard, most of those FFVs will be sold by the Big Three - a shot in the arm for them, our economy and the national interest more generally.

An additional benefit for an Obama administration concerned with alleviating world poverty is that the adoption by this country of an Open Fuel Standard will have the effect of establishing it as a global standard. Car manufacturers will sell their FFVs all over the world, enabling about 100 countries to grow the fuels they need to power them, ending their dependence on foreign oil and reducing dramatically the petro-wealth transfers being used by freedom's enemies to our collective detriment.

Call it the silver lining of the autos' perfect storm.

Mark Twain is usually credited with the quip that "Everybody talks about the weather, but nobody does anything about it." The same is certainly true of our dependence on foreign, and often unfriendly, sources of energy – particularly when gas prices soar and every American feels the pinch.

The difference, of course, is that we actually could do something about energy freedom – a status that might not render us totally independent of all foreign sources of oil, but that would leave us vastly less dependent than we are today and, therefore, far more secure.

But will we? Or more precisely, will be before it becomes absolutely necessary to do so?

Obviously, we will take whatever steps are necessary once imported oil ceases, for whatever reason, to be available in the quantities or at prices to which we are accustomed. At that point, we will have no choice but to wean ourselves from a costly and strategically reckless dependency on such fuel.

But achieving such energy freedom at that point will be much more difficult and entail much more hardship than if we do it before such a dreaded – but absolutely predictable – calamity befalls us. Whether as a result of actions taken by terrorists or their state-sponsors, by an OPEC oil cartel likely to come increasingly under the sway of rabidly anti-American Islamists like the Muslim Brotherhood and their allies in Iran, or by Mother Nature, the only responsible working assumption has to be the following: At some point, there will be serious shortfalls in supplies of foreign energy and far higher prices associated with obtaining whatever continues to be available.

President Obama has only made this problem worse with his administration's decisions to: limit exploration and exploitation of offshore and Arctic oil deposits; block a pipeline that would tap oil from Canadian shale – a foreign source, to be sure, but a far more reliable one than those of Saudi Arabia and other OPEC suppliers; and his release of 30 million barrels from the Strategic Petroleum Reserve, which had no enduring effect on either the price of oil or its availability, but reduced our cushion against the aforementioned day of reckoning.

The good news is that we can dramatically increase our energy self-sufficiency in the transportation sector where we currently consume 70 percent of the oil, some two-thirds of which is imported. All it will take is to equip our vehicles to use fuels we have, or can readily make, in abundance.

Such fuels include natural gas, methanol (which can be produced from anything with carbon in it, including natural gas and coal) and ethanol (which can be generated from sources other than corn, particularly as cellulosic technologies come on stream). Already, thanks to the price differentials between these American-available fuels on the one hand,

and gasoline and diesel obtained from oil on the other, there is a growing interest on the part of consumers and businesses in having what has been called "fuel choice" – the ability to use alternatives to oil-based transportation fuels, as well as those derived from petroleum.

Some believe that market forces alone will give the American public such energy freedom. When oil prices are high, that confidence seems warranted. Unfortunately, history suggests that whenever the nation contemplates serious actions to reduce its addiction to petroleum, OPEC steps in to manipulate the market and keep us hooked.

Even if that were not the case, waiting for the private sector to act in a comprehensive and sustained fashion sufficient to reduce our vulnerabilities to disruptions in our energy supplies from overseas is a formula for being overtaken by such disruptions. Simply put, we cannot afford to wait for the market to provide energy freedom.

The federal government can and should play a catalytic role in affording the public fuel choice. It need not tell them what kind of fuel to use, just help ensure that they and the U.S. transportation sector can use something other than oil-based products.

For example, a federal requirement that new cars sold in America be capable of using methanol and ethanol, as well as gasoline, would create markets for such alcohol-based fuels and competition that will drive down gas prices. Some recoil at the idea of such a government "mandate" as is contained in the bipartisan Open Fuel Standard Act (H.R. 1687). But, such a capability is very inexpensive to include in new cars and, as President Reagan's National Security Advisor, Robert "Bud" McFarlane, wrote last week in the Wall Street Journal: "Neglecting to require auto companies to open their vehicles to fuel competition is to mandate a continued monopoly by oil."

Another sensible step would be for the government to encourage the manufacture of big trucks powered by natural gas. My friend Boone Pickens has proposed tax credits that would incentivize industry to produce 140,000 such trucks. While some libertarians rail against the bill Mr. Pickens supports, the NAT Gas Act (H.R. 1380) for including what they characterize as "subsidies," no less a small-government man than Rep. Ron Paul (R-TX) endorses it. He draws a sensible distinction between subsidies that amount to "government taking money from people and giving it to a favored interest" and incentives that allow "industries, businesses and individuals…to keep more of the money they have earned."

It's time to stop talking and start securing energy freedom.

Economic Security

The Clinton transition team has made clear the president-elect's intention to create as one of his first initiatives a new Economic Security Council (ESC). If we are lucky, the ESC will actually give due weight to economic security issues. This would represent a significant break with Bush administration policies that frequently pursued narrow, parochial economic interests despite their adverse strategic implications for the nation as a whole.

This practice has been particularly evident in Bush decisions about the transfer of sensitive dual-use technologies to potential adversaries. While reports concerning the sale of strategic equipment and know-how to Saddam Hussein (including some of value to his nuclear weapons program) prior to Iraq's invasion of Kuwait have been particularly titillating, the lax attitude reflected in such transfers has of late become the rule - not the exception to it.

Indeed, the outgoing administration has presided over the virtual dismantling of the multilateral export control regime known as COCOM. It did so thanks largely to intense pressure from Germany and other allies – nations prepared to sell just about anything to anyone.

The lengths to which allied governments have been prepared to go in accommodating their exporters' desires for dangerous overseas sales has recently been on vivid display in Great Britain. The government of Prime Minister John Major is reeling from revelations that he and other Cabinet officers knew a British company, Matrix-Churchill Ltd., was supplying Iraq with an array of technologies applicable to building, among other things, weapons of mass destruction. In fact, it has been established that Her Majesty's Government actually intervened on several occasions to facilitate such transfers.

While the British may have been uniquely (and incomprehensibly) maladroit in putting the government's role in such transactions on public display, they are hardly alone in aiding and abetting traffic in sensitive dual-use technologies to dangerous actors around the world. The German, French and Italian governments have been every bit as assiduous in promoting their respective corporations' interests at the expense of the world's stake in keeping chemical, biological and nuclear weapons-related technology out of unfriendly hands.

U.S. exporters meanwhile, understandably concerned about losing international market shares to foreign competitors, have become a powerful domestic lobby in favor of the removal of many sensitive technologies from COCOM's export control list. Like our leading allies, these American business interests have generally found constraints on strategic trade to be inconvenient. They seized upon the "end of the Cold War" to argue forcefully that the multilateral technology control arrangements forged during its heyday should now be dispensed with.

Unfortunately, one fact of life about the so-called post-Cold War world should now be obvious to Western governments - even if those with a vested interest in unconstrained exports refuse to recognize it: The threat posed by the proliferation of militarily relevant technologies has, if anything, been exacerbated by the breakup of the Soviet Union. It certainly has not been not ended by it.

The ascendancy in Russia of "Civic Union" - the self-styled "centrist reformers" who actually represent the last bastion of central economic control and communist orthodoxy, the Soviet military-industrial complex - means that dual-use technology flowing to Moscow will surely wind up in the wrong hands. That will be the case even if, against all odds, such equipment and know-how miraculously does not translate into a more sophisticated and menacing Russian military.

It will, in any event, be sold for hard currency to other malevolent actors in Iran, Libya, Syria, China, North Korea, Cuba, etc. After all, militarily relevant high technology is just about the only commodity the former Soviet republics can export at the moment. Its value is all the greater if it has Western origins.

Under these circumstances, it is ludicrous to believe that Russia and the other Soviet successor states will institute and enforce stringent export controls that might preclude such profitable transactions. And yet, this is the premise upon which the United States and its COCOM partners have invited the former U.S.S.R. "inside the tent."

At a recent meeting in Paris, the ex-Soviets were for the first time permitted to participate in deliberations about the West's export control policies. The practical effect of this step will be to make it vastly more difficult for COCOM in the future to adopt controls that would deny technology transfers to those states. In exchange for this extraordinary concession, the Soviet successor states were obliged to do little more than make a vacuous commitment to exercise greater control over their own dual-use technology exports.

If President Clinton is as concerned about the growing danger posed by proliferation of weapons of mass destruction as Candidate Clinton claimed to be, a first order of business for his Economic Security Council should be to take a fresh look at the Bush policy in the area of export controls. A review should consider not only the wisdom of liberalized trade in strategic technologies to Russia under present and prospective circumstances, however. It also should assay the wisdom of other proposed transfers of sensitive dual-use technology.

These include selling communist China the $2 billion in advanced semiconductor manufacturing technology Beijing seeks - a dubious proposition on both commercial and strategic grounds. It also should entail a review of the advisability of permitting the sale of sophisticated U.S. surveillance satellites to nations like Spain, the United Arab Emirates and South Korea.

An early indication of Mr. Clinton's abilities in managing the nation's international relations and striking a prudent balance between competing economic and national security interests will be found in his approach to these and other export control questions. We can only hope his stewardship in this area will be more visionary than that of his predecessor.

The new Bush-Cheney team has rightly made rebuilding the U.S. military one of its top priorities.

Unfortunately, its predecessor's legacy is not only one of leaving the armed forces in a deplorable state requiring such repairs; Bill Clinton and Al Gore also did much to diminish - and, in many cases, to eliminate altogether – the defense industrial base that will be needed to effect the rebuilding.

This was not, as the Leninists say, "an accident, comrade." Early in the first Clinton administration, then-Defense Secretary Les Aspin convened what came to be known as the Last Supper for the nation's defense contractors. He advised them there would not be enough work for all of them in the post-Cold War future. They were put on notice that there was going to have to be a significant contraction in the number and production capacity of their firms.

In the years that followed, some went out of the defense business; many others were gobbled up by a few conglomerates. Recent, grievous depreciation of stock values imperils the viability of one or more of even these giant concerns.

Perhaps even more troubling was the encouragement the Clinton team gave to foreign acquisition of U.S. defense contractors. This practice often conduced to the transfer of key research and development and manufacturing capabilities overseas - further exacerbating the worrisome trend toward ever-greater Pentagon dependence on overseas suppliers for its gear. At the Conservative Political Action Conference last Friday, Elaine Donnelly of the Center for Military Readiness, pointed out a relatively benign, if absurd, example this phenomenon: the black berets the Army has decided to issue to all its soldiers – despite nearly universal opposition to the idea of degrading this traditional symbol of the service's elite Ranger units - will be bought from Communist China.

Unfortunately, there are many other instances in which far more sensitive military requirements are becoming reliant upon foreign manufacturers. These include: precision gears and gear boxes; certain types of sophisticated microchips used in guidance systems and other weapons applications; pan carbon fiber, the precursor to "stealth" composites; and computer monitors and printed circuit boards. There are obvious national security implications involved in having U.S. combat capabilities depend to a critical degree on companies - and, in some cases at least, countries - who may not prove reliable suppliers in time of need. As the military increasingly turns to commercial off-the-shelf technologies, this trend will only grow.

Matters are made still worse by another consideration: Foreign purveyors of sensitive dual-use technology (that is, equipment and know-how relevant to both military and civil applications) are, as a general rule, willing to sell their goods not only to the United States but to the military-industrial complexes of U.S. enemies, as well.

The Clinton Defense Department's response to such developments was like that of Mad Magazine's Alfred E. Neuman: "What, me worry?" To the extent the subject received any policy consideration at all, the administration's willingness to promote trade and "globalization" at the expense of American sovereignty and prudent security practices usually was sufficient to trump misgivings expressed by more sober policy-makers in the executive branch and Congress.

Today, Clinton appointees who have burrowed into various agencies around town, including notably Pentagon official David Tarbell, will be meeting in the hope of adding yet another U.S. technology of critical importance to the American military to the list of foreign-supplied equipment. This afternoon, the Committee on Foreign Investment in the United States (CFIUS) will hold discussions with representatives of the Netherlands' company known as ASML, the world's second-largest manufacturer of lithography machines used to produce high-quality silicon chips. ASML is trying to buy Silicon Valley Group (SVG) - the planet's most creative innovator in lithography technology and the last American supplier of such equipment. If approved by CFIUS, the Dutch would also pick up SVG's subsidiary, Tinsley Laboratories, which manufacturers state-of-the art mirrors and lenses for the nation's spy satellites and other military users.

Without assured access to the fruits of the work done by SVG and Tinsley, such priority Bush programs as effective missile defenses and information-based "revolutionary" weaponry would be rendered problematic. Should ASML wind up selling these companies' high-tech products to China - as the Dutch (and many others) have done - moreover, such technology could well wind up being used against American personnel and interests.

A growing chorus from Capitol Hill, led by Sen. Robert Bennett, Utah Republican, and Reps. Jim Gibbons, Nevada Republican, and Duncan Hunter, California Republican, is calling on the Bush administration to take charge of the CFIUS process on the SVG deal. This can most easily be done by taking another 45 days to conduct a more formal investigation of this proposed transaction. This would, in addition, afford Donald Rumsfeld and his counterparts at other agencies a chance to put in place subordinates who share their commitment to rebuilding, rather than selling off, America's defense capabilities. As today's meeting of the CFIUS will underscore, there isn't a moment to lose.

As America grapples with a two-front challenge - the global war on terror and the need to reinvigorate the U.S. economy - its leaders are hoping that expanded international trade can help solve both problems.

Unfortunately, if the machinations of the Chinese conglomerate Hutchison Whampoa are any indicator, an indiscriminate approach to trading with potential enemies could cost the United States dearly on both fronts.

Recent debates over granting President Bush Trade Promotion Authority [TPA], according Communist China permanent "Normal Trade Relations" status and permitting taxpayer subsidized trade with Cuba have all implicitly, if not explicitly, shared a dubious conviction: Since overseas commerce is an inherently good thing, the more of it the better.

This sentiment takes an extreme form among those who favor what might be called a "trade uber alles" philosophy. These advocates tend to be less than sensitive, to put it charitably, to the potential national security risks associated with putting their philosophy into practice. Even the relatively tangible repercussions - such as the loss of indigenous industrial capability and the attendant, increased reliance on foreign suppliers for key components of weapon systems - are typically dismissed, or at least subordinated to the perceived greater good of developing globalized relationships with trading partners.

To be sure, the most doctrinaire of Free Traders typically try to conceal their insouciance about the defense implications of their policies.

They often assert that trading with authoritarian regimes that are either our enemies today or that might become foes in the future can be safely undertaken since it will inexorably transform them by creating a middle class imbued with capitalist impulses and, in due course, with irresistible democratic aspirations.

This thesis may even be true in the long run. The problem is that in the short- to medium-term, ill-advised trading with potential adversaries can serve not only to prop up their regimes, but afford them opportunities to do us great harm.

A case in point would appear to be Hutchison Whampoa, a Hong Kong-based commercial empire founded and largely owned by a Chinese multibillionaire named Li Ka-shing. Li, who U.S. intelligence believes is closely tied to the communist leadership in Beijing, has turned Hutchison into a global colossus described in a recent company press release as having "over 120,000 employees worldwide, operat[ing] and invest[ing] in five core businesses in 37 countries: telecommunications; ports and related services; property and hotels; retail and manufacturing; and energy and infrastructure."

As noted in this space last month, one of Hutchison's subsidiaries secured long-term leases at either end of the Panama Canal two years ago and is currently hard at work acquiring a presence for China at other strategic "choke points" around the world, including notably the Caribbean's Bahamas, the Mediterranean's Malta and the Persian Gulf's Straits of Hormuz. At a moment inconvenient to the United States, such access could translate into physical or other obstacles to our use of such waterways.

An even more troubling prospect arises from a bid Hutchison Whampoa and two partners [one an American company called Savi Technology] are making to win U.S. government contracts to enhance security at American ports. The lack of such security is widely understood to be one of the most serious vulnerabilities facing those charged with homeland defense. Turning over the design of a cargo-monitoring system to a company closely tied to the regime in Beijing could mean affording the latter insights into how that system can be defeated.

It would be decidedly in the interest of the Chinese People's Liberation Army and its clients - which include all the world's terrorist-sponsoring states – to know how to circumvent the techniques used by the United States to protect American harbors from deadly attacks using containers and/or the vessels that transport them. But it is certainly not in our interest.

The same probably can be said of Hutchison Whampoa's just-announced purchase of a 61.5 percent majority interest in the bankrupt Bermuda-based telecommunications firm, Global Crossing Ltd. Global Crossing was the original winner of a 10-year, $450 million contract to operate a high-speed classified research network for Pentagon scientists. After the company went belly up, WorldCom got the deal last April.

Even before the latter's corporate financial meltdown, however, Global Crossing and other telecommunications companies were demanding that the award be reconsidered. With Li Ka-Shing's infusion of $250 million into Global Crossing, it may be seen as a viable competitor, assuming security considerations are not allowed to get in the way. And why should they? If Mr. Li and his friends are considered a safe enough bet to be put in charge of monitoring what is coming into our ports, how could anybody object to fiber optic cables he controls being used as the conduit for classified Defense Department secrets?

There is surely a place for genuinely free and fair trade in America's war on terror. Those who are truly, as President Bush put it, "with us" in that war should be among the beneficiaries of our efforts to maximize reciprocal access to markets. However, some 30 years of ever-expanding Chinese opportunities to sell in the United States have yet to translate into comparable opportunities for American companies in the PRC - let alone transformed the government in Beijing into one that is reliably on our side in the present global conflict, to say nothing of democratic.

Trade uber alles means, by definition, subordinating national security considerations to the ambitions of those who seek profits through commerce. In a time of war like the present, we simply cannot afford to pursue such a policy to its illogical, and potentially highly destructive, conclusion.

American relations with the world's largest democracy, India, were much in the news last week. Secretary of State Condoleezza Rice made a stop in New Delhi, and spoke enthusiastically about the two countries' shared values and improving ties. Shortly after, confidence in both were shaken when an American company's plant in India was sacked by demonstrators angry that a prominent Indian politician (who happens to be Hindu extremist associated with past sectarian violence) was denied a visa to tour the United States.

Another story that could have far-reaching and possibly very adverse implications for Indo-American relations went nearly unremarked, however – apart from attention from CNN's Lou Dobbs and his intrepid investigative staff: The impending transfer, at fire-sale prices, of a strategically vital, American-owned global fiber-optic network to an Indian concern with close ties to its government and military. The Indians appreciate owning such a network, built out over four years at a cost of some $3.4 billion, is an essential building block to commercial pre-eminence in the 21st century. The growing demands of the U.S. military for the bandwidth necessary to transfer in a secure fashion immense quantities of video and other data in real-time to commanders and forces all over the world transform this fiber optic infrastructure being sold by Tyco into something else altogether - a force-multiplier of immeasurable value.

That would, of course, only be true if two conditions apply:

(1) The owners of the fiber-optic network are willing to have our armed forces utilize their cable. It is noteworthy that the Indian company trying to buy the Tyco infrastructure, VSNL, several years ago refused to allow a fiber-optic connection to be made to the U.S. base at Diego Garcia.

(2) The U.S. military must have confidence its message traffic will not be intercepted. The beauty of fiber-optic communications systems is that they are very hard to penetrate - unless, that is, you own the infrastructure and, therefore, physically control its cable lines. If the next owner of Tyco's global network is a company 26 percent owned by the Indian government and a major supplier to India's military and intelligence services, the Pentagon could not be sure its "mail" will not be read by potentially unfriendly eyes.

Strategically minded national security types hope India will prove in the future a reliable, democratic friend of the United States. But, it could turn out otherwise. While the Indians have as much, if not more, to fear from China's increasing power-projection capabilities and expansionist ambitions, growing trade and warming political relations between the two emerging giants may obscure that danger. There are also worrying Indian energy partnerships being formed with Iran, even as India has retained close Kremlin ties forged during the Cold War.

In short, the United States cannot afford to view the proposed sale of the Tyco Global Network as it has too many similar fire sales of sensitive American-owned assets in recent years (including, notably, IBM's transfer to Communist China of its personal computer division). It is not merely another commercial transaction, one in which vital U.S. economic and national security interests will be assured by whatever outcomes are determined by globalized market forces.

For example, the reported price of $130 million would be less than a third what it will cost the Defense Department just to provide secure, high-bandwidth fiber-optic links between various components of the nation's new missile defense system in the South Pacific, Alaska and the continental United States. The cost is unclear if the U.S. military must replicate the full Tyco network - even if it can obtain the myriad approvals required from other countries to do so.

Unfortunately, at present, the only impediments to the early transfer of a true national asset to a potentially problematic foreign owner are two, all too often pro forma bureaucratic exercises: the grant of a Federal Communications Commission license to transfer ownership and a possible Committee on Foreign Investment in the United States (CFIUS) review.

Last Thursday, the FCC agreed to consider VSNL's request for the former under "streamlined" procedures. Whether the secretive CFIUS is even considering this sale is now unknown. Even if it is, the committee has scarcely ever rejected such transactions. This is hardly a surprise, given that CFIUS is chaired by the Treasury Department - an agency charged with encouraging the repatriation of U.S. dollars by selling American properties to foreign investors.

In the Tyco Global Network case, though, too much is riding on the outcome to allow this national asset to be turned over to non-American owners without real and rigorous adult supervision. The executive branch and, if necessary, Congress should consider alternative arrangements to preserve full, unrestricted and secure U.S. use of this fiber-optic infrastructure - not least by the American military.

There are ample reasons to want improved relations between the world's most powerful democracy and its most populous one. Fortunately, there are also plenty of ways to do that without holding a fire sale to India of one of this country's strategic assets and true national treasures.

How would you feel if, in the aftermath of September 11, 2001, the U.S. government had decided to contract out airport security to the United Arab Emirates (UAE), the country where most of the operational planning and financing of the attacks occurred?

My guess is you, like most Americans, would think it a lunatic idea, one that could clear the way for still more terror in this country. You probably would want to know who on earth approved such a plan - and be determined to prevent it.

Of course, no such thing occurred after September 11. In fact, the job of keeping our planes and the flying public secure was deemed so important the government itself took it over from private contractors who were seen as not rigorous enough.

Now, however, 4 1/2 years later, a secretive government committee has decided to turn over management of six of the nation's most important ports - in New York, New Jersey, Philadelphia, Miami, Baltimore and New Orleans - to Dubai Ports World following the UAE company's purchase of London-based Peninsular and Oriental Steam Navigation Co., which previously had the contract.

This is not the first time this interagency panel - called the Committee on Foreign Investment in the United States (CFIUS) - has made an astounding call about the transfer of control of strategically sensitive U.S. assets to questionable purchasers.

In fact, as of last summer, CFIUS had, since its creation in 1988, formally rejected only one of 1,530 transactions submitted for its review.

Such a record is hardly surprising given that the committee is chaired by the Treasury Department, whose institutional responsibilities include promoting foreign investment in the United States. Treasury has rarely seen a foreign purchase of American assets it did not like. And this bias on the part of the chairman of CFIUS has consistently skewed the results of the panel's deliberations in favor of approving deals, even those opposed by other, more national security-minded departments.

Thanks to the secrecy with which CFIUS operates, it is not clear at this writing if any such objection was heard to the idea of contracting out managing six of our country's most important ports to a UAE company. There would certainly appear to be a number of grounds for rejecting this initiative, however:

- America's seaports have long been recognized by homeland security experts as among our most vulnerable targets. Huge quantities of cargo move through them every day, much of it of uncertain character and provenance, nearly all of it inadequately monitored. Matters can only be worsened by port managers who might conspire to bring in dangerous containers, or simply look the other way when they arrive.

- Entrusting information about key U.S. ports - including, presumably, government-approved plans for securing them - to say nothing of responsibility for controlling physical access to these facilities, to a country known to have been penetrated by terrorists is not just irresponsible. It is recklessly so.

- At the risk of being politically incorrect, the proposed new management will also complicate the job of assuring that the personnel working in these ports pose no threat to their operations - or to the rest of us. To the extent we must remain particularly vigilant about young male Arab nationals as potential terrorists, it makes no sense to provide legitimate grounds for such individuals to be in and around some of this country's most important strategic assets.

- Of particular concern must be the implications for energy security as a very large proportion of the nation's oil imports come through the Atlantic and Gulf State ports that the UAE company hopes to take over. For example, Philadelphia handles some 85 percent of the oil coming into the East Coast; New Orleans is responsible for a seventh of all our energy imports.

Given such considerations, how could even a stacked deck like the Committee on Foreign Investment in the United States find it possible to approve the Dubai Ports World's transaction?

Could it have been influenced by the fact a former senior official of the UAE company, David Sanborn, was recently named the new administrator of the Transportation Department's Maritime Administration? Mr. Sanborn is former DP World director of operations for Europe and Latin America.

Or is it because the U.S. government views - and is determined to portray - the United Arab Emirates as a vital ally in this war for the Free World? A similar determination has long caused Washington to treat Saudi Arabia as a valued friend even as the Saudis play a double game, working simultaneously to repress terrorism at home and abet it abroad.

Whatever the explanation, the nation can simply no longer afford to have the disposition of strategic assets - including those with a military or homeland security dimension - determined by a Treasury-dominated panel in secret without congressional oversight.

Congress should see to it that the United Arab Emirates is not entrusted with the operation of any U.S. ports, and that the Treasury Department is stripped of the lead role in evaluating such dubious foreign investments in the United States.

A likely upshot of President Bush's meetings this week with his Canadian and Mexican counterparts in Montebello, Canada, will be a further impetus to the effort to engage in what is euphemistically called the "harmonization" of the three countries' economies, regulatory systems and policies. The effect will be to contribute to what is on track to become one of the most worrying legacies of George W. Bush's presidency: a significant, and possibly irreversible, erosion in the nation's sovereignty.

Sovereignty is an abstraction to which few Americans give much thought. We take it for granted, like the air we breathe or the water we drink. Yet, the essence of the most successful political experiment in history - the United States of America - is the sovereign power entrusted by the people via our Constitution to our elected, accountable representatives.

Unfortunately, such sovereignty is endangered by those who believe the world of nation-states is too disorderly for efficient global commerce and the peaceable resolution of disputes. Call them the Transnational Progressives (conservative wit John O'Sullivan coined an abbreviation he insists must be spelled Tranzies). They prefer supranational arrangements like the European Union, run by wholly unaccountable bureaucrats.

The trouble for the Tranzies is that a lot of folks who value their freedoms - notably, the American people and many who represent them in Congress - generally don't fancy such arrangements. They see them for what they are: big government on steroids, unwieldy, unchecked and unresponsive to the will of the ruled.

So it is necessary for the Tranzies to resort to extraordinary means to supplant national governments. The European Union's architects have acknowledged privately they could never have pulled it off if the publics of the Continent's various nations understood what was afoot.

Today, we know a similar effort is at work behind the Security and Prosperity Partnership (SPP) on the agenda at the Montebello Summit. In fact, thanks to Freedom of Information Act requests doggedly pursued by Judicial Watch, we know there are some two-dozen trilateral "working groups" whittling away our sovereignty - er, "harmonizing" our rules and regulations on immigration, the environment and health care with those of Mexico and Canada. This effort, as one of the SPP's admirers has put it, involves the nation-state's "erosion by stealth."

The way this is being done in the U.S. is by having the working groups operate secretively, with essentially no transparency or accountability to Congress, the media or the public.

In fact, even some proponents of the SPP and the North American Union (NAU) it ultimately seeks to institute, Greg Anderson of the University of Alberta and Christopher Sands of the Hudson Institute are beginning to worry about an approach they describe as "eschewing the more traditional diplomatic and trade negotiation models in favor of talks among civil service professionals and subject matter experts within each government . . . [which] places the negotiation fully within the authority of the executive branch in the United States"

They went on in a paper prepared for a recent Hudson event to declare "the [SPP negotiating] process must be made more transparent to answer legitimate citizen concerns about potential outcomes . . . The design of the SPP is flawed by the exclusion of Congress from the process"

At the same time the Bush administration is complicit in stealthy negotiations eroding U.S. sovereignty in our hemisphere, it is responding to aggressive behavior by others in ways that seem sure to encourage still more such erosions - if not vast new threats to our security.

For example, Russia's KGB thug-turned-president, Vladimir Putin, has announced his country would resume its Cold War practice of sending nuclear-capable, long-range aircraft on forays into or near the airspace of various Free World nations, including ours. According to the New York Times, during such a mission in July near U.S. bases on Guam, the Pentagon says it did not even bother scrambling fighters to intercept the Russian bombers.

A White House spokesman pooh-poohed this ominous behavior, saying "Militaries around the world engage in a variety of different activities" and that "it is not entirely surprising" that the Russians would engage in this one.

Meanwhile, The Washington Times' Bill Gertz reports the Chinese military recently proposed that the Pacific be divided into spheres of influence. Presumably, what the PRC has in mind is getting the part that includes Korea, Japan, Taiwan, Southeast Asia and the Philippines and acceding (for the moment at least) to the United States having Hawaii. While a senior American general scoffed at the idea, Mr. Gertz says: "Some pro-China officials in the U.S. government . . . are said to favor the Chinese proposal"

Then, there is the Tranzies' defective Law of the Sea Treaty (LOST). The Bush administration hopes to get it ratified this fall with help from senators willing to join in entrusting 70 percent of the world's surface - its oceans and can't impinge upon our sovereignty? In fact, LOST lends itself to myriad erosions of U.S. sovereign conduct via the treaty's provisions with sweeping environmental, tax, business-related and military implications.

The 2008 presidential election is an opportune moment for a national debate about safeguarding America's sovereignty. The question is: Will there be much of it left to safeguard 14 months from now?

The question on Wall Street in the wake of the latest meltdowns in the U.S. financial sector is "Who's next?" The more important issue is not which of the major banks or investment firms will follow Lehman Brothers into bankruptcy or Merrill Lynch into fire sale. Rather, the question should be "What's next?"

After all, the problem afflicting so much of the U.S. capital markets - and, therefore, those around the world - is not one of individual corporations hitting a rough patch and requiring bail-outs from the federal government or the private sector. It is, instead, the result of a reckless disregard for sound investing practices in the unscrupulous pursuit of profit. In a word, the last "what" was "subprime."

As we all know by now, the practice of building financial houses of cards on various investment instruments based in nontransparent and problematic subprime mortgage-backed securities was a formula for disaster. It induced firms that not only should have known better but are required to behave better to perform unconscionably. In the process, they violated industry standards and government regulations with respect to transparency, disclosure, due diligence, good governance and accountability.

Tragically, in the process of leaping out of the scalding subprime frying pan, Wall Street is heading directly into a fire that promises, if anything, to be more devastating than the present disaster. Incredibly, it bears all the hallmarks of subprime with respect to a lack of transparency, a systematic failure to disclose and an utter absence of due diligence, good governance and accountability. The next "what" is called Shariah-Compliant Finance (SCF).

Shariah, of course, is the term the Islamists use to describe the ruthlessly repressive, totalitarian program they believe should govern every aspect of the lives of faithful Muslims. It is also the instrument they intend to use to rule the world. The first clue that something is wrong with Wall Street's next big thing is that it is Shariah-compliant.

The next clue is how Shariah-Compliant Finance works. Like subprime, it is a black box, in which management and investors alike are told to trust in the experts. In this case, the experts are Shariah authorities who are accorded exclusive responsibility for determining whether investments are "pure" (halal) and therefore acceptable, or "impure" (haram) and not.

As an important monograph on the subject recently issued by the McCormick Foundation and the Center for Security Policy (for copies contact the Center at www.SecureFreedom.org) makes clear, these authorities are, unsurprisingly, adherents to Shariah. A number of them explicitly embrace its call to jihad (including a former senior member of the Dow Jones Islamic Index, Sheik Taqi Usmani). This "holy war" is to be waged where possible through violent means, where necessary through "soft" means like Shariah-Compliant Finance. For this reason, such Islamists call SCF "financial jihad."

Earlier this year, David Yerushalmi, a litigator specializing in securities law and an expert on Shariah, produced a riveting legal memorandum (soon to appear in the University of Utah Law Review) examining the civil and criminal exposure inherent in Shariah-Compliant Finance. His conclusion: banks and investment houses offering SCF products may be enabling or engaging in the following: racketeering, antitrust activity, securities fraud, consumer fraud and/or material support for terror.

What makes Shariah-Compliant Finance even more dangerous than subprime is that, in its effort to legitimize and institutionalize Shariah in America, it is advancing a criminal conspiracy whose purpose is the violent overthrow of the United States Constitution and government in favor of Islamic rule. That would make it sedition.

For these reasons, we should be especially wary of the purported silver lining to the current Wall Street crisis: the infusion of vast quantities of petrodollars, primarily from the Organization of Petroleum Exporting Countries' Saudi Arabia and other Islamist nations in the Persian Gulf. It is bad enough that these putative rescuers of our subprime-fueled liquidity debacle are buying up engines of our capital markets for pennies on the dollar. Worse yet, they are, in the process, putting themselves in a position to promote Shariah-Compliant Finance and the seditious theo-political agenda it serves.

A forthcoming book about SCF by Center for Security Policy Vice President Alex Alexiev offers a further, sobering thought about the fire next time: It is becoming ever-harder to differentiate between the Gulf states' so-called Sovereign Wealth Funds (actually they are the slush funds of the sovereigns) and Shariah-Compliant Finance. The former is increasingly being invested in ways that promote the latter, adding unfathomably large pools of funds to what is estimated already to be an $800 billion global industry.

The Center for Security Policy has sent copies of David Yerushalmi's legal memorandum to the heads of scores of Wall Street firms and the nation's leading commercial banks, warning them of the ominous similarities between subprime and SCF. Interestingly, only the late Merrill Lynch bothered to respond, albeit with a vacuous note blithely affirming its concern about terrorism.

Fortunately, Congress is beginning to recognize the possible peril in what may happen next to Wall Street. Notably, last month, a senior and highly respected member of the Senate Finance Committee, Arizona Republican Jon Kyl, wrote Securities and Exchange Commission Chairman Chris Cox, Federal Reserve Chairman Ben Bernanke, Treasury Secretary Henry Paulson and Attorney General Michael Mukasey, asking them to respond to Mr. Yerushalmi's analysis of Shariah-Compliant Finance.

The question occurs: Will they encourage or discourage the capital markets' leap into the fire via a headlong plunge into subprime on seditious steroids?

American capitalism - led by and caricatured as the financial industry centered on Wall Street - is predicated on the notion that the market is driven by fundamentally economic motives. To its admirers, that means its dynamics are dictated by profit motivation. Wall Street's critics call it greed.

The rules and regulations that govern our stock transactions largely reflect this assumption. We discourage undesirable behavior primarily by levying fines and otherwise making it costly to engage in it.

Forgive the obviousness of this question but, what if actors who are interested in affecting our stock market and economy more generally are motivated not by making money but by some larger strategic interest? In that case, financial disincentives are likely to prove completely ineffectual.

For example, would our present Maginot Line of financial defenses - much of them constructed by legislators bearing names such as Christopher Dodd, Barney Frank, Paul Sarbanes and Michael Oxley - protect us if avowed enemies of this country sought to inflict a major, and possibly decisive, blow against us and didn't care if they lost money in the process?

This proposition is explored in a riveting book that will be published this month by one of my colleagues, Kevin D. Freeman, a senior fellow of the Center for Security Policy. In fact, as the title of "Secret Weapon: How Economic Terrorism Brought Down the U.S. Stock Market and Why It Can Happen Again" suggests, Mr. Freeman's thesis is that it already has occurred, with devastating effect, and that worse may be in the offing.

By training a certified financial analyst who worked for a decade with one of the giants of modern finance, investment maven Sir John Templeton, the author knows his stuff. Among other things, Mr. Freeman reminds us that U.S. enemies - potential and actual - have served notice repeatedly that they understand our market's vulnerabilities to attack.

For instance, in 1999, two senior Chinese colonels wrote an officially sanctioned book titled "Unrestricted Warfare." It identified "bear raids" on stocks to trigger a market collapse as the first in a long list of unconventional weapons that could devastate America.

Another threat of financial warfare was issued by al Qaeda leader Osama bin Laden, who boasted that his jihadists were as "aware of the cracks in the Western financial system as they are aware of the lines in their own hands." That from a man who selected the World Trade Center as a target for the Sept. 11 attacks so as to do massive economic harm to the United States. It was not lost on bin Laden - or America's other enemies - that when the U.S. economy declines, calls intensify for cutting back spending on America's defenses.

No less troubling should be the fact that a very-much-alive spiritual leader of the

Muslim Brotherhood, Sheik Yusuf al-Qaradawi, has described the use of proceeds from Shariah-compliant finance as "jihad with money."

Worse, Sheik al-Qaradawi is a top Shariah authority for the sovereign wealth fund of Qatar. That position and his preeminence in Islamic jurisprudence worldwide (thanks in part to his popular jihadist program broadcast by Al-Jazeera Arabic TV) has helped make Sheik al-Qaradawi a driving force in what is now said to be a trillion-dollar "Islamic finance" industry. Under his influence, Islamists have successfully enlisted Western capitalists to help them exploit free markets as a strategic tool for promoting and insinuating their toxic, supremacist politico-military-legal doctrine throughout the Free World, including the United States.

Incredibly, this stealth jihadist is the man the Obama administration reportedly has tapped to help broker peace talks with the Taliban on Afghanistan. It is presumably no accident that the latter has chosen to set up a diplomatic mission in Sheik al-Qaradawi's adopted hometown, the Qatari capital of Doha.

Is it a coincidence that, as the Wall Street Journal reported in August 2007, Shariah authorities gave their blessing to the practice of "short-selling" just as the stock market was peaking?

As even former Obama economic guru and Treasury Secretary Lawrence H. Summers has observed, sovereign wealth funds serve the interests of the sovereign first, and profit second. Mr. Freeman believes we face a particular danger from the fact that most of the world's wealth-fund sovereigns are in China and the Middle East - the latter increasingly governed by the dictates of Shariah-compliant finance.

I have accompanied Mr. Freeman in briefings he has conducted at senior levels in official Washington and with top financial players in New York, Dallas and Houston. Those of his interlocutors in the national security community seemed, without exception, to accept that economic threats to the United States could come from quarters not interested in monetary returns. Unfortunately, such folks typically lack Mr. Freeman's deep understanding of financial markets, their vulnerabilities and how they could be exploited.

By contrast, when Mr. Freeman has presented his findings to financial market participants, they rarely get it. They typically fall back on the traditional assumption that anyone who buys Credit Default Swaps, stocks or bonds has an exclusively economic motive. The idea that these instruments could be used as weapons is so foreign to them that they often push back angrily, denying the obvious.

Despite willful blindness and blistering attack, Mr. Freeman's warnings stand up to scrutiny. His "Secret Weapon" should receive it at the highest levels of both the national security and financial security communities and at once.

Technology Security

"TECH DEAL THAT WOULD HELP THE KGB WITH ITS SPYING?" | MARCH 8, 1994

Less than 48 hours after a key CIA operative was arrested for allegedly doing great harm to U.S. security by spying for Russia's intelligence service, the Clinton administration took steps that seemed designed to make it up to the KGB.

After all, the administration's newest legislative proposal would greatly assist the KGB in accomplishing one of its principal, and abiding, duties - acquiring sensitive "dual-use" technology from the United States and other Western nations. So great is the strategic significance of this concession that the Kremlin might view it as more than offsetting the loss of even so valuable an agent as Aldrich Ames.

Such a dramatic conclusion derives from the fact that the draft legislation introduced by the administration on Capitol Hill on Feb. 24 would have the effect of largely eviscerating U.S. national security export controls. To date, these controls have appreciably contributed to U.S. and multilateral efforts to preserve the qualitative edge long enjoyed by Western military establishments.

At a minimum, past use of export controls has imposed significant delays and monetary costs on adversaries attempting to gain access to the West's superior technology. Consequently, the KGB has historically given a very high priority to defeating these measures.

Unfortunately, Russian intelligence - and its clients in the military-industrial complex -have benefited from two trends in recent years: First, reduced tensions between the West and Russia after the collapse of the Soviet Union have encouraged some to believe that the diversion of Western high technology was no longer a cause for concern. This notion translated into repeated initiatives by the Bush and Clinton administrations and by the Congress to liberalize the technology transfer regime administered by the Coordinating Committee for Multilateral Export Control (COCOM) as well as national export control arrangements.

Second, in the name of encouraging democratic and free market reforms in Russia, Washington and its allies have provided Moscow with billions of dollars worth of largely unconditioned, undisciplined and inadequately monitored aid. Such nontransparent hard currency flows provided the KGB and other instruments of the Soviet Old Guard the means to underwrite certain malevolent activities - notably, espionage and strategic technology acquisitions.

The Clinton administration's new proposal for reauthorizing the Export Administration Act will make matters much worse by largely eliminating the president's authority to prevent the export of U.S. goods and technology unilaterally. In the place of this presidential discretion, the administration proposes to rely upon what unnamed officials have called "a heavy emphasis on the multilateral process."

This notion is even more insidious than the general "mindless multilateralism" Clinton security policy-makers like Morton Halperin and Strobe Talbott ("Halbotts," for short) have evinced since coming to office. After all, on March 31, 1994, COCOM - the only effective multilateral export control organization upon which "heavy emphasis" might be placed - will cease to exist. It will give new meaning to April Fool's Day if it marks the beginning of an era in which the Clinton team is claiming multilateral arrangements will protect Western export control interests just as those arrangements are vaporized.

Make no mistake about it: The elimination of COCOM before a successor multilateral export control organization can be put into place is nothing less than recklessly irresponsible. Even if the follow-on entity were up and running, moreover, its utility would be highly questionable. After all, the world's most aggressive diverter of strategic technologies, Russia, is supposed to be a charter member of the organization!

The Clinton administration's decision to gut what remains of the U.S. and multilateral export control apparatus is, regrettably, but the most recent in a series of steps that subordinate the national interest to the parochial concerns of special interests. Shrill protests from exporter groups claiming that the Halbotts have not gone far enough in dismantling this apparatus seem transparently calculated to make the administration appear moderate and responsible.

In fact, the special interests have gotten far more than they have any right to expect - and than the nation can afford to give them.

Reacting to the Ames scandal and the Russian leadership's cavalier response to it, thoughtful members of Congress - for example, Sens. Robert Dole, Kansas Republican, and Dennis DeConcini, Arizona Democrat - have called for a freeze on U.S. foreign aid to Russia. The Clinton White House has, as Mr. Dole put it recently, "moved too far, too fast in assuming that changes in Russia have permanently altered the international landscape." The truth of the matter though is that undisciplined, unconditioned aid (as opposed to targeted, monitorable assistance) to Russia should be permanently halted - not just frozen pending a needed re-examination of the premises used to justify U.S. taxpayer assistance to Moscow.

Messrs. Dole and DeConcini should go beyond their initiative aimed at restricting only ill-advised aid flows, however: They must now seek to curb the Clinton administration's bid to provide Russia with what is, arguably, an even more precious - and certainly more dangerous - commodity: militarily relevant high technology. The place to start is by blocking the president's proposal to destroy the Export Administration Act and to deny the United States the effective national security tool export controls have consistently proven to be.

Reduced to its essence, the crisis with North Korea is not about arms control - even though it does demonstrate clearly the inability of the Nuclear Non-Proliferation Treaty to prevent those who want nuclear weapons from getting them. This is true whether or not Pyongyang remains a nominal member of the International Atomic Energy Agency.

It is not even principally about the psychopathic dementia that has characterized the rule of Kim Il Sung and his son, Kim Jong Il - although the first Communist dynasty's proclivity to aggression and terrorism inflames anxieties about its access to nuclear weaponry.

Instead, the prospect that North Korea is acquiring nuclear weapons is a first-order crisis because of the quantum increase it represents in the destructive potential of the world's bad guys. It also translates into a corresponding erosion in the qualitative edge in military technology upon which the good guys have relied to deter - and, if necessary, to defeat – their enemies.

These are not academic abstractions. The war with Saddam Hussein would have been a very different affair had the Iraqi despot been able to threaten Rome, Paris or London - to say nothing of Washington - with nuclear-armed ballistic missiles. Indeed, it might not have happened at all, as the United States, or at least members of the grand coalition it assembled, quailed at the risks involved in fighting an adversary capable of exploiting their absolute vulnerability to such attacks.

This consideration is certainly at work in the present set-to with North Korea. South Korea and Japan are behaving like states that feel distinctly vulnerable to a changed "correlation of forces." In part, of course, this perceived new correlation is a function of the diminished quantity of U.S. military power in the region. In part, it is the by-product of our allies' lack of confidence in President Clinton, arising from his inconstancy and fecklessness.

But the most significant factor is the perceived impact of a qualitative difference in the character of the threat posed by North Korea. Put simply, we are seeing in the crisis over Pyongyang's nuclear capabilities an adverse impact on American interests and alliance relationships that is the predictable result of an adversary reducing the gap between the technological capabilities of their military and ours.

Unfortunately, this is only the beginning - and not just because North Korea is expected to sell whatever nuclear weaponry and ballistic missiles it can get its hands on to rogue nations elsewhere, for example, Iran and Syria in the Middle East. The proliferation of these and other weapons of mass destruction is also picking up steam due, in no small measure, to monstrously shortsighted U.S. policies on controlling the export of related technologies.

In September 1993 and again in March 1994, the Clinton administration took gigantic steps toward dismantling the national and multilateral arrangements used to limit the transfer of strategic technologies to potential enemies. These measures built upon - and greatly exacerbated - the effect of similar decisions made during the Bush presidency.

Taken together, these initiatives have, among other things: eliminated government controls on the export of virtually all dual-use technology incorporated in current operational U.S. defense systems; made widely available immensely powerful computers and machine tools; essentially decontrolled microelectronics manufacturing technology, including that involved in the promising fields of microsensors and micromachines; and facilitated the transfer of inexpensive laser technology with worrisome military applications.

Worse yet, Reps. Sam Gejdenson, Connecticut Democrat, and Toby Roth, Wisconsin Republican - the chairman and ranking minority member respectively of a key House Foreign Affairs subcommittee - are pushing legislation that would go even further towards eliminating what remains in the way of U.S. export controls for national security purposes.

Their bill, H.R. 3937, would for example: remove the Pentagon from key decision-making concerning export controls; let Russia - a chronic diverter of strategic technologies - have access to virtually any Western technology it wants; dramatically reduce U.S. intelligence capabilities by proliferating unbreakable communications encoding software; and automatically decontrol highly sensitive technology if more modern equipment becomes available or if others overseas are said to manufacture comparable systems.

Fortunately, there is some hope that these misbegotten executive and legislative initiatives may finally get some adult supervision. Today the House Armed Services Committee is considering important amendments to H.R. 3937 that would preserve - and possibly strengthen - the Pentagon's role in evaluating the wisdom and implications of militarily relevant technology transfers.

Members of the Armed Services Committee appear to appreciate far better than their colleagues on the Foreign Affairs panel that the United States literally cannot afford to promote the proliferation of strategic technologies. The costs of emboldening the likes of Kim Il Sung could be very great. The costs of reestablishing the qualitative edge enjoyed by the U.S. military prior to such transfers will be greater still, and probably be paid for not only in national treasure but in the lives of our servicemen and women.

These are unbudgeted, unnecessary and unsustainable expenses in the present period of draconian defense cuts. We can only hope that the House Armed Services Committee - and its Senate counterpart - will thwart this and similar misguided catalysts to proliferation in North Korea, and beyond.

Legend has it that Lenin once ridiculed Western capitalists for being willing to sell the communists the rope with which the latter would hang them. While this story may be apocryphal, it nonetheless accurately describes a time-honored practice by communist and other totalitarian regimes: Exploit the West's willingness to disregard legitimate security concerns in its pursuit of commercial transactions involving the transfer of militarily relevant (or "dual-use") technology. By so doing, even governments lacking enormous resources can acquire advanced equipment and know-how needed to field militaries capable of posing powerful threats to the interests of the selling nations.

It seems unlikely that even the cynical Lenin could have imagined the absurd lengths to which the Clinton administration would be willing to go in the rope-selling business, however. This week in Paris, it is setting the stage for making the Kremlin a formal member of a new international technology transfer control mechanism - the so-called "New Forum." This entity is intended to succeed the now officially defunct Coordinating Committee on Multilateral Export Controls (COCOM). If all goes according to plan, starting in January, Moscow will have an equal say about the length and strength of the high technology "rope" to be sold - and who gets it.

By definition, bringing Russia inside the tent in this fashion ensures that it will be given access to detailed information about sensitive Western technology. As a practical matter, moreover, it will be difficult - if not impossible - to deny the Kremlin access to such technology. And the Russians will, of course, be in a position to block efforts to produce a Western consensus against selling dual-use equipment or know-how to the world's rogue nations. As the case of the Russian-Iranian reactor deal graphically demonstrates, Moscow has proven reluctant to deny its clients whatever hardware they want. At a minimum, Moscow can be expected to serve as the middleman for transfers of any technology that might yet be denied the likes of Iraq, Iran and North Korea, but that can be sold to the former Soviet Union.

Matters are made worse by two related developments. First, the Clinton administration agreed in March 1994 to dismantle COCOM before any successor institution was in place. As a result, multilateral controls on strategic dual-use technology - for example, those governing exports of advanced multi-axis machine tools, underwater exploration equipment, aviation and naval propulsion systems, telecommunications, supercomputers, etc. - have been largely dismantled.

Of particular concern is the resulting absence of pre-notification of sensitive exports. In the past, such notice has been indispensable to U.S. attempts to dissuade its allies from selling "rope" to the bad guys. At this writing, it is not clear whether the parties to the New Forum will agree even to give notice of technology transfers after the fact. As one concerned official put it, "We'll just have to wait until we learn about these dangerous transactions from intelligence - assuming we find out about them."

The New Forum will also leave to "national discretion" decisions about what to control and how rigorously to enforce such controls. Given the proclivities of the Germans and other Europeans (to say nothing of the Russians), "national discretion" amounts to a licence for wholesale national indiscretions with respect to the exports of sensitive technology to rogue nations.

This initiative has been made even more problematic, thanks to the administration's second mistake: It has undercut its own leadership position by engaging in some of the most irresponsible technology transfers on record. Washington has, for example, unilaterally and greatly expanded the performance standards of supercomputers available for export. This is an area of genuine U.S. market dominance at the moment, so the oft-cited excuse of foreign availability does not apply. Indeed, that fact - combined with the enormous military potential of powerful supercomputers for such applications as nuclear weapons design, effects simulation and operational planning, dual-use air traffic control, undersea warfare, etc. - may explain why Japan and other allies were willing to maintain significant export controls in this area.

With the Clinton administration's decision to sell advanced supercomputers to China (among a host of other technologies enabling the Peoples' Republic to build, for example, advanced, long-range and highly accurate cruise missiles), it has persuaded the other advanced industrial nations that literally anything goes. The result is certain to be a buyer's market for the componentry and manufacturing systems needed for tomorrow's world-class weaponry.

Naturally, the administration would have us believe that, in the post-Cold War world, we need not be concerned about selling high technology "rope" to former communists in Russia or "reform" communists in China. This is, of course, nonsense - not because of ideology but for two practical reasons. First, both countries are actively hawking everything from ballistic missiles to nuclear hardware to anyone with cash. And second, both are engaged in behavior that makes future conflict with them possible, if not inevitable. Third, the two are actively sharing military technology and data.

Under these circumstances, the administration's technology transfer policies cry out for adult supervision from Capitol Hill. A good first step would be to establish that national security considerations, and not simply trade promotion priorities, must be factored into export control decision-making. If there were no other justification for dismantling the Commerce Department - which has traditionally thwarted efforts to address the former in its monomaniacal pursuit of the latter - the evisceration of its Bureau of Export Administration would be sufficient grounds for doing so.

Responsibility for running a restructured security-minded interagency export licencing process should be placed where it belongs: in the Defense Department. Also in order are urgent hearings into the cumulative, detrimental impact of the administration's technology transfer policies.

If corrective action on export controls is not taken promptly by either the executive or legislative branches, the steps being mapped out this week will probably facilitate a grave new impetus to international proliferation. There will be nothing funny on the Clinton administration's way to the New Forum.

When the final net assessment is performed on the immense harm done to U.S. national security by the Clinton-Gore administration, the cause of the most grievous, long-term damage may come as a surprise: The most serious and enduring harm may prove to have resulted from the systematic, purposeful and wholesale dismantling of U.S. export-control mechanisms and multilateral arrangements that until 1992 governed the transfer of militarily relevant or "dual use" technologies.

The question that is now arising is whether this evisceration of U.S. export controls will be attributable solely to Clinton administration machinations? Or will certain Republican lawmakers - even some with conservative credentials —now looking to captains of industry for campaign contributions give invaluable political cover to Al Gore with respect to one of his greatest vulnerabilities?

As things stand now, the vice president is fully and uniquely implicated in the practice of giving priority to politically influential companies' desire for short-term profits in overseas markets, without regard for the larger national interest. This practice has jeopardized the U.S. military's qualitative edge - the access to superior technology that allows U.S. armed forces to fight and prevail even when substantially outnumbered.

In addition, as successive reports performed or commissioned by Congress (notably, those produced over the past two years by the House select committee chaired by Rep. Chris Cox and blue-ribbon panels chaired by former Secretary of Defense Don Rumsfeld and former CIA Director John Deutch) have documented, eased access to sophisticated U.S. equipment and know-how is giving rise to unprecedented new threats to national security from developing nations and even subnational groups.

Given this record, it is stupefying that the Senate is expected this week to consider legislation that would greatly compound this problem. Were this bill - the Export Administration Act (EAA) (S.1712) - actually to pass unchanged, moreover, the Republican-led Congress would become fully implicated in what is, arguably, the Clinton-Gore administration's most reprehensible act of purposeful malfeasance.

It is noteworthy that this legislation is being brought to the Senate floor over the strenuous objections of all four authorizing committees with jurisdiction over national security matters: the Senate Armed Services, Foreign Relations, Intelligence and Governmental Affairs committees. As recently as Feb. 29, the chairmen of these four committees (Republican Sens. John Warner of Virginia, Jesse Helms of North Carolina, Richard Shelby of Alabama and Fred Thompson of Tennessee, respectively), together with six other influential committee or subcommittee chairmen (Republican Sens. Jon Kyl of Arizona, Pat Roberts of Kansas, James M. Inhofe of Oklahoma, Robert C. Smith of New Hampshire, Connie Mack of Florida and Orrin Hatch of Utah), wrote Majority Leader Trent Lott warning that "S.1712 fails to protect U.S. national security interests" and opposing consideration of the EAA "at this time."

The reasons for such opposition are not hard to divine. This legislation is designed to make it exceedingly difficult - if not, as a practical matter, impossible - to impose export controls on strategically sensitive technologies. Months of behind-the-scenes negotiations by these legislators and their staff with the EAA's proponents, primarily Texas Republican Sen. Phil Gramm's Banking Committee, have to date left such serious problems as the following uncorrected:

- S.1712 would confirm in law the Clinton practice of precluding executive branch agencies responsible for national security from exercising real influence over the export control process. For instance, the Commerce Department will have, for all intents and purposes, sole authority over which technologies are subjected to high-tech transfer restrictions. The bill would also confer on the Banking Committee sole jurisdiction for areas clearly within the purview of other Senate committees charged with oversight of the defense, foreign policy and intelligence portfolios.

- The bill unduly restricts the circumstances under which export controls can be imposed. This is done to such an extent that the next president may be hamstrung should he believe, unlike the incumbent, that the transfer of certain dual-use U.S. technology should be blocked from going to undesirable end-users.

It would, for example, be illegal to do so if would-be exporters claim that foreign competitors can offer a comparable product. (Under S.1712, another loophole would be created if the product is not available overseas but is widely available domestically.) If the EAA were in force, the president would be prohibited from blocking the export unless he could establish both that U.S. security would be harmed and that foreign availability can be eliminated via multilateral controls in under 18 months - neither of which are likely to be demonstrable in advance.

In an important address to the Heritage Foundation on Friday, one of those most concerned about this defective legislation, Sen. Thompson, declared: "We need strong, principled leadership from the president and Congress on these national security matters. We can start by passing an Export Administration Act that balances trade with national security - as opposed to the current, proposed legislation that would loosen export controls further than has the Clinton administration."

The nation may long suffer the consequences of the Clinton-Gore team's failure to strike such a balance. It seems equally certain that neither the "common defense" nor Republican electoral prospects will be advanced if the Senate disregards the judgment of Mr. Thompson and its other experts on national security in an effort to out pander the vice president for the contributions and support of high-tech businesses determined to sell their wares without regard for the dangers such sales might entail for the rest of us.

The Pentagon has had a dirty little secret for years now: Foreign suppliers are an increasingly important part of the industrial base upon which the U.S. military relies for everything from key components of its weapon systems to the software that runs its logistics.

With the Air Force's Feb. 29 decision to turn over to a European-led consortium the manufacture and support of its tanker fleet - arguably one of the most important determinants of U.S. ability to project power around the world - the folly of this self-inflicted vulnerability may finally get the attention it deserves from Congress and the public.

The implications of such dependencies were made clear back in 1991 during Operation Desert Storm. In the course of that short but intense operation, American officials had to plead with the government of Japan to intervene with a Japanese manufacturer to obtain replacement parts for equipment then being used to expel Saddam Hussein's forces from Kuwait.

The obvious lesson of that experience seemingly has been lost on the Pentagon. In the nearly two decades after, it has sought to cut costs and acquisition timelines by increasingly utilizing commercial, off-the-shelf (or COTS) technology. Under the logic of "globalization," COTS often means foreign-supplied, particularly with respect to advanced computer chips and other electronic gear.

Such a posture raises obvious questions about the availability of such equipment should the United States have to wage a war that is unpopular with the supplier's government or employees. Then there is the problem of built-in defects such as computer code "trap doors" that may not become obvious until the proverbial "balloon goes up" and disabling of U.S. military capabilities becomes a strategic priority to foreign adversaries, or those sympathetic with them.

Even the Pentagon and intelligence community recognized this sort of train-wreck was in prospect had Huawei, a company with longstanding ties to the Chinese People's Liberation Army, been allowed to buy 3Com. The latter's "intrusion prevention" technology is widely used by the U.S. government to provide computer security against relentless cyber attacks from, among others, Communist China.

Now, unfortunately, the Air Force has set in motion what might be called a "plane-wreck." Opposition is intensifying on Capitol Hill, on the presidential hustings and across America to the service's decision to make the European Aerospace, Defense and Space (EADS) consortium the principal supplier of its aerial refueling capabilities for the next 50 years.

There appear to be a number of questions about the process whereby the decision was made to reject the alternative offered by the nation's historic supplier of tanker aircraft - the

Boeing Co. These questions (for example, concerning the ability to operate on relatively short and austere runways) seem likely to result in that corporation protesting the source-selection of a much larger Airbus aircraft over Boeing's modified 767.

Even more telling may be other considerations that argue powerfully against a reliance on the EADS-dominated offering. A number of these considerations were identified in a paper issued by the Center for Security Policy in April 2007 and re-released last week Evidently these were not taken into account by the Air Force:

- One of the owners of EADS, the government of France, has long engaged in: corporate other acts of espionage against the United States and its companies; bribery and other corrupt practices; and diplomatic actions generally at cross-purposes with America's national interests.

- The Russian state-owned Development Bank (Vneshtorgbank) is reportedly the largest non-European shareholder in EADS with at least a 5 percent stake. It is hard to imagine that, just when Vladimir Putin and his cronies are becoming ever more aggressive in their anti-Americanism and efforts to intimidate Europe, we could safely entrust such vital national security capabilities as the manufacture and long-term support of our tanker fleet to a company in which the Kremlin is involved.

- The enormous U.S. taxpayer-financed cash infusion into EADS will probably not only translate into more money for the slush funds the company has historically used to bribe customers into buying Airbus planes rather than Boeing's. It will also help subsidize the Europeans' space launch activities - again at the expense of American launch services.

- EADS has been at the forefront of European efforts to arm - over adamant U.S. objections - Communist China, Hugo Chavez's Venezuela and Iran.

- As the Center for Security Policy paper points out: "Through its aircraft production division, EADS is a huge jobs program for anti-American labor unions that form the backbones of some of Europe's most powerful socialist parties. By purchasing products that employ these workers, we will be feeding those who would rather bite our hand than shake it."

These and other aspects of the selection of the Airbus tanker - notably preposterous claims about the number of American jobs that will be created by contracting out our tanker fleet to the Europeans - seem to assure that this decision will indeed be a political plane-wreck.

The tragedy is that the replacement of our obsolescent aerial refueling fleet has already been unduly delayed. The further deferral that now seems inevitable may mean we wind up literally sacrificing aircraft and their crews or at least the national power-projection capability we need while this mess is sorted out.

Last summer, a Chinese telecommunications giant founded by a former People's Liberation Army (PLA) engineer was rebuffed in its effort to sell vast quantities of equipment to Sprint Nextel - an American company that provides communication services to the U.S. Defense Department and other government agencies. An interagency group known as the Committee on Foreign Investment in the United States (CFIUS) took a hard look at the proposal and, quite sensibly, rejected it on national security grounds.

Unbeknownst to CFIUS at the time, Huawei was making another, unscrutinized and problematic investment in the United States. It bought pieces of 3Leaf, a now-insolvent pioneer in "cloud computing" technology, including intellectual property with obvious military applications.

When this transaction serendipitously came to the Pentagon's attention, alarm bells went off. CFIUS took a look at it as well and came to the same conclusion as it had with the Chinese company's previous play with Sprint Nextel and two earlier initiatives - its effort to buy a stake in 3Com and bid to invest in some of Motorola's assets: No way.

Initially, Huawei declared that it intended to appeal to President Obama to overrule his interagency experts. Perhaps in doing so, it was counting on his well-established proclivity to yield to Chinese demands. Perhaps the company was banking on the political influence of the prominent former American officials it had indirectly hired through a firm called Amerilink to tamp down their successors' security concerns about Huawei. These advocates include: a former Vice Chairman of the Joint Chiefs of Staff, Adm. William Owens; a former House Majority Leader, Rep. Richard Gephart; and a former Deputy Secretary of Defense, Gordon England.

Five days after floating this idea, however, the Chinese were persuaded to abandon their latest gambit. Presumably, Huawei's American guns-for-hire or perhaps Obama's own advisors impressed upon them that President Obama could hardly afford to ignore CFIUS' conclusions in order to do the PRC's bidding.

Now, Huawei is trying a new tack. Its deputy chairman, Ken Hu, published last week an audacious open letter on the corporate website. Hu professes the company's commitment to free enterprise and insistently denies any wrongful expropriation of proprietary information or ties to the PLA. He decries the "longstanding and untrue rumors and allegations" that, among other things, suggest the company would use access to U.S. computer networks for nefarious purposes. He goes so far as repeatedly to call on Washington to conduct a "thorough government investigation [that] will prove that Huawei is a normal commercial institution and nothing more."

Essentially, Hu has challenged the U.S. government to make public what it knows about the security threat posed by this Chinese behemoth.

What a splendid idea! The more the American people know about Chinese enterprises like Huawei and the full extent of their efforts to penetrate the U.S. market (for example, for the purpose of acquiring technology, both legally and illegally) and the security implications of our relying upon their products and services, the better.

Here are a few suggestions concerning information - at least some of which has evidently driven past CFIUS decisions to parry Huawei's U.S. machinations - that it would be helpful to share with the American people:

- What is the actual relationship between Huawei and the Chinese government? Hu declares that his enterprise is "a private company owned entirely by its employees." While he acknowledges that it benefits from tax incentives and loans made available to its customers from China's "commercial banks" - read, state-owned enterprises routinely used as financial instruments of the communist government in Beijing - Hu suggests that there's nothing for us to worry about. That is assuredly not the case, and we need to know the truth.

- How about the true extent of ties between the People's Liberation Army and Huawei? At a moment when the PLA is increasingly ascendant and aggressive, both at home and abroad, Hu's assurances of no connection beyond its founder's past service in the military's now-disbanded engineer corps ring hollow. Huawei's massive state-supported telecommunications research and development activities have clear military applications. And its commercial transactions assuredly afford Chinese intelligence opportunities for insinuating trap doors and other means of penetrating Western computer and communications networks.

- What has been Huawei's record elsewhere overseas? The company has been implicated in selling sophisticated equipment to the Taliban, Saddam Hussein's Iraq and the Iranian Revolutionary Guard Corps, in part, to improve their military capabilities. Aiding and abetting America's enemies is not something we can safely ignore, especially since it is both suggestive of Huawei's utility to the Chinese government and adds further reason to be concerned about the role it might play if allowed to expand its operations here.

Evidently, China is prepared to play hardball. It has announced that it will establish an inter-ministerial committee similar to CFIUS. Presumably, it will become an instrument for selectively restricting foreign investment in the PRC - retaliating against U.S. business interests in the event of future CFIUS rejections on security grounds and creating still-greater leverage on U.S. companies to support its predatory trade and "commercial" activities. Only by making plain what Huawei and similar enterprises are up to can the threat they pose be properly understood - and countered. The place to start is by saying "No way, Huawei."

Space

Today, NASA Administrator Daniel Goldin is expected to make what may be the most far-reaching space-related initiative since President Kennedy declared the goal of putting a man on the moon. With his announcement of a winner in a competition to design the X-33 - a flying prototype for a reusable launch vehicle (RLV) - Mr. Goldin is taking a step that promises, at last, to give the United States reliable, inexpensive and prompt access to space. As such capabilities are likely to prove indispensable elements of the United States' future civilian technological competitiveness and a robust national security posture, much is riding on his decision and on its implementation.

Mr. Goldin will be picking among three dramatically different design approaches: The first, designed by McDonnell Douglas, involves a cone-shaped vehicle that would take off and land vertically. This would enable it to operate from austere launch pads virtually anywhere, independent of the expensive complexes traditionally used to send expendable rockets or reusable shuttles into space.

The feasibility of such a radical launch-and-recovery concept has been demonstrated by a series of remarkable flights performed over the past few years using a test article recently dubbed the Clipper Graham in honor of one of the program's greatest champions, the late retired Army Lt. Gen. Daniel Graham. The Clipper Graham also demonstrated impressive progress toward meeting a critical test for what are known as single-stage-to-orbit (SSTO) spacecraft: achieving the high readiness and reliability and fast turn-arounds with low manpower requirements typical of modern commercial aircraft but heretofore largely unknown with space launch systems.

The other two designs would be launched vertically but land horizontally, like the existing space shuttle. Lockheed Martin's concept involves a flat-bottomed, wingless rocket known as a lifting body. Rockwell's approach resembles somewhat the existing space shuttle, which it also built, although it would operate without the shuttle's externally mounted rockets and fuel tank.

The demanding performance requirements with respect to responsiveness and cost-effectiveness are particularly crucial insofar as Mr. Goldin's stated purpose is to get NASA out of the business of owning and operating rockets in favor of an exclusive focus for his agency on research and development activities. According to his plan, once NASA and its selected industry partner have produced a workable SSTO system, the latter would be expected to raise the capital necessary to produce reusable launch vehicles.

In theory, RLVs will prove so efficient as to enable them strongly to compete with existing space launch services - even the massively underpriced ones offered by the command-style economies of Russia, Ukraine and China, to say nothing of France's somewhat more expensive, but state-subsidized Ariane family of rocket boosters. As a result, charges to private sector and government customers would be expected to enable the RLV to operate as a viable commercial endeavor.

The challenge will be to keep the program on track and consistent with its remarkable genesis: The Clipper Graham went from paper concept to launch in just 18 months at a cost of only $60 million. While its design objectives were modest compared to the X-33 and operational successors, this remarkable achievement illustrates what it will take to bring SSTOs to life.

First, the NASA bureaucracy - much of which regards the whole RLV concept as a threat to its institutional "rice bowl" - must not be allowed to conduct "business as usual" with respect to this development program. While Mr. Goldin has managed to date to keep the R&D program leading up to the X-33 choice quite streamlined, once the selection of a design is made bureaucratic sclerosis is a real danger. This problem is already evident in some of the key subsystem technologies such as avionics, thermal materials and engines where large NASA infrastructures are adding much to the cost of the program without contributing much to the needed developmental progress.

Second, a focus on deliverables is needed. An early test of the prospects for realizing Dan Goldin's vision for the X-33 will be whether the winning contractor is obliged to begin providing actual hardware in a timely fashion - for example, in as little as six-to-eight months from contract award.

And third, the U.S. military must recognize that it has an enormous stake in the prompt, successful realization of the promise of the X-33 program. An operational vehicle offering the characteristics envisioned for the reusable launch vehicle could transform the Pentagon's ability to accomplish such missions as flexible, global reconnaissance; rapid, intercontinental-range precision-strike; ballistic missile defense; reconstitution of intelligence and other space assets; and space control. Defense Department orders for such RLVs could, moreover, assure the viable private sector production base needed to realize Mr. Goldin's dream of weaning NASA from such functions.

This, in turn, will require the Pentagon to devote resources and consolidated, aggressive management to a supporting role for the NASA effort and to its own streamlined acquisition program. The outgoing commander of the U.S. Space Command, Gen. Joseph Ashey, accorded such actions a high priority. His successor, Gen. Howell Estes, must be encouraged to do no less.

If these steps are taken, the announcement Mr. Goldin makes today could well usher in a golden age for U.S. achievement in space unrivaled since President Kennedy set his sights on the moon.

"RISKY SPACE AGENDA REVEALED WITH VETO" | OCTOBER 21, 1997

In 1991, the United States decisively won a war against a dangerous and well-armed adversary. It did so with extraordinary speed and minimal loss of American lives. While these feats are widely recognized and admired, the strategic factor that did much to make them possible is almost unknown beyond military circles: exclusive U.S. control and use of outer space.

America's orbiting satellites provided its forces on the ground in the Persian Gulf with timely intelligence about the disposition of enemy forces. Other space assets told allied forces their exact location in the desert, on the seas and in the air and helped some of those famous precision-guided munitions to find their targets. Still other satellites provided warning of Saddam Hussein's ballistic missile launches, affording a modicum of warning to target areas and units tasked with intercepting such missiles.

Given other advantages, it is probably the case that the United States and its allies would have prevailed even if Saddam had enjoyed a similar capability to use space as a theater of military operations. There can be little doubt, however, that the cost of victory - whether measured in terms of lives, national treasure or the duration of the conflict - would have been far greater than was the case in Desert Storm.

To cite just one example, if Iraqi forces had access to "real-time" intelligence from space-based reconnaissance assets, the element of surprise necessary to Gen. Norman Schwartzkopf's "Hail Mary pass" would have been denied. Unable to execute the end-around maneuver that flanked Saddam's entrenched forces and mine fields, coalition armies would have been obliged to mount bloody assaults on stronger points in Iraq's defensive line.

Further evolution of the art and technology of war since the conflict in the Gulf has, if anything, made space an even more critical component of successful combat operations for the future. Innovations that promise to add enormously to the lethality of American military power - such as the "fusion" of telecommunications, geographic and intelligence flows in data streams that can be provided directly to front-line commanders and even individual units – depend critically upon sensors, relays and other assets based in outer space.

On the other hand, an enemy able to disrupt or destroy such assets may be able to stymie, if not defeat, U.S. forces on the ground, in the air or at sea. In fact, recent war games conducted by the Army demonstrated that the U.S. ability to make undegraded use of outer space - and, just as importantly, to deny such use to its adversaries - would be absolutely critical to the conduct of conflicts on the ground.

Reflecting this reality, the Air Force, which takes pride in being the most innovative of the armed services, has adopted a new doctrine that casts itself as an air-and-space force.

By so doing, it has explicitly recognized the imperative of U.S. control of space in time of war - both as a vantage point from which to monitor and guide terrestrial combat, as a venue hostile powers must not be allowed to use for similar purposes, and, in due course, as a locus for weapons that can prevent missile attack and project American power.

Unfortunately, the Clinton-Gore administration last week took steps that will deny the U.S. military the means with which such a farsighted and necessary doctrine can be implemented. In the first declared exercise of the line-item veto for "policy reasons," President Clinton deleted space control-related programs from the fiscal 1998 Defense Appropriations Act that were included at congressional initiative. Thanks to his deletion of the Clementine II program, the Kinetic Kill Anti-Satellite (ASAT) system and the Military Space Plane, the United States may be find itself utterly unable to exercise the necessary control of space in the next war.

Clementine II is the successor to an award-winning scientific endeavor that inexpensively and quickly mapped the entire lunar surface while validating hardware, software and concepts relevant to space-based ballistic missile defenses. This spacecraft would further refine the latter while providing invaluable astrophysical data in the course of a planned intercept of a fast-flying asteroid. Mr. Clinton reaffirmed his determination to rely upon a treaty rather than effective anti- missile protection for the American people when he cited concerns about this program's compliance with the 1972 Anti-Ballistic Missile Treaty to justify his veto.

The administration has adopted a no less irresponsible head-in-the-sand posture with respect to the Army's Anti-Satellite program. This system represents one of only two near-term techniques available to the United States to neutralize enemy satellites; the other, a laser system in New Mexico, remains untested in this role. Incredibly, the National Security Council's Robert Bell declared in announcing the veto on Oct. 19: "We simply do not believe that this ASAT capability is required, at least based on the threat as it now exists and is projected to evolve over the next decade or two."

Finally, the Air Force's new doctrine clearly contemplates capabilities that could only be provided by a space plane configured for and dedicated to military missions. In the relatively short-run, such a vehicle would be capable of launching payloads into orbit and on ballistic trajectories virtually on demand. Over time, it could serve as a means of operating in and from space.

In the final analysis, the problem with these three programs is not that they are irrelevant to national security. Rather, these programs fall afoul of a core belief of administration arms control zealots like Vice President Al Gore, namely that space is not now and must not be "militarized." In the face of abundant evidence to the contrary, they insist on preventing the United States from developing and fielding systems that will enable it to dominate what is likely to be the future's most important theater of operations. They prefer that U.S. security be based instead on demonstrably unverifiable and ineffective arms control agreements.

This predilection lends itself to exploitation by potential adversaries. It is, as the communists used to say, "no accident, comrade," that Boris Yeltsin last month secretly proposed negotiations on a treaty that would ban anti-satellite weapons. While such a ban cannot be either effective or verifiable given the myriad ways in which satellite operations can be interrupted or terminated (including some that are essentially undetectable), it will assuredly have one effect: It will introduce new impediments to U.S. development and deployment of space control technologies since practically all such devices could be used as ASAT systems. In fact, the president's pre-emptive deletion of the three space-control programs may represent the Kremlin's first exercise of a line-item veto in the U.S. budget.

In a statement issued to the press on Oct. 19, President Clinton said, "I have been assured by the secretary of defense that none of the cancellations would undercut our national security or adversely affect the readiness of our forces or their operations in defense of our nation." At least with respect to the three space-related cancellations, this proposition is so manifestly untenable as to demand congressional hearings aimed at exploring the basis for such a conclusion - and an immediate effort aimed at overriding line-item vetoes that may prove extremely injurious to U.S. security.

In the summer of 1998, the Clinton-Gore Administration was suddenly traumatized by a man named Donald Rumsfeld. For the preceding five years, its senior officials had been manfully arguing that the Nation faced no threat from ballistic missile attack. They even manipulated the available intelligence data and analyses to support the party line that such a danger would not materialize for at least 15 years.

For five years, it worked, and the administration was able to stave off successive efforts by congressional Republicans to deploy anti-missile defenses.

Then suddenly everything changed. A blue-ribbon commission, comprised of members appointed by both Republicans and Democrats and brilliantly led by former Defense Secretary Rumsfeld, rendered its findings. The Rumsfeld Commission concluded that the evidence and more realistic assumptions made it likely that, in addition to existing threats to the American homeland from Russia and China, the United States would face the possibility of ballistic missile attack from Iran and North Korea within as little as five years of a decision by these rogue states to acquire long-range missiles. Since the U.S. could not be sure when such a decision was taken, the commission warned that the nation could have "little or no warning" that a threat was emerging from these quarters.

Within a month, the Rumsfeld Commission's "second opinion" was confirmed. North Korea demonstrated it had mastered the capability to design, produce and fly a three-stage ballistic missile. Thanks to this technology, Pyongyang – and anybody dictator Kim Jong-il cared to share it with -could quickly have an intercontinental range missile capable of attacking the United States with weapons of mass destruction. The debate in this country changed profoundly; today, with the imminent installation of President-elect George W. Bush, the nation is at last poised to begin deploying defenses against such a threat.

I mention all this because the Clinton-Gore team appears to have learned its lesson about Don Rumsfeld. Earlier this year, Congress turned to the former defense secretary once again to lead yet another high-level, bipartisan effort. This one is charged with sorting out the facts and recommending changes with regard to a national policy issue every bit as momentous as defending America against missile threats: This country's urgent - and growing - need to be able to exercise space power.

Broadly defined, space power requires having assured access to and use of space - and the ability, if necessary, to deny such access and use to potential adversaries. The United States' dependence upon outer space for both its national and economic security is immense. Prospective adversaries recognize this as a potentially decisive vulnerability; several are working hard at acquiring the means to impede, if not to deny altogether, America's exploitation of space and/or to use space against us (for example, by acquiring near-real-time intelligence about U.S. force movements) in any future conflicts.

Unfortunately, the Clinton-Gore administration has left the Nation ill prepared to exercise space power. Before the Supreme Court took away the line-item veto, Mr. Clinton used it to try to terminate three Defense Department programs that would have afforded some limited capability to operate in and control outer space. Despite its laudable rhetorical policies concerning the need for American space power, the administration has yet to provide the capabilities needed to implement such policies.

Nowhere is this more true than with respect to the necessary, if not sufficient, precondition to space power: reliable, ready and affordable access to space. The United States today is locked into space launch systems and their large and ponderous infrastructure that have had problems with reliability, are incapable of rapidly placing payloads in orbit and are staggeringly expensive to operate.

The administration has made matters worse by encouraging the use of foreign launch services. It has, notably, transferred militarily relevant space technology to Communist China so Beijing can offer access to space to American businesses and other users - effectively precluding the sort of indigenous U.S. launch industry upon which the country's future economic competitiveness and national security will depend.

Given the composition of the current Rumsfeld Commission - an impressive array of knowledgeable and thoughtful national security practitioners - and its chairman's demonstrated leadership abilities, it seems highly likely that their findings about the need for space power will be roughly as momentous as the earlier Rumsfeld panel's conclusions about the missile threat.

In particular, the current effort will surely conclude that the United States must have the means to get into space whenever the need arises. Done properly, this would mean having access to the exoatmosphere comparable to that afforded by military, or even commercial, aircraft to the endoatmosphere - that is, employing reusable spacecraft on a sortie-like basis. The result would be rapid turnarounds and costs so low that not even the heavily subsidized expendable launch systems of socialist nations would be able to compete. The technology for such a revolutionary capability and the space power it would afford the United States could be rapidly brought to bear were there a will to do so.

Unfortunately, the Clinton-Gore administration hopes this week to pre-empt the new Rumsfeld Commission. It intends to sign a bilateral agreement with the Russians that would oblige the United States to provide between 30 days and 24 hours advance notice of virtually any space launches. The practical effect of such an arrangement - which the administration hopes shortly to multilateralize - would be to lock the nation into the existing way of doing business, precluding sortie-like operations in space and, thereby, creating new bureaucratic impediments to giving such an approach to space access the priority and funds

452

it requires.

This is too high a price to pay for a Clinton "legacy." The deal with Russia should be put on ice at least until after the current Rumsfeld Commission issues its report in mid-January. All we are saying is give space power a chance.

This will be a big week for Donald Rumsfeld, President-elect Bush's choice to head the Pentagon. Before it is over, he will have undergone what may be a contentious examination of his record and views by members of the Senate Armed Services Committee charged with considering his nomination.

History will probably assign much greater importance, however, to another date this week on Secretary-designate Rumsfeld's calendar. On Thursday, he will unveil the report of a blue-ribbon, congressionally mandated Commission on National Security Space Management and Organization - a panel assigned the momentous task of evaluating the need for U.S. space power, and how it can be assured.

It remains to be seen precisely what the latest Rumsfeld Commission will recommend. But its chairman gave an indication of the thrust in his remarks after Mr. Bush announced his nomination on Dec. 28:

"We are in a new national security environment. We do need to be arranged to deal with the new threats, not the old ones . . . with information warfare, missile defense, terrorism, defense of our space assets and the proliferation of weapons of mass destruction throughout the world.

"History teaches us that weakness is provocative. The task you have outlined is to fashion deterrence and defense capabilities, so that our country will be able to successfully contribute to peace and stability in the world."

Just as some - including, in all likelihood, at least a few senators –bridle at the idea of defending the American people against ballistic missile attack, the notion that we should protect our "space assets" is sure to provoke criticism from the usual suspects. After all, they say, space must not be "militarized" and that arms control agreements preventing anti-satellite weapons and other uses of space for military purposes is a far more sure way to safeguard our equities there.

As it happens, the naiveté and recklessness of such an approach was made clear last week by a report out of Hong Kong to the effect that Communist China has completed ground tests of "an advanced anti-satellite weapon called 'parasitic satellite' which will be deployed on an experimental basis and enter the stage of space test in the near future."

In fact, on Jan. 5, the newspaper Sing Tao Jih Pao revealed that: "According to the well-informed sources, to ensure winning in a future high-tech war, China's military has been quietly working hard to develop a symmetrical combat capability so that it will become capable of completely paralyzing the enemy's fighting system when necessary by 'attacking selected vital points' in the enemy's key areas. The development of the reliable anti-satellite 'parasitic satellite' is an important part of the efforts in this regard.

"It is reported that the 'parasitic satellite' is a micro-satellite which can be launched to stick to an enemy satellite; and in time of war, it will jam or destroy the enemy satellite according to the command it receives. As a new-concept anti-satellite weapon, the 'parasitic satellite' can control or attack many types of satellite, including low-orbit, medium-orbit and high-orbit satellites, both military and civilian satellites, single satellite and constellated satellites. An enemy satellite, once locked on by 'parasitic satellite,' cannot escape being paralyzed or destroyed instantaneously in time of war, no matter how sophisticated it is, and no matter whether it is a communications satellite, early-warning satellite, navigational satellite, reconnaissance satellite, radar electronics jamming satellite, or even space station or space-based laser gun."

The Rumsfeld Space Commission will doubtless take note of this, and other, ominous developments - just as did a symposium on space power convened last month by the Center for Security Policy (a summary of whose proceedings is being released today). After all, U.S. intelligence has become increasingly concerned over the fact that, thanks to collaboration between Britain's University of Surrey and the Chinese People's Liberation Army, Beijing has made great strides in the development of micro-satellites capable of performing the sort of space control functions described above.

As the once-and-future defense secretary fully appreciates, given the immense dependence of both the United States' military and economic competitiveness upon unencumbered access to and use of space, the nation can no longer afford to indulge in wishful thinking that those equities will remain inviolable indefinitely. And inherently unverifiable and unenforceable international agreements cannot be relied upon to protect space assets from "parasite satellites," jamming, lasers and other types of interference and/or attack that may be exceedingly difficult to detect.

The time has come for a concerted national effort to assure that the United States enjoys and can reliably exercise space power. This will require first and foremost an appreciation of what is at stake, as well as a clear program for enhancing the survivability of existing satellites and greatly improving the nation's ability to get into and exercise power in and through outer space. We can only hope that Don Rumsfeld's latest, immense contribution to the common defense will be the catalyst for such urgently needed activities.

Just when you thought Barack Obama's toadying to Islam could not get any worse, now comes this: The President directed the new administrator of NASA, retired Marine Major General Charles Bolden, as "perhaps [his] foremost" charge to "find a way to reach out to the Muslim world and engage more dominantly Muslim nations to help them feel good about their historic contribution to science...and math and engineering."

This comment came in an interview the NASA chief conducted with al-Jazeera while touring the Middle East to mark the first anniversary of Mr. Obama's much-ballyhooed Cairo paean to Muslims. Bolden elaborated, "It is a matter of trying to reach out and get the best of all worlds, if you will, and there is much to be gained by drawing in the contributions that are possible from the Muslim (nations)."

In an address to the American University in Cairo, Bolden added that Mr. Obama has "asked NASA to change...by reaching out to 'nontraditional' partners and strengthening our cooperation in the Middle East, North Africa, Southeast Asia and in particular in Muslim-majority nations." He declared that "NASA is not only a space exploration agency, but also an Earth improvement agency."

Now, when one thinks of the "contributions" to our space program that are possible from Muslim nations, the one that comes to mind is the literal kind - recycled petrodollars - since their "contributions to science, math and engineering" for several hundreds of years have been, to put it charitably, underwhelming.

As it happens, the NASA Administrator made it pretty clear in his remarks to al-Jazeera that the U.S. space program is not going anywhere without foreign help. That will soon be literally true since, with the retirement of the last space shuttle this fall, we will be entirely dependent on Russian launchers to put people into space.

Such a state of affairs will persist unless and until experimental American rockets being developed by private American concerns pan out. Or the Chinese offer us a ride.

Unfortunately, the prospect of America's space program relying - like a fading superpower version of A Streetcar Named Desire's Blanche DuBois - on the "kindness of strangers" is the inevitable result of programmatic decisions being taken by the Obama administration.

The most obvious one was the cancellation earlier this year of NASA's Constellation program, which was intended to provide a "man-rated" expendable rocket to replace the shuttle as America's means of putting humans into space. The national security and commercial implications of this decision have been exacerbated, however, by two other, seemingly unrelated actions: President Obama's decision to stop producing long-range missile defense interceptors and to defer indefinitely any replacement of our aging nuclear-armed intercontinental ballistic missile force. As a result, real concerns are beginning to be expressed about the viability of the U.S. industrial base for solid-fuel rocket motors. Without government procurements in one or more of these areas - possibly for years to come, America will see at a minimum the continuing attrition of domestic suppliers for vital components and the steady erosion of the skills required to manufacture boosters capable of reliably lofting large payloads.

Matters would be made worse when one combines this reality with another Obama priority: relaxing export controls on sensitive dual-use technologies. The argument usually made is that such steps are necessary to ensure that American producers can compete in world markets and that "higher fences around fewer technologies" can safeguard what absolutely must be protected, and allow easier transfer of products that need not be.

In practice, it is predictable that the result of this policy will be that manufacturing jobs associated with presently controlled technologies will move offshore, where production can take place at lower cost. And the price that will surely be extracted by Saudi Arabia and other wealthy Muslim nations from whom NASA will be seeking "contributions" will be access to know-how and possibly space-launch-related production capabilities currently deemed too sensitive to transfer.

It would be bad enough if the results of such initiatives would be simply to build up America's commercial competitors. Given that many of the relevant technologies are inherently applicable to military uses - notably, delivering nuclear and other weapons of mass destruction over long distances via ballistic missiles - these steps will ineluctably result in greater threats to American citizens, interests and allies, as well.

Worse yet, in a recently unveiled policy pronouncement, President Obama has expressed an openness to exploring Russian and Chinese ideas for new, multilateral space arms control negotiations. As Moscow and Beijing have long appreciated, unavoidable verification and definitional problems ensure that, as a practical matter, any treaty likely to emerge from such talks would further weaken America's ability to protect its interests in space and on the ground - without denying such advantages to our potential adversaries.

As in so many areas, it seems President Obama's space policies and programs are designed to "fundamentally transform" America from a preeminent world power to just another nation, dependent on the good will and assistance of others to safeguard its interests. To the extent that such reliance is placed on sources like the Russians, the Chinese and "the Muslim world" that have made little secret of their ambition to weaken, if not destroy, the United States, it is likely to end badly, as it did for poor Blanche DuBois.

Intelligence

In congressional testimony today, Central Intelligence Agency Director James Woolsey is expected to unveil the most sweeping reorganization of the CIA since the early 1980s. Some critics of U.S. intelligence will doubtless suggest that this effort amounts to rearranging the proverbial deck chairs on the Titanic.

In fact, the proposed reorganization appears to me to be more like the iceberg - and the consequences bearing down upon it are likely to be just as dire for the Central Intelligence Agency as for that ill-fated ship.

The impetus for the radical changes that are envisioned in the CIA's analysis arm, known as the Directorate of Intelligence (DI), come from two sources - the Clinton White House and Congress. The former has been infuriated by an intelligence service that continued to serve up assessments of international developments that did not conform to the administration's Pollyannish worldview. Indeed, they often gave critics of President Clinton's myriad foreign policy failures grist for the mill.

A seminal event in this regard, and case in point, were the briefings supplied to Congress last fall by the national intelligence officer for Latin America, Brian Latel. These briefings raised serious questions about the mental stability, behavior and policy predilections of ousted Haitian President Jean-Bertrand Aristide. The analysis and judgments - and leaks to the press about them - offered by Mr. Latel greatly sharpened congressional opposition to the Clinton policy aimed at restoring Mr. Aristide to power, no matter what. No less unwelcome were CIA assessments suggesting that administration strategies for dealing with North Korea, Somalia, Bosnia, China and Russia were equally flawed. Administration officials started to argue that CIA was not providing them with "the proper support."

Meanwhile, many of the CIA's critics in Congress have seized upon the catastrophe of the Aldrich Ames spy case to press their arguments for a radical overhaul - if not the complete dismantling - of an organization believed to be an anachronism of the Cold War. Never mind that Ames worked in the operations - or covert - side of the agency, not the analysis side. To appease, or at least placate, those on Capitol Hill demanding massive budgetary reductions and bureaucratic changes, the CIA's senior management has suddenly whipped up several ominous proposals.

These initiatives - which will affect the DI's organization, products and links to senior policy-makers - have a common attribute: A conscious effort will be made not to serve up bad news to officials disposed to construe such information as evidence of "disloyalty" to the administration and its purposes. DI analyses will be strictly limited to factual statements; the sorts of forecasts and informed, if necessarily somewhat subjective, judgments that have traditionally been ingredients in CIA analyses are now being dismissed as "crystal ball-gazing" and to be left out of future DI papers. Reporting on politically sensitive "sore spots" will not be routinely provided to the president and his subordinates. Briefers will be chosen who need not be reminded to avoid such tackiness. Those who cannot or will not adapt to this "new look" of intelligence analysis are being demoted, reassigned or sent abroad.

Particularly troubling is the announced desire of the deputy director for intelligence, Douglas MacEachin, to "purge" the agency of the "culture of the 1980s." Mr. MacEachin's precise intent is somewhat unclear. On the one hand, it could mean that the administration wants to be seen as eliminating a "Cold War mindset" from DI products. On the other hand, the "1980s culture" the DDI wants to purge may be that instituted under former CIA Directors William Casey and Robert Gates - designed to maximize the quality and utility of intelligence analysis by encouraging competition in analysis, incorporating alternative scenarios and publishing dissenting points of view.

Either way, this reorganization of the Central Intelligence Agency will not provide the hardheaded, critical intelligence support Mr. Clinton and his team so desperately need. Instead, it will institutionalize pandering to policy officials who become spiteful when confronted with bad news concerning their assumptions and decisions.

For example, the kind of rigorous analysis that U.S. policy-makers and commanders will have to have in the event of an invasion of Haiti will not be produced under this plan. Similarly, CIA analysis of many other issues this administration finds politically neuralgic - for example, North Korea's nuclear weapons program; the resurgent anti-Western forces in the former Soviet Union; the potential for further, strategically significant conflict in the Persian Gulf; the long-range problems for U.S. interests in East Asia and beyond arising from China's economic growth and military build-up; and the need for effective missile defenses - are also likely to suffer as a result of this scheme.

CIA officials may think that such a plan will spare them the budget cutter's ax by winning favor with the administration. In the long run, however, by creating conditions under which the agency becomes, at best, irrelevant and, at worst, a contributor to ill-considered policy decisions, they may well be writing the CIA's epitaph.

461

To hear the Clinton administration tell it, in the wake of the terrible damage done by Aldrich Ames' unauthorized disclosure of classified information, there's going to be no more of that sort of thing. A new politicized management team has been hired to shake up, purge and otherwise discipline the CIA's covert operations directorate. This is being done in the name of preventing such disastrous compromises of U.S. intelligence and the "sources and methods" by which it is acquired - usually at great expense to the taxpayer and often at considerable risk.

Yet, there appears to be one important exception to this policy: If the compromise occurs as the predictable result of sharing intelligence with the United Nations, it seems the Clinton administration is inclined to regard that as an acceptable cost of doing business.

This point was brought home graphically a few months ago when it came to light that U.N. personnel in Somalia had been, to put it delicately, rather casual about safeguarding classified information supplied by the United States. In fact, had it not been for a chance discovery by a U.S. diplomat literally turning out the lights as the U.N. bailed out of Mogadishu, sensitive data - some of which reportedly identified the Somali sources - would have been compromised. Those Somalis would have probably met the same fate as did the agents sacrificed by Aldrich Ames.

Unfortunately, a postmortem on the Somali fiasco by Sen. Olympia Snowe, Maine Republican, revealed it was not an isolated problem. There have been at least four incidents in which the United Nations has breached the security of classified documents provided by the United States. More appalling still, Mrs. Snowe discovered that there was no agreement in place obliging the United Nations to provide for the protection of intelligence supplied by the United States. When the administration was challenged on this point, it indicated it would be demeaning to the secretary general even to ask for such an agreement.

Mrs. Snowe correctly thought this absurd. At her initiative, the Senate Foreign Relations Committee, on which she serves, amended the Foreign Relations Revitalization Act - which is expected to be taken up by the full Senate today -to conform U.S. intelligence-sharing practices with the United Nations with those observed elsewhere. The Snowe amendment blocks the provision of U.S. intelligence information to the United Nations, its employees, or any associated organization unless mechanisms "have been formally agreed to and implemented by the United Nations for protecting intelligence methods and sources." Such mechanisms would require, among other things, that the United Nations must: adopt background investigation and security violation investigation procedures comparable to those employed by the United States government; agree to protect U.S.-provided intelligence in a similar manner; immediately notify Washington if there has been a security breach with regard to such information and cooperate in U.S. law enforcement investigations thereof; and ensure that U.S. classified data is not given to nationals ineligible for access to such information - including those from states sponsoring terrorism.

It is instructive that the Clinton administration, which professes to be so concerned about Aldrich Ames' compromising of U.S. intelligence, is vehemently opposed to Mrs. Snowe's efforts to prevent the United Nations from becoming the vehicle for similar travesties in the future. This opposition was expressed, for example, at a meeting last month with Senate staffers. On that occasion, the administration's case was presented by Michael O'Neill - the new chief of staff in John Deutch's CIA who previously ran highly partisan anti-agency actions for then House Speaker Tom Foley - and Dr. Toby Gati, the assistant secretary of state for intelligence and research. (The latter, a friend of Bill and Hillary, was judged qualified for this senior intelligence post by her background as a professor at Columbia and as a spokesperson for the multilateralist United Nations Association.)

According to participants, Mr. O'Neill evinced little concern that the United Nations could do much damage to U.S. interests. He minimized the problem of leaks of intelligence shared with the United Nations, even as he acknowledged that some were inevitable and unavoidable.

Tobi Gati went even further. She claimed it was important for the United States to provide intelligence to the United Nations "even when it is not in the U.S. interest." Her rationale? "The medium is the message." In other words, by sharing sensitive information in those circumstances, we can increase the chances that the United Nations will use American intelligence when U.S. interests will be served by doing so. The lack of judgment evident in Dr. Goti's reasoning -and the behavior she attempts to justify with it - has alarmed many of her colleagues in the intelligence community.

Incredibly. Sen. Arlen Specter, chairman of the Senate Intelligence Committee and a candidate for Mr. Clinton's job, is reportedly considering an administration request that he offer his own amendment to strike Mrs. Snowe's language. Alternatively, Dr. Gati's friends on the House Intelligence Committee hope they can have it excised when the bill goes to conference later this summer.

Could undisciplined, indiscriminate sharing of classified information with the United Nations ultimately harm security by compromising our sources and methods as comprehensively as Aldrich Ames did? Perhaps not. But if any lesson is to be learned from the Ames disaster, it is that such capabilities are highly perishable and, once exposed, are gone for good. Olympia Snowe should be commended, and strongly supported, in her efforts to prevent further squandering of the intelligence assets (both human and technological) and the considerable resources required to field them, that America is likely to need in the future more than ever before.

The phenomenon of a presidential nominee feverishly trying to recast long-held positions and obscure his established record on the eve of his consideration by the Senate is not new. In fact, this sort of "confirmation conversion" is often a telltale sign that a candidacy is in serious trouble. Frequently, it has the opposite of the intended effect - sinking a nomination, rather than saving it.

This may be the case with President Clinton's latest candidate for the office of director of central intelligence (DCI). The spectacle of Anthony Lake's attempted makeover is only reinforcing senators' fears that the former national security adviser is too political, too facile, in short too untrustworthy to hold what is, by definition, a position of ultimate trust. After all, the DCI works not just for the president but for the legislative branch, as well. Congress simply cannot afford to turn over the CIA to a man in whose judgment, independence or integrity it lacks confidence.

Manifestations of Mr. Lake's confirmation conversion are not hard to find. In backgrounding sympathetic press outlets and damage-control conversations with senators, the DCI-designate and his supporters have made, among others, the following representations:

- A few weeks ago, Mr. Lake responded to a direct question on "Meet the Press" about whether he thought Alger Hiss was a Soviet spy by saying: "I've read a couple of books that certainly offered a lot of evidence that he may have been. I don't think it's conclusive." When this astounding statement precipitated sharp criticism in the media, among U.S. intelligence and counterintelligence operatives and on Capitol Hill, Mr. Lake put out the word that (according to the Dec. 30 issue of U.S. News & World Report) "[he] does believe in the former diplomat's guilt - but did not think that a television interview following Hiss' recent death was the appropriate venue in which to express it."

- Tony Lake played a central role in preventing the responsible congressional committees from knowing about the administration's fateful decision to acquiesce in radical Islamic Iran's effort to penetrate the European Continent through arms shipments and military cooperation with the Bosnian government. So much so that he is cited by name in a criminal referral from the House select subcommittee seeking Janet Reno's appointment of a special counsel to investigate the legality of administration actions in the Iran-Bosnia affair. Not surprisingly, this episode engenders unease in the Senate about how forthcoming a DCI Lake would be with Congress regarding politically sensitive covert initiatives.

- In a classic instance of confirmation conversion, Mr. Lake has reportedly told senators he now believes it was a mistake to have withheld information about the Clinton role in Iran's equip-and-train program in Bosnia. Even President Clinton has been brought into the act, declaring on Dec. 16 that he "accepts" Mr. Lake's statement that "it probably would have been better to inform key members of Congress on a confidential basis."

- When challenged about his statement at the time he was nominated about the importance he attached to collecting "intelligence" on the environment, Mr. Lake has suggested that this was nothing more than a sop to Vice President Al Gore. In fact, as former Defense Secretary Caspar Weinberger and Peter Schweizer recently noted in National Review - on Tony Lake's watch, CIA resources have been massively diverted from monitoring military threats to addressing precisely the sorts of "global issues" so dear to the Vice President's heart (for example, the extent of ecological degradation taking place in Lake Victoria). This could prove to be an expensive "sop" - particularly if it were to continue at a Lake CIA so Al Gore won't "get mad" at the director.

- Over the past year, National Security Adviser Tony Lake has joined other administration officials who professed confidence in the conclusions of a controversial 1995 National Intelligence Estimate (NIE). This NIE arrived at the preposterous conclusion that there would be no threat of ballistic missile attack against the United States for at least 15 years. The NIE became a cornerstone of the Clinton stonewall against prompt deployment of anti-missile systems to protect the American people. When combined with concerns about the NIE's contents, the use to which this estimate was put reinforced the perception that the administration was brazenly politicizing the U.S. intelligence community.

- Mr. Lake now claims he agrees with the findings of a special panel commissioned by departing DCI John Deutch and chaired by former DCI Robert Gates. Presumably, that is because the Gates panel claimed the NIE was not, strictly speaking, "politicized." It nonetheless found that the NIE's methodology, assumptions and conclusions were sufficiently flawed as to make the estimate deficient as a basis for policy-making about deploying missile defenses. Even by the standards of past confirmation conversions, it would be a stunning reversal if Tony Lake were actually to embrace this critique.

Mr. Lake's makeover also involves demurrals about his past associations with the radical left Institute for Policy Studies, a "university" it ran and one of its spinoff organizations, the Center for National Security Studies. Like other statements made in a bid to shore up support for his nomination, these demurrals - which bear directly on the DCI-designate's historic views of, for example, covert operations and counterintelligence activities - will have to be carefully evaluated by the Senate Select Committee on Intelligence.

One thing is clear already, however: A man with a demonstrated reluctance to tell the truth - lest he, by so doing, hurt others' feelings, engender the anger of his executive branch bosses or complicate the president's political and/or policy agenda - should be considered wholly unfit for the job of director of central intelligence.

"DEAD MAN WALKING... THE CONFIRMATION PLANK?" | MARCH 11, 1997

As long-awaited hearings begin today on Anthony Lake's controversial nomination to become the next director of central intelligence (DCI), the suspense over whether he can successfully run the Senate gauntlet has largely disappeared. Tony Lake's prospects are becoming those of a Dead Man Walking.

The more interesting question is: How much damage will Mr. Lake inflict on the Clinton-Gore team's triage operation - aimed at stanching the hemorrhage of ruinous revelations about communist Chinese influence operations - in the process of proving that he cannot be confirmed?

After all, Tony Lake will be the first senior Clinton administration official to appear under oath before a Senate committee with a responsibility - and, one must expect, a keen interest - to discover the extent to which Beijing's agents successfully gained access to the White House, to John Huang's Commerce Department and to congressional offices like those of California's Democratic Sens. Dianne Feinstein and Barbara Boxer.

Last Tuesday, I suggested in this space that Tony Lake presided as national security adviser over what appears to be the most successful penetration of the White House by an unfriendly foreign government since the British took the place in the War of 1812. Information that has subsequently come to light only compound concerns about entrusting such a man with the job of assessing and countering hostile foreign intelligence activities.

This information also raises a host of questions about what President Clinton knew about China's offensive, and when he knew it. On Saturday, an unnamed White House official backgrounded The Washington Post that: "The White House was unaware of alleged Chinese efforts to funnel money into presidential campaigns [sic] until reading news accounts last month." By Sunday, however, this line of defense began to crumble.

After Vice President Al Gore's former chief of staff and President Clinton's outgoing counsel, Jack Quinn, used this line on the record, ABC News' evening report featured further backgrounding to the effect that administration officials on the political side were kept in the dark about the FBI's information about Chinese penetrations. The story now goes that only the foreign policy side of the house knew about them, as long ago as June 1996 – and they failed to relay the information to the president.

If true, it is a scandal for Tony Lake, his former deputy and successor as national security adviser, Sandy Berger, and their NSC team. The latter would include not only those senior officials with responsibility for counterintelligence but also those handling the East Asia portfolio who met with the likes of Pauline Kanchanalak, a Thai businesswoman with ties to China and a Democratic donor of suspicious funds.

On the other hand, if, as seems far more likely, the FBI warnings about Chinese activities were passed from the NSC to the political types, but were ignored by the latter as inconvenient in the midst of a campaign determined to raise money from any source - including convicted drug dealers, Russian arms proliferators and, it appears, Chinese intelligence - the scandal is vastly more serious.

Mr. Clinton is not a man given to profound personal loyalties when his own interests are in jeopardy. Time and again, the plug has been pulled on Cabinet and sub-Cabinet positions when they proved controversial. None of the controversies to date, however - not the nanny problems, not the Radical Leftist writings, not the problematic records of two previous candidates for the DCI job - have posed anything like the possibly mortal peril to Mr. Clinton's own future that the China-Lake issue does.

Consequently, the president seems likely to conclude that Tony Lake is expendable. In fact, Saturday's New York Times reported that "Mr. Clinton has not done much to promote Mr. Lake's confirmation," regarding the CIA job as "a step down" from the position of national security adviser and a post for which Mr. Lake is "overqualified." This smacks of an administration maneuvering to cut its losses.

Interestingly, it comes as the New Republic - a magazine reputedly considered required reading by Mr. Clinton, Mr. Gore and other self-styled "New Democrats" - published this week a devastating cover story titled, "The Great Equivocator: Why Tony Lake Should Not Run the CIA." While the author, Jacob Heilbrunn, takes pains to disassociate his criticisms from those of Mr. Lake's more conservative critics, he nonetheless arrives at basically the same bottom line: Tony Lake's record is one marked by dismal policy judgments, a lack of vision or the courage of his convictions and a seeming inability to make tough, to say nothing of sound, decisions. As Mr. Heilbrunn puts it: "Lake's view of the world, decisively shaped by the central event of his young adulthood, the Vietnam War, is rooted in moral ambiguity and ambivalence. From

Cambodia to the Soviet Union, from Bosnia to the Middle East, Lake's career long penchant has been to evade unpleasant realities and elide the differences imposed by clear moral choices."

(Interestingly, Mr. Heilbrunn notes that, "as one of the architects of the [Clinton] administration's China policy, Lake has been at the forefront in coddling Beijing. Lake, who has adopted the Clintonite obsession with markets - the term appeared 41 times in a recent speech - has insisted that the U.S. refrain from exposing Chinese efforts to export nuclear materials to Third World countries. No country will loom larger in the CIA's future calculations than China." As The Washington Times observed yesterday, this obsession with trade has seen the Clinton administration turn over one of the nation's premier military installations, the Navy base at Long Beach, Calif., to the Chinese merchant marine without a formal review of the obvious, adverse national security implications of doing so.)

These are qualities that would be undesirable in a director of central intelligence under any circumstances. Such an individual is clearly an unacceptable candidate for that post under the very difficult circumstances in which the U.S. intelligence community is currently operating.

Whether President Clinton decides to pull the plug on Anthony Lake's nomination as part of his own damage-limitation operation or the Senate concludes that Mr. Lake lacks the judgment, integrity and independence to serve as an effective DCI, the net result is likely to be the same: Tony Lake will not be allowed to make matters worse at the CIA.

Chairman Richard Shelby and his colleagues on the Senate Intelligence Committee must work to ensure, however, that two positive things come out of this dismal nomination: First, the present hearings must thoroughly examine what just occurred with respect to China's efforts to advance its interests by, among other things, buying access and influence in Washington on Tony Lake's watch. And second, a high standard must be set so the nation can be assured that future nominees to run the American intelligence community do not have Mr. Lake's serious liabilities.

A "need to know" is one of the most time-tested principles of information security. According to this principle, if you don't have such a need, you should not be given access to classified or other sensitive data.

Even if you think you have a "need to know," moreover, unless appropriate background checks have been performed - establishing that you can be trusted to treat such information confidentially - and the requisite security clearances (known in the government as "tickets") issued, you do not qualify. In sum, the basic rule has been: No tickets, no access.

That, at least, was the general practice until the Clinton administration came to office, empowering a number of individuals who were critical of governmental secrecy in general and the so-called "abuse" of classification procedures in particular. Madeleine Albright, Tobi Goti, Hazel O'Leary, Anthony Lake, Morton Halperin and John Podesta were among the senior officials who, during the Clinton years in one way or another, pursued a different approach.

For example, former Secretary of State Albright, and her department's intelligence chief, Mrs. Goti, believed "sharing" sensitive U.S. intelligence with other nations would demonstrate the validity of American charges about their involvement in proliferation. The predictable result was confirmed in a front-page article The Washington Post on Sunday about Russian-Iranian missile cooperation over the past decade: The recipients of such information were generally more interested in ascertaining - and terminating - the ways in which it was obtained than in ending their proliferation activities. All too often, putting them "in the know" meant that, thereafter, we would be kept in the dark, having lost irreplaceable intelligence collection "sources and methods."

Then there was the security-wrecking operation engaged in by former Energy Secretary O'Leary and the anti-nuclear activists she chose to staff key jobs in her department. For instance, she blithely ended the nuclear weapons laboratories' traditional practice of giving different colored badges to lab personnel based on their "need to know" and levels of security clearance. Her rationale? It would be discriminatory to those (notably, Chinese, Russian, Iranian and other foreign nationals) who had neither. We may never fully know how much damage was done as a direct or indirect result of the climate of insecurity and dysfunctionality created in the nuclear weapons complex by O'Leary and Company.

An even more ominous legacy, however, may be that resulting from the compulsory declassification requirements promulgated by President Clinton at the urging of his then-National Security Adviser Tony Lake, Mort Halperin (at the time one of his chief lieutenants on the NSC staff) and John Podesta, who ultimately served as White House chief of Staff.

According to the champions of this approach, everybody had a "need to know" about most government secrets; Mr. Clinton directed that - in the interest of good government - after a certain number of years, basically all of them were to be put into the public domain.

In some cases (prominent among them the Energy Department), the arbitrary deadline and the quantity of secrets to be revealed meant that those responsible for declassifying old, but potentially still highly sensitive, information were obliged to give documents containing such data only the most cursory of security reviews. As a result, whole boxes full of classified information were sometimes summarily deemed declassified and made accessible to anyone who wanted to review their contents. Presumably, among that number were scientists from nuclear wannabe states like North Korea, Iran and Iraq. Findings in the caves of Afghanistan suggest they may have included operatives of al Qaeda and other terrorist organizations, as well.

Fortunately, to build even primitive atomic weapons, let alone thermonuclear arms, one must have not only knowhow but access to fairly complex and expensive manufacturing capabilities. The bad news is that is not the case with biological weapons (BW). Knowledgeable people can use commercially available fertilizer and pharmaceutical equipment to create batches of viruses that can be employed with devastating effect.

Now, the New York Times reports that the Clinton declassification requirements have caused U.S. government agencies to make publicly available what amount to BW "cook books" - "hundreds of formerly secret documents that tell how to turn dangerous germs into deadly weapons." According to Sunday's Times, "For $15, anyone can buy 'Selection of Process for Freeze-Drying, Particle Size Reduction and Filling of Selected BW Agents,' or germs for biological warfare. The 57-page report, dated 1952, includes plans for a pilot factory that could produce dried germs in powder form, designed to lodge in human lungs." In the wrong hands, this recipe could enable a future terrorist attack that would make the recent anthrax letters, and even the destruction of the World Trade Center, pale by comparison.

In a number of areas, the Bush administration has, since coming to office a year ago, taken steps to undo lunatic policies inherited from its predecessor. These include, notably: the unworkably expensive and inequitable Kyoto Protocol; business-crippling ergonomics rules; open-ended adherence to the vulnerability-dictating Anti-Ballistic Missile Treaty; inaction on the Yucca Mountain repository for nuclear waste and other impediments to national energy self-sufficiency; and an invitation to industrial and governmental espionage masquerading as a protocol to the Biological Weapons Convention.

A no-less-worrisome legacy is the Clinton declassification agenda. Particularly in the midst of the war on terrorism, it is imperative that President Bush re-establish proven and prudential information security practices. Given the very serious stakes, should Mr. Bush fail to take corrective action on this score, the American people will certainly have a legitimate need to know why.

Nearly two years ago, in the immediate aftermath of the September 11 attacks, official Washington was seized with the question: Had there been prior warning of these devastating acts of terror? And, if so, could it have been acted upon so as to prevent the premeditated murder of thousands of Americans?

The recently released report of a joint congressional intelligence committee's investigation into this topic confirms what many experts had assumed: Of course there were warnings of these attacks - both of a general and even of a somewhat specific nature. The problem was, as is usually the case, differentiating before the fact such salient information from what the intelligence professionals call the "noise" - the background clutter that is irrelevant or at least uninformative.

The investigation also confirmed that matters were made worse by various bureaucratic, regulatory and procedural arrangements that impeded such action as might have been taken to disrupt the hijackers' plot before it was perpetrated. In short, there were "dots" that might have been connected but built-in impediments made even more problematic the always-difficult task of connecting such dots without the filtering benefit of hindsight.

Ever since September 11, the Bush administration has recognized that, as important as the events and lessons of that day may be, there is an even-more-pressing task: Figuring out how to discern - and draw appropriate connections between - the pieces of information that suggest the nature and timing of possible future terrorist attacks. The absence to date of more deadly incidents in this country is, in part at least, a reflection of this focus [together with the president's offensive strategy aimed at disrupting enemy networks and making it harder for them to operate with impunity in our homeland].

As the Bush team sought to enhance the government's ability to connect the dots for counterterrorism purposes, it was fortunate to secure a return to public service of one of the nation's most formidable national security practitioners: Retired Navy Adm. John Poindexter.

A top graduate of the Naval Academy, Adm. Poindexter had an exemplary career in his service and would likely have retired as one of its few four-stars but for his answering the call to help run the National Security Council under President Reagan. In the course of that assignment, he became embroiled in decisions aiding pro-U.S. Nicaraguan freedom fighters that the then-Democratic-controlled Congress was determined to abandon. For those who have had the privilege of knowing and working with him, the vitriolic, demeaning and career-terminating treatment to which this outstanding military officer was subsequently subjected was the real scandal, not what happened on his watch at the NSC.

It was, therefore, highly gratifying that at a moment of national crisis, Donald

Rumsfeld's Pentagon was able to enlist Adm. Poindexter once more in the service of his country. Drawing on his vast experience with defense, intelligence and information technologies, the admiral was given a post at one of the most creative and productive organizations in the federal government, the Defense Advanced Research Projects Agency. His assignment: Develop ways to improve our ability to connect the dots.

In this capacity, Adm. Poindexter has been a driving force behind two promising initiatives: the Total Information Awareness [TIA] project and the Policy Analysis Market [PAM]. The former envisioned using commercially available data-mining techniques to discern and assimilate terrorism-relevant information from government and private sector sources. The latter proposed to utilize well-established market techniques to draw out and evaluate information about possible terrorist scenarios.

Critics have cast these two initiatives in a very different light. The TIA project has been portrayed as "Big Brother" incarnate, a wholly unaccountable means for government to collect and utilize private information without regard for Americans' civil rights. For its part, PAM precipitated a firestorm of criticism on Capitol Hill and in the press after it was caricatured as a government-sponsored "terrorism futures market."

John Poindexter's association with these ideas was invariably used by their opponents to further their demands that the programs be terminated. One such critic, Sen. Barbara Boxer, California Democrat, went so far as to say of PAM that Congress should "end the careers of whoever it was who thought that up."

Unfortunately, Mrs. Boxer has gotten her wish. Adm. Poindexter announced last week that he will once again be leaving government service. This decision had to be all the more painful for it being accompanied by a truncation of his Information Awareness program, a smoking crater where the PAM project was to be and his reputation once again sullied by people who are unworthy to hold his coat.

Such people will doubtless be among the first to find fault the next time there is a terrorist attack and the dots that might have prevented the ensuing death and destruction were not connected. Should such an attack occur, however, the blame will likely lie at least in part with them for impeding effective use of tools that can and should be properly used to anticipate and address terrorist threats - and not with a patriot named John Poindexter who advanced them when, to his credit, he once again selflessly and creatively answered his nation's call to service.

The heat is on. Advocates of history's most sweeping and least-considered "reform" of the U.S. intelligence community are intent on having their way. In recent days, members of the September 11 Commission and leading legislators of both parties have taken to the media with warnings of dire consequences if their bill is not passed - and utterly preposterous promises of good things if it is.

The former include the claim - mostly advanced by Democrats - that President Bush will be discredited, if not politically emasculated, if he cannot compel balking Republican members of Congress to enact this legislation. The latter include assertions that passing the intelligence reform bill is necessary to "keep the American people safe." The public - 80 percent of whom we have endlessly been told favor this measure - could reasonably be under the illusion its adoption will prevent future terrorist attacks against this country.

Of course, none of this is true. Mr. Bush will be strengthened, not hurt - and more importantly, so will the national interest - if he recognizes the wisdom of many on Capitol Hill, in the intelligence community and, yes, inside his own administration who know this bill is too defective to warrant enactment.

Take, for example, the hotly contested issue of whether the bill's proposal to reassign management control and budgetary authority for three Defense Department intelligence agencies to a new director of national intelligence will impair our military's operations and security. Rep. Duncan Hunter, California Republican, the chairman of the House Armed Services Committee, and all the Joint Chiefs of Staff are convinced it will. The bill's proponents insist it will not, often averring they would never support legislation that would do such a thing, and suggest their opponents are motivated by parochial interests.

Happily, one man in America has unique credentials that allow him to address the matter objectively: James Schlesinger, a former intelligence chief and past defense secretary.

Mr. Schlesinger told the Senate Armed Services Committee Aug. 16: "Intelligence is increasingly interwoven with military operations. We must always have in mind the crucial role of intelligence in support of the war fighter. The advance of military technology and its embodiment in our military forces have made intelligence ever more integral to our military strategy and battlefield tactics and to this country's immense military advantage . . . In all of this, the accuracy, the immediacy and the believability of intelligence is crucial . . .

"It has taken many years to persuade military commanders that national assets will reliably be available to them in the event of conflict. To shift control over crucial intelligence assets outside the Department of Defense risks weakening the relative military advantage of the United States - and at the same time creates the incentive to divert resources into (likely inferior) intelligence capabilities, which would further reduce the available forces."

Mr. Schlesinger concluded his Olympian testimony last August with a call for Congress to "remember Hippocrates' injunction: 'First, do no harm.' In altering the structure of the intelligence community, it is essential to deliberate long and hard - and not to be stampeded into doing harm . . . Reform may now be necessary. Yet, in the vain pursuit of a perfect intelligence organization, do not shake up intelligence in a way that does do harm - and in pursuit of this will-of-the-wisp, damage in particular those military capabilities that we alone possess."

Fortunately, this eminently sensible advice to "do no harm" has recently been echoed by two highly influential, yet politically divergent editorial pages.

On Nov. 22, the Wall Street Journal observed: "Congress wrapped up its weekend lame-duck session without passing intelligence reform, and you will no doubt be reading outraged editorials and political moans that the country is now less safe. Don't believe it. The opposite may be closer to the truth, since the proposed reshuffling of the intelligence bureaucracies would have taken months, if not years, to carry out - and certainly would have turned some of our spy agencies' attention away from the actual collection and analysis of intelligence . . . If this reform is really so vital, it will get done, but better to do it in more considered fashion next year."

Then, on Nov. 24, The Washington Post editorialized: "Last weekend, Congress passed up the opportunity to adopt, after scant consideration, the largest reorganization of the U.S. intelligence community in half a century - a measure that was rushed through both houses with election-year zeal and then concocted by a conference committee into a 500-page omnibus that hardly anyone had read, much less considered . . . A better solution would be to pause, let this election-year stampede subside and urge a new Congress to try again."

Perhaps the real reason some in Congress are so intent on passing "intelligence reform" legislation now is that considering this matter next year would almost certainly require action they are resisting and have not addressed in the current bill: Much-needed streamlining and other improvements in legislative oversight of the intelligence community. That possibility to do real good is another excellent reason for our leaders to avoid doing harm to American intelligence when the lame duck session resumes next week.

Philosopher George Santayana said, "Fanaticism consists in redoubling your effort when you have forgotten your aim." By that definition, there seems to be an outbreak of fanaticism in official Washington as proponents of the so-called "intelligence reform bill" insist it be enacted this week - even though, in at least two important ways, it no longer would help reduce America's vulnerability to renewed terrorist attack.

First, the bill was not supposed to aim only at intelligence reform. It was intended to carry out the September 11 commission's various recommendations - including some not dealing with changes to the U.S. intelligence community.

Arguably far more important in terms of reducing the chance of another terrorist attack on the American homeland are a set of commission recommendations some members of Congress have no interest in adopting. These pertain to border security, changes to policies and practices governing legal and illegal immigration and standards designed to make state-issued drivers licenses less susceptible to fraud and abuse.

I appeared last week at a Capitol Hill press conference with five members of September 11 Families for a Secure America who oppose the bill in its present form. This group represents some 300 of the families who lost loved ones on September 11, 2001 - far more than any other group and most especially the handful of self-appointed spokesmen calling themselves the "9/11 Family Steering Committee" who campaigned for John Kerry and now insist the bill be enacted as is.

It turns out vastly more of those whose lives were shattered by the terrorists on September 11 recognize a political certainty: If the present legislation does not make our borders less porous, or improve the government's ability to monitor aliens here legally and remove those who are not and prevent terrorists' use of identity and document fraud, provisions to do so are unlikely to ever pass.

Though polls indicate the vast majority of Americans want more robust policies toward illegal aliens, leading politicians of both parties choose to ignore such constituents. Instead, they defer to those who advocate on the illegals' behalf - notably, well-heeled immigration lawyers, prominent Latino organizations and various industries whose profits depend on cheap labor.

Consequently, all other things being equal, if any bills dealing with immigration issues are taken up next year, they will likely be about "legalizing" aliens who have come here without permission. Whether called amnesty or not, that will be the legislation's perceived purpose. The mere prospect will create new incentives to gain access to and/or remain in this country illegally - exactly the opposite of what the September 11 Commission had in mind, and sure to compound the illegal activities that made possible the last terrorist attacks.

The only chance to do something constructive about borders, immigration and drivers license and other document security is by embedding these elements in must-pass September 11 legislation. If elected officials get away with claiming their bill rewiring the Intelligence Community's organizational chart is the only necessary response to the commission's recommendations, you can forget about any action on this other, critically important front. House Judiciary Committee Chairman James Sensenbrenner and those of his colleagues who are not interested simply in paying lip service to the idea of "making the American people safer" but actually doing so, understand this and must be supported in holding the line.

The second argument for killing the present bill is that the effect of its changes to U.S. intelligence are likely to worsen, not improve, matters. It will create more bureaucracy and more "stove-piping," which are likely to produce more "groupthink" and less timely and actionable intelligence. These are precisely what reformers say they want to avoid. And we can ill-afford in time of war to create new chains of command for the Defense Department's intelligence agencies. No one - least of all House Armed Services Committee Chairman Duncan Hunter - should be under any illusion that presidential assurances or minor language changes will correct a fundamental flaw in this bill, one likely to harm our men and women in uniform.

Legislators have no higher obligation than to make our country truly safer. If there is a significant danger a bill will not actually advance that aim, it is incumbent on them to address the identified defects carefully and deliberately - an impossibility in the last hours of a lame duck session.

The American people want and expect their elected officials not simply to get this bill done but done right. True presidential leadership will be demonstrated by recognizing that can only be accomplished next year.

For some politicians, it is tough under the best of circumstances to do the right thing when it comes to national security. Posturing about "peace dividends" chronically results in defense budgets and end-strengths insufficient to deter future acts of aggression and fight the ensuing wars.

Intelligence programs are compromised by self-serving leaks and press-driven legislative responses. Pentagon leaders are savaged in public by legislators who thereby underscore their lack of understanding of the threats besetting our country, and the fact they have no better answers to the challenges thus posed.

Unfortunately, a congressional by election season in the second term of a presidency confronting widespread public misunderstanding of, and fatigue with, a global war is far from the best of circumstances. It is in such a season that President Bush confronts the determination of several members of his party in the Senate to do the politically popular rather than the necessary thing with respect to legislation that would govern the detention, interrogation and judicial review of captured al Qaeda terrorists and other unlawful enemy combatants.

Worse yet, these senators John McCain, John Warner and Lindsey Graham are not only encouraging fellow Republicans to join them in breaking with President Bush. They are giving political cover to Democrats gleeful at the chance to conceal their readiness to do the wrong thing on national security by lining up behind McCain and Company, whose number includes former Secretary of State Colin Powell. The latter supports the McCain legislation that offers enemy detainees more rights and more sharply circumscribes their interrogation than the Bush administration believes is consistent with the national security since, says Mr. Powell, the world is less persuaded of the moral legitimacy of our actions.

Unfortunately, due to such machinations, a legitimate, important but basically technical disagreement over procedures has been blown wildly out of proportion. To hear the dissident Republican senators' partisans on editorial pages and talk shows tell it, their efforts are all that stands between civilized norms of behavior toward al Qaeda and other terrorist detainees and the Bush team's rampant torture, judicial mayhem and the shredding of international law (notably, the Geneva Conventions).

Poppycock. As best-selling author Richard Miniter recently reported in the New York Post on his return from a visit to the detention facility at Guantanamo Bay, the Defense Department is bending over backward to avoid any appearance of mistreatment of these unlawful enemy combatants.

For example, detainees at "Gitmo" are supplied with three square meals a day made up of foods to their liking (all "halal," conforming to Islamic food regulations, and a choice of vanilla or chocolate ice cream); expensive medical care (including colonoscopies, dental work and prostheses); extensive legal representation (an average of 2.2 lawyers for every detainee); and extraordinary latitude for the practice of their faith (for example, interrogations are interrupted for prayers).

Moreover, as Rear Adm. Harry Harris, commander of the Guantanamo facility, makes clear in an interview with the Wall Street Journal over the weekend, detainees have repeatedly attacked their guards, seeking to kill or at least maim them using improvised weapons fashioned from fans, cameras, plumbing and light bulbs. Lately, detainees rewarded for good behavior with more lenient treatment have also taken advantage of their conditions to savagely attack their guards. Some of their lawyers are suspected of facilitating terrorist communications.

Unfortunately, far from debunking charges of abuse and ending talk of the need to close this and other vital interrogation facilities, the coddling of prisoners at Gitmo seems to be intensifying the sanctimony of Bush administration critics. They insist on blurring the lines sensibly drawn by the Geneva Convention between prisoners of war (namely, military personnel from states parties who conform to the laws of war by wearing uniforms, displaying their arms, and adhering to an identified chain of command) and unlawful enemy combatants (who do not). And they adopt a posture of contemptuous moral superiority over those who disagree.

We need to remove the sanctimony from this debate. Reasonable people can come to different conclusions about the extent of the rights that should be enjoyed by people believed to be among the most dangerous Islamofascist terrorists on the planet. Those who recognize the importance of neither compromising classified information and the sources and methods by which it is obtained nor making inevitable the unwarranted release of such individuals are not indifferent to human rights. Those who appreciate the need to use methods of interrogation more aggressive than those employed at Gitmo are not in favor of torture.

By the same token, those on the other side of these issues do not have an exclusive claim to morality's high ground. If, thanks to the absence of interrogation techniques that make detainees uncomfortable but fall well short of already prohibited torture, Americans are condemned to death (perhaps, ironically, in the course of a successful terrorist attack on the U.S. Capitol), those responsible for denying our government such tools will bear a heavy moral burden.

At that juncture, of course, it will be easy enough yea, even politically correct to blame legislators who unilaterally disarmed America in critical ways. By that time, however, it will be too late for some of us.

So, as the Senate deliberates this week whether to adopt John McCain's approach to detainee-related issues or the more robust version favored by President Bush, let us hold the senator from Arizona and his colleagues on both sides of the aisle accountable. For all of our sakes, they should err on the side of protecting the national security. Congress should swiftly enact legislation that actually protects America by establishing sensible, practicable guidelines for: use of aggressive, non-torture interrogation methods where absolutely necessary; legal protections for those charged with performing such interrogations; and the limitation, if essential to protect sources and methods of intelligence, of evidence shared with detainees in the course of their prosecution.

The announcement last week that the Obama administration would turn over the job of preparing National Intelligence Estimates to a man whom Saudi Arabia, China, Iran and Hamas surely consider an agent of influence calls to mind an old axiom about Charles "Chas" Freeman's new line of work — "Garbage in, garbage out."

The expression captures an immutable reality. The quality of the output of intelligence collection and analysis is only as good the inputs.

So, if you have a spymaster who unwittingly relies on double agents feeding the CIA enemy disinformation rather than accurate intelligence, conclusions drawn from such data will be erroneous, possibly dangerously so.

Similarly, if the chairman of the National Intelligence Council (NIC) - the organization responsible for producing the National Intelligence Estimates (NIEs) that are supposed to reflect the best insights of the intelligence community as a whole and that usually guide U.S. government security decision-making - has a well-established and anti-American policy agenda, he will likely try to discount or exclude insights from NIEs that conflict with his biases. Such a politicization of intelligence would have far-reaching implications for American interests and security.

Could this happen? In fact, it did in 2007 under the Bush administration. In December of that year, the National Intelligence Council - then under the leadership of another product of the State Department, Thomas Fingar - produced an NIE that declared "with high confidence" that the Iranian mullahs had halted their nuclear weapons program in 2003. An unclassified summary of that estimate was made public with much fanfare, and with a transparent political purpose: To deny President Bush grounds for attacking Iran so as to prevent the regime there from getting the bomb.

At the time, many intelligence and defense experts challenged the Iran NIE's much-ballyhooed conclusion as preposterous and misleading. It was even belied by findings elsewhere in the estimate. Today, however, no sentient being thinks this National Intelligence Estimate's principal finding was accurate.

Indeed, the chairman of the Joint Chiefs of Staff, Adm. Mike Mullen, declared in recent days that the mullahs now have enough enriched uranium to produce a nuclear weapon and are working to do so. Maybe that development would have occurred in the absence of a flawed NIE. Given Tehran's announced ambition to "wipe Israel off the map" and bring about "a world without America," though, it was entirely predictable once such a skewed estimate was publicly released with the desired effect.

Unfortunately, the December 2007 NIE may look like the gold standard compared with what we can expect from a NIC process run by Chas Freeman. Like his boss, Director of National Intelligence Dennis Blair, and CIA Director Leon Panetta, Mr. Freeman has long been a consumer of intelligence, but not a professional in the spy business. In fact, in the course of a long career in the Foreign Service, Mr. Freeman served in capacities - notably as ambassador to Saudi Arabia and as the No. 2 man in Embassy Beijing - where the job often is seen as representing the host government to his own, rather than the other way around.

Worse yet, in the years since he left government service, Mr. Freeman has repeatedly espoused policy views that are profoundly troubling in their own right and that should simply be disqualifying for the position of objective arbiter of the most sensitive national intelligence assessments.

For example, Mr. Freeman has viewed the Middle East through the prism of one of Foggy Bottom's most successful Arabists. He justifies Arab enmity towards us on the grounds that we are associated with Israel. He decries the liberation of Iraq for having "catalyzed anarchy, sectarian violence, terrorism, and civil war in that country." He makes excuses for "democratically elected" Hamas and urges its embrace by the United States.

Worse yet, through his organization, the Middle East Policy Council, he has been a paid shill for Saudi Arabia - from whence millions of dollars have flowed to pay for Mr. Freeman's excuse-making for the Saudis. Mr. Freeman has also served on the board of the Chinese National Offshore Oil Corporation (CNOOC), a notorious state-owned arm of Chinese colonialism in Africa and Asia - a vantage point from which he could and did flak for Communist China.

Then, as is made clear in a paper by Clare Lopez about what Tehran calls "the Iran Lobby" in America released by the Center for Security Policy last week Mr. Freeman has been a frequent apologist for Iran, as well. Like others who make up that "lobby," Mr. Freeman has repeatedly and in numerous forums parroted the mullahs' party line, insisting that the United States must engage diplomatically with Iran, not attack it.

It strains credulity that a man with such pronounced - and anti-American - policy views can serve effectively, let alone objectively, as the arbiter of National Intelligence Estimates. Perhaps they are not really his views and that he was simply what amounted to a paid lobbyist for deeply problematic causes and countries. The evidence suggests that he is what he appears to be: an aggressive partisan in the service of many of America's most dangerous actual or potential adversaries.

Either way, it is malfeasance to entrust the National Intelligence Council to him. It speaks volumes about Barack Obama's judgment and policy proclivities that he would even consider such an appointment.

After all, this is a vital post at the very pinnacle of the U.S. national security establishment. It is not a job for a garbage collector - or purveyor.

King Solomon was immortalized for saving a baby's life by threatening to split it between the real mother and a pretender. President Obama may become *in*famous for actually *splitting the baby* with his decision Friday to praise, and then undermine, critical intelligence collection operations conducted by the National Security Agency.

In fact, much of the speech could have been given by any national security-minded American leader. It was full of the sort of statements that are not heard often enough these days, particularly from this Commander-in-Chief: "Throughout American history, intelligence has helped secure our country and our freedoms...Emerging threats from terrorist groups and the proliferation of weapons of mass destruction place new and, in some ways, more complicated demands on our intelligence agencies."

Mr. Obama added: "They were now asked to identify and target plotters is some of the most remote parts of the world and to anticipate the actions of networks that, by their very nature, could not be easily penetrated by spies or informants. And it is a testimony to the hard work and dedication of the men and women of our intelligence community that over the past decade we've made enormous strides in fulfilling this mission."

The money quote in this part of the speech would seem to have been: "I did not stop these [intelligence collection] programs wholesale, not only because I felt that they made us more secure, but also because nothing in that initial review and nothing that I have learned since indicated that our intelligence community has sought to violate the law or is cavalier about the civil liberties of their fellow citizens."

Then, there was the other part of the speech. It unveiled a series of decisions that would, if not stop, certainly will compromise those programs – seemingly without regard for the consequences the President warned against in the rest of his address. That was the part with the operational – rather than rhetorical – passages.

If there were any lingering doubt that there is national security fraud being perpetrated by Team Obama, the newly announced policy on intelligence collection should put it to rest.

For example, there was Mr. Obama's change to the so-called Sec. 215 programs, whereby the NSA collects and analyzes what is known as phone record "metadata" – numbers called by whom, when and for how long. The President declared that they would immediately begin transitioning to a new arrangement for holding and accessing such information. The problem is that the President not only dispensed with the present practice – whereby the government obtains such data from phone companies and internet providers, and is able to examine it, but not the contents of conversations, without the time-consuming court orders that might be the difference between life and death in countering terrorist plots. He also rejected the two obvious alternatives: the companies that generate the records holding them or some new, private third-party entity doing so.

In addition, Mr. Obama extended some ill-defined privacy rights to "ordinary people" overseas. The dangers with these pledges should be obvious. Terrorists hide among "ordinary people" – especially when the Obama Justice Department now says that "religion" can no longer be used as an indicator for investigators. Since the administration does not understand that the Islamic doctrine of shariah is a supremacist *political* agenda that requires its adherents to engage in holy war or jihad, not constitutionally protected religious practice, those charged with protecting the rest of us are being further blinded and hobbled in their missions.

The President also declared that NSA would stop eavesdropping on "friendly and allied" foreign leaders. The obvious question is: Does that rule out monitoring communications between adversaries like China's Xi Jinping and "friends" like Germany's Angela Merkel about collaboration that may conflict with our vital interests? It is a serious mistake to rule out any opportunity to have what the military calls "situational awareness" about such adversaries, especially if they are making inroads in undermining our alliances.

Less obvious is what happens when a foreign leader is a putative ally, but does not behave like one. Mr. Obama says that Turkish Prime Minister Recep Tayyep Erdogan is one of his closest friends among counterparts overseas. Yet, Erdogan has been fundamentally transforming his country's secular Muslim democracy into an Islamist autocracy with close ties to the Muslim Brotherhood and even al Qaeda. Again, he should be monitored closely, not give a pass by U.S. intelligence.

Some intelligence professionals are consoling themselves with notion that the President could have done even more damage, for instance, by going after national security letters the FBI uses to inform investigations and barring NSA's efforts to break foreign encryption programs. Unfortunately, things will almost certainly get worse as Mr. Obama entrusted implementation to Attorney General Eric Holder – including defining an alternative approach for the Section 215 programs by March 28th.

The good news is that, on the eve of the President's address and under the sponsorship of the Center for Security Policy, a distinguished group of national security and intelligence professionals offered in an open letter to Mr. Obama principles and recommendations that would provide a far more sound basis for guiding our necessary collection programs and policies. The Center also produced last week a white paper critiquing the "reform" proposals of a like-minded group the President commissioned, proposals he partly adopted. It is to be urgently hoped that Congress will draw on such guidance as it must now perform damage control on the harm Team Obama is inflicting.

Barack Obama has split the NSA baby. Split babies die. Unforgivably and needlessly, so may innocent Americans.

AFTERWORD

On re-reading these columns, in many cases for the first time in years, I am struck by the fact that the views I expressed in them have stood up pretty well over time. To be sure, many describe events and decisions long lost to memory and in that sense might seem passé. Yet, most – if not virtually all – have an abiding relevance to the security policy choices being made today.

I think that is so primarily because they reflect what is, in my view, the essential ingredient in any effective policy: common sense. There is no greater danger in my experience than heeding the counsel of those in government, the media and most especially academia who insist on the superiority of their recommended courses of action on the grounds that they are products of other factors.

Typically, these authorities dismiss commonsensical approaches with blithe assurances that they are inferior to those rooted in such things as: anthropological insights into foreign cultures and societies; the art of diplomacy; requirements imposed by international law; or, worst of all, the theories propounded by political scientists. To the extent that such factors are at odds with, let alone *defy*, common sense they should be assiduously abjured.

The good news is that the American people are still imbued with abundant common sense. That is so despite concerted efforts made over the past few decades to wean it out of them (for example, by Common Core-style educational engineering and curricula manipulation) or otherwise to induce them to defer to the "smart people" with their fancy government titles, tenured professorships or celebrity status.

The trick is to ensure that the public has the information they need to arrive at commonsensical decisions about who to vote for and what platforms or initiatives to endorse. This has, until recently, been made difficult because of the gate-keeping role on news and other information flows played by the so-called "mainstream" media.

It has lately become a commonplace that the advent of alternative media and information sources has challenged and perhaps begun permanently to end the sort of information dominance that enables the formulation and adoption of policies actually inimical to the national interest and security. I have witnessed this phenomenon firsthand from my vantage point on the Commentary pages of one of the earliest and most important of alternative media in the nation's capital: the *Washington Times*.

But for the *Times* and the challenge it posed to the media preeminence and party line-promotion of the capital's other newspaper, the *Washington Post* – many of the points of view that have been essential to a proper debate about national security over the past twenty-five years, my own among them, would not have seen the light of day.

I hope that the next twenty-five years will witness a further, quantum expansion in the number of platforms and vehicles for expressing such points of view in the service of securing freedom, and pray that I will be able to continue to contribute to that noble and vital mission.

Made in the USA
Middletown, DE
05 April 2015